Ritual, Violence, and the Fall of the Classic Maya Kings

Maya Studies

UNIVERSITY PRESS OF FLORIDA

Florida A&M University, Tallahassee
Florida Atlantic University, Boca Raton
Florida Gulf Coast University, Ft. Myers
Florida International University, Miami
Florida State University, Tallahassee
New College of Florida, Sarasota
University of Central Florida, Orlando
University of Florida, Gainesville
University of North Florida, Jacksonville
University of South Florida, Tampa
University of West Florida, Pensacola

Ritual, Violence, and the Fall of the Classic Maya Kings

EDITED BY GYLES IANNONE,
BRETT A. HOUK,
AND SONJA A. SCHWAKE

Diane Z. Chase and Arlen F. Chase, Series Editors

University Press of Florida
Gainesville · Tallahassee · Tampa · Boca Raton
Pensacola · Orlando · Miami · Jacksonville · Ft. Myers · Sarasota

Copyright 2016 by Gyles Iannone, Brett A. Houk, and Sonja A. Schwake
All rights reserved
Printed in the United States of America on acid-free paper

This book may be available in an electronic edition.

First cloth printing, 2016
First paperback printing, 2018

23 22 21 20 19 18   6 5 4 3 2 1

Library of Congress Cataloging-in-Publication Data
Names: Iannone, Gyles, editor. | Houk, Brett A. (Brett Alan), 1967– editor. | Schwake, Sonja A., editor.
Title: Ritual, violence, and the fall of the classic Maya kings / edited by Gyles Iannone, Brett A. Houk, and Sonja A. Schwake.
Other titles: Maya studies.
Description: Gainesville : University Press of Florida, [2016] | Series: Maya studies | Includes bibliographical references and index.
Identifiers: LCCN 2015038628 | ISBN 9780813062754 (cloth : alk. paper)
ISBN 9780813064055 (pbk.)
Subjects: LCSH: Mayas—Kings and rulers. | Mayas—Politics and government. | Mayas—Social conditions. | Ritual—Mexico—History. | Ritual—Central America—History. | Violence—Mexico—History. | Violence—Central America—History. | Mayas—Antiquities. | Indians of Mexico—Antiquities. | Indians of Central America—Antiquities.
Classification: LCC F1435.3.P7 R58 2016 | DDC 972/.6—dc23
LC record available at http://lccn.loc.gov/2015038628

The University Press of Florida is the scholarly publishing agency for the State University System of Florida, comprising Florida A&M University, Florida Atlantic University, Florida Gulf Coast University, Florida International University, Florida State University, New College of Florida, University of Central Florida, University of Florida, University of North Florida, University of South Florida, and University of West Florida.

University Press of Florida
15 Northwest 15th Street
Gainesville, FL 32611-2079
http://upress.ufl.edu

To all of the Maya people, past and present, in appreciation of their amazing resilience across centuries of environmental, social, and political change

Contents

List of Figures ix
List of Tables xi
Foreword xiii
Christopher C. Taylor

1. Introduction 1
   Gyles Iannone, Brett A. Houk, and Sonja A. Schwake

2. Cross-Cultural Perspectives on the Scapegoat King: The Anatomy of a Model 23
   Gyles Iannone

3. Killing the "Kings of Stone": The Defacement of Classic Maya Monuments 61
   Eleanor Harrison-Buck

4. Concepts of Legitimacy and Social Dynamics: Termination Ritual and the Last King of Aguateca, Guatemala 89
   Takeshi Inomata

5. The Life and Afterlife of the Classic Period Piedras Negras Kingdom 108
   Charles Golden, Andrew K. Scherer, Melanie Kingsley, Stephen D. Houston, and Héctor Escobedo

6. Destruction Events and Political Truncation at the Little Kingdom of Minanha, Belize 134
   Sonja A. Schwake and Gyles Iannone

7. The Collapses in the West and the Violent Ritual Termination of the Classic Maya Capital Center of Cancuen: Causes and Consequences 159
   Arthur A. Demarest, Claudia Quintanilla, and José Samuel Suasnavar

8. Social-Political Manifestations of the Terminal Classic: Colha, Northern Belize, as a Case Study   187
   Palma J. Buttles and Fred Valdez Jr.

9. Signs of the Times: Terminal Classic Surface Deposits and the Fates of Maya Kingdoms in Northwestern Belize   203
   Brett A. Houk

10. Events and Processes Leading to the Abandonment of the Maya City of Blue Creek, Belize   223
    Thomas H. Guderjan and C. Colleen Hanratty

11. Dynamic Transitions at El Perú-Waka': Late Terminal Classic Ritual Repurposing of a Monumental Shrine   243
    Olivia C. Navarro-Farr

12. Lords of the Life Force and Their People: Reflections on Ritual Violence and Reverence in the Maya Archaeological Record   270
    David Freidel

References   285
List of Contributors   339
Index   343

Figures

1.1. Map of the Maya area showing sites discussed in this volume and selected other major sites   9
3.1. A carved limestone tablet with a portrait of K'inich Ahkal Mo' Nahb' III   71
3.2. Locations of terminal deposits in Central Acropolis Court 5D-2 at Tikal   76
3.3. Front of Stela 32, Naranjo   77
3.4. Distribution of sites with termination deposits, monument defacement, and Terminal Classic circular shrines in the Maya Lowlands   79
4.1. Map of the Aguateca epicenter   94
4.2. Dense deposit of artifacts found south of the stairway of Structure L8-6   97
4.3. Stairway of Structure L8-7 after removing the pile of stones viewed from the west   98
4.4. Fragment of a carved limestone object found in the deposit of Structure L8-6   101
5.1. Map of the northern portion of the Piedras Negras epicenter   114
5.2. Throne 1 at Piedras Negras   115
5.3. Fragment of modeled stucco head discovered in the collapse of Structure J-4 in the Acropolis of Piedras Negras   116
5.4. Map of the southern portion of the Piedras Negras epicenter   119
5.5. Structure O-7 at Piedras Negras   120
6.1. Map of the Vaca Plateau and adjacent areas showing the location of Minanha   136
6.2. Rectified isometric plan of the Minanha epicentral court complex   137
6.3. Remnants of the razed 38J-3rd shrine   143
6.4. Components of the buried penultimate royal residential courtyard at Minanha   147
6.5. Butt of Stela 4 at Minanha   149

7.1. Map showing the principal western exchange routes of the Pasión, the highland route, and the "transversal" 161
7.2. Maps of Classic period trade hegemonies 165
7.3. Panel 3 and Altar 2 of Cancuen 169
7.4. Plan view of the royal palace at Cancuen 170
7.5. Purely highland-style feasting ball court at Cancuen 175
7.6. Southern cistern in front of the entrance to the royal palace at Cancuen 178
7.7. Palace cistern deposits and example of a perimortem wound from the large-scale sacrifice of nobles 179
8.1. Map of northern Belize 191
8.2. Colha skull pit and fire-shattered wall 192
8.3. Colha skull pit 193
8.4. Colha skull pit illustration/drawing 193
8.5. Colha composite of skull cut marks 195
9.1. Map of Dos Hombres 204
9.2. Map of Chan Chich 212
9.3. Map of La Milpa 216
9.4. Figurine and whistle fragments from Terminal Classic surface deposits 220
10.1. The central twenty square kilometers of Blue Creek showing known residential groups 226
10.2. Plan view of U Xulil Beh showing locations of house mounds and terraces 231
10.3. Elevated view of Structure 50 after excavation 236
10.4. Detail view of Termination Deposit at Structure 50 236
10.5. Photo of round Yucatecan-style shrine at the Rosita Group 239
11.1. Central Zone at Waka' 245
11.2. Plan view of Structure M13-1 at Waka' 246
11.3. Waka' Stela 9 and Stela 10 257
11.4. Waka' Stela 6 and Stela 34 258
12.1. James Garber excavating an above-floor deposit on Structure 4, OP 22, Cerros 277
12.2. Excavating sherds from termination rituals at Structure 6F-68, Yaxuna 277
12.3. Royal crown worn by a sacrificed young woman, Burial 24, Yaxuna 280

Tables

3.1. Maya lowland sites with terminal deposits 67
4.1. Frequencies of ceramic sherds found in different areas of Aguateca 99
11.1. Ceramic sequence for El Perú-Waka' 248
11.2. Categories of evidence for desecratory, reverential, and/or both forms of ritual termination 255

Foreword

Anthropological models tend to have very short shelf lives. It has been at least two decades, for example, since the terms "mechanical solidarity" and "organic solidarity" were used in anything but history of anthropology courses. Today, in sharp contrast to models that once focused on social cohesiveness and the nature of shared phenomena, as in "collective representations," anthropology has turned in the direction of concepts that probe the nature of conflict, dissension, and individual action. In the anthropology of today, no social formation exists or has ever existed that operates or operated like a smoothly working machine. Instead, topics of interest are more likely to be agency, multivocality, domination, and resistance. This shift toward methodological individualism, provoked by an earlier anthropology that all too frequently failed to critically examine dominant ideologies and their degree of unanimity, may also have led us to a kind of presentism. We simply reject everything that our predecessors had to say, merely because they said it so long ago. Granted, evolutionism, diffusionism, functionalism, and structuralism all had their flaws, and their practitioners often blithely pushed their explanatory frameworks into domains where they should not have gone or ignored things that with the benefit of hindsight now seem obvious. But was that sufficient reason in all cases to throw the baby out with the bath water?

It is the premise of this volume that one of these hastily discarded babies, divine kingship, merits a closer look, in particular kingship as practiced by the Maya until the apparent widespread demise of this institution in the ninth century AD. The early theorist most closely associated with divine kingship was Sir James Frazer, someone whom many scholars today would consider to be an antediluvian. And who could deny that he was an unabashed unilineal evolutionist and an undisciplined comparativist? In reading *The Golden Bough* one is likely to encounter examples from

Classical Greece thrown in with examples from Africa, South America, and Asia, with little or no attention paid to historical context. But was Frazer completely wrong? When he talks about divine kingship and its connection to what he calls "life" (meaning fertility and prosperity), one is obliged, in my view, to acknowledge that Frazer was on to something that was not just a figment of his imagination.

The area with which I have most ethnographic experience is Rwanda, and Rwanda was once ruled by a "sacred king." Here Frazer's work has relevance, as does that of Luc de Heusch. Rwanda's kings were "sacred" rather than "divine." Heusch, in talking about African kings, distinguishes between those treated as if they were deities on earth, such as Egyptian pharaohs, whom he would call "divine," and those treated as extraordinary beings by virtue of their privileged relationship with the supernatural but not deities in themselves, whom he would call "sacred." Rwandan sacred kingship endured until 1931, when the Belgian tutelary authorities and the Rwandan Catholic Church overthrew Mwami Musinga and replaced him with his mission-educated son, Charles Rudahigwa. Kingship of a sort held on in Rwanda until the social revolution of 1959–1962, when the majority Hutu ethnic group overthrew the king and Tutsi ethnic domination and replaced them with a Hutu-dominated presidential system. Kingship representations, however, did not disappear. In other work, I attempt to show that Rwanda's last Hutu president, Juvénal Habyarimana, whose assassination in 1994 triggered the genocide, was like a "sacred king," as he was often depicted in political media with symbols that derive from Rwandan sacred kingship. We may believe that there are no longer any sacred or divine kings, but many modern dictators come very close.

Rwandan sacred kings and Maya kings shared many characteristics. Both were believed to promote prosperity and fertility by virtue of their special relationship with the supernatural. Both were also thought to be candidates for physical elimination—the king as scapegoat—in the event that their relationship with the supernatural was perceived to fail. Environmental calamities could cause this, as could military defeat. Whether this occurred in all cases with all kings is, however, unclear. This is why this monograph is so welcome. Only empirical data of an historical nature can answer many of the questions Frazer's model left open, and in the absence of textual, linguistic, and ethnographic material, archaeological evidence is often the only type available.

The Maya kings discussed in this volume are deemed to have been sacred or divine due to their special ritual status and their association with prosperity and fertility. However, by the end of the ninth century most of the kings were gone and the kingship institution was moribund. This book asks the question why, but it does not stop at an overarching hypothesis of environmental failure; instead, it offers several Maya polities as examples of precisely what happened at different times and in different places. In some cases, the kings, members of their family, and their retinue were eliminated but were also carefully buried with ceremonial objects, and in other instances the sites of king sacrifice showed signs of violence and desecration. Sometimes the kings and their institution appear to have been suddenly extinguished and in other instances they seem to have faded away slowly and gradually.

This monograph also attempts to shed light on a question Frazer's evolutionism and later functionalist descriptions could not address—legitimacy—and the degree to which Maya kings were supported by their subjects. When one speaks of kings, one wonders if everyone among the Maya believed that the king actually possessed supernatural powers. Where there is domination there is invariably resistance, and there are usually other ways by which subordinate people imagine their relationships to nature and to fertility. Did these alternative ways require hierarchy? Once again, in the absence of textual and other materials, archaeological data is about the best we have to address questions of this sort. This volume will not answer all the questions anthropologists have about sacred and divine kingship, but its great merit lies in the fact that the authors attempt to take the lessons of modern anthropology seriously while not simply rejecting divine kingship out of hand as just another worn-out paradigm, just another dated "grand narrative."

Christopher C. Taylor
Author of *Milk, Honey, and Money: Changing Concepts in Rwanda Healing* and *Sacrifice as Terror: The Rwandan Genocide of 1994*

Introduction

GYLES IANNONE, BRETT A. HOUK,
AND SONJA A. SCHWAKE

Archaeological efforts to explain the dissolution of early state formations have always been rooted—at least to some degree—in contemporary circumstances. In the case of the ancient Maya, this was clearly illustrated three decades ago by Richard Wilk (1985), who demonstrated how shifting concerns in American society influenced what were considered to be valid interpretations for the collapse of a large number of southern lowland kingdoms during the ninth century AD. Prevailing concerns with climate change and the propensity to see droughts as the primary causal factor in the demise of these same Maya kingdoms (e.g., Gill 2000; Kennett et al. 2012) continue to illustrate how current issues can bias our interpretations of the past (Iannone, Yaeger, and Hodell 2014; Yaeger and Hodell 2009). That is not to say that droughts did not play a significant role in the downfall of the various Maya kingdoms, only that we need to be more critical with respect to the implicit (and often untested) aspects of our interpretive frameworks (Iannone 2014).

One such implied (and often unverified) component of many models for the collapse of early state formations—including those of the Maya—is the concept of the "scapegoat king," first promoted by James Frazer (1993 [1922]) in his still-influential volume, *The Golden Bough*, and subsequently elaborated on by many others (see chapter 2). In its original formulation, this model emphasized two different yet complementary themes, both of which continue to pervade many models of societal collapse (Hansen and Stepputat 2006, 298–299; see also Abercrombie and Turner 1978, 154–155; Plant 1980, 345; Quigley 2000, 239). The first theme suggests that kings are intrinsic to their kingdoms and that as the embodiment of these kingdoms, they reflect the shared, collective will and well-being of the people who inhabit their realms. The second theme implies that kings are extrinsic to their kingdoms because they have special characteristics, unique origins, and unusual powers and that this allows them to assume the dangerous task of carrying the moral transgressions and impurities of their kingdoms and to assume the role of guarantor of prosperity for their followers because of the special relationship they have with the supernatural forces that are responsible for fertility. The latter qualities relate to the notion of the "divine" king who is different, powerful, vital, and potentially dangerous (Trigger 2003, 79–87). Both the intrinsic and extrinsic characteristics of kings are usually highlighted in unison in efforts to illustrate the unique roles these individuals play within society (Hansen and Stepputat 2006, 299), and to explain why kings are often perceived to be at fault when kingdoms begin to show signs of declining prosperity, and ultimately collapse[1] and thus are treated as scapegoats, resulting in their removal from power using prescribed ritual practices and sometimes even violent acts (as is documented in the various cross-cultural examples presented in chapter 2).

At least since the initial formulation of J. Eric S. Thompson's (1954) "peasant revolt" model, Mayanists have frequently used the scapegoat king trope in their explanations for the ninth-century collapse, sometimes explicitly (e.g., Freidel and Shaw 2000; Iannone, Chase, et al. 2014; Lucero 2002, 2006; Moyes et al. 2009; Webster 2000, 2002a, 2002b) but far more often implicitly. Although this model seems to draw the various environmental and sociocultural data sets into a coherent whole that accounts for how and why the various Maya kingdoms met their demise, as an explanatory device it has rarely been vigorously tested (but see Moyes et al. 2009). As Takeshi Inomata underscored in his commentary on the first draft of this volume, while the divine king model may be quite useful for understanding the ancient Maya, whether the scapegoat king trope is useful for conceptualizing the ninth-century Maya collapse remains to be demonstrated.

Returning to the idea that our contemporary circumstances often influence what we consider to be valid interpretations of past events, one wonders whether our attraction to and uncritical application of the scapegoat king model relates, on some level, to our perception that contemporary governments are mismanaging resources and are generally unresponsive to issues that are of concern to the general public. That such sentiments are not unique to our own sociopolitical milieu may explain why the scapegoat king model has had such a long and often uncritical explanatory reign within the social sciences. Nevertheless, the persistence of such views does not, in and of itself, confirm the efficacy of the explanatory framework. From an archaeological standpoint, the tenets of the scapegoat king model need to be critically evaluated using the range of data sets available to us. In doing so, particular emphasis must be placed on the material correlates that support the idea that ancient rulers—including the Maya kings who are the focus of this volume—symbolized the well-being of their communities, assumed the role of guarantor of prosperity and fertility for their kingdoms, and were therefore treated as scapegoats when it was perceived that they were no longer effective in these roles.

This, then, is the explicit goal of this volume: to assess the explanatory power of the scapegoat king model using detailed data sets from a number of Maya centers, all of which show evidence for ritual and/or violence that correlates in space and time with the fall of kings and the demise of the traditional institution of kingship in the early ninth century AD.

Critique of the Scapegoat King Model

Although many believe that the scapegoat king model has substantial explanatory power with respect to understanding societal collapse—as is amply demonstrated by the many cross-cultural analyses discussed in chapter 2—some significant issues lurk beneath the surface of this interpretive framework. Criticisms center on a series of interrelated issues, many of which are rooted in Weberian approaches to power and legitimacy (e.g., Abercrombie and Turner 1978; Brenner 1994; Hansen and Stepputat 2006; Heath 2010; Rudolph 2006). To reiterate, several of these concerns were raised by Takeshi Inomata as we worked our way through the first iteration of this volume, and his insights were integral to framing the final version of the monograph. In broad terms, the main issue concerns the fact that most of the models that employ the concept of the scapegoat king are based on questionable notions of how legitimacy would have been cultivated and maintained in past societies.

To begin, it is clear that the scapegoat king model is overtly *functional*; it is often based on the notion of a sacred covenant that binds the supernatural powers, elite managers, and mass of producers under a social contract that promotes solidarity by assigning each component of this tripartite relationship specific yet complementary roles (e.g., Joyce 2000, 75; Monaghan 2000, 39; cf. Houston and Inomata 2009, 28, 36–42). In the scapegoat king models, solidarity diminishes when: 1) the gods decide not to provide the sun, rain, and fertile soils that are vital to the productivity of the producers and overall health of the kingdom (which initiates the crisis); 2) elite managers fail in their tasks of properly sustaining and eventually placating the gods through their ritual practices (which initially stimulates and in the end perpetuates the crisis); and 3) the mass of producers eventually decide to withhold and redeploy for their own direct benefit the natural and human resources they would have normally provided to an effective ruler so the latter could properly nourish and pacify the supernatural forces (which exacerbates the crisis). In other words, loss of solidarity results when ineffective kings fail in their chief roles, as defined by the principles of the sacred covenant. According to the scapegoat king model, when this occurs, kings can suffer from a legitimacy crisis (Habermas 1975), which, if it cannot be dealt with through an effective strategy of containment (Jameson 1981), ultimately leads to their removal from power. The latter may be achieved through a variety of means and may involve ritual termination events and even violent acts (see chapter 2).

Whether the ability to do so is framed in ideological terms or in more tangible expressions, it is true that good rulers keep their supporters' well-being in mind when governing. However, the idea that kings lose power simply because they are perceived to be poor managers is an obvious oversimplification (Brumfiel 1992, 556–557). Models that emphasize external causes for declining prosperity and hence the removal of a scapegoat king and the concomitant fall of their kingdom—whether this is the result of shifting trade networks, defeats in warfare, or various environmental causes (i.e., drought, resource degradation)—also underestimate the role internal factors play in a collapse and generally undervalue the dynamic character of social change (Middleton 2012, 257). In reality, societies—especially those that are highly differentiated and pluralistic—are not systems that exhibit long-term equilibrium punctuated by periodic, externally stimulated, legitimation crises but are rather social formations that perpetually lurch from crisis to crisis (Abercrombie and Turner 1978, 152; Brumfiel 1992, 558). The fluid, conflictive, negotiated, and multivocal nature of societies and communities is ignored in the more functional applications of the scapegoat king model.

Most interpretations that employ the idea of the scapegoat king can also be characterized as *normative* because they imply significant levels of collective adherence to and belief in a dominant ideology imposed from above (Heath 1999, 2; Rudolph 2006, 3). We use the term ideology here in a very strict manner, one that adheres to how it is employed in the various applications of the scapegoat king model, as opposed to the broader way it has been applied in other discussions of legitimacy, where it encompasses "*any* aspect of symbolic systems, ritual, religion, or belief, and . . . associated features of politics or economy" (Demarest 2013, 372, emphasis in original). Within the scapegoat king framework, ideologies are characterized as being inherently political and dominant ideologies serve specifically to inhibit a true understanding of the world, leading to a false consciousness wherein the privileged position of the elite is justified as natural and unquestionable and as related to their special, nontechnological control over nature and hence to their ability to provide for the needs of their followers simply by conducting the appropriate rituals, using the requisite symbols within the proper settings, as in the sacred covenant discussed above (McGuire 2002, 105–106; McGuire 2008, 54; see also Abercrombie and Turner 1978, 161–162, 166; cf. Demarest 2013, 377).

Significantly, although kings may marshal a wide range of symbols and ritual settings to promote their claims that they have an integral role in making sure the sun rises every day and sufficient rains arrive at the correct times and in the correct amounts to water the fertile soils, they do not really control these natural forces and they therefore also have to provide some more tangible benefits to their followers, such as planning, organization, and protection, in order to justify their privileged position and overall legitimacy (Childe 1950, 13). The inability to provide the latter benefits may be just as detrimental to a king and court as the perceived failure to deliver the former ones.

The normative aspects of the scapegoat king model also downplay the existence of diversity, special interests, and the ability of subordinates to both penetrate and resist the dominant ideology and to eventually transcend the false consciousness that the dominant ideology cultivates in order to transform society through collective action (Houston and Inomata 2009, 63; McGuire 2002, 79, 142, 165; McGuire 2008, 38–39; Van Buren and Richards 2000, 10). It is, in other words, erroneous to assume that legitimacy and authority are simply imposed from above and willingly accepted by the masses because such acceptance unknowingly promotes stability (Abercrombie and Turner 1978, 154, 166; Houston and Inomata 2009, 44). Legitimacy is always negotiated based on ever-present conflicts, contradictions, accommodations, and crises (Abercrombie and Turner 1978, 152).

Viewed another way, it is equally significant that applications of the scapegoat king trope ignore the possibility that elites may be better integrated with the dominant ideology than subordinate groups (Abercrombie and Turner 1978, 149), a fact that has a direct bearing on the types of political truncation we often see in the initial stages of a collapse (i.e., where kings, royal courts, and the institution of kingship are the first casualties in the dissolution of a complex society). Alternatively, others suggest that the real problems occur when non-elites "buy into" dominant ideologies to a greater degree than the elites do (Lucero 2006, 17). It is also true that a great deal of apparent support for a dominant ideology may be automatic and habitual and thus lacking in pure intentionality (e.g., Bourdieu 1977; Houston and Inomata 2009, 38). Individuals and the groups of which they are part may also have ulterior motives for purposely promoting the symbols and ethos of the dominant ideology (Dornan 2002, 318–321).

For these reasons, our interpretations must reflect the idea that there is no shared understanding of or access to the consequences of social structures (Dornan 2002, 318). Equally important is the notion that resistance to dominant ideologies and structures can vary considerably within a single community and (especially) across communities, no matter how oppressive these ideologies and structures may be. We must also remember that human actions in the past were grounded in a "situationally rational practice" that differs considerably from our contemporary, scientific, ego-focused, often skeptical, and equally situational way of viewing the world and engaging with issues such as inequality (Deetz 1996, 34; Dornan 2002, 318, 324).

Finally, the scapegoat king model can be criticized for being *neo-evolutionist* and *essentialist* because it is blatantly static and generalizing, promoting a stratagem for legitimacy that fits *all* societies exhibiting king-based governance structures no matter how far apart they are in time or space, with little regard for historical contingency or context (Brenner 1994, 680, 688; Rudolph 2006, 10). In addition, it is a *centralist* model, in that it focuses authority and agency in particular centers and specific individuals (i.e., a court complex and a king) and thus fails to acknowledge the agency, motivations, and goals of subordinate communities and actors. The focal monuments and rituals kings sponsored and hosted do more than foster integration; they also "emphasize ethnic, regional, and local distinctions" (O'Connor 1983, 111) and provide the settings for active resistance (Dirks 1987; McAnany 2010, 196–198).

In the end, the scapegoat king model fails to recognize that kingship is a "tentative and always emergent form of authority" (Hansen and Stepputat 2006, 298). Does this mean that this interpretive framework has no explanatory value? Not necessarily. However, these criticisms force us to critically evaluate the model so we can determine its utility for elucidating the causes for the collapse of specific early state formations, including the ninth-century Maya kingdoms.

To quote Randall McGuire (2008, 84), "One of the main purposes of theory is to define the questions we ask about the social world." Some of the questions that emerge from our critical assessment of the scapegoat king model and that guide the considerations of the various data sets presented in this volume include the following.

- Does the cross-cultural model of kingly legitimacy, prosperity, and scapegoating hold in all times and all places?
- What are some of the material correlates that support the premise that legitimacy and prosperity are linked in societies ruled by kings?
- Is legitimacy solely invested in an individual charismatic male king or is it attributed to a broader governance structure and thus a wider cadre of actors exhibiting diverse roles, statuses, and genders?
- Are power and legitimacy centered entirely in the kingly body or are they also invested in specific places (palatial residences or cities), relics, and regalia that transcend the kingly person?
- To what degree do subordinates accept the dominant ideology—in this case the institution of divine kingship—and how might we recognize covert resistance to it archaeologically?
- What crises would justify the removal of a king, given that crises were omnipresent?
- What circumstances could potentially lead to the removal of a king without subsequently replacing him with a new ruler (i.e., what would cause an entire governance structure to be treated as a scapegoat)?
- What strategies of containment might be adopted to avoid the removal of a king and/or the collapse of an entire governance structure?
- Do ritual terminations and/or violence always accompany the removal of a king, and, if so, why are such acts a necessary part of the process of deactivating divine authority?
- What testable implications and material correlates can archaeologists use as evidence for the removal of a scapegoat king due to declining prosperity?
- Are there other events or processes that coincide with the demise of kingly authority?

Gyles Iannone considers these questions in more detail in chapter 2, using a wide range of cross-cultural data. The chapters that follow also generate insights that, although they are more specific to a particular site or region, are still useful for contemplating these broad issues.

Volume Summary

This volume brings together a number of pertinent archaeological case studies and researchers who have all, in one way or another, been investigating ritual, violence, and the fall of the Classic Maya kings (figure 1.1). These studies reflect a subtle shift that has emerged in the past decade or so concerning how archaeologists interpret the data associated with the abandonment of Classic Maya urban centers. This has allowed the various contributors to take a closer look at the processes and events associated with the fall of a series of kingdoms situated in different parts of the ancient the Maya world. By querying their detailed data sets in a variety of ways, each contributor is able to assess whether the scapegoat king model has explanatory power with respect to the specific collapse sequence(s) they have documented. These evaluations are guided by the following questions.

> Was the collapse of the kingly governance structure a protracted process (e.g., AD 750–1050), or do the key events suggest a comparatively short period of demise (e.g., AD 800–830)?
> Does the duration of the collapse have a bearing on the applicability of the scapegoat king model to the specific case study in question?
> What specific events and material correlates mark the dissolution of kingly governance?
> At whom were the events and the actions that constituted these events aimed (i.e., just the king or a broader range of political agents, spaces, and symbols)?
> Do these events reflect the types of activities one would expect given the tenets of the scapegoat king model?
> What specific crises stimulated the documented events and did these crises relate in any way to declining prosperity?
> Why did these particular crises lead to the end of divine kingship as an institution rather than simply the removal of an individual king and the installation of a new ruler?
> Does the scapegoat king model have explanatory value for the case study in question?

The current chapter introduces the main theme of the volume and provides a critical discussion of the relevant theoretical issues concerning the scapegoat king model, with particular emphasis on its applicability to the various Maya case studies that form the bulk of the monograph.

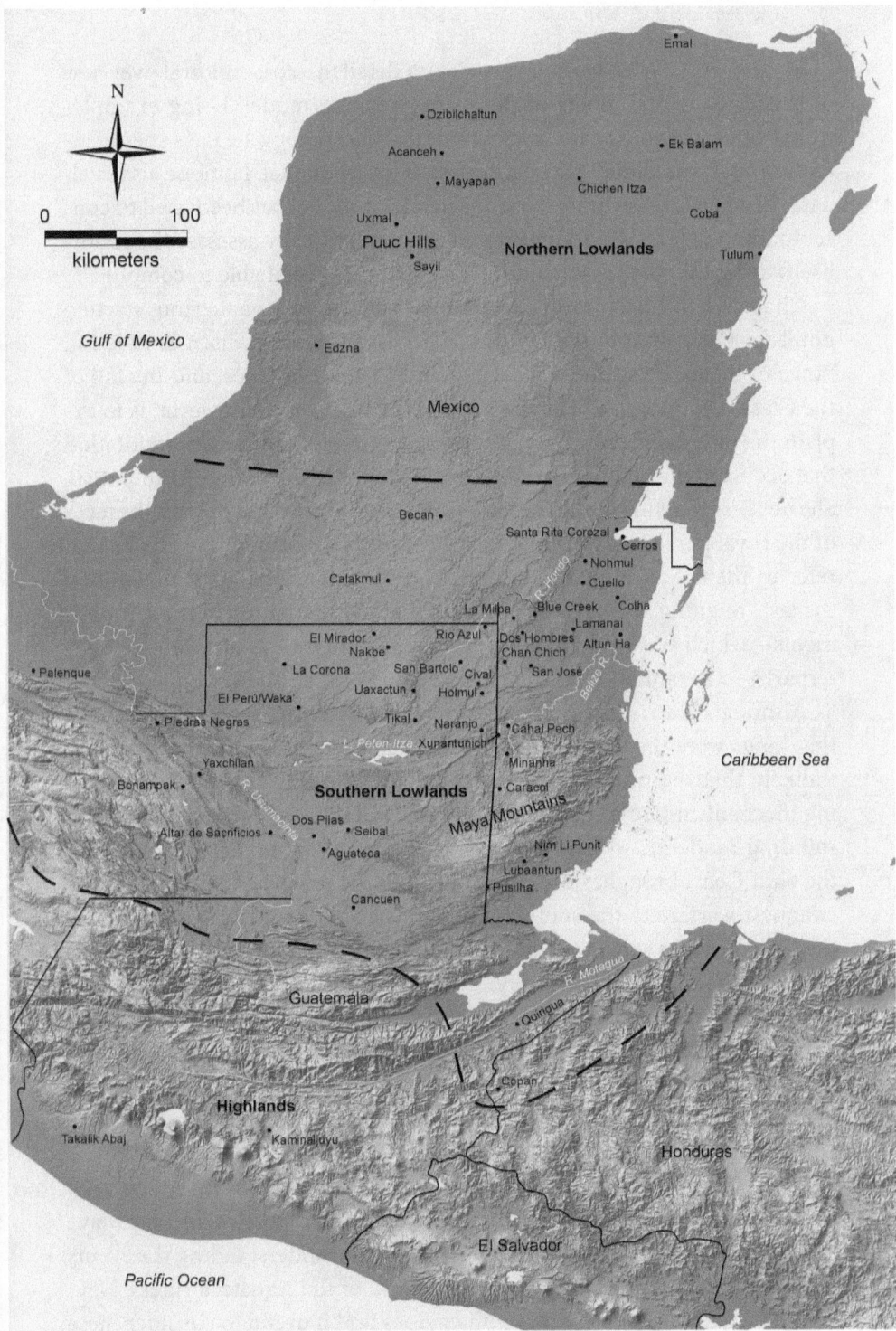

Figure 1.1. Map of the Maya area showing sites discussed in this volume and selected other major sites. Base map courtesy of NASA JPL, SRTM mission. After Houk 2015, Figure 1.1.

In chapter 2, Gyles Iannone provides a detailed, cross-cultural overview of the fundamental tenets of the scapegoat king model. Using examples from both archaeology and sociocultural anthropology, he pays special attention to the potential material correlates of the model. Iannone also evaluates in a general way how the scapegoat king model has been used to conceptualize ancient Maya kingship. Finally, he critically assesses the model itself, using the vast cross-cultural data set he has been able to compile.

Chapter 3, by Eleanor Harrison-Buck, provides an advantageous starting point for our shift into the various Maya case studies; it discusses the full range of material residues associated with "ritual, violence, and the fall of the Classic Maya kings." Harrison-Buck's principal goal, however, is to explain the rationale behind a widespread program of monument mutilation that occurred throughout the southern lowlands in the period AD 810–830. She believes that this mutilation, especially the destruction of both the faces of the royal personages depicted on these monuments and the glyphs that refer to them, was aimed at terminating specific individuals, most often the last "reigning kings." She concludes that the mutilation of these monuments—which served as perpetual proxies for their flesh-and-blood counterparts—was tantamount to inflicting "soul loss" on them.

Although Harrison-Buck's interpretation fits quite well with the idea that kings were the embodiment of their kingdoms, she believes that it is unlikely that the monument mutilation was a result of some scapegoating mechanism tied to declining prosperity. Rather, she resurrects a long-standing model in which an intrusive group of Chontal-Itza Maya from the Gulf Coast brought new forms of economic practice and pan-regional conquest warfare to the southern lowlands. According to Harrison-Buck, they also brought a form of "questionnaire" with them that they used to ferret out unworthy local leaders. She posits that the various termination and destruction events may, in this light, be evidence of "malevolent rituals" aimed at permanently incapacitating these unsatisfactory local lords.

In chapter 4, Takeshi Inomata picks up on the theme of conquest in his consideration of the fall of the Aguateca royal court around AD 810, although in this instance the antagonists were likely regional enemies as opposed to foreigners. Inomata suggests that, although various aspects of the scapegoat king model help us understand the nature of ancient Maya kingship, in his mind the model is less useful for understanding the events leading up to and culminating in the demise of the Aguateca rulers. Nevertheless, like Harrison-Buck, Inomata does find it useful to consider these events in light of the idea that the Aguateca rulers were perceived to be the physical embodiments of their kingdoms. As a result, it is not surprising that the conquest of Aguateca involved focused destruction (i.e., tearing away cut stones and opening sealed rooms), burning, and deposition of termination deposits within rooms and on stairways, all in association with the royal-residential palace complex and main plaza, the buildings and spaces most closely connected to the kingdom's last ruler.

As in Harrison-Buck's interpretation, the ritual destruction at Aguateca is not thought to reflect the demise of a king who had lost his legitimacy and was subsequently treated as scapegoat due to mismanagement and declining prosperity. Rather, because the last king was considered to be the embodiment of the Aguateca kingdom, buildings in the royal-residential palace complex and main plaza that were intricately linked with him were physically and symbolically desanctified by aggressive invaders in order to deactivate all manifestations and claims to power by local authorities and to ultimately destabilize the kingdom as a whole. These efforts were apparently successful, as they resulted in the complete abandonment of the Aguateca epicenter.

The focus of chapter 5 is Piedras Negras, another center that witnessed various termination events dating to around AD 810. According to Charles Golden and colleagues, these events include the partial dismantling and burning of buildings and the destruction of friezes, thrones, and monuments. With respect to the latter, efforts seem to have been focused on defacing images of royal personages, as was previously discussed by Harrison-Buck. Finally, trash seems to have accumulated or to have been purposely deposited in some of the key buildings in the royal acropolis, and "near-surface" deposits containing human bone and ash were dumped in various places throughout the epicenter.

Golden and colleagues conclude that although scapegoating may have played a role in the fall of the Piedras Negras kingdom, this remains hard to prove, especially since it remains difficult to chronologically correlate the fall of the ruler with specific destruction and termination acts. In the end, there is little evidence to suggest that declining prosperity or environmental issues contributed to the demise of the Piedras Negras kingdom, although in the final decades of the kingdom some building projects were never completed and there were greater disparities in diet. Apparently, no single legitimation crises brought down the royal court. Rather, various internal issues, which may have been exacerbated by regional warfare, likely played the most significant role in the decline. In fact, the epigraphic record shows that the last known king of Piedras Negras, the physical and symbolic embodiment of the kingdom, was captured by rival Yaxchilan in AD 808, apparently around the same time that the various destruction events were carried out. Golden and colleagues posit that following this devastating loss, surviving elites enacted a program of ritual termination in order to desanctify the spaces and objects most intricately associated with the defeated king and his royal court prior to attempting to resurrect the kingdom in another part of the center that was associated with the earliest foundations of royal rule at Piedras Negras. This attempt at rejuvenation was not entirely successful.

Ultimately, unlike Aguateca, Golden and colleagues see the fall of Piedras Negras as being much more drawn out, spanning much of the seventh through ninth centuries. They also emphasize that there was a greater degree of community continuity at Piedras Negras after the termination of the buildings and monuments associated with the defeated king in AD 808. Specifically, they document the persistence of earlier community practices until the final abandonment of Piedras Negras in the early tenth century.

Chapter 6 takes the reader farther to the east, to the Vaca Plateau center of Minanha. Here, Sonja Schwake and Gyles Iannone document two major destruction events associated with the center's royal residential courtyard and principal eastern shrine complex, the second of which is postulated to have occurred around AD 800. At this time the upper portions of the stelae associated with the eastern shrine were broken off and removed and the largest administrative range structures in the epicenter were decommissioned through the deposition of termination deposits containing broken ceramics and other artifacts in liminal spaces such as doorways, the removal of structural elements to hasten the collapse of vaulted roofs, and/or complete burial beneath new (albeit much simpler) architecture.

The most significant events were associated with the royal residential courtyard, which was first swept clean to purify it. Its vaulted rooms were then carefully filled in from the inside to keep them intact. Finally, the entire courtyard—except for the very top of one temple (Structure 38J)—was methodically and apparently quite carefully buried beneath five meters of rubble fill. Prior to this, the stucco friezes associated with the temple were dismantled and broken up and the pieces were scattered among the courtyard fill. This was not the end of Minanha as a community, however. A new, albeit rather small and impoverished, residential courtyard was built on top of the once-grandiose royal residential space. A diverse population continued to live on in the vicinity of the Minanha ruins for another three centuries or so.

As at Piedras Negras, the factors that led to the demise of the Minanha royal court and the destruction of symbols and desanctification of space once closely associated with the last king were complex. Schwake and Iannone posit that there may have been some declining prosperity as a result of overuse of the small pockets of land suitable for terracing and the drain on water sources brought on by drought conditions. Nevertheless, whether the king was considered responsible for these issues is difficult to determine. As in many of the other case studies, it does appear that regional warfare was at least partially responsible for the fall of the Minanha king and the subsequent destruction of the stelae and friezes that were symbolic of their royal pedigree. Nevertheless, the care taken to bury Minanha's royal residential complex also points the finger at local agents who at the same time that they seized the opportunity to increase their autonomy following the defeat of their king still carried out the infilling with a significant level of respect for the powerful forces they were encapsulating.

In chapter 7, Arthur Demarest and colleagues document some of the most extensive and dramatic termination deposits found in the southern lowlands. In their research at Cancuen, the authors have found evidence for the blockage of entrances into the royal-residential palace, the defacing of monuments, and the remains of the violent massacre of the king, the queen, and many members of their royal retinue. Many of the bodies were deposited in full regalia, along with offerings, within a sacred cistern near one entrance to the palace, thus terminating the cistern's usage. The remainder were unceremoniously interred beneath a layer of mud at another entrance. These actions occurred around AD 800. As at Aguateca, these acts prompted the total abandonment of the Cancuen epicenter.

Demarest and colleagues argue that the dramatic end of Cancuen was the culmination of a protracted period of "fragmentation" that may have begun with Tikal's defeat of Calakmul in AD 695 (see also Schwake and Iannone). This defeat, and the disintegration of the two principal power blocs that had existed since Early Classic times (ca. AD 250–550), ushered in a period of balkanization that spawned a greater number of kingdoms, both large and small. This period was characterized by increased competition and status rivalry, more regular and significant warfare campaigns, and ultimately myriad legitimation crises as power and prosperity diffused out and away from the traditional centers of power. This occurred both on the regional scale, as Cancuen slowly but surely lost control of precious trade routes, and on the local scale, as upstart nobles gained greater control over Cancuen's ports and assumed certain functionary roles, such as war leaders. According to Demarest and colleagues, such competition within and between polities would have eroded the legitimacy of Cancuen's king. The growing autonomy of neighboring trading partners and local nobility ultimately forced Cancuen's kings to adopt a strategy of containment involving symbolic imagery that advertised the ruler's role as a water lord, the initiation of new monumental building projects, and the devolution of greater powers and rights to the increasingly emboldened nobles.

Unfortunately for the Cancuen king, the various economic, ecological, political, and ideological crises were too much to overcome, and he paid the price. According to Demarest and colleagues, it was likely the neighboring and once closely allied trading partners in the adjacent highlands who brought down the Cancuen kingdom. Although the execution of the various members of the royal court involved little ritual and was clearly violent, it still may have been carried out ceremoniously, as is attested by the associated offerings and by the fact that the victims were interred in their finery. Thus, there was still a reverential character to the execution, one that reflected the Cancuen king's once-vaunted position as a divine lord.

Palma Buttles and Fred Valdez discuss a similarly dramatic example of possible royal execution at the small center of Colha in chapter 8. Here, archaeologists discovered a skull pit at the base of an elite residence. The residence had been burned around AD 800, and collapse debris from the destruction had covered the skull pit, preserving it until its discovery. Buttles and Valdez propose that the burning of the elite structure and decapitation and flaying of thirty individuals at the onset of the Terminal Classic period potentially represents an instance of internal revolt and scapegoating against the Colha royal family by a population pushed to the brink by a variety of factors, including drought, declining agricultural productivity, high populations, and possibly declining health.

Buttles and Valdez conclude that the execution is best viewed as a ritual termination of elite identity (by "defacing" them) and power. Significantly, the disarticulated and comingled remains of twenty-five additional individuals were found at the base of a nearby ceremonial structure, suggesting that, as at Cancuen, the program of executions, whether the result of internal revolt or warfare, was focused on a large number of Colha community members (minimally fifty-five). Following these executions, Colha was rapidly abandoned.

In their efforts to contextualize what happened at Colha, Buttles and Valdez stress the various pressures at work across the lowlands (i.e., the failing economic and social systems), noting that despite the unique combination of events associated with the abandonment (or survival) of each Maya center, the interdependence among various kingdoms—and especially their rulers—was an important factor in the broader processes associated with the collapse and the fall of the scapegoat kings.

In chapter 9, Brett Houk provides a critical overview of the rather ubiquitous "termination deposits," which differ from normal middens because they are usually found blocking stairs or entranceways (instead of constituting dumps behind structures). These often contain human remains and exotic or elite objects and generally lack ceramic refits and faunal materials (which are discussed in many of the case studies in this volume). Using data from three centers in northwestern Belize, Houk demonstrates that such surface or near-surface deposits require closer scrutiny if we hope to understand the rationale that lead to their deposition.

Houk first describes a destructive act that took place in association with the acropolis at Dos Hombres. Dated by ceramic types to ca. AD 800, thousands of ceramic vessels and other elite artifacts were smashed in the entrance courtyard of the acropolis, effectively terminating the use of the complex and ushering in the abandonment of the ceremonial precinct.

Houk then goes on to describe a different type of deposit found at Chan Chich and La Milpa. These are associated with elite but perhaps nonroyal contexts and also date to the period just prior to center abandonment. At La Milpa, archaeologists excavated a dense surface deposit at a small courtyard attached to the second-largest plaza at the site. Although arguably not a royal compound, the location of the courtyard in the heart of the epicenter suggests that its occupants had strong ties to the ruling powers. The deposit draped the inside and outside of a low wall along one edge of the courtyard and accumulated over several centuries, beginning at the end of the Late Classic and extending into the Postclassic.

Houk describes similar surface deposits of scattered elite artifacts at Chan Chich that were located on the steps to palace structures in the western part of the site. Dated to ca. AD 850 by the presence of Fine Orange pottery, it is not entirely clear if the Chan Chich deposits represent desecratory or reverential ritual behavior or both.

Houk concludes that although there is some spatial and temporal consistency with respect to these three "midden-like" deposits, the agents and motivations that lead to the deposition of these artifact assemblages likely varied, and they should thus not be lumped together as examples of a single, unambiguous category referred to as either a dedicatory or a desecratory assemblage. He also suggests that although it is difficult to connect these motivations to a desire to remove a failed ruler (i.e., through the scapegoating mechanism), there is likely some form of "guilt by association" at play in all three case studies. Finally, although these assemblages seem to date, at least partially, to the period of declining prosperity leading up to the demise of the region's kings (as implied by contemporaneous examples of poor construction techniques and/or construction projects that were never finished), Houk contends that non-elites continued to contribute to these assemblages over time, possibly in efforts to tap into the once-great portals of power that had been central to each kingdom.

Chapter 10 shifts our attention slightly eastward, to the center of Blue Creek. Here, Thomas Guderjan and Colleen Hanratty discuss surface deposits similar to those Houk detailed. The Classic period rulers of Blue Creek were exceptionally prosperous, as evidenced by their access to exotic material goods such as jadeite, their monumental architecture, a fertile agricultural system, and their strategic position in the landscape with respect to trade networks. The authors argue, however, that different lineage groups in the Blue Creek polity competed with one another and that the material evidence from a series of Terminal Classic ritual deposits indicates that some groups were excluded from kingly wealth, power, and authority.

Some of these surface deposits were laid down in Blue Creek's central precinct, in association with the stairways and doorways of key public spaces and buildings closely connected with the ruler, including elite residences. Such deposits were also discovered in association with a series of elite residences at Kín Tan, the residence for a powerful but nonroyal lineage. These "termination deposits" are considered to be the result of deliberate ritual events tied to the termination of use of the plazas and courtyards in question. Because no human activity occurred at these loci following deposition of the termination deposits, the authors posit that they mark the onset of complete abandonment of specific elite-oriented architectural settings at Blue Creek around AD 810. Significantly, other non-elite architectural units in the vicinity of the Blue Creek epicenter do not have termination deposits, and many demonstrate continued occupation beyond the key date of AD 810.

The impetus for the rituals, artifact deposits, and ultimate abandonment, according to Guderjan and Hanratty, was likely a complex set of problems, including rising populations, declining agricultural productivity, and shifting trade networks. Unable to mitigate these issues, kings and other closely aligned elites who had previously used exclusionary tactics to their own benefit found themselves on the outside looking in. The previously excluded segments of society were able to persist for decades afterward.

Chapter 11 focuses on Waka', a large center situated in northwestern Petén, Guatemala. Continuing with the theme of the previous two chapters, Olivia Navarro-Farr discusses the diverse and complicated surface deposits and reset monuments at Structure M13-1, Waka's principal civic-ceremonial temple and possibly a key fire shrine, or Wite' Naah. She eloquently illustrates how these assemblages demonstrate not only the varied responses to the decline of royal power at Waka' but also the challenges archaeologists face as they try to interpret their significance. Based on ceramic data, AMS dates, stratigraphy, and context, Navarro-Farr argues that some of the deposits were likely laid down in the Late Classic, at the time of the demise of royal authority, while others date to the early Terminal Classic, suggesting that nonroyal and perhaps even non-elite members of the Waka' community continued to conduct rituals at Structure M13-1 after the royal dynasty at the center had collapsed. Although some of the deposits are thought to represent desecratory acts aimed at the failed ruling line, Navarro-Farr considers other deposits to be the product of reverential activities.

For example, based on the idea that reverential and desecratory acts were not necessarily mutually exclusive in ancient Maya world view, Navarro-Farr considers the overlapping and varied ritual deposits as acts of healing aimed at restoring the soul force of Structure M13-1. The intent behind these ritual practices was the desire to perpetuate some aspects of traditional royal praxis associated with fertility and prosperity or at least to engage with the memory of such praxis, in direct association with the former architectural setting most closely associated with it, despite the absence of true royal agents. Navarro-Farr posits that the intentions behind the surface deposits and reset monuments reflect an important and complex nonroyal response to the tumultuous events and conditions of the Terminal Classic period.

In the end, Navarro-Farr makes a strong case for some degree of ideological and ritual continuity at Waka'. Nevertheless, it is also clear that most of the reset monuments at the center had been broken at an earlier time (at the time of the demise of royal authority, during the Late to Terminal Classic transition), thus implying that a significant disjunction also occurred at Waka' that was likely similar in temporal and behavioral terms to what occurred at the other centers discussed in the preceding chapters.

In chapter 12, David Freidel considers how the case studies in this volume demonstrate the ability to detect the relationships between divine kings and their subjects through archaeological excavations even in the absence of hieroglyphic texts. Freidel's thoughtful chapter closes the volume by exploring the evolution of divine kingship from its Preclassic roots to its Terminal Classic demise, considering the cosmological centrality of the office of king and the relationships between kings and their followers, and contemplating the fragile, complicated, and often incomplete archaeological record that tells their tales.

Conclusions

The various case studies in this volume, deriving from many parts of the southern lowlands, show significant patterning in terms of:

- *Material/spatial foci*: including portable powerfacts (exotic and elite objects), monuments, friezes, liminal spaces (stairs and doorways), buildings (temples), and especially royal-residential courtyards, all of which were closely associated with the institution of kingship, and often specific kings
- *Behavioral residues*: specifically, the deposition of distinct artifact assemblages consisting of purposely broken and often burned items (including objects of prestige value and in many instances fragments of human bone); the burning of courtyards and buildings; the defacing of monuments, thrones, and friezes; the undermining of architectural elements so as to facilitate building collapse; the infilling of courtyards; and the execution of elite personages, including kings
- *Temporal range*: acknowledging the difficulty that often exists with regard to correlating specific acts of ritual and violence with the relatively short time frame during which a particular king was removed from office, *most* of the events discussed in the various case studies are thought to date to the period from AD 800 to 830
- *Intent*: although the perpetrators of the ritual and/or violence vary by case study, the intent seems to consistently be aimed at physically and symbolically removing specific rulers from power and desanctifying the politically and ideologically charged spaces and objects that were most vital to their claims to power and to the institution of kingship in general

Character: regardless of the level of violence and destruction exhibited, all of the case studies demonstrate some level of ritual praxis, and thus reverential behavior, implying that just as there were proper procedures for installing a new king, there were also appropriate techniques for removing them, regardless of the antagonist

Irrespective of these areas of general agreement, there are some differences of opinion concerning more specific areas of interpretation. Some of these relate to whether researchers see the various ritual and/or violent events as being representative of a rapid and tumultuous era of significant change leading to abandonments (Buttles and Valdez, Demarest et al., Inomata) or whether they are thought to mark a more subtle period of transition within a developmental sequence marked by considerable continuity (Golden et al., Navarro-Farr). The two camps are clearly influenced by the nature of events that occurred at particular archaeological sites; some were clearly more intense and others were much more understated (e.g., McAnany 2010, 197).

Our own opinion is that, even though many Maya centers now demonstrate considerable demographic continuity across the Late to Terminal Classic transition, we should not underestimate just how tumultuous, and thus significant, the period from AD 800 to 830 was, even for those who survived this era (Houston and Inomata 2009, 295, 300; Middleton 2012, 264). Consider the economic collapse of 2008. Will this economic decline and reorganization—which obviously had deleterious impacts on the lives of many citizens around the world—register in the archaeological record to the same degree as the material residues associated with the fall of the Maya kings during the thirty-year period in question? Not likely. We have long been fascinated by what happened at this time in Maya history precisely because the material indicators imply that this was a momentous disjuncture in a long developmental sequence marked by less dramatic ups and downs.

Nevertheless, this does not give us license to invoke apocalyptic scenarios in our efforts to reconstruct the circumstances related to the economic, political, and ideological changes that took place in the early ninth century. The contributions that highlight the dramatic events that seemingly imply significant discontinuities while also positing demographic and socio-cultural continuities likely capture the experiences of the majority—though clearly not all—of the southern lowland kingdoms in the AD 800–830 era (Guderjan and Hanratty; Harrison-Buck; Houk; Schwake and Iannone).

The contributors to this volume also disagree about the utility of the scapegoat king model for explaining what happened during the infamous Maya "collapse." To reiterate, most would agree that in ideological terms kings were the embodiment of their kingdoms and that most of the ritual and violence that characterized the period from AD 800 to 830 was therefore understandably focused on rulers and those most closely associated with them. Indeed, the latter may have been targeted because they suffered from a kind of "guilt by association" or possibly because they were considered "part of the king's regalia" (as Iannone discusses in chapter 2). The overall pattern seems to fit with the "centralist" aspects of the scapegoat king theory and does imply that rulers were more integrated with the dominant ideology than their followers, many of whom outlived them.

Be that as it may, the contributors all struggle with the issue of causation. Some seem more comfortable invoking economic and environmental decline and a failed response to an unsurmountable legitimation crisis tied to declining prosperity as the *ultimate* cause of the demise of the failed rulers (Buttles and Valdez; Demarest et al.; Guderjan and Hanratty; Schwake and Iannone). This stance does not, however, rule out warfare, intracommunity strife, or a combination of both as having been significant, albeit *proximate*, causes of the rapid dissolution of kingship governance in the specific case studies in question.

Others do not see declining prosperity as key to the demise of the kings. Rather, they invoke interkingdom warfare (Inomata; Golden et al.) or even conquest warfare led by agents from outside the Maya lowlands (Harrison-Buck) as their key explanatory devices. Nevertheless, it is not always clear what stimulated such endemic warfare. It is plausible, for instance, that the most aggressive kings were pressed into warfare precisely because they were struggling to maintain legitimacy due to declining prosperity in their own kingdoms. Attacking other kingdoms is, after all, one of the better-documented strategies of containment in the scapegoat king model (see Iannone, this volume). From this perspective, the destruction inflicted on other kingdoms and the ritual acts aimed at silencing them forever can again be viewed as *proximate* causes of the fall of specific kings; declining prosperity—whether economic, environmental, or a combination of both—was the *ultimate* cause.

In closing, it is important to consider why, unlike earlier examples of similar sets of ritual practices, which removed a sitting ruler in preparation for the installation of a new one, the ritual and violence that occurred between AD 800 and 830 spread rapidly through the southern lowlands, effectively bringing an end to Classic style kingship governance. Why did new kings not step in to fill the void, as had happened in the past? This is a difficult question to answer, but it undoubtedly has a lot to do with the changing world order. For one, environmental and economic issues may have become insurmountable, meaning that not only did competition for resources reach a previously unknown level (which only exacerbated the situation) but also support populations and less powerful but more resilient community leaders (i.e., lineage heads) may have considered the institution of kingship to be a drain on the system rather than an effective means of guaranteeing prosperity for all (e.g., McAnany 2010, 197). These traditional power brokers may even have been culpable, if only partially, in the removal of their own scapegoat rulers.

In addition, the endemic warfare kings carried out against other kings—likely part of a strategy of containment that became increasingly common in the late eighth to early ninth centuries—may have not only created a situation where there were fewer "rulers in waiting" than ever before but also the extensive destruction and ritual desanctification of powerfacts and places of power may have symbolically removed the precise tools that any prospective ruler would have needed to jump-start their kingdoms. If traditional power brokers (i.e., lineage heads) played a role in this process of deactivation in some cases, they were likely reluctant to help those with kingly intentions to simply "keep on carrying on" (e.g., Golden et al. this volume).

Still, even though the crucial AD 800–830 era can be seen as a time of intense environmental, economic, social, political, and even ideological change—resulting in the "ritual, violence, and fall of the Classic Maya kings" that is the focus of this volume—the places and objects of power, now broken, burned, buried, and unkempt, continued to resonate for the members of the surviving communities. As such, these powerfacts and monumental edifices were still periodically tapped into and manipulated in efforts to guarantee a productive and happy life in a world no longer dominated by divine kings and kingly governance structures.

Acknowledgments

We would like to thank Meredith Babb, our editor, and all of the other members of the University Press of Florida for their encouragement throughout the original formulation and ultimate revisions to this volume and their continued support for the project.

Note

1. The term *collapse*, as used in this volume, refers to a marked decline in sociopolitical complexity, normally over the course of two or three generations (Tainter 1988, 193; Tainter 2000, 332), that has negative impacts on human well-being (that is, at least for some segments of society), is unwanted, and cannot be avoided by implementing gradual changes to the current governance and/or economic systems (Young et al. 2007, 450).

2

Cross-Cultural Perspectives on the Scapegoat King

The Anatomy of a Model

GYLES IANNONE

The highly popular scapegoat king model is grounded in the belief that the legitimacy of those we have come to refer to as "kings" is closely tied to the actual *and* perceived prosperity of their kingdoms (Quigley 2005). Kings are required to 1) feed the gods by sponsoring and carrying out rituals in sanctified, often monumental spaces; 2) serve as the superlative symbolic representative of their kingdoms, as exemplified by demonstrations of their vigor, health, and prowess; their elaborate dress; the ornate symbols of prestige and authority they are adorned with and surrounded by; and the grandiose settings they build and act through; and, 3) redistribute prosperity by bestowing titles, emblems, and land and labor grants on their clients (Feeley-Harnik 1985). Maintaining legitimacy through these actions is easier during times of plenty. But, according to the model, problems arise during times of socioecological stress because the ability of kings to maintain the illusion of prosperity can be compromised, and they may therefore face a "legitimation crisis" (Habermas 1975; Zhao 2009), forcing them to adopt a "strategy of containment" in order to hold onto power (Jameson 1981). This stratagem often involves a ramping up of the same set of activities and symbolic displays as outlined above. Clearly, these customary responses have the potential to exacerbate an already difficult situation because the actions that are associated with them are major drains on the kingdom's finances, even in the best of times. The fundamental premise of the scapegoat king model is that when these strategies of containment fail, it is the kings who are ultimately held responsible, and as a result they are often literally and figuratively removed from power.

In this chapter I explore these ideas through a cross-cultural examination of the tenets of the scapegoat king model, with particular emphasis on the assumption that kings establish, maintain, and lose legitimacy within this analytical framework. The themes presented here are potentially relevant to our understanding of how the institution of kingship developed in the Maya area and why this mode of political authority fell out of favor during the early ninth century AD. Nonetheless, there are still some issues concerning the overt functionalism inherent in this model (see chapter 1), and its explanatory power should not be simply assumed but rather critically evaluated, as is done at the end of this chapter.

Legitimacy, Order, and the Creation of a King

According to Norman Yoffee (1979, 15), a state is a sociopolitical formation that "depends on its ability to express the legitimacy of differentiated social elements, acting through generalized structures of authority by which it transcends the various societal components and gives an order to the stratification of those components." Here, legitimacy refers to "the institutionalization of people's acceptance of, involvement in, and contribution towards order" (Baines and Yoffee 2000, 15). In early stratified societies, maintaining the legitimacy of the hierarchical system, with all of its inequalities and ideological underpinnings, was the raison d'être of the political actors we refer to as kings. These individuals were "owed service" precisely because they were perceived to be "the guarantors of earthly law and order" (Yoffee 2000, 46). The term "king," according to Claessen (2005, 233–234):

> refers in the first place to the ruler of a kingdom.... Whatever symbols and rituals are found in connection with kingship—a king is in the first place a ruler, a specific type of ruler, distinguishable from a chief or head man on the one hand, and a president on the other.... [A king is] a supreme, hereditary ruler of an independent stratified society, having the legitimate power to enforce decisions... According to this definition, the distinction between head man and chief on the one hand and king on the other hand can be readily established: head men or chiefs do not have the legitimate right to enforce decisions, even though they sometimes do.... The distinction between king and president is equally clear: a president is elected[;] heredity does not play a role.... Thus kingship is, or was, a specific type of sociopolitical leadership distinguished from chiefship and presidency.

By means of example, Angkorian kingship has been described in the following manner:

> The State is the King, whose power is limitless, and who is the absolute leader of the country, of its armies, of all its political and administrative affairs. The sovereign appoints and dismisses all dignitaries, great mandarins and provincial governors; he establishes and shares out taxes in fixed shares, and disposes to his liking the kingdom's revenues, of which he is the great usufructor. Supreme judge, he has the power of life and death, of mercy, of revision and judgments.... Unique legislator, his ordinances have the force of law; he makes and revises codes, he promulgates them in solemn audience [Aymonier as quoted in Coe 2003, 135].

Creating the "Stranger King"

Historically, the institution of kingship has manifested itself in varying ways around the world. Usually, however, kings are created as a result of some form of installation ritual that is aimed at transforming a "normal" person into someone who is different from all others (Feeley-Harnik 1985, 275–287; Quigley 2005, 4). On a philosophical level, the installation ritual symbolically kills the individual, who is subsequently reborn as a new being, now separated from his/her own kin group (Quigley 2005, 3). For example, among the Akwapim of southeastern Ghana it is believed that to become a king it is not sufficient to simply be born into an important lineage; the individual must also go through a series of rituals aimed at separating himself from others. The candidate for king is "metaphorically put to death in the installation rite.... He is then a living-dead man" (Gilbert 2008, 172–173). This transformation is effectively captured by the "stranger-king" model, which stresses the idea that the rituals create a stranger, someone who is no longer the same person he once was (Feeley-Harnik 1985, 280; Helms 1993). The sanctified installation rituals create not only a "stranger" but also someone who is now invested with legitimate, divine authority (Feeley-Harnik 1985, 275–287; Trigger 2003, 79–87).

Divine or Not Divine? That Is the Question

It has been suggested "that the segregation of the king's person and his dependence on others for the satisfaction of his simplest needs is a direct consequence of the extraordinary powers he is believed to embody" (Drucker-Brown 2005, 182). These powers derive not only from the fact that the king exhibits the qualities of an "other" (Helms 1993; Trigger 2003, 79–87) but also because he is conceived of as a "living ancestor" who is in direct contact with the cosmological forces that created the universe (Helms 1999, 199). These are the god-kings, or divine kings, whose images and deeds have left an indelible mark on history (O'Connor 1983, 33; Trigger 2003, 79–87).

Divine kings are often thought to be the offspring of the gods or earthly manifestations of gods. As a result, they share a bond of kinship with and therefore become the community's strongest link to the supernatural realm. As quasi-supernatural beings, kings therefore have the potential to affect people's lives in the same way that a god does (e.g., they can promote fertility and military success [Trigger 2003, 79–87]). According to Virginia Fields (1989, 9):

> The capacity of rulers to interact with supernatural powers, to intercede between humans and gods for the good of the populace, is a primary characteristic of divine kingship, a phenomenon commonly associated with societies making the transition from simple and egalitarian to complex and hierarchical. In divine kingship, ruling elites utilize notions of cosmic order to sustain the structure of their earthly domains.

Examples of divine kings can be found throughout the world. Egyptian kings were conceived of as living gods (Fagan 1999, 110), more specifically as the "the god Horus on earth, holding exclusive ability to liaise with supernatural forces and divine beings" (Richards 2000, 38). Among the Pallavas of South India, the "king was seen as descended from one of the great gods of the parānic tradition, Visnu or Siva" (Dirks 1987, 28). The neighboring Cholas also considered their kings to be like gods; they believed them to be the holy "possessors of the earth" (Heitzman 1997, 62). In Southeast Asia, the lives of the "god-kings" were believed to be "modelled on a still higher world of the gods," as were their royal courts and exemplary capitals (O'Connor 1983, 33). Kings in Tahiti and the Tonga Islands were also believed to be "descended from the gods. . . . Because of this descent they had a direct connection with the gods and ancestors, and hence they could influence fertility and well-being" (Claessen 2005, 243–244). Finally, Inka kings were thought to be the divine offspring of the sun god (Van Buren 2000).

In the case of the ancient Maya, David Freidel and Linda Schele (1988a, 1988b) argue that during the Late Preclassic period (400 BC–AD 250), certain buildings adorned with masks of gods began to serve as stages for a new type of leader who wished to express close ties with the supernatural forces. By the Early Classic (AD 250–550), there was a shift toward depicting actual human faces on these buildings, which likely marks the appearance of divine rulers or, in other words, the first true Maya kings (e.g., McAnany 2010, 38). By the end of this period many of these kings begin to use the title *k'uhul ajaw*, which implies that they were indeed presenting themselves as "divine lords" (Houston and Inomata 2009, 132; McAnany 2010, 168). Some kings even started to include references to the Sun God in their names, using the appellation *k'inich* (Houston and Inomata 2009, 141).

Other key representations of Maya divine kingship were also firmly established by the Early Classic (McAnany 2010, 38). The special relationship between kings and the supernatural powers was highlighted in symbols of authority, iconography (McAnany 2010, 166), royal titles, and texts (Demarest 2013, 374). These confirm that Maya kings served as intermediaries between their communities and the supernatural forces that guaranteed fertility and prosperity (Houston and Inomata 2009, 63). For example, David Freidel and Justine Shaw (2000, 278, 280) underscore that many kingly rituals, especially those related to maize, were tied to the time of creation and highlighted control over the "forces of prosperity" (see also Freidel and Shaw 2000, 278, 292; McAnany 2010, 166).

The shift in social logic associated with the emergence of divine kingship in the Maya world did not mean that non-elites stopped carrying out small-scale, localized rituals aimed at beseeching the supernatural powers to provide the sun and rain required for plentiful crops (Lucero 2006, 28). However, it seems clear that by the Early Classic period, the power of Maya kings and their ability to legitimately demand the natural and human surplus of their supporters were increasingly based on their claim to close connections with the supernatural powers, whom they personally petitioned and accessed through state-sponsored rituals (Freidel and Shaw 2000, 278, 280; Lucero 2006, 183). Such powerful intermediaries were likely deemed useful because gods were often unpredictable, spiteful, petulant, and generally disorderly, although this also meant that they did not make the best model for kingly behavior (Houston and Inomata 2009, 34). Ultimately, Maya gods were not conceived of as being infallible, and thus neither were their kings (Houston and Inomata 2009, 34; Webster 2002b, 440).

Considering this issue more broadly, many have questioned whether in fact any king, anytime or anywhere, was ever really conceived of as a "divine" being with powers on par with those of the gods. Luc de Heusch

(2005, 34) has argued that there is in fact considerable variability when it comes to the purported divine nature of those we call kings. This is because the institution of kingship is "shaped by historical, political, and cultural factors" (Brisch 2008, 8). For example, "The king is not assimilated with a divinity in traditional black Africa as he was in ancient Egyptian civilization, which presents a variant type of sacred kingship that can be found elsewhere in the Middle East" (Heusch 2005, 25). Likewise, "Persian kingship is characterized by a special relationship between the ruler and the gods, although no divine descent or god-like qualities are attributed to the king" (Wiesehöfer 2009, 88). It is also unlikely that kings in India or Southeast Asia were perceived as gods. They may have been treated as such, but this was often a formality (De Casparis and Mabbett 1992, 322–323). For instance, although the Chola kings of south India were given names with the suffix *dēva*, meaning "god"—implying that they had some "divine attribute"—these appear to be coronation names rather than titles used throughout the king's life. Alternatively, we are told that although *some* Angkorian kings were referred to as "the god who is king" during their lives, for *most* rulers, divine titles were attributed to them only after death (Higham 2001, 151, 248). Similarly, although to be considered legitimate a Burmese king had to be an "amalgam"—at once "a deity, a human, and superhuman" (Aung-Thwin 1985, 68)—the people were often reluctant to stress the king's superhuman qualities, even in the context of public documents (Aung-Thwin 1985, 61). Ultimately, in Southeast Asia, the degree of divineness varied from region to region (De Casparis and Mabbett 1992, 322–323).

According to Peter Bedford (2009, 35), "While the king was the supreme human being in Assyrian thought, he was mortal all the same, and Assyrians resisted the deification of their ruler, which had been known in Sumer and early Babylonia." Still, Yoffee (1979, 18) argues that although they may not have been conceptualized as truly divine, in mid-third-millennium Mesopotamia "the rulers [still] *attempted* to depict themselves as the legitimate representatives of the deities" and thus the rightfully designated authority that could "mobilize resources from the temple estates" (emphasis mine). Reinhard Bernbeck (2008, 160) concurs, suggesting that

> deification of kings in ancient Mesopotamia may . . . be conceptualized as a means towards an end, the maintenance of extreme distance by a ruler to his immediate subjects, a shielding off for the protection of individual power. It is not so much the king's transcendent status

as god, but rather the ritualization of government practices that guarantees the stability of political power relations within the institutional apparatuses of government through constant interpellation of those who deal with the king on a daily basis.

Likewise, in a more general statement on divine kingship, J. G. De Casparis and Ian Mabbett (1992, 323–324) conclude that "it is necessary to remember that, whatever it implies for the notion of royal divinity, it did not mean that any ruler once crowned was treated by everyone with awe-filled veneration and unquestioning obedience.... The significance of divine kingship then, is not as an instrument of enhanced power. It is, rather, a ritual statement."

Live Long and Prosper

Regardless of the degree to which individual kings were considered divine beings, cross-culturally, the institution of kingship has traditionally centered on three main issues: administration of the sacred, force, and prosperity (Feeley-Harnik 1985). My focus here is the last aspect, which some have gone so far as to suggest is the principal factor that creates the institution of kingship (Feeley-Harnik 1985; Quigley 2005). When one consults the literature, various examples emerge to support the consistent associations among kings, legitimacy, and prosperity (Lucero 2006, 21) and the notion that the leaders of early states were obliged to guarantee the well-being of their followers (Lucero 2006, 17).

Kingship and Prosperity

We are told that Egyptian rulers were the "very essence of the divine order of a prosperous world nourished by a bountiful river" (Fagan 1999, 110). The Egyptian king's special connection to fertility is exemplified by a macehead that depicts the "scorpion king" digging an irrigation canal (Hughes 2001, 39). Egyptian kings also built granaries to deal with poor harvests (Hughes 2001, 40). Kings in other African societies, such as those of the Jukun, were also intricately tied to notions of fertility, especially the productivity of plants (Heusch 1997, 217). Elsewhere in Africa, Bemba kings were perceived to be "rainmakers," and their health and behavior was thought to reflect that of the kingdom as a whole (Heusch 2005, 27). In the Sudan, "kings are answerable to their subjects on the state of the weather.... [They are] known as 'rainmakers.'... The security expected from the King includes protection from violence by enemies, but also from epidemics, earthquakes, droughts, pests and plagues" (Simonse 2005, 70). Christopher Taylor (2010, 254) has recently provided a good example of the close ties between kingship and prosperity in Rwanda (see also Taylor, this volume):

> In early Rwanda collective care for the fertility of the land, people, and livestock was one of the most important values held by all ethnic groups. The king's role in ensuring fertility was perceived as indispensable. Through the rituals prescribed by complex dynastic code, the king presided over the descent of *imaana* (fertility or divine beneficence) from sky and earth. The king's capacity to accomplish this was contingent on the degree to which he successfully embodied the ideals of kingship. Liquids—including rain, milk, honey, semen, blood, and even rivers—were important as symbols of these ideals. For example, the king was the foremost rainmaker for the kingdom and risked his throne in the case of prolonged drought. He also risked it in the case of too much rain. The orderly flow of fertility from sky to earth involved the king's maintenance of ritual purity and the eradication of impurity.

Turning to Southeast Asia, we are told that starting as early as the eleventh century AD, Burmese kings regularly dressed up as the god Sakka (i.e., Indra) to conduct the *laythwan maṅgalā*, "the auspicious ploughing ritual to insure the arrival of the monsoons" (Aung-Thwin 1985, 49). Brigitta Hauser-Schäublin (2005, 748) has recently uncovered evidence to suggest that Balinese kings also "acted as a prime promoter of fertility for the benefit of [the] people, their fields, and their livestock" (see also Hauser-Schäublin 2003, 166). At the great Khmer center of Angkor, an inscription presents Yashovarman I "as the husband of the earth, who filled it with virtue, pleasure and fecundity" (Higham 2001, 159). All Khmer rulers apparently tried to maintain good rice crops by dealing with unpredictable rainfall (Higham 1989, 350). The close relationship between kingship and prosperity among the Khmer is summarized by Charles Higham (1989, 350), who concludes that "it is important to realize that the Angkorian *Mandala* was underwritten by the production of rice to feed the elite, the bureaucrats, specialists and the corveé labour force.... Royal, and that is synonymous with divine, intervention to counter unpredictable rainfall was one of the hallmarks of Angkor." An excellent summation of the connection between kings and fertility in Southeast Asia has been provided by Kenneth Hall (2011, 110):

In traditional Malay belief, both the source of the river waters and the home of the ancestral spirits were high on the upstream mountain slopes; the highest reaches of the mountains were thought of as the holiest places and the source of beneficial forces that bestowed well-being upon the people. . . . The Srivijayan king drew upon these beliefs as he took the title "Lord of the Mountain." . . . But he was also "Lord of the Isles" and able to commune with the "spirits of the waters of the sea," a dangerous force that had to be propitiated and whose powers had to be absorbed by the king. . . . Thus he presumably linked the spirits of the upstream and downstream in the person of the king. . . . The king's magical powers, closely associated with fertility, were also linked with the river. The magic of the association between the king and the water was so strong that it was dangerous for the king to bathe in ordinary water for fear of causing a flood. His bath water had to be treated with flower petals before it was safe. And there were other fertility taboos. On a specific day each year the king could not eat grain. If he did, there might be a crop failure. Nor was he able to leave his realm, for if he did, the sun's rays might go with him, the skies would darken, and the crops would fail.

Elsewhere, the Mahayana Buddhist kings of Java were expected to ensure the well-being of their realms and to help their followers achieve Nirvana (Dumarcay 1978, 8). Such expectations were also common in other Buddhist kingdoms across Asia. Among the Silla of Korea, the "King told the future by looking at the wind and the clouds, and it was said that he knew in advance if there would be calamity from flood and fire and if the harvest would be bountiful or poor" (Nelson 2008, 188). Rulers in Korea and Japan both discovered "the intent of the spirits through séance and divination, as well as by making the proper sacrifices to produce the desired outcome. The well-being of the community—and eventually the continuation of the state itself—depended on the knowledge of the shaman leaders" (Nelson 2008, 228).

According to James Frazer (1993 [1922], 292), Greek kings were also held responsible for both the crops and the weather. Similarly, Inka rulers used gold sticks to break the earth during the festival of the sun, marking the new agricultural year (Van Buren 2000, 80). Elsewhere, in Tonga and Tahiti, the supreme rulers were "sacred, guaranteed fertility and well-being, and handed out rewards and punishments" (Claessen 2005, 243–244).

Finally, iconography and textual data support the idea that the principal roles of Maya kings were to guarantee water and food during times of need and to be able to maintain the agricultural and water-management systems that facilitated such beneficence, even though they may not have legally owned or even controlled these "critical" resources (Demarest 2013, 375–376, 393–394; Freidel and Shaw 2000, 274, 277, 291; Lucero 1999; Lucero 2006, 2; McAnany 2010, 43). There are, as in other parts of the world, textual metaphors that conflate the rituals of Maya kings with activities associated with agriculture, such as planting and harvesting (Houston and Inomata 2009, 145). Like their Burmese counterparts, Maya kings also regularly impersonated gods during their ritual performances, including some directly associated with prosperity (i.e., Chak, the rain god; Itzam-Yeh, the magical bird and source of prosperity; and, Hun-Nal-Yeh, One Maize; Freidel and Shaw 2000, 278, 280).

Kings as Environmental Stewards

In terms of some early examples of "stewardship" (Redman 1999, 22), Donald Hughes (2001, 40) reminds us that in "the Biblical story of Joseph's interpretation of Pharaoh's dream, and his advice to build granaries to prepare for hard times . . . the pharaoh and governmental officials tried to even out fluctuations of supply and demand by storing surplus in good years and distributing it when the harvests failed." Yoffee (1979, 21), in discussing mid-third-millennium Mesopotamia, relates that "if the state did not maintain the balance between the goods and services that could be mobilized from locally organized units and those that remained properly embedded within them, then instability, disintegration, and even environmental degradation were the likely results." In the Archaemenid/Persian Empire, kings were "obliged to protect the god's good creations" (Wiesehöfer 2009, 88), and they apparently traveled around their realms to make sure that their governors were using resources efficiently and sustainably. If they were not, the king could remove them and replace them with a new governor (Hughes 2001, 59). Both the Greeks and the Romans understood that intensive agriculture could lead to decreasing yields over time, and they therefore developed various means to maintain production such as manuring, fallow periods, and terracing (Redman 1999, 20). In ancient Athens, kings were required to manage resources effectively—including agricultural lands, water, and trees—although it is true that they often did not do a very good job of this (Hughes 2001, 59–66). In China, kings ruled through a "mandate of heaven," and the underlying philosophy—even to this day—is that it is the ruler's responsibility to manage the state's resources in an efficient and sustainable manner (e.g., Hughes 2001, 69; Ponting 2007, 127–128; Zhao 2009), although here too damage to the environment often occurred under the king's watch (Redman 1999, 23; Ponting 2007, 127–128). Finally, the three main monotheistic religions—Judaism, Christianity, and Islam—all refer to a general ethos of respect for nature and the thoughtful use of resources, even if it is true that in practice this ethos was not always achieved (Hughes 2001, 58; Redman 1999, 22).

Summary

As these myriad examples demonstrate, although kings may be incredibly wealthy, the institution of kingship is really founded on the idea of broader prosperity for all (Quigley 2005, 2). There is, however, a significant degree of what Henry Orenstein (1980) has called "asymmetric reciprocity" at play in most kingdoms, wherein the ruler of the state receives the lion's share of material wealth and in return gives back mainly nonmaterial items, such as ideological guarantees (e.g., guarantees of fertility [for women, crops, animals], peace, and prosperity; see also Claessen and van de Velde 1991, 8–19). That said, no king reigned for long without providing some tangible benefits to his followers, such as lavish feasts and ceremonies, gifts, protection, and the redistribution of surplus produce and labor (Lucero 2006, 31; Webster 2002b, 443).

With specific reference to the scapegoat king model, it is posited that the three principal ways that kings have traditionally demonstrated their vital role in maintaining the prosperity of their kingdoms are by 1) feeding the gods; 2) presenting themselves as the superlative representative of their polities; and 3) redistributing prosperity (Feeley-Harnik 1985).

Kings Feed the Gods

The legitimacy of kings has always been closely connected to their role in sustaining the gods. Within many belief systems around the world there is some concept of "original debt," which centers on the idea that humans are indebted to the gods for producing and reproducing their existence on a daily basis (McAnany 2010, 68). In order to service this debt, people from all segments of society carry out various forms of ritual, including sacrifice, to help circulate some form of "cosmic energy" that both sustains the gods and animates the universe (Bloch and Parry 1982; Trigger 2003). In many cultures the circulation of this cosmic energy is structured, in ideological terms, around a social contract referred to as the "sacred covenant" or "universal contract" (Joyce 2000, 75; Monaghan 2000, 39). This covenant outlines obligations and expectations for the gods, commoners, and kings. In essence, gods provide part of themselves, in the form of sun, rain, and fertile earth—in the correct amounts—so that commoners may produce and perpetuate themselves, and they in turn supply surplus produce and labor to the king, who is charged with using this tax or tribute wisely to build sacred spaces and carry out the required rituals that sustain the gods (see also Trigger 2003, 473–475, 490). According to Patricia McAnany (2010, 90), "We need to envision the past replete with ritual practice—particularly offerings—designed to ameliorate the impact of humans on the earth and to compensate earthly deities for such invasive practices."

An example from the Chola kingdom of South India succinctly captures the expectations of the universal contract: "The people of the kingdom came to the king to proffer gifts in the form of personal service and the earth's bounty. In return, the ruler as possessor re-endowed his subjects with gifts in the form of protection and enjoyment of the earth" (Heitzman 1997, 62). Another example from the Chola region underscores that "dues from land were gifts to the overlord, in the way worship was given to the gods" (74). Ultimately, "the Cholas defined political power as the ability to protect and propagate dharma [power that upholds the natural order of the universe] throughout the world, and the legitimate ruler as the person who most effectively carried out this work" (217).

Among the Maya it was believed that when humans died, their flesh entered the ground as the ultimate repayment for supernatural beneficence (Houston and Inomata 2009, 37). The Maya also practiced many forms of sacrifice to service their original debt to the supernatural forces (McAnany 2010, 97) and to release *ch'ulel*, or "cosmic energy," back into the universe (Freidel et al. 1993, 205; Schele and Miller 1986). These practices included 1) burning incense; 2) making sacrificial offerings of food, animals, alcohol, captives, and themselves; and, 3) holding feasts and smashing the material items used in these ceremonies (McAnany 2010, 281). Maya kings were legitimately able to acquire tax and/or tribute because they were charged with carrying out the most awe inspiring and potent sacrifices and rituals, all of which were aimed at servicing the original debt of the kingdom (Demarest 2013, 375; McAnany 2010, 67–69). To underscore their special role in the social contract, Maya kings took sacrificial practices to an extreme, through various forms of auto-sacrifice, usually some form of bloodletting (Freidel et al. 1993, 205).

In summary, the social contract that emerges as a result of the sacred covenant links the various components of the universe into a single, hierarchical system in which the gods are the most powerful and important entities: "Humans may eat the gods, but it is the gods who do most of the eating" (Monaghan 2000, 39). One should not, however, underestimate the key role that kings assume in the sacred covenant. Although everyone in a community can conduct rituals that help sustain the universe and therefore guarantee prosperity, it is the rulers of polities who are charged with carrying out the most potent rituals and sacrifices. They also control the most sacred settings and the most powerful sacrificial materials, and they have the loudest voices when it comes to attracting the god's favor (Baines and Yoffee 2000, 17; Trigger 2003, 486–490). In other words, in times of stress—such as periods of declining prosperity—it is the king's voice that has the best chance of being heard. For this reason, although much of the load for supporting the ritual practices of the state fell on the backs of commoners—the state's primary producers—kings, in particular, played a crucial role in helping cosmic energy flow throughout the universe (Trigger 2003, 486–490; see also Errington [1989] for the Sulawesi of Indonesia; Freidel et al. [1993] for the Maya; and O'Connor [2000] for Egypt).

Kings Are Symbolic of Their Kingdom's Prosperity

Kings are also the superlative symbolic representative of their polities (Feeley-Harnik 1985; Frazer 1993 [1922]; Quigley 2005). Their legitimacy and the prosperity of their kingdom is invariably reflected in 1) the construction of public works, such as temples, palaces, roads, hospitals, defensive walls, and reservoirs; 2) the hosting and financing of extravagant ceremonies (rituals, feasts, etc.); 3) the king's extraordinary attire and accoutrements, including clothing, jewelry, and symbolically charged emblems; and 4) the overall appearance of the king and the royal court, which should appear strong and vibrant (Frazer 1993 [1922]; Trigger 2003, 79–87).

Kings have regularly enhanced their own prosperity and that of their kingdom through the effective use of labor. As a result, public works, especially those related to ritual practices, emerge as key symbols of the prosperity of a kingdom (Childe 1950, 16; Feeley-Harnik 1985; Quigley 2005). That this connection developed very early on is attested by the fact that it was often the "first-generation" states that built the largest and arguably most impressive temple structures (Flannery and Marcus 2012, 411). Examples documenting the connection between public works and prosperity can be found throughout the world.

The Epic of Gilgamesh provides us with a perspective from ancient Mesopotamia:

> I will proclaim to the world the deeds of Gilgamesh. . . . In Uruk he built walls, a great rampart. . . . Look at it still today; the outer wall where the cornice runs, it shines with the brilliance of copper; and it has no equal. Touch the threshold, it is ancient. . . . Climb upon the wall of Uruk; walk along it, I say; regard the foundation terrace and examine the masonry: is it not burnt brick and good? (Sandars 1972 as quoted in Hughes 2001, 34)

For South India, Nicholas Dirks (1987, 65) emphasizes that "the excellence of the city . . . is a direct extension of [the king]. . . . The decoration of these avenues and gateways are the ornaments of the king. . . . The city is beautiful as much because it exudes prosperity in every corner as because it is beautifully decorated and symmetrical in its design."

Turning to Southeast Asia, Higham tells us that

> Angkor was essentially the centre of a court society involved in the pursuit of perfection. The successive temple-mausolea constructed there represented heaven in stone, and they were built to house the immortal essence of successive overlords. They were also centers for ritual performances, reviews and displays of wealth and munificence which advertised the overlord's god-like status. (1989, 352)

It is said that for the Khmer, "ambrosia flowed from the temple-city out into the country-side" (O'Connor 1983, 35). In fact, across Southeast Asia it was believed that the higher the temple, the greater the merit accrued by its sponsor and the greater its attraction to others who wished to partake in its splendor (36). In essence, temple construction was a "moral achievement" that not only transformed the kingly sponsor's wealth, influence, and resources into status (35–36) but also benefited the kingdom as a whole.

Documents also indicate that after the Burmese king Aniruddha "killed his brother in fair combat for the throne," he was urged by the god Sakka (i.e., Indra) to take the following remedial action:

> O King, if thou wouldst mitigate thine evil deed in sinning against thine elder brother, build many pagodas [tiered or cone-shaped

temples], gu [hollow temples], monastaries, and rest houses, and share merit with thine elder brother. Devise thou many wells, ponds, dams, and ditches, fields and canals, and share the merit with thine elder brother. (Aung-Thwin 1985, 63)

This passage clearly outlines what types of infrastructure projects were expected of a legitimate Burmese king.

Finally, it is also apparent that Maya kings regularly presented themselves as the superlative symbols of their kingdom's prosperity by building impressive architectural features, such as temples, ball courts, and palaces, and public works, such as terraces, roads, and reservoirs (Flannery and Marcus 2012, 385; McAnany 2010, 277–281). Monumental architecture and the associated plazas and courtyards provided the settings for opulent ceremonies that legitimized the accrual of surplus by community leaders (Demarest 2013, 373–374). The various water-management features may have been particularly important to the legitimacy of ancient Maya rulers, given the seasonality of rainfall in the tropics (see Demarest 2013, 375–376, 393–394; Lucero 1999, 2006; McAnany 2010, 93; Scarborough 1998).

According to Bruce Trigger (2003, 89–91), kings also consistently legitimize their special position in society through their extravagant lifestyle (see also O'Connor 1983, 106–110), one that very few get to see and most just dream about. Royal court complexes, which included palaces, temples, abundant servants, exotic beasts, gardens, and feasts, symbolize the uniqueness of the king. The strength and prosperity of the kingdom is presented to the world by the elaborateness and complexity of its royal court, and courtly activities and styles become something to emulate. Kings and their courts are perceived as the "epitome of civilization" (O'Connor 1983, 33).

A good example of such outward displays of prosperity is related to us by Zhou Daguan, a Chinese emissary who visited Angkor in AD 1297:

All the ministers, officials, and relatives of the king were in front, riding elephants. Their red parasols, too many to number, were visible in the distance. Next came the king's wives and concubines and their servants, some in palanquins and carts, others on horses or elephants, with well over a hundred gold filigree parasols. Last came the king, standing on an elephant, the gold sword in his hand and the tusks of his elephant encased in gold. He had more than twenty white parasols decorated with gold filigree, their handles all made of gold. Surrounding him on all four sides were elephants in very large numbers, with soldiers to protect him as well. (Harris 2007, 83)

Zhou Daguan's firsthand observations highlight the important role fancy clothes, baubles, trinkets, crowns, staffs, and other objects serve in kingly legitimization (see also Trigger 2003, 89–91). Such items of royal regalia have been termed "powerfacts" by Michael Hoffman (1979, 294) because they "embody and personify the sovereign status of the ruler" (Fields 1989, 13). For example, Khmer kings wielded the *preah khan*, "the sacred sword and symbol of kingship" (Higham 2001, 154). Similarly, according to Zhou Daguan (1296):

> Only the king can wear material with a full pattern of flowers on it. On his head he wears a gold crown, like the crown worn by the Holder of the Diamond. Sometimes he goes without a crown, and simply wears a chain of fragrant flowers such as jasmine wound around the braids of his hair. Around his neck he wears a large pearl weighing about four pounds. On his wrists and ankles and all his fingers and toes he wears gold bracelets and rings, all of them inlaid with cat's-eye gemstones. He goes barefoot, and the soles of his feet and the palms of his hands are dyed crimson with a red preparation. When he goes out he has a gold sword in his hand. . . . Senior officials and relatives of the king can wear cloth with a scattered floral design, while junior officials and no others can wear cloth with a two-flower design. Among the ordinary people, only women can wear cloth with this design. (Harris 2007, 50–51)

Likewise, among the Swazi of southern Africa, certain animal species, such as eagles and lions, are considered to hold particular powers and characteristics, and thus their feathers and pelts could only be worn by kings because these animals were thought to "personify the traits of ideal rulers" (Fields 1989, 13).

Elizabeth Brumfiel (2000, 134) describes the importance of specific items of regalia to the legitimacy of Aztec kings:

> In the official ideology of the Aztec state at the time of European contact, order, legitimacy, and wealth were very closely linked. According to the Aztecs, the world order depended upon the circulation of *tonalli*, a heat-light-energy force that was indispensable for existence. . . . Aztec rulers claimed to be endowed with greater *tonalli* than their subjects. . . . The ruler's *tonalli* was evident in his

royal raiment. . . . Rulers were garbed in elite craft products that radiated light. Metal objects and gem stones were polished until they gleamed . . . feathered headdresses and standards were arranged so that they shimmered. . . . Even stone sculptures and wooden objects were finished to a high luster. When the ruler donned his royal finery, metal, stone, and feathered objects radiated sparks of divine fire. The strength of the ruler's *tonalli* was manifest.

In the Maya world, sumptuous feasts and grandiose ceremonies celebrated the magnificence of the king and the kingdom at the same time that these events blatantly reaffirmed and built on sociopolitical differences (Dietler 2001, 85–88; McAnany 2010, 163). Maya kings also differentiated themselves from their supporters by their lavish residential compounds, their ability to sponsor artisans of great skill and renown, and display of the results of such artistic production on their person and on monumental architecture, which might even contain their personal image (Lucero 2006, 31; McAnany 2010, 159, 195–196). The grandeur of the monumental precincts and the rituals they were the setting for signified not just a vigorous king but also a strong kingdom; the two were inextricably linked (Lucero 2006, 153).

In the same way, in the Maya world the most commonly referred to tribute items were not food staples but emblems of authority and power, such as cacao, quetzal feathers, *spondylus* shells, jadeite, or cloth (McAnany 2010, 286–288). Many of these items became key components of a king's regalia, the sum total of which resplendently displayed his power and vivacity (McAnany 2010, 277–281). Donning the costume of the maize god, orating from a temple adorned with ritually charged iconography, or having green quetzal feathers, water lilies, or fish attached to their costumes were particularly palpable ways through which Maya kings underscored their key role in maintaining fertility and prosperity (Freidel 2008, 192, 194; Lucero 1999, 2006; McAnany 2010, 154, 166; McAnany and Gallareta Negrón 2010, 157–158).

Finally, it has also been suggested that the king's "regalia" also included certain functionaries, at least according to Clifford Geertz (1980, 126), who posits that

> in Bali, as in most of the rest of Southeast Asia . . . the king, no mere ecclesiarch, was the numinous center of the world, and the priests were the emblems, ingredients, and effectors of his sanctity. Like the heirlooms already mentioned, like his sarongs, his umbrellas, his palanquin, and his jewelry, like his palace, his wives, his linggas, his

cremation tower, his fetes, his wars; indeed . . . like the realms as a whole—priests were parts of the king's regalia.

Beyond the regalia itself, the king's body, and physical appearance was also very closely connected to perceptions of legitimacy and strength. As the physical manifestation of a kingdom's success and prosperity, the health and welfare of a king is a direct embodiment of the state itself; this is why kings are consistently portrayed as young, powerful, and vigorous, rather than as old and feeble (Trigger 2003, 79–87). With few exceptions where rulers did not lead their armies into battle, such as the Neo-Assyrian Empire (Bedford 2009, 35), kings were considered to be the supreme military leaders of their kingdoms, and to be considered legitimate they often had to be successful warriors, as was true for the Aztecs (Smith 2008, 89). Among the Maya, capturing the lords of other polities and ransoming them or their body parts for tribute was also an effective means of demonstrating the strength and vitality of a king. Such military successes also brought additional natural and human resources to the conqueror (McAnany 2010, 278–281). Tribute finance would have been especially important in tropical lowland environments, where long-term storage is a problem (McAnany 2010, 291).

As Richard O'Connor (1983, 20) has succinctly described, in Southeast Asia, those who exhibited "prowess," especially those that were capable of subduing their political foes and who were therefore perceived to dominate the physical and spiritual world, attracted followers who wished to partake in their influence. Subordinates also made offerings at the temples such overlords controlled, again in efforts to tap into the latter's power. In discussing how these principles manifested themselves among the Khmer, Wolters (1979, 435) concludes that "society . . . would also have been perceived as the scene of relationships between those with different capacities for achievement, enabling the man of superior prowess to provide those of lesser prowess with opportunities for achieving within their capacity."

From a different but related perspective, the literature is quite consistent in stating that because the king's body represented the kingdom as a whole in many parts of Africa (Heusch 2005, 27; Gilbert 2008, 184), if they were ill or old, the king had to be killed or removed. In some parts of Africa it was also believed that kings absorb the sins and deaths of their subjects, so they must be repeatedly purified or sacrificed as a scapegoat (Heusch 1997, 217). As Michelle Gilbert (2008, 184) informs us, "If the king becomes ill, Odiwra [purification] cannot be performed and it is believed that grave misfortune will follow. Should the illness persist, something must be done. While the Shilluk [in the Sudan] would ritually strangle their sick or impotent king to save the kingship, in Akropong [southeastern Ghana] the solution was 'voluntary' abdication."

In Southeast Asia, especially the Buddhist kingdoms, the state of a person's physical body was also a sign of his or her "moral status" (O'Connor 1983, 104), the implication being that legitimate kings needed to appear beautiful and vigorous.

Similarly, the "symbolic association of the ruler's body and its fluids were part of the corporeal conception of the sacredness of Maya rulers" (Demarest 2013, 375). Their bodies could also be connected to the sun, specifically its "radiance" or its "vital force," and references and iconography underscore the beauty of the king's body and its connection to pleasing fragrances, such as those coming from flowers (McAnany 2010, 168). Maya kings also had special diets, as demonstrated by iconography and isotope studies (169–174). Finally, Maya kings were expected to be superlative performers (174–176).

Kings Redistribute Prosperity

Finally, the legitimacy of kings is also closely connected to their ability to redistribute prosperity (Helms 1993, 87; McAnany 2010, 17). Kings habitually bestow titles and emblems on their clients—generally referred to as "symbolic capital" (Bourdieu 1990, 112–121; McAnany 2010, 17) or "social currency" (Reents-Budet 1994)—as well as land and labor grants in order to cultivate and maintain their sometimes far-flung patron-client networks (Dirks 1987, 28). Although such relationships appear at first glance to be inherently hierarchical—whether they are framed using the traditional patron-client trope or the increasingly more common "great king–little king" construct (Bedford 2009, 49–50, 53; Iannone 2009; Schnepel 2002, 2005; Wiesehöfer 2009, 68–69, 79)—there was a certain degree of heterarchical fluidity present in these relationships in most early state formations. This is because the patron needed the loyalty and support of his client as much as the client depended on the munificence and exemplary model provided by the patron. This complex relationship is captured quite well by the fact that kings were referred to as "father" in many parts of Southeast Asia, including Java, Myanmar, and Thailand (O'Connor 1983, 44–45).

The politically charged "gifts" (Mauss 1954) patron-kings bestowed upon their followers often included ideologically significant items from distant lands (Helms 1993, 87). In some cases, as in ancient Myanmar, South India, and China, dyadic gifting also involved strategic "donations" that directly enhanced the merit accumulation of the king's subjects, thereby contributing to better futures and even good rebirths for both parties (Adamek 2005, 135; Aung-Thwin 1985, 47; Scott 1972, 92–93 Talbot 1991, 308).

India provides myriad examples of such politically charged gifting. In fact, Nicholas Dirks (1987, 128) posits that "the royal gift was basic to statecraft in all of the kingdoms of the old order in southern India" (see also Talbot 1991). Dirks (105) has documented a good example of how such gifting occurred, in this case how one of the great kings of South India rewarded a little king for assistance in war:

> The king put on a feast for him at the palace, and gave him horses, elephants, and many beautiful garments; he also gave him the title Tirumalai Cetupati (i.e., a title incorporating his own name); and in addition gave him his own lion-faced palanquin, along with many banners and emblems and a canopy.... [He also received] lands [on which he did not have to pay any tax or tribute].... From that time onward the Cetupati ruled over his kingdom without paying any tribute.

Dirks (91) also describes a case in which two elephants were brought to a south Indian court to fight, but one escaped and began to wreak havoc. Eventually, a little king who was attending the festivities was able to tame the beast. For this act, the great king rewarded him by

> [mounting] him on the same tamed elephant which was duly decorated with many emblems, flags, and banners, including the howdah [the elephant carriage], a pair of fly whisks, the five-coloured shawl, the tiger flag, and he was sent off to the accompaniment of drums and musical instruments, after having been given the title: "he who caught and subdued the royal elephant."

James Heitzman (1997, 180) informs us that elsewhere in South India, Chola kings "used religious donations to establish their legitimate claims to overlordship" and that "the collection of honours, the giving of gifts, and the assumption of titles ... were modes of achieving legitimacy." The importance of kingly gifting has also been well documented for the kings of Orissa (Dirks 1987, 126–127; Schnepel 2002, 216).

In the kingdoms of Southeast Asia, subordinates also sought to benefit from the gifts that a lord of "prowess" could provide, including titles, roles, symbols, and privileges (O'Connor 1983, 20). "People literally carried their status with them, while the lack of such symbols told you who the commoners were" (104). According to O'Connor, throughout the region individuals literally "disappeared into their royal titles as though such honours said everything there was to say about them" (104). The ostentatious lifestyle of the Southeast Asian kings and their courts was also a sign of worthy rulers and were something to emulate (107). Great kingdoms were therefore "replicated" by smaller and smaller courts and their little kings, the only major difference being "size and elegance" (i.e., real importance was assigned to the size and elegance of the court of a great king) (109).

Higham (2001, 151–152) outlines how gifts of land, titles, and duties were crucial to building and maintaining relationships between Khmer kings and their clients (see also Mabbett 1978). A case in point is Kambu, a subordinate of a tenth-century Angkor king who was given "a grant of land, a gold palanquin, gold cup, a white parasol, another with peacock feathers and a spittoon" (Higham 1989, 345). The firsthand account of Zhou Daguan (1296) highlights how clearly individual ranks were signified by a specific types of emblems that Khmer kings gave as gifts:

> In going out and about, the insignia and retinues of these officials vary by rank. The most senior are those with a palanquin with gold poles and four parasols with gold handles. Next in rank are those that have a palanquin with gold poles and two gold-handled parasols. Next down are those with a palanquin with gold poles and one gold-handled parasol; and next again, those with just one gold-handled parasol. At the lowest level are those who just have a parasol with a silver handle and nothing else. There are also those who have a palanquin with silver poles. (Harris 2007, 51–52)

Turning briefly to other parts of the world, we see that in the Achaemenid/Persian Empire, kings rewarded their subjects "in the form of tax exemptions . . . special proximity to the king, or gifts such as landed property (or its proceeds or incomes), valuable objects, horses with golden bridles, or merely a seat at the royal banquets" (Wiesehöfer 2009, 79). There is also evidence to suggest that Tongan kings "guaranteed fertility and well-being, and handed out rewards and punishments" (Claessen 2005, 243–244). Similarly, in order to quell opposition Aztec rulers granted land and titles, such as "He of the Twisted Water" or "He of the House of Darkness"; these titles "referred to sacred places and forces, and placed the title-bearer in a broader cosmological scheme" (Brumfiel 2000, 137).

Finally, the legitimacy of Maya kings was also strongly linked to the effective reallocation of "symbolic capital" or "social currency" (Demarest 1992; McAnany 2010, 17, 133, 304; Reents-Budet 1994). Like their counterparts in other parts of the world, the rulers of Maya polities held feasts and gave land, labor, titles, and emblems as gifts (Demarest 1992, 2013, 392–393; cf. Freidel 2008, 194). Some particularly relevant research has been done with regard to sourcing ceramics with primary standard sequences in order to explore gifting and alliance building (Reents-Budet 1994). Great kings also seem to have been present at the installation ceremonies of little kings, and some titles suggest patron-client relationships, such as *Usajal* (his noble?) and *Yajaw* (his *ajaw*?) (Martin and Grube 2008).

Legitimation Crises, Containment, and the Scapegoat King

As Declan Quigley (2005, 1) underscores, for many people past and present, "kingship provides an indispensable mechanism for transcending political division and underwriting stability and harmony." The integral role kings play as guarantors of prosperity for their subjects has been amply demonstrated in the previous discussion. It is now possible to assess their likely response to crisis and to begin to build a more nuanced understanding of why kings become scapegoats when their kingdoms start to exhibit problems.

Legitimation Crisis

Of relevance to understanding how and why kings fall out of favor is the concept of the "legitimation crisis" (Habermas 1975; see also Peregrine 1999, 2012, 178; Zhao 2009). This refers to a crisis resulting from the inability to maintain the required level of "mass loyalty" needed to uphold a specific governing system (Habermas 1975, 46). According to Peregrine (2012, 178), "Where it is part of a political leader's job to ensure economic stability, to ensure, at minimum, that people have enough to survive, a legitimation crisis may ensue far sooner than an economic crisis if the people perceive an economic crisis is imminent, or even possible." In fact, according to Habermas (1975), legitimation crises are far more likely to prompt a political collapse than any form of economic or environmental crisis (see also Peregrine 2012, 178).

Strategies of Containment: Keep Calm and Carry On

In efforts to reduce the effects of a legitimation crisis, kings may implement what Fredric Jameson (1981) refers to as a "strategy of containment."

Specifically, "leaders facing potential crisis will adopt strategies . . . that they can implement without much social endorsement; that is, ones they can implement largely by themselves" (Peregrine 2012, 178). In the early state formations in question, these were invariably the broadly sanctioned activities that were traditionally associated with the office of kingship.

What were these traditional means of containment? In the ancient Maya world, such strategies of containment often included continued sponsorship of elaborate rituals and ceremonies, the commissioning of new temples, and the capturing of rival kings who could be held for ransom and/or sacrificed (e.g., Lucero 2006, 195; McAnany 2010, 281, 196–198). Maya kings also used trade, gift giving, and risk management to mediate the deleterious effects of declining prosperity resulting from poor crop yields or diseases (Freidel and Shaw 2000, 279–280). Ultimately, it appears that through their sponsorship of greater numbers (and in some cases more elaborate versions) of architectural, artistic, and ritual expressions during the eighth century, Maya kings adopted a strategy of containment based on traditional practices, all of which were specifically aimed at demonstrating their continued, vital role in the sacred covenant with the gods and their followers (Freidel and Shaw 2000, 279).

The Scapegoat King

To reiterate, given the principles of the sacred covenant, it seems plausible that a legitimation crisis will stimulate a king to adopt a strategy of containment that involves increasing efforts to appease the apparently disgruntled gods. It is, after all, the supernatural's responsibility to provide the correct amount of sun, rain, and fertile earth so that the commoners can sustain themselves and produce enough to provide tax and tribute. If this is not happening, the kings themselves can be seen as the culprits—they are the ones who are supposed to keep the gods happy—and they therefore need to be proactive in their response to stress. In other words, a fundamental premise of the scapegoat king model is that "political elites lose their power because their rituals fail to reach the gods" (Lucero 2006, 24).

Ultimately, "what is at stake in royal etiquette are not power relations between people, but a much wider fear of a breakdown of the universe" (Bernbeck 2008, 160). According to Arlene Rosen (2007, 10):

> Responses to harsh environmental change are very much related to how a particular community views the reasons for this transformation. Many times, rainfall, drought, heat, storm intensity, and so on,

are viewed as an integral part of the cosmology, and solutions to problems of adverse weather and climate change must make sense within that framework. For example, if rainfall is a divine gift, then solving the problems related to drought must involve dealings with the supernatural in the form of pleasing the deity responsible. Failure to adjust to environmental stress is as much a social and cosmological problem as an environmental one.

The logical response to such legitimation crises is a strategy of containment that involves the ramping up of the same set of activities that are used to build and enhance the king's legitimacy in the first place: 1) the initiation of more public works projects, especially the construction of larger and more elaborate temple complexes aimed at "feeding," and thus sustaining, the apparently discontented gods; 2) the financing and hosting of increasingly more grandiose ceremonies and feasts; 3) the instigation of wars to conquer significant enemies, or at least transform them into more stable tributary states; 4) the gifting of additional titles, emblems, land and labor grants in order to secure the economic and political support of key subordinates; 5) the donning of more ostentatious attire and commissioning of more flamboyant emblems of authority; and 6) greater efforts to present the king as strong, vigorous, and in command of the situation.

In the past, these would have been rational (in emic terms) responses to periods of crisis; it is inherently unfair to evaluate them from the perspective of the contemporary world. However, our etic perspective is useful for understanding the consequences of these actions, in the sense that the responses of troubled kings, if they indeed fit the pattern outlined above, would have served only to put increasing stress on human and natural resources, thus escalating the crisis. This situation appears to be a classic example of what has been called the "sunk-cost effect," which refers to a situation where systems get locked in to a particular way of doing things. As Marten Scheffer (2009, 251) notes,

> The historical cases suggest some fundamental characteristics of societal response to problems that are deeply rooted in human nature, as revealed by studies of modern human behavior. The main pattern I want to stress here is the tendency to become increasingly rigid and adhere to old structures and habits as a sense of crisis tightens. Evidence suggests that this may reduce the chance for innovative solutions and much needed change in behavioral patterns.

What happens when the sunk-cost effect takes hold and the strategy of containment a king adopts only serves to exacerbate the crisis? As has been demonstrated in many parts of the world, at times like this the blame for declining prosperity is laid directly at the feet of the throne and the kings themselves become the scapegoats (Frazer 1993 [1922]; Gilbert 2008; Trigger 2003, 490–424; Webster 2000; Zhao 2009).

An example of a scapegoat king who was confronted with a legitimation crisis and adopted an ineffectual strategy of containment based on traditional symbols and ideological notions derives from the Burmese kingdom of Bagan. We are told that as a result of declining prosperity brought on by a long-term program of tax-exempt donations to religious institutions, which drew wealth away from the state, unrelenting investments in monumental architecture as a means to demonstrate his continued vitality, and increasing attacks by Mongols (Aung-Thwin 1985, 194; Aung-Thwin and Aung-Thwin 2012, 103–106), King Narathihapade (AD 1254–1287) "became the scapegoat for the 'fall' of the Pagan kingdom. He was given the epithet 'the king who fled the Chinese' by later chronicles" (Aung-Thwin and Aung-Thwin 2012, 99).

In his discussion of the decline of Bagan, Michael Aung-Thwin (1985, 185) concludes that

> as the [king] became less able to retain his economic (and ideological) monopoly over the distribution of wealth (and merit), his power diminished while at the same time his image corresponded less with society's expectation of legitimate kings. No longer was he perceived as having that limitless reservoir of *kutho* (merit) and *phun* (glory) around which the politically ambitious gathered, nor was he any longer able to generate that quality that had convinced others (and possibly himself) of his role as intermediary between heaven and earth. The awe with which his followers had once regarded him also dissipated. It was therefore not surprising to find King Narathihapade, in the latter part of whose reign the state showed the most obvious signs of decentralization, attempting to recapture those symbols of kingship, to such an extent that their artificiality was obvious even to his contemporaries.

A recent consideration of troubled Maya kings concludes that

> divine kingship is a double-edged sword: it carries great privilege and unlimited power but also demands that a ruler deliver munificence to

their people as would a god. A string of military defeats or seasonal droughts can do much to damage the credibility of a divine ruler, who must shoulder the blame for such misfortune.... From all indications, Late Classic times—with large populations to feed, possible cyclical droughts, and conflictive martial activity—would have been a challenging time in which to rule. (McAnany and Gallareta Negrón 2010, 157–158)

When confronted with perturbations, Maya kings would have responded through their own perceptions of the world, not ours (Freidel and Shaw 2000, 280). For them, it may have been entirely rational to believe that their sacrifices played a role in promoting fertility and productivity (Houston and Inomata 2009, 56). Their strategy of containment was therefore a ritual one, shaped by conceptions of the creation (Freidel and Shaw 2000, 291). In adopting such a response, they may have ultimately forgotten (or not even considered) that the material conditions of life—the ability to feed ones' people and maintain their well-being—could not be guaranteed purely through rituals and ceremonies (Freidel and Shaw 2000, 292).

Ultimately, "those who claim they control the cosmos and the future of the civilization survive only as long as they are able to command the loyalty of their subjects" (Fagan 1999, 96). As Quigley (2005, 20) notes, "the scapegoating mechanism . . . acts to protect and rejuvenate the kingship when an individual king fails in health and deed." There are many examples of kings who were killed when their powers or strength were perceived to be waning or even at the end of a fixed term (Frazer 1993 [1922], 265–277, 283). In some instances kings are even killed when they are still young and vigorous, in an effort to remove them long before they begin to exhibit characteristics of decline (Westermark 1908, 22).

For instance, the rulers of many Chinese dynasties were often deposed when their "mandate of heaven" was thought to have dissipated, as implied by declining environmental, economic, and social prosperity (Zhao 2009). James Frazer (1993 [1922], 292) notes that Greek kings were "responsible for the weather and crops, and . . . [they] may justly pay with [their] life for the inclemency of the one or the failure of the other." In the Lambayeque Valley of Peru's North Coast, the last ruler, Fempelle, apparently had the audacity to move the idol of the dynasty's founder, which prompted the offended gods to unleash uncommonly heavy rains for thirty days and nights. In response to the resulting floods, the king's subjects tied his hands and feet and threw him into the ocean in an effort to appease the supernatural forces (Fagan 1999, 96).

In Africa, sick or elderly kings are often forced to abdicate the throne or are sacrificed as a scapegoat, as has already been discussed (Heusch 1997, 217; Gilbert 2008, 184). In additional African examples, Jukun kings, who are closely connected to the plants that are cultivated, can be treated as a scapegoat and killed in secret if there is a persistent drought or a bad harvest. These calamities are thought to reflect the king's weakened spiritual/ mystical power (Heusch 1997, 217, 2005, 30). Similarly, Simon Simonse (2005, 73) concludes that in the Sudan,

> in the process of identifying the cause of disaster, kings and subjects stand face-to-face. The understanding between king and people stipulates that if no other agents are left to be identified, it is the king who carries the blame. It is this ultimate responsibility that motivates the king to do everything in his powers to mend the situation: by directing the blame onto others, by performing sacrifices and by praying to his father for assistance.... If no rain falls... the only course of action left to his subjects is to seek his death.

Taylor (2010, 266) tells us that in Rwanda,

> One of the sacred king's responsibilities was to direct and control [droughts and floods].... Yet the king also ran the risk of being perceived as the one responsible for complete cessation of beneficial flows in times of crisis, in which case he might be judged to be an inadequate embodiment of *imaana* and thus a candidate for elimination.

In summary, in the African contexts, "regicide is [often] the outcome of a reactive process to protracted drought in which the king, considered guilty of the situation, gradually becomes the sole target of a slowly intensifying, condemning consensus of ever larger sections of the population affected by droughts" (Simonse 2005, 84).

Maya kings were also held responsible for weather and crop-related events, and they not only benefited during times of prosperity—the good times may have even have cultivated in them a level of arrogance and even a belief that they controlled the supernatural powers (Freidel and Shaw 2000, 277, 291)—they also felt the brunt of dissatisfaction when prosperity failed due to increased competition and warfare, drought, resource degradation, declining agricultural yields, growing populations, and shifting trade networks (Demarest 2013; Dunning et al. 2012, 3654; Freidel and Shaw 2000, 277, 291; Lucero 2006, 184; Webster 2002a).

Why did the scapegoat king mechanism take effect in the Maya world at the beginning of the ninth century? At the end of the day it was because when severe instability set in, the question shifted from "Why is this occurring?" to "Who is responsible?" As long as the producing households continued to meet the tax/tributary demands of their rulers, they could not be held accountable. Thus, blame fell at the feet of the rulers or the gods (Webster 2002a, 343–347). But because the disgruntled gods were only the proximate cause of the calamity (i.e., they withheld the forces that fostered fertility), the kings were viewed as the ultimate cause (i.e., their rituals were unable to maintain the benevolence of the supernatural powers). Under these circumstances, it is understandable why it would seem reasonable to assume that it was the kings who became the scapegoats for their kingdom's problems (Iannone, Chase, et al. 2014; Lucero 2002, 2006; Moyes et al. 2009, 175; Webster 2002a, 2002b).

When such dire circumstances took hold, many Maya commoners may have migrated away from their kingdoms in search of greener pastures, sometimes found within other kingdoms that were believed to be ruled by more effective rulers, in other cases to hinterlands where the reach of the ineffective kings was significantly diminished (Lucero 2006, 191, 195, 200). Illegitimate kings and the symbols and edifices that had previously supported their claims to divine rule did not get off unscathed, however. The various chapters in this volume document the range of events that were potentially associated with the removal of a scapegoat king, including the apparent symbolic closing off of royal residential courtyards through the deposition of ritual artifact dumps at key access points, the physical infilling and/or the razing and burning of these courtyards or other buildings or monuments closely connected with the divine rulers, and possibly even the massacre of royal families (see also Adams et al. 2004, 337–339; Graham 2004; Guderjan et al. 2003, 40; Hammond 1999a, 1999b:13; Hammond and Thomas 1999; Houk 1996, 2000; Iannone 2005; Inomata and Houston 2001; Inomata and Triadan 2003, 162–163; LeCount et al. 2002, 44; Mackie 1985, 48–49; Mock 1998b; Webster 2000, 75; Yaeger 2010). Finally, an interesting ethnohistoric example may provide a glimpse into the circumstances associated with the removal of a scapegoat king during the chaos of the early ninth century:

Maya rulers of the contact period were held responsible through their conduct and ritual knowledge for the manner in which the weather and crop-related prophecies of the katuns unfolded.... The consequence of drought and famine for such rulers, in one case, is interrogation for failure of ritual knowledge and evidently sacrifice on posts or scaffolding in a public space. (Freidel and Shaw 2000, 277)

Of Scapegoats and Turncoats

According to the scapegoat king model, a king's essential strength is also, unavoidably, their Achilles' heel. They present themselves as the ultimate moral and ritual authority in their kingdom (Webster 2002a, 346). As a result, regardless of whether they are competent or whether they are puppet rulers whose decisions are made by their advisors, the ruler as an individual is still the focal point of the kingdom. When times are good, kings benefit enormously because of their privileged position. But when things begin to unravel, they also take the full brunt of the dissatisfaction as the state's prime scapegoat. Kings can be perceived to be improperly carrying out their roles in keeping the universe functioning smoothly (i.e., a lack of prosperity) and therefore can be challenged by those below them. This is because subordinate groups are always able to "penetrate," to varying degrees, the ideologies of their superiors (Van Buren and Richards 2000, 10). As a result, even though little kings, lesser nobles, and commoners are often economically and politically disenfranchised—and taking into consideration that they also likely see the benefits of the social contract that linked them to both their overlords and the supernatural powers (this is why revolution is not a common thing)—they still have avenues of resistance and the ability to undermine an ineffective ruler.

Paradoxically, during times of crises, one of the responses of embattled kings is to increase tax and tribute demands in order to maintain—and in some cases enhance—their ability to meet their mandate as guarantors of prosperity. Such requests inevitably put additional stress on subordinates and support populations, often leading to discontent. As a result, some portion of the tax and tribute—in the form of gifted titles, emblems, land grants, and tax exemptions—invariably has to circulate back to allied little kings, lesser nobles, and local leaders in efforts to placate them and suppress dissent. Unfortunately, not only does this draw much-needed resources away from the overlords, it also emboldens and empowers subordinates and amplifies their ability to resist the increasingly onerous demands of an ineffectual ruler. These centrifugal forces only serve to exacerbate an already difficult situation because they promote political and economic fragmentation that thwarts efforts aimed at consolidation.

The centrifugal forces of decentralization that emerge when kings become scapegoats are well documented throughout history. For Angkor, we are told that "with time, increasing amounts of land passed into the hands of grandee families, which opened up the possibility of pursuing power through religious munificence in competition with the central overlord. This, in turn, required the overlord to outperform them" (Hagesteijn 1984 as quoted in Higham 1989, 355). The history of South India is replete with similar examples. According to Dirks (1987, 47), "The more gifts of honours and rights the overlord makes to his subordinate, and—in what is a logical and political consequence of this—the more the subordinate participates in the sovereignty of his overlord, the more the subordinate is represented as a sovereign in his own right." Another example comes from ancient Myanmar, where the downfall of the Second Pegu/Toungoo dynasty was apparently hastened by its own governors from the centers of Toungoo, Prome, and Ava (Aung-Thwin and Aung-Thwin 2012, 138).

In the ancient Maya world, Late Classic kings faced similar challenges. By the turn of the eighth century, as a result of increased warfare, political balkanization (Iannone 2005, 2010), and possibly even a growing penchant for polygamy among the royals that produced an increasing number of "cadet lineages" (Dunning et al. 2012, 3654), there was a growing number of kingdoms of varying size (many so small most members could gather in one large plaza; Houston and Inomata 2009, 40), all vying for basic resources, tax, and tribute and all of whom claimed some level of divine authority (Lucero 2006, 42; Webster 2002b, 449). This sociopolitical landscape is confirmed by the various titles and types of relationships referred to in the epigraphic record, including the notion of "overlordship," which suggests that there was a "subtle hierarchy of rulers" (Houston and Inomata 2009, 135, 141). There is also evidence that lesser Maya nobles and/or little kings could (and often did) oppose the overlords they served (Houston and Inomata 2009, 63).

Ultimately, during the crises of the early ninth century, increasingly powerful Maya nobles and/or little kings likely saw little benefit in supporting an overlord. They may have, in fact, actively attempted to destabilize them and in doing so promoted themselves as the obvious leaders of choice in the changing political landscape. However, because they also inherited the roles and responsibilities of their defunct overlords, their legitimacy continued to be tied to notions of prosperity, and many of them eventually became scapegoats too, especially in regions where troubles persisted.

The Scapegoat King through a Critical Lens

Having documented the tenets of the scapegoat king model and provided a plethora of examples from different parts of the world that seem to support its efficacy, we are still left with a question: How much explanatory power does this construct really have? On one hand, it appears to have some cross-cultural validity in terms of how inequality was rationalized in early state formations. It is also perceptibly functional because it emphasizes the managerial qualities of individual kings rather than the exploitive character of the institution of kingship, favors group solidarity over social conflict, and promotes the power of a dominant ideology to mask inequalities over the ability of subordinates to penetrate, challenge, and/or manipulate this ideology for their own benefit. In the following discussion, I reflect on the strengths and weaknesses of the scapegoat king trope using a series of general questions originally presented in chapter 1. Informed by the cross-cultural data presented in this chapter, my goals are to draw out some of the more useful aspects of this explanatory framework and to highlight some areas of divergence from the ideal model.

Does the cross-cultural model of kingly legitimacy, prosperity, and scapegoating hold in all times and all places (i.e., is there spatial and temporal variation)? There is considerable overlap, not simply in the way various scholars employ the scapegoat king model but also in terms of how many cross-cultural data sets appear, at least to some degree, to support the associations among legitimacy, prosperity, and fertility. At the same time, the details do imply some divergences from the ideal model. For example, there is a range of ideas concerning the extent to which kings were considered divine, whether kings need to lead their armies into battle to demonstrate their prowess and vigor, and the degree to which a king is considered *the* center of his kingdom as opposed to simply being one of many things that could potentially be the foci of power, legitimacy, and prosperity.

What are some of the material correlates that support the premise that legitimacy and prosperity are linked in societies ruled by kings? There are various textual and iconographic references to kingly participation in key moments of the agricultural cycle (first planting), the storage of agricultural surplus (granaries), control of weather (especially rain making), various aspects of water management (the building of reservoirs and canals), and success in warfare. There are also myriad examples of kings being responsible for the well-being of their supporters and controlling key titles, emblems, and land and labor grants, all of which were tied to prosperity. Finally, it was also quite common for kings to assume the identity of supernatural forces associated with fertility through appellations and the donning of costumes during performances and in iconographic depictions.

Is legitimacy solely invested in an individual charismatic male king or is it attributed to a broader governance structure and thus a wider cadre of actors exhibiting diverse roles, statuses, and genders? The evidence suggests that although in theory the king is often the principal focus of power and legitimacy, in practice a broader range of actors share in these aspects of divine rule. This is true for the various functionaries who, as has been suggested, may even have been perceived as part of the king's regalia and the subordinates who accepted titles and emblems from the king in order to enhance their own status and identity. It should also be noted that although the language surrounding the scapegoat king model tends toward the androcentric, women also served as regents (Flannery and Marcus 2012, 390, 417–420) and even as rulers who led their armies into battle. Thus, women too could assume the central role as the principal guarantor of prosperity and legitimacy for kingdoms. It may be significant that female rulers seem to have become increasingly popular in the tumultuous two centuries immediately preceding the ninth-century Maya collapse (Freidel et al. 2013, 246–247; Reese-Taylor et al. 2009; cf. Houston and Inomata 2009, 146–148), and they may also have been more common in pre-Angkorian Cambodia, also during "exceptional political and social circumstances" (Jacobsen 2003).

Are power and legitimacy centered entirely in the kingly body or are they also invested in specific places (palatial residences or cities), relics, and regalia that transcend the kingly person? It is clear that although in many instances the kingly body does serve to contain a significant portion of a kingdom's power and legitimacy, the degree to which the individual king is conceptualized as *the* center of the kingdom varies considerably. For example, O'Connor (1983, 62–67) has documented great diversity in terms of who or what was the precise center of the Southeast Asian kingdoms. In some instances, the center was the king (among the Malays), in others it was the palace (in Java), and in some cases it was actually the city (among the Thai and Burmese). In the latter two instances, the loss of a "place" or even the capture, destruction, or holding hostage of particular images, symbols, idols, or regalia were potentially more significant blows to a kingdom than the loss of a specific kingly person. This may help explain the rationale behind some of the termination and/or destruction events we see in the Maya world during the early ninth century. In considering this issue, it is not insignificant that Maya kings and their courts appear to have been "strongly tethered" to specific places on the landscape that often held the remains of their ancestors. Courts did move, but it was hard to effectively transfer sacred powers from one place to another (Webster 2002b, 449–450b).

To what degree do subordinates accept the dominant ideology—in this case the institution of divine kingship—and how might we recognize covert resistance to it archaeologically? Within the early state formations that are the focus of this study, monumental buildings and symbol systems were employed to promote the dominant ideology, which in turn publicized the legitimacy of the elites (Childe 1950; Gečienė 2002; Smith 2009, 13). Much of the labor that was employed to build the monumental constructions was of the corvée (tax) variety, but this does not mean that the laborers were fully alienated from the results of their labor. Through the construction process they "may have developed an emotional tie to these symbols of authority" (Smith 2009, 21). Similarly, subordinates, especially little kings, lesser nobles, and local leaders, often became entangled in the dominant ideology because the gifts of titles, emblems, and land and labor grants their overlords provided were also integral to their own identity as guarantors of prosperity for their followers. As a result, they too had a vested interest in perpetuating the symbols and beliefs associated with the dominant ideology. For this reason, it would be erroneous to assume that even if subordinates were able to fully penetrate the dominant ideology of divine kingship, they would necessarily actively work against it. Agency does not equate with resistance, and conformity does not imply intentionality (Dornan 2002, 318–321).

This does not mean that the ideology of divine kingship, as it was manifest in places such as the ancient Maya world, served to promote "solidarity" in an uncontested way (e.g., Lucero 2006, 22, 28). Maya society was undoubtedly quite conflictive in nature; it was characterized by factionalism, contradictions, and constant negotiation (Houston and Inomata 2009, 28, 34–42). Still, resistance to a dominant ideology is complicated by the fact that those most able to resist—little kings, lesser nobles, and wealthy local leaders—are invariably caught up in the same social contract as their overlords. At the same time, and to confound matters further, the degree to which these agents are entangled with the ruling regime itself can vary considerably. It is plausible that subordinates at the two ends of the "loyalty spectrum"—those who are the most loyal and those whose loyalty is most in question—receive the greatest quantity and quality of gifts from the overlord (for different reasons, obviously), whereas individuals and groups whose loyalty is more ambiguous receive less beneficence. Yet those who are least loyal may ultimately be emboldened to resist further precisely because they have accrued more titles, emblems, and land and labor grants from their overlord, all of which heightens their autonomy. Those with more equivocal loyalties may increase their opposition for different reasons, mainly because they are increasingly excluded from cultivating their own power and legitimacy through the acquisition of political gifts. The question remains, however: In such situations, are these factions resisting the regime itself or are they resisting the dominant ideology?

It is quite telling that there is no good archaeological evidence for political action on the part of subordinates against the notion of divine kingship in the Maya world (Webster 2002b:444). As discussed above, for many, covert resistance was likely more about trying to obtain as many titles, emblems, and land and labor grants as one could from the overlord without having to provide the overt loyalty and full level of tax or tribute their patron demanded. In most instances, this resistance seems to have been enacted using the traditional rules of the game, which were not only based on the doctrines of the sacred covenant but also adhered to the customary principles of patron-client relationships. In other words, during the lifespan of most kingdoms, conflict and resistance were likely less about challenging the dominant ideology and more about clients trying to free themselves from their patrons so that they could, in turn, foster their own power and legitimacy and, in some instances, even assume the overlord position in a newly reconfigured set of patron-client relationships. The latter would, however, have been based on the same ideological codes as the ones they replaced.

For these reasons, the material correlates of resistance remain difficult to determine, because resistance is not a one-dimensional process. It may appear in quite diverse ways in the archaeological record; two very different assemblages may signify similar levels of opposition to an overlord. Alternatively, loyalty and opposition may look very much the same in the archaeological record, for example, where loyal and disloyal agents both accumulate and display similar sets of emblems and titles, all acquired from the same overlord but for different reasons (i.e., in the first case to reward loyalty and in the second to cultivate it). It is, unfortunately, difficult to dig up the residues of motivation and intentionality.

What crises would justify the removal of a king, given that crises were omnipresent? The review of the cross-cultural literature suggests that kings could in fact be removed at any time if it was felt by some that a political change was desired, regardless of whether the king was young or old, weak or strong. Perceptions of a forthcoming crisis was often enough to stimulate removal of a king, even if the king was still youthful and vigorous. Nevertheless, kings seem to have become scapegoats principally when it was perceived that there was some kind of cosmological crisis, one that signaled that the kingdom had fallen out of favor with the supernatural powers and that negatively impacted the kingdom as a whole because of its duration, magnitude, or complexity, regardless of whether the causes were environmental, economic, political, or a combination of these.

That said, environmental issues seem to dominate many of the examples of scapegoating. Prolonged drought and floods appear to have been particularly significant. Such environmental disturbances could not be effectively addressed through a strategy of containment based simply on the ramping up of ritual activities. Nonetheless, falling out of favor with the supernatural forces called for just such a ritual response, and adopting this tactic would have only made a bad situation worse for the kings who implemented it because it would have led to an even more tenuous grasp on power and legitimacy and, for many, their eventual removal from office.

What circumstances could potentially lead to the removal of a king without subsequently replacing them with a new ruler (i.e., what would cause an entire governance structure to be treated as a scapegoat)? When a crises is of such magnitude, duration, or complexity that it cannot be seen to be resolved simply by replacing one king with another—principally because the replacement would be informed by the same ideological principles and thus be predisposed to respond in the same ways to the issues at hand— it is plausible that the perceived breakdown of the social contract would also necessarily undermine the legitimacy of a much broader assemblage of royal personages, functionaries, and political leaders who are entangled with the regime and the belief system upon which it is based. This could, in turn, usher in a period of chaos and eventually stimulate significant structural changes that would result in an entirely new world order. It is telling that the ruptures we recognize as collapses do tend to coincide with such significant ideological shifts (Butzer 2012, 3638). These collapses also serve to "wipe away old [social and factional] distinctions and so let a ruler start afresh" (O'Connor 1983, 59), even though it may be some time before that new ruler and governing structure emerges.

For example, the ninth-century Maya collapse has often been considered the result of "failed social institutions" (Freidel and Shaw 2000, 279) that resulted in the demise of the institution of kingship as it had been practiced during the Classic period (Lucero 2006, 200; Webster 2002b, 450–451). On one level, it was kings and royal families who paid the price for endemic crisis (Sharer 1982, 375; Webster 2002a, 343–347). Equally significant, however, is the fact that as part of this reorientation of Maya governance structures, there were widespread termination rituals and destruction events associated with specific places, particular buildings, and certain powerfacts, all of which were closely connected to the wider institution of kingship (as detailed in the various chapters in this volume). This implies that it was the institution that was treated as a scapegoat, not just specific kings. Also of note is the fact that following the ninth-century collapse, Maya conceptions of history became less linear and more cyclical and more clearly focused on famines and population movements resulting from natural disasters, such as droughts, pandemics, and hurricanes (Freidel and Shaw 2000, 273). These beliefs may harken back to the tumultuous times that the Late Classic kings and their broader governing apparatus were not able to deal with in an effective manner.

What strategies of containment might be adopted to avoid the removal of a king and/or the collapse of an entire governance structure? It seems that, cross-culturally, the most common response to crises was to ramp up the traditional ritual practices that framed the king's role within the sacred covenant. However, the examples of stewardship that are discussed—although varying in their effectiveness—do suggest that kings did at times understand the actual material conditions of the crises they faced and that they did try to prepare for them in a proactive way. Nevertheless, it is also clear that this goal was rarely achieved.

Do ritual terminations and/or violence always accompany the removal of a king, and if so, why are such acts necessary parts of the process of deactivating divine authority? Cross-culturally, kings were created through prescribed ritual processes. For this reason, one can assume that the removal of a king would follow a similarly sanctioned set of procedures. Removing a king would have likely involved deactivating the various places and powerfacts most closely associated with him or her (i.e., residences, principal temples, celebratory texts and iconography, and emblems of authority).

The destruction of the material symbols of one's enemies has a long, cross-cultural history. As Randall McGuire (2008, 26) stresses, such actions are "not something apart from real politics but, rather, is real politics expressed in powerful and consequential ways."

What testable implications and material correlates can archaeologists use as evidence for the removal of a scapegoat king due to declining prosperity? From an archaeological perspective, one might expect termination events and ritual destruction to focus on the kinds of buildings, monuments, and powerfacts discussed above. In other words, the focus would likely be the things most closely related to kingly authority and the power and legitimacy of a ruler (e.g., McGee 1998, 42; Mock 1998a; Stross 1998, 37). In addition, actions more accurately interpreted as being desecratory in nature, involving burning and other acts of violent destruction (Freidel 1998, 190)—including the killing of members of the royal family—would likely be more common during such periods of dramatic political change. Events such as these, examples of which are the focus of the various chapters in this volume, are highly significant and require more focused attention from archaeologists.

Are there other events or processes that coincide with the demise of kingly authority? If the legitimacy of a particular king comes into question, supporters may also chose to emigrate (Lucero 2006, 191, 195, 200). If this occurs to a significant extent it may be just as effective as killing a king. This is particularly true for contexts where human labor is crucial to the vitality of a kingdom, as was the case in the various tropical civilizations, including that of the Maya (Lieberman 2003, 2009, 764–765, 2011; Scarborough and Burnside 2010, 180).

Conclusions

> With divine kingship came great responsibilities for the well-being of subjects, who accepted social inequality as the price for the role of a privileged intermediary with the capricious forces of nature. The illusion worked most of the time, until destruction or starvation made the people think their lords had failed them. Then thousands went hungry and the ruler paid the price. (Fagan 1999, 96)

In this statement, Brian Fagan succinctly captures the basic tenets of the scapegoat king model. As the examples in this chapter illustrate, scholars focusing on numerous culture areas and various time periods have often used this trope—sometimes explicitly, but more often implicitly—to capture the unique roles a king plays as the central focus of a kingdom and to explain why kings often felt the brunt of dissatisfaction during times of crisis. Although the scapegoat king framework has considerable explanatory power, it also has some inherent limitations that need to be addressed when it is applied to specific case studies, as is underscored in the previous discussion. The chapters that follow explore these issues in more detail using a series of archaeological examples from throughout the ancient Maya world. The ultimate goals are to provide a better understanding of just what happened to the various Maya kingdoms in the first few decades of the ninth century AD and to assess whether the rulers of these kingdoms were conceived of and treated as scapegoats during these troubled times.

3

Killing the "Kings of Stone"

The Defacement of Classic Maya Monuments

ELEANOR HARRISON-BUCK

Epigraphers suggested some time ago, based on their decipherments of ancient Maya hieroglyphic texts, that sacred objects such as monuments were "ensouled" via precious royal blood, copal, and other prescribed ritual offerings (Freidel et al. 1993, 181–224; Houston and Stuart 1996, 294–295; Schele and Miller 1986, 175–185; Stuart 1996, 160). In the case of stone monuments, David Stuart (1996, 160) further suggested that the carved images of Maya kings were not just elite portraits but were seen as actual extensions of the royal self. Like humans, these "kings of stone" were named, clothed, nurtured with offerings, and acquired a *ch'ulel*, or inner life force (Stuart 1996, 157; Vogt 1998, 21). According to numerous ethnographic accounts, the *ch'ulel* "constitutes a part of the soul and inhabits the blood of all humans" (Houston and Stuart 1996, 295; see also Freidel et al. 1993, 181–185). Following Vogt (1965a, 33) and others, the term "soul" is used advisedly here as it inherently distorts the nuances of indigenous belief. Most scholars of Maya ethnography and archaeology (including epigraphers) still use the term "soul" but acknowledge the limitations of its use. Although it may have gone by a different name, the concept of a *ch'ulel* is likely rendered in antiquity as droplets of blood in the iconography and it is also found in the epigraphy, where it forms the glyphic element for *k'ul* (or *ch'ul*), meaning "sacred," "divinity," or "holiness" (Freidel et al. 1993, 182; Houston and Stuart 1996, 294–295; Stuart 1984). As active participants, stone monuments, or *ch'ul lakamtun* ("holy big stones"), were engaged members of ongoing ritual performance that involved human and nonhuman social actors and, like rulers, could effect change in the world (Stuart 1996; see also Gillespie 2001, 2008; Harrison-Buck 2012a, 103). Despite these and other breakthroughs in the hieroglyphic decipherments, few Maya archaeologists have seriously considered the role(s) such nonhuman agents played as social actors in ancient Maya society.

Here, these ideas concerning the Maya self, nonhuman agency, and the construction of personhood are explored and the agency of monuments are considered in the context of their defacement. This work builds on a previous study of a series of patterned terminal deposits that contain in some instances evidence of smashed and defaced monuments (Harrison-Buck 2012a). Elsewhere, I have suggested that these deposits are the causal remains of "termination rituals" found at sites across a broad area of the Maya lowlands dating to the transition from the Late to the Terminal Classic (AD 750–850) (Harrison-Buck 2012a; Harrison-Buck et al. 2007). Termination rituals are distinguished from middens or reverential deposits on the basis of several contextual criteria that Pagliaro and colleagues have outlined (2003, 79–80). These include intensive burning, structural damage, pot smashing and scattering, rapid deposition of material, dense concentrations of large sherds with sharp, angular breaks, and large quantities of "elite" artifacts. Unlike most domestic trash deposits, a key feature of desecratory (as opposed to reverential) termination deposits is primary- or secondary-context human remains; such deposits may involve "purposeful disturbance and/or desecration of elite burials as well as the remains of ritually sacrificed elite inhabitants of a Maya community" (Pagliaro et al. 2003, 80). Instead of being along the side or behind structures, as is typical of middens, desecratory termination deposits are usually located at key points of transition, in areas that block access to rooms or elite residential plaza groups, and/or on the front steps of buildings (see Houk this volume). Of relevance here is the defacement and mutilation of carved monuments, another key feature of termination rituals that often coincides with the destruction of portable objects and buildings (Freidel and Schele 1989; Mock 1998a, 5).

I argue that mutilated monuments were the victims of "soul loss" aimed at terminating the final reigning Maya kings and their ancestral lineages. I begin with a discussion of the epigraphic and ethnographic references that shed some light on nonhuman agency among the Maya and of the ancient practice of monument mutilation as a method of soul displacement. I then present a detailed study of several defaced monuments dating to the end of the Classic period that have been documented at Piedras Negras, Dos Pilas, Palenque, Tikal, and Copan, among other Classic Maya centers (table 3.1). In the case studies presented here, the ruler's residence and associated temples show evidence of purposeful destruction and the king's monuments have been desecrated. Carved portraits on columns, lintels, freestanding monuments (stelae), and royal thrones have been smashed, and portraits (particularly the faces) show signs of purposeful mutilation, suggesting a targeted attack on the royal elite. Defaced monuments are interpreted in various ways, but most scholars link them to violent, conquest-related events. Some argue that such evidence is indicative of long-term interpolity conflict and internecine warfare among kings that eventually led to the demise of dueling Classic Maya centers (Demarest 1997, 2004a, 2006; Demarest et al. this volume; Golden 2003; Golden et al. this volume; Houston et al. 1998). Here I propose an alternative interpretation and suggest that broader shifts in regional power stemming from the Gulf Coast and northern Yucatan may have brought about changes in warfare practice—where conquered sites fail to recover—and contributed to the ultimate political and economic downfall of Classic Maya aristocracy. I conclude that monuments are but one of many receptacles or thresholds where human and nonhuman social agents interacted and where conflict was played out in ancient Maya society.

Killing the "Kings of Stone": Theorizing Nonhuman Agency in Monument Defacement

In Evon Vogt's (1969, 371) seminal ethnographic study of the Tzotzil Maya, he concludes that "the most important interaction going on in the universe is not between persons nor between persons and material objects, but rather between souls inside these persons and material objects." This may explain why monuments and other sacred objects "are the principal concern of most of the extant Maya [hieroglyphic] texts, rather than the deeds and histories of royal figures" (Stuart 1996, 151). Both the ethnographic and epigraphic data suggest that Maya objects may have been of central importance in the hieroglyphic texts and highly valued in life because they served as "bodily" receptacles for souls that were awakened through sacrificial blood, copal, and other precious substances. The concept of a soul or animate co-essence awakened through bloodletting and other self-sacrifice appears to have deep roots that go back to Preclassic times (Schele and Miller 1986, 179–180). Both Maya ethnography and epigraphy suggest that the concept of a relational co-essence and an "extrasomatic" self is fundamental to Maya thought (Gossen 1994, 1996; Houston and Stuart 1996, 292; Vogt 1965a, 1976, 1998; Watanabe 1992). Both contemporary and ancient

Maya sources offer archaeologists rich emic accounts to mine, specifically with regard to nonhuman agency. Yet relatively few archaeologists have seriously considered in their theorizing and interpretations the role(s) nonhumans played as social actors in ancient Maya society (for some notable exceptions, see Brown and Emery 2008; Duncan and Hofling 2011; Freidel et al. 1993; Geller 2012; Gillespie 2001, 2008; Harrison-Buck 2012a, 2012b; Hendon 2010, 2012). This is surprising given the amount of recent theorizing in anthropology about the power and agency of objects (e.g., Brown 2001; Fowles 2010; Hodder 2011; Knappett and Malafouris 2008; Latour 1993; Olsen 2007).

In this study, personhood is considered as a *symmetrical* process (sensu Witmore 2007) that was not necessarily restricted to one type of entity (i.e., living biological human beings) or ontological status (see also Harrison-Buck and Hendon 2013). Maya ethnographic accounts suggest that what constitutes a *living* body (of a human or nonhuman) was determined by its ability to retain a soul and all its parts (Vogt 1976, 22–24). Although this study focuses on monuments as receptacles of important nonhuman social actors, in fact, it is its relational ontological status that is of prime importance, more so than the object itself (for other examples of this idea, see contributions in Watts 2013). Maya monuments are probably best viewed as one of many receptacles or thresholds where the numinous comes to reside and interact with other human and nonhuman persons. Thus, the fractal parts of the soul or spirit *thing* are irreducible to objects and approximate the object/thing dialectic that Bill Brown (2001, 4) describes in his "story of how the thing really names less an object than a particular subject-object relation."

The subject-object relationship was fluid and ever changing. This is particularly apparent in cases of soul loss among the contemporary Maya. In his ethnographic study of the Tzotzil Maya in the Chiapas Highlands of Mexico, Evon Vogt (1969, 370–371) describes the thirteen parts of the Zinacanteco soul: "The soul, while temporarily divisible into parts in the various kinds of 'soul-loss' that can occur, is believed to be eternal and indestructible" (Vogt 1969, 370). Although Maya believed (and believe today) that soul parts cannot be permanently destroyed, they can be displaced from a receptacle. For both ancient and contemporary Maya, these receptacles are not exclusively living human bodies but can also include valued materials and important objects, such as domesticated corn, musical instruments, wooden crosses, or stone monuments, among other precious things (Stuart 1996; Vogt 1969, 371). Soul displacement or loss is a serious condition that can lead to sickness or even death. Among the contemporary Zinacantan, certain receptacles, such as a newly constructed house or the body of a newborn child, are particularly vulnerable to soul loss and must be carefully nurtured to ensure that the soul becomes "fixed" (Vogt 1976, 18). In order to retain the parts of the soul and avoid the death of the receptacle-body, these co-essences must be cared for and nurtured through prescribed rituals (for an ancient example, see Eberl 2013).

The ethnographic and epigraphic data suggest that both contemporary and ancient Maya share the ontology of a divisible soul that is transformative in nature and dangerous if and when it becomes detached from its receptacle-body (Houston and Stuart 1989). Typically, only shamans or divining priests who tend to have a stronger co-essence (or *nagual*) are capable of initiating and sustaining an interaction with the detached soul or other powerful co-essences (Reina and Monaghan 1981, 18; Vogt 1976, 24). In some cases, malevolent "witchcraft" aimed at displacing and harming the soul is carried out and can pose a serious threat that can lead to sickness that requires shamans to perform curing ceremonies to avoid death of the receptacle-body (Vogt 1969, 406–415). One example of a malevolent ritual is the *mal entierro* that is practiced among the contemporary K'iche' Maya in the Guatemalan highlands (Brown 2004). Also referred to as an "evil burial," these rituals are aimed at causing death to one's enemies and often are accompanied by *tulac* or malicious incantations (52). The prescribed ritual involves smashing and burning artifacts. For the K'iche', these deposits sometimes include animal sacrifice and/or the incorporation of human bone fragments from the dirt of a freshly dug grave (40). "By interring and smashing deposits, ritual practitioners bury and destroy the enemy, whereas by including pieces of clothing or hair of the intended victim, the ritual practitioner personalizes the rite and directs forces and deities to one particular individual" (51). These rituals are carried out at mountain shrines in the highlands, places that are regarded as thresholds of powerful interaction between human and other-than-human agents. Despite the differences in location, the artifact assemblages and their contexts—(re)interred offerings in pits with smashed and scattered surface deposits including human remains—bear a strong resemblance to ancient desecratory termination deposits discussed below that contain smashed and defaced monuments.

The targeted mutilation of monuments that deface portraits of a specific ruler may be analogous to the personalized *mal entierro* rituals that Brown (2004, 51) describes, which were directed toward one intended victim. The bodies of kings and particularly the facial features on stone monuments appear to be the target of mutilation. This practice of facial and bodily mutilation appears to have roots in Preclassic times. For instance, most Olmec colossal heads show pockmark scars on the faces due to purposeful mutilation (Coe and Diehl 1980; Grove 1981). Mock (1998b, 118) equates the ancient Mayas' "destruction of the face with the erasure of social identity and the dispersal of *ch'ulel*." The decapitation of an individual and the flaying of an individual's face may be equivalent to the mutilation of faces on stone monuments; both resulted in soul loss whereby the victims became "nonpersons" as "the potent force of their self-identity was ritually terminated" (Mock 1998b, 119; for some cross-cultural comparisons, see Iannone this volume). Below I present a series of case studies that lend support to the notion that portrait defacements and the destruction of the king's residential and religious architecture (as documented in various chapters in this volume) were targeted attacks aimed at killing parts of a ruler's soul or co-essence at the end of the Late Classic period.

Case Studies

Table 3.1 shows where evidence of defaced monuments, burning, and building destruction are found associated with termination deposits from elite contexts at sites across the Maya lowlands. Smaller Maya sites typically do not contain evidence of carved monuments in the form of lintels, panels, thrones, and stelae. Therefore, monuments that show signs of purposeful destruction are restricted to larger Classic Maya centers. The types of defaced monuments range from thrones to freestanding stelae to columns that served as building supports for vaulted roofs. Defaced monuments are found at sites across a broad area of the Maya lowlands, including the Usumacinta-Pasión (Palenque, Piedras Negras, Yaxchilan, Dos Pilas, Cancuen, and Altar de Sacrificios), Motagua (Copan and Quirigua), and Petén regions (Tikal, Naranjo, Xultun, and Ixtonton). Below I discuss some of the best-documented examples found in published reports that date toward the end of the Late Classic period.

Usumacinta-Pasión Drainage

Piedras Negras

At Piedras Negras, excavations of the main acropolis in the 1930s and in the 1990s have revealed the destruction of a royal throne (Throne 1) dated

Table 3.1. Maya lowland sites with terminal deposits

Site	Date of Elite Abandonment (AD)	Defaced Monuments	Smashed Ceramics	Fortification Walls	Human Remains	Building Destruction	Evidence of Burning
Aguateca	810	X?	X	X	X	X	X
Altar de Sacrificios	830	X	X		X	X	X
Altun Ha	850		X		X	X	X
Blue Creek	850		X		X?	X	X
Cancuen	800	X (Panel 3 and ball court markers)	X	X	X	?	?
Calakmul	810–849	?	X		X		
Caracol	895	?	X		X	?	X
Chan Chich	800–850		X		X	X?	X?
Colha	780–830		X		X	X	X
Copan	820–822	X (Stela 11—pier of Temple 18)	X		X	X	X
Dos Hombres	840–850		X		X	X?	X
Dos Pilas	760–830	X (throne and banner stone of Structure N5-3A)	X	X	X	X	X
El Perú-Waka'	800	X	X		X	X	X
Hershey	830	X? (slate fragments in North Plaza)	X	X?	X	X	X
Ixtonton	800–825	X (Stela 2 of the East Temple)	X		X	X	X
Minanha	810		X		X	X	X
Nakum	800–850	?	X		X	X	X
Naranjo	820–830	X (Stela 32 of Str. C-9)	?	?	?	?	?
Palenque	815	X (XIX pier, XIX and XXI thrones)	X		X	X	X
Piedras Negras	810	X (Throne 1 in palace gallery J-6)	X			?	X	X

(*continued*)

Table 3.1—*Continued*

Site	Date of Elite Abandonment (AD)	Defaced Monuments	Smashed Ceramics	Fortification Walls	Human Remains	Building Destruction	Evidence of Burning
Río Azul	840	?	X		X?	X	X
Tikal	850–869	X (Stela 24 and paired Altar 7 of Temple 3)	X	X	X	X	X
Xultun	810	X (Stela 9 of Str. A-4)	?	?	?	?	?
Xunantunich	780–800	?	X	X?	X	X	X
Yaxha	850	X?	X		X?		X
Yaxchilan	810	X (Stela 24)	?		?	X?	?
Yaxuna	850–900		X	X	X	X	X

Source: Adapted from Harrison-Buck (2012a, Table 1).

to AD 785 and associated with Ruler 7, the final reigning king of Piedras Negras (Houston, Escobedo, Child et al. 2000; Satterthwaite 1937; Weeks et al. 2005). Site abandonment is dated to AD 810 based on the last recorded monument at the site and is described as a rapid and violent end based on the evidence of building destruction, burning, and smashed monuments (Martin and Grube 2008, 153). Although conservators have reconstructed the throne (see figure 5.2b), the royal portraits on its back were defaced in antiquity (Sharer and Traxler 2006, 431). The throne was found smashed and scattered across the palace gallery J-6 throne room in the main acropolis (see figure 5.2a). In addition to destroying the throne, individuals purposely defaced carved panels on the facades of the palace building depicting this ruler (Golden 2003, 43; Martin and Grube 2008, 153). My understanding from the reports is that images and glyphs of the ruler were selectively defaced but that images and glyphs of deities were apparently left intact, suggesting that the perpetrators were literate in Mayan iconography and hieroglyphic writing. The royal palace building appears to have been purposefully destroyed and burned (Houston, Escobedo, Child et al. 2000; Martin and Grube 2008, 153; Sharer and Traxler 2006, 431; Weeks et al. 2005). Excavators in the 1930s noted that the piers and lintels at the door of the throne room were purposefully undermined to force the building to collapse (Houston, Escobedo, Child et al. 2000). Similar patterns have been noted at Chichen Itza (Ruppert 1952), Copan (Andrews and Fash 1992), and Palenque (Straight and Marken 2007), where doorway piers and lintels "were purposefully destroyed with the intent of undermining structural integrity as part and process of site abandonment" (Golden 2002, 84).

Dos Pilas

Dos Pilas is another site in the Pasión region where the destruction of monuments is associated with the last known ruler (Ruler 4) and marks the termination of the epicenter at the end of the Classic period. Demarest and colleagues (2003, 128–132) describe the desecration of the throne of Ruler 4 and the toppling of an associated banner stone inside the throne room (Structure N5-3A), which was adjacent to the N5-3 presentation palace structure (Demarest et al. 2003, 128–129, Figs. 5.3, 5.5, and 5.7). Excavations determined that this palace was the principal royal residence in the time of Ruler 4 (Demarest et al. 2003, 131). Inside the palace throne room, three whole vessels were found on the floor along with three unbroken obsidian blades near the banner stone, and the throne slab had been flipped over and broken into over a dozen fragments (Demarest et al. 2003, 129, Fig. 5.7). The investigators interpret the monument destruction and associated ceramic and obsidian deposits as evidence of termination rituals associated with conflict-related events. "The throne and banners of a ruler were the preeminent symbols of sovereignty and would be the first targets of destruction and defacement" (Demarest et al. 2003, 130). There was no evidence of Late Classic (late facet Nacimiento phase) ceramics, and no Terminal Classic (Sepens phase) material was found associated with this deposit (Demarest et al. 2003, 132). Based on the ceramic data and the last dated monument associated with the termination deposit, Demarest dates the overthrow of Ruler 4 to between AD 761 and AD 780 (Arthur Demarest, personal communication, December 2012).

The pattern of monument defacement found at Dos Pilas is strikingly similar to others documented here. Like Piedras Negras, the throne desecration at Dos Pilas is attributed to Classic period Maya warfare, although the details in the epigraphic record of this supposed conflict remain unclear and the identity of the perpetrators is unknown. Demarest and his team documented fortifications at Dos Pilas that they suggest were built in the period AD 760–830 (Demarest et al. 1997). According to the investigators, the efforts of the elite to defend themselves failed and they were ousted by the end of the eighth century, perhaps two or three decades earlier than most of the sites considered here (see table 3.1).

Palenque

Patterns of destruction that targeted the royal elite and their associated monuments at Piedras Negras and Dos Pilas resemble finds from Palenque in Chiapas, Mexico. Like Dos Pilas, these events appear to have taken place in the Late Classic period, during the second half of the eighth century. Excavations from 1998–2002 in the southeastern part of Palenque revealed two contemporaneous palace buildings—Structures XIX and XXI—in the Cross Group/South Group that were ritually terminated. These include the remains of defaced monuments (for a map of this area, see Stuart 2007, Fig. 11.1).

Structure XIX was completely collapsed but originally had a double-vaulted roof across the front and rear galleries of the structure and seven columns running along its central axis (Straight 2007, 184, Fig. 10.6). Only the central pier of the seven columns showed evidence of decoration, an elaborately carved limestone tablet with a portrait of K'inich Ahkal Mo' Nahb' III, the fourteenth ruler of Palenque (figure 3.1). Prior to its destruction, the portrait of the standing ruler faced a wide central doorway and would have been immediately visible to anyone entering the room of Structure XIX. The central doorway is unusually wide, 5.3 meters across, and the jambs were probably capped with a perishable lintel made of *chico zapote* wood (Straight 2007, 190). On the left-facing side of the central pier was a modeled and painted stucco panel with an image of a striding male individual named Upakal K'inich, the son or brother of K'inich Ahkal Mo' Nahb' III and the heir to the throne (Stuart 2007, 209). Both the carved stone and stucco panels were broken off from the central pier and purposefully smashed in antiquity. Tearing down the central masonry pier undermined the doorway, its large lintel, and the double-vaulted roof and would have encouraged the ultimate collapse of the building. The fragments of carved stone and modeled stucco were found associated with several discrete terminal deposits purposefully scattered throughout the room that contained broken ceramics, obsidian, and other elite items (Straight and Marken 2007).

Also inside the large open space in the northeast corner of the room of Structure XIX, a sculpted bench or throne with carved panels was found defaced (Miller 2000). According to Miller's (2000) report of the 2000 season of the Cross Group Project at Palenque, a large gaping hole had been made in the interior of the sculpted bench. Excavation inside the hole revealed portions of a ceramic vessel (Special Deposit 2000-3). More of

Figure 3.1. A carved limestone tablet with a portrait of K'inich Ahkal Mo' Nahb' III, the fourteenth ruler of Palenque, originally from a central pier of Structure XIX. Photograph by Jorge Pérez de Lara Elías in Stuart 2005, Figure 4. © Jorge Pérez de Lara, by permission.

this same vessel was found in a deposit of smashed and scattered artifact remains, including human bone, found on the floor in front of the throne. Based on the contextual association, it seems likely that these terminal deposits are coeval with the defacement of the sculpted throne. The pit dug into the throne may represent a cache or tomb that was looted in antiquity as part of this terminal event. Large pieces of carbonized wood may be the remains of wooden beams and lintels, suggesting that the building was burned as part of the termination event.

A somewhat smaller bench or throne that is very similar in style was found in nearby Structure XXI, also in the Cross Group/South Group at Palenque. It contains carved panels that mention both K'inich Ahkal Mo' Nahb' III and Upakal K'inich (Stuart 2007). Structure XXI is a double-vaulted room with a series of four central piers along its long axis. A bench or throne in the southeastern corner of the large open room is stylistically the same as the one in Structure XIX (in fact, David Stuart [2007, 209] suggests they were likely made by the same sculptor). A text band dates the throne in Structure XXI to AD 736 and is coeval with hieroglyphic dates found associated with Structure XIX. Like the Structure XIX bench, the slab, which measures approximately 3 meters by 1.7 meters, was smashed and the fragments were stacked on the south side, indicating that it was purposefully destroyed in antiquity (González Cruz 2003; Marken and Straight 2007, 309, note 17). The monuments of K'inich Ahkal Mo' Nahb' III and Upakal K'inich, who reigned in the first half of the eighth century AD, were the targets of destruction in both Structures XIX and XXI. The epigraphic dates of these two structures are the latest recorded dates associated with architecture at Palenque (Marken 2007, Table 4.5). Following K'inich Pakal II, only scant epigraphic references mention three more kings—K'inich Kan Bahlam III, K'inich K'uk' Bahlam II, and Janaab Pakal III—who apparently ruled Palenque until at least AD 814. Then the record falls silent (Martin and Grube 2008, 174–175).

The pattern of monument defacement and destruction of the elite buildings at Palenque, where the piers and lintels were purposefully undermined and the associated thrones within were desecrated, sharply parallels the types of violent destruction events that occurred elsewhere in the Maya area in the late eighth to early ninth century AD (as documented in the various chapters in this volume). The exact dates of the termination events at Palenque are unknown, but it is assumed to have taken place sometime after AD 736 based on the final dates on the associated monuments in Structures XIX and XXI (Straight 2007, 187, 190). The excavators state that both of these buildings were purposefully dismantled, based on the dispersed fragments of the carved stone and stucco. The investigators suggest that this was part of a reverential termination, rather than a violent desecratory act committed by enemies. Straight (2007, 189) attributes faulty construction to "the partial loss of structural integrity . . . prompting an immediate and dramatic 'killing' of the entire building." The investigators report evidence of "architectural growth and continuous habitation" in the Cross Group/South Group, continuing through Late Classic (Balunte) times, ca. AD 750–820 (Straight 2007, 176). If the destruction of this and other important royal buildings occurred during the site's heyday in the mid-eighth century, the investigators fail to explain why they were both "reverentially" destroyed and not rebuilt, particularly given that they appear to have functioned as the royal residence and as part of an extended court complex through Balunte times (Marken and González Cruz 2007, 151).

Motagua Valley (Copan)

Monuments often are just one component of a larger terminal deposit that is usually focused on a royal elite courtyard and palace complex. In some cases, associated ceremonial temple buildings linked with the final rulers also were victims of desecration. This was the case at Copan, where Stela 11 (which dates as late as AD 820) was snapped in half and found at the base of Temple 18 (otherwise known as Structure 10L-18), a modest memorial ceremonial shrine. Temple 18 is the last known building that was dedicated by Yax Pasaj, the final reigning king of Copan (Fash et al. 2004, Fig. 12.1). Like the central pier in Structure XIX at Palenque, Stela 11 was not a freestanding monument but was originally part of a column that supported the doorway of the temple. It "depicts a bearded Yax Pasaj in the guise of the aged Maize God" (Martin and Grube 2008, 212). This and another column that shows Yax Pasaj performing a war dance once supported the roof of the temple and were purposefully dismantled, broken, and (in the case of Stela 11) physically removed from the interior of the shrine (Fash 1991, Figs. 107 and 108). Notably, Schele (1991, 4–5) interpreted the accompanying inscriptions on Stela 11 as *u lob*, or "he defaced him" (Mock 1998b, 118). References in the text to "the toppling of the Foundation House" have been interpreted as evidence of an overthrow of the founder's lineage that perhaps relates to the political collapse of the city itself (Martin and Grube 2008, 212). Inside Temple 18, a crypt that may be the final resting place of Yax Pasaj was looted in antiquity (Fash et al. 2004, 267). This desecration of Yax Pasaj's royal tomb appears to have accompanied the termination of the ruler's shrine building and his portraits on the supporting columns.

Nearby, there are signs of deliberate destruction and burning of the royal residential compound of Yax Pasaj, known as Group 10L-2 (Fash et al. 2004, Fig. 12.1). Most of the vaulted elite buildings within this compound were cleared in the 1890s, and if similar termination rituals existed, it is possible they were unreported (Fash et al. 2004, 272). All four of the vaulted structures (10L-2, 10L-22A, 10L-29, and 10L-33) that have been recently excavated in Group 10L-2 show signs of purposeful desecration in the form of intentional fires, and dense deposits of "domestic refuse" were found covering the floors (Andrews and Fash 1992; Fash 1991; Fash et al. 2004). In Structure 10L-29, the building collapsed after the supporting beams, including the lintel above the doorway, were intentionally exposed to fire and the wall and vault above it could no longer support the weight of the roof (Fash et al. 2004, 272). The excavators report a similar destruction pattern for another house of the Yax Pasaj lineage, Structure 10L-33, where the lintel above the doorway was intentionally burned, undermining the vaulted roof. Likewise, Structures 10L-41 and 10L-32-1st (the latter of which has been identified as the royal residence of Yax Pasaj) show signs of intentional burning and deliberate destruction, although this is less certain because both of these buildings were cleared in the 1890s. However, more recent excavations on the back side of Structure 10L-32 have revealed a layer of burning beneath the collapse of the wall stones, suggesting that it met the same fate as the other desecrated buildings in Group 10L-2 (Fash et al. 2004, 272).

The deliberate destruction of the royal residence and temple of Yax Pasaj marks the end of Copan's long line of kings that began with the founding ruler, Yax K'uk Mo'. The abandonment of the site core at around this same time at end of the Late Classic period has led some to suggest that warfare may have "contributed to the downfall of the Copan kingdom" (Webster et al. 2000, 208). More recently, however, investigators have also cited environmental degradation of the Copan Valley as another possible contributing factor to the political collapse in this area (Webster 2002a).

Petén Region

Tikal

Similar to Copan, the site of Tikal shows paired destruction of both the royal residence and the temple associated with the ruler Dark Sun, one of the final Classic Maya kings at Tikal. Both the ruling residence in Group 5D of the Central Acropolis and the nearby Temple 3 were the focus of termination rituals at the end of the Classic period and mark the abandonment of the site core. Stela 24, which in AD 810 commemorated the nineteenth K'atun, was found at the base of Temple 3 paired with Altar 7. The two monuments associated with Dark Sun were both purposefully smashed and damaged in antiquity (Martin and Grube 2008, 52). This ruler's residence in the Central Acropolis—Court 5D-2—also appears to have been targeted for destruction (figure 3.2). Peter Harrison (1999) documented a series of terminal deposits restricted to particular areas within the Central Acropolis, many of which appear to be blocking passageways that served as entrances to the main elite residence, Structure 5D-46, which was also strewn with debris. These thick deposits, some measuring 1.8 meters deep, contain elite ritual and rare items of wealth (many still useable) and disarticulated human bone, some of which shows signs of cut marks (Harrison 1999, 198). Peter Harrison (1999, 198) reports that parts of the same vessel were found in the upper and lower levels of the thick deposits. As Suhler and Freidel (2003, 144) note, the location, context, and contents of these deposits sharply resemble termination deposits found associated with site abandonment elsewhere in the Maya lowlands. Although Peter Harrison (1999, 194) interprets these deposits as squatters' refuse, this explanation is difficult to support given the nature of these deposits, which suggest a single event rather than gradual accumulation. Furthermore, some of these terminal deposits are found on the tops of buildings and pyramid summits, which are unlikely locations where a squatter might throw his or her trash (for further discussion, see Stanton et al. 2008).

Naranjo

Relatively close to Tikal, in the Petén, there is additional evidence of defaced monuments found at the site of Naranjo. Stela 32 (figure 3.3) depicts the final reigning king of Naranjo, Waxaklajuun Ubaah K'awiil (Martin and Grube 2008, 83). The monument shows the targeted mutilation of the ruler's body. There is merely an outline of where the body once was, but the remainder of the carved portrait is intact. Since the 1970s, Naranjo has been ravaged by looters, and many monuments were stolen or damaged in that decade. However, the damage on Stela 32 is present on Maler's (1908) original negative from 1905, and this suggests that the defacement of the ruler's portrait on the monument occurred in antiquity. The stela was found at the base of Structure C-9, the largest pyramidal structure at Naranjo, located in

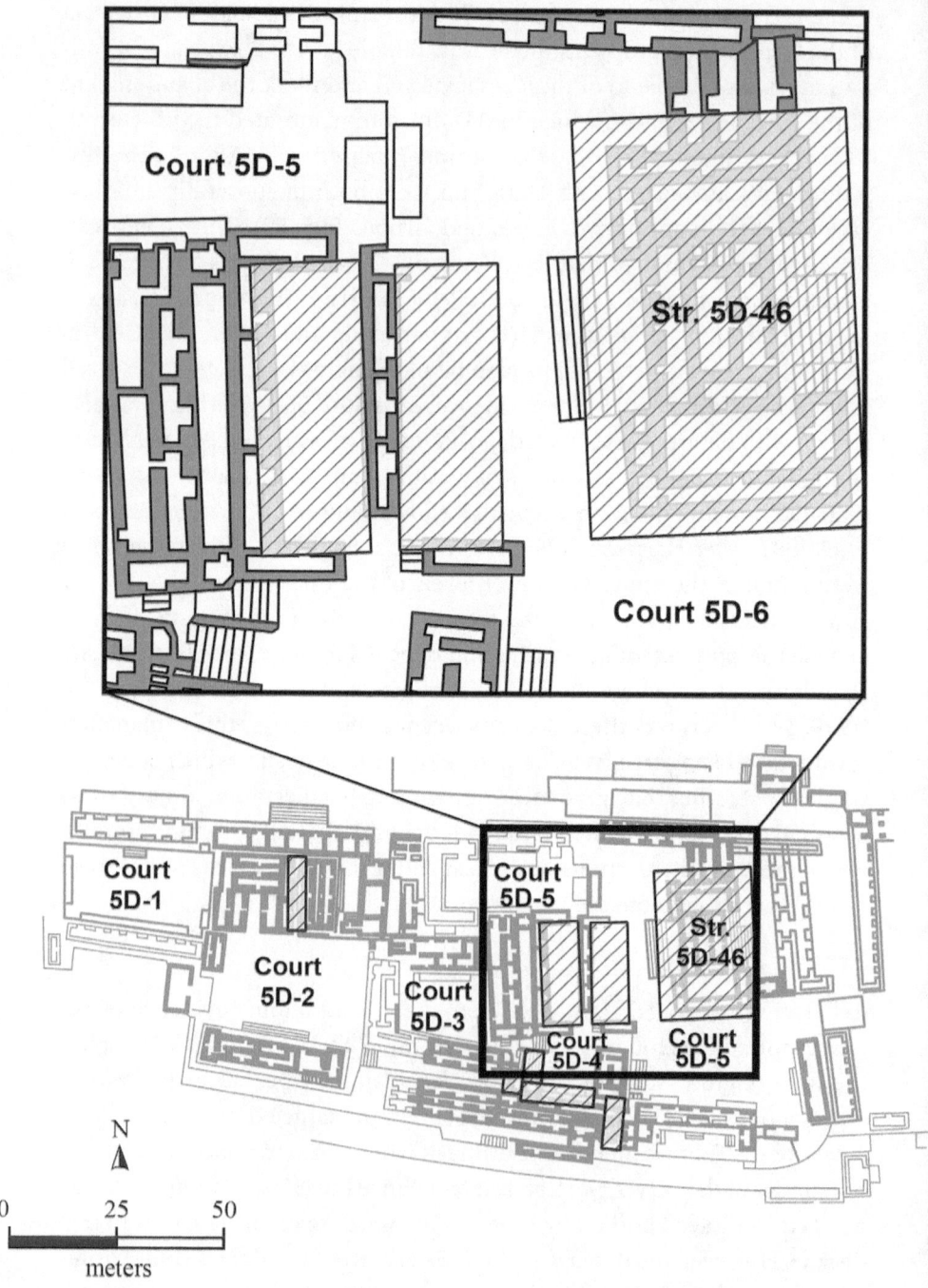

Figure 3.2. Locations of terminal deposits in Central Acropolis Court 5D-2 at Tikal (adapted from Harrison 1999, Figure 118). Illustration by Marieka Brouwer Burg.

Figure 3.3. Front of Stela 32 at Naranjo. Drawing by Ian Graham. © President and Fellows of Harvard College, Peabody Museum of Archaeology and Ethnology, PM# 2004.15.6.3.14 (digital file# 99200065).

the Triadic Acropolis in the easternmost part of the site (Tokovinine and Fialko 2007, 3).

Investigations are ongoing at Naranjo, but to my knowledge evidence of termination deposits have not yet been reported. However, excavations have been primarily focused on recording the extensive looter's tunnels, conserving buildings and monuments, and determining overall site chronology through deep vertical testing (Tokovinine and Fialko 2007; Fialko 2009). If termination deposits exist at this site, I would anticipate that they are located around Structure C-9 and in and around the palace acropolis, namely within the royal residence (Structure B-15). In clearing several looter's pits in Palace B-15, Fialko (2009, 44–57) did note evidence of collapsed vault stones and plaster stucco elements, infilling events, and burned timbers in precincts 3 and 4 that may point to such events toward the end of the Late Classic period. However, this remains speculative until further investigation is carried out at the site.

The Fall of the Classic Maya Kings: Where, When, Who, and Why?

The vast majority of termination activity presented here coincides with site abandonment and typically targets the last reigning king. This is evident in the purposeful destruction of his monuments, residential compound, and temple buildings. In many cases, the lintels and piers of vaulted structures were the focus of destruction. They were torn out, smashed, scattered throughout the room, and sometimes physically removed from the buildings. Without the roof support, the undermined buildings ultimately collapsed. Often thick layers of debris containing unbroken elite items were deposited inside these buildings (just prior to their collapse) and along their front steps, physically blocking access into them. The strong patterns in the archaeological record suggest that the terminal events recorded in table 3.1 were "ritual" in nature, seemingly based on widely shared and understood ideological practices (but see Demarest et al. this volume). In contrast to dedicatory events or venerative termination, desecratory termination activities often contain evidence of human remains suggestive of the brutal killing of the royal elite family, as in the case of Cancuen (see Demarest et al. this volume) or the disentombment of royal ancestors, both suggestive of a violent termination of the reigning king and a process of marked institutional change in Classic Maya aristocracy (Harrison-Buck et al. 2007, 82).

The distribution of terminal deposits with evidence of defaced monuments dating to the end of the Late Classic period is widespread across

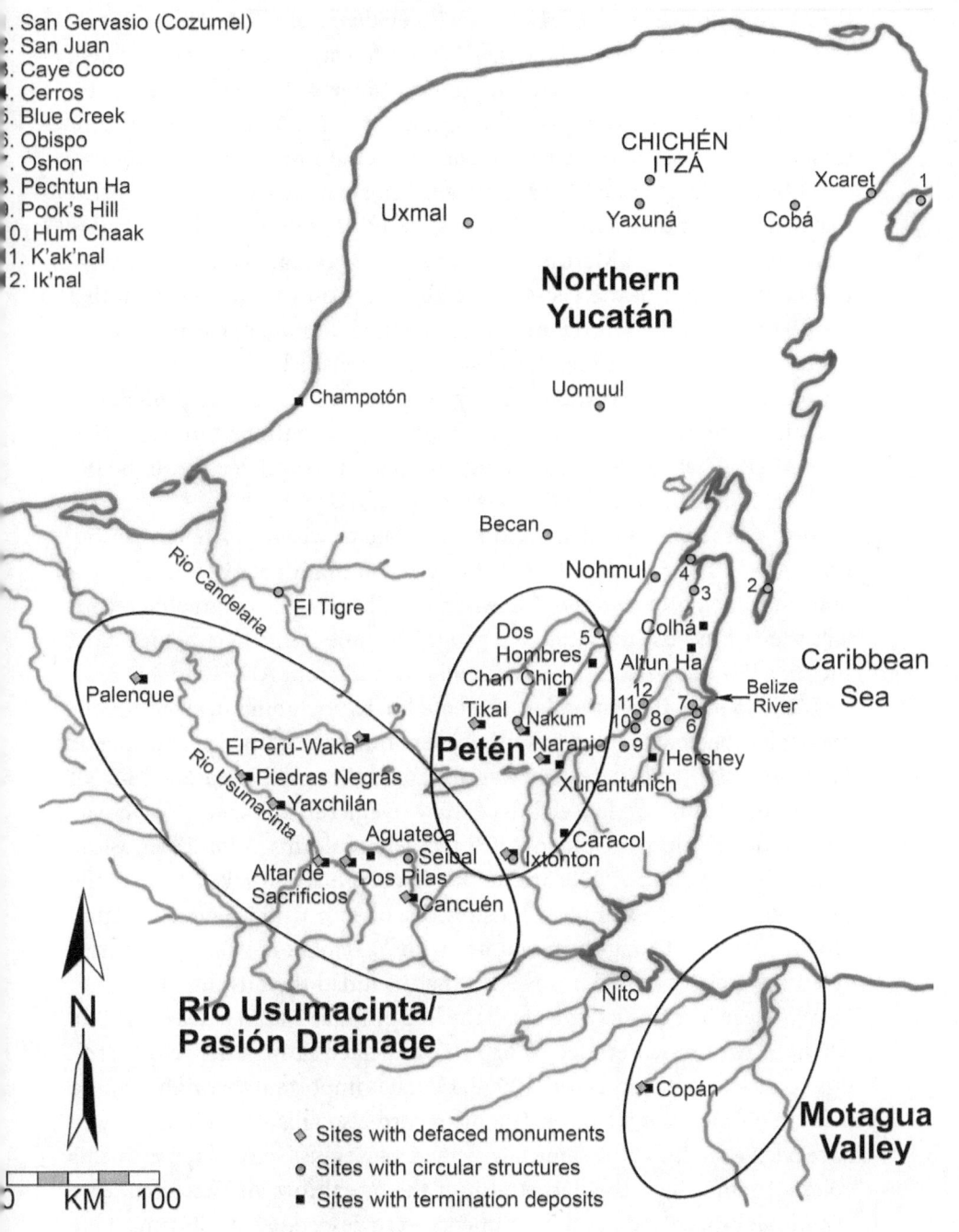

Figure 3.4. Distribution of sites with termination deposits, monument defacement, and Terminal Classic circular shrines in the Maya Lowlands.

the Maya lowlands (figure 3.4). Sites with evidence of defaced monuments are typically restricted to the larger Classic Maya centers, where emblem glyphs and vaulted architecture are found (table 3.1). Smaller Maya sites typically lack evidence of carved monuments and vaulted masonry construction with carved stone lintels, piers, panels, thrones, and stelae.

Although the list in table 3.1 is certainly not exhaustive, it is noteworthy that nearly every one of the major Classic Maya centers whose hieroglyphic texts are discussed in Martin and Grube (2008) reveal evidence of termination at the end of the Classic period. Only Tonina and Quirigua that are discussed in the Martin and Grube volume do not appear in table 3.1. In those two cases, I did not have access to published reports of the excavations to verify termination activity. It is worth noting that Tonina, like Ceibal, is one of the few sites where monuments continued to be erected after AD 830, while Quirigua shows a similar pattern of decline in the period AD 810–830, based on the cessation of texts.

Most of the deposits discussed herein date to within a 70-year period, from AD 760 to 830, based on a combination of radiocarbon dating, ceramic chronologies, and the date when the Classic-style epigraphic record falls silent. If we use the latter as a gauge, the time frame narrows for most sites to a 20-year period (a Maya *k'atun* interval) from AD 810 to AD 830.

The evidence of termination presented here, including defaced monuments, has been attributed to both local commoner uprisings and Classic Maya intersite "status rivalry" warfare among kings that spiraled out of control by the mid- to late eighth century (Demarest 2004a, 2006; Demarest et al. this volume; Golden 2003; Golden et al. this volume; Houston, Escobedo, Child et al. 2000; Schele and Grube 1995; Schwake and Iannone this volume). For example, Houston, Escobedo, Child, and colleagues (2000) argue that long-term warfare with Yaxchilan is what finally triggered the collapse at Piedras Negras that included the ousting of Ruler 7. Yet it is clear that this city survived the loss of Ruler 7 until at least AD 810, when the now-much-eroded Altar 3 was dedicated at this site (Golden et al. this volume; Martin and Grube 2008, 153). It is important that right around this same time, Yaxchilan's epigraphic record also falls silent. It appears to have been a victim of the same fate as Piedras Negras (see Golden et al. this volume) rather than the perpetrator of the overthrow. At Yaxchilan, elite ceremonial space and royal monuments were desecrated at this time. Like Piedras Negras and Dos Pilas, simple houses were built on top of the open plaza spaces, and royal monuments, including Stela 24, which depicts the final king's father (Itzamnaaj B'alam III), were found broken up and buried in the rubble foundations of these intrusive houses. The evidence suggests that warfare with Yaxchilan was not the ultimate cause of the downfall of Piedras Negras and that another force was at work in the demise of these and other Maya centers. For the Pasión, Demarest (2004a, 102, 109) argues that status rivalry warfare produced "structural vulnerabilities" for the Classic Maya aristocracy. This may have been the case not only in the Pasión but also throughout the Maya lowlands, where epigraphic texts document rivaling elite centers. Yet the evidence of patterned termination deposits, dating to a relatively short period of time and occurring at the vast majority of major (and minor) centers across the lowlands, brings into question whether localized internecine warfare between rivaling kings is what caused the ultimate demise of the Classic Maya kings. If this were the case, we would expect the victors of these long-standing rivalries (e.g., Yaxchilan, Tikal, Naranjo, Aguateca) to survive longer than the others. Yet they all seem to have experienced a similar fate of political disruption and collapse, most occurring around the same time. It seems equally unlikely that these patterned termination events were the causal remains of random, haphazard uprisings indicative of a peasant revolt. The targeted monument defacement points to a literate elite group rather than to dispersed commoners or secondary elite. For example, in the case of the monument defacement at Cancuen in the Pasión (noted in Demarest et al. this volume), selective facial mutilation targets two secondary nobles—a *sajal* and an *ahjkuhuun* (Demarest, personal communication, December 2012).

While these "conquest" events at the end of the Late Classic period in many ways resemble the targeted captive taking that was characteristic of Classic Maya warfare, they had much more profound repercussions. Unlike Classic Maya warfare, cities rarely recovered following the ousting of the royal kings (Inomata 2008a, 287). While this type of warfare is not characteristic of the southern Lowland Maya "star wars" it is often associated with other Maya groups to the north, namely the Itza of northern Yucatan and the closely related Chontal Maya of the Gulf Coast. Based on his reading of the ethnohistoric accounts, J. Eric Thompson (1970) made famous the "Putun-Itza" hypothesis where he suggested that the Itza from Chichen Itza were Chontal-speaking Putun people whose origins were in the Gulf lowlands (see also Scholes and Roys 1968, 23–24). Thompson (1970) and others argued that these Chontal-speaking Maya warrior-merchants introduced a series of "non-Classic" features into the southern Maya lowlands that resulted in successive waves of so-called Mexicanized Maya influence beginning in the mid- to late eighth century and continuing as late as the early tenth century (e.g., Ball and Taschek 1989; Kowalski 1989; Sabloff and Willey 1967; Vargas 2001). Among these are fine paste ceramics, such as Pabellon Modeled-carved types thought to originate in the Gulf Coast (Adams 1973a; Sabloff 1973, 123–124; Thompson 1970, 38–39), although more recent sourcing suggests that many were probably produced both upstream and downstream along the Usumacinta-Pasión drainage (Bishop 1994). Other non-Classic features include the so-called Cycle 10 iconography beginning around AD 810–830 and continuing through AD 889–909, which displays a distinctive iconographic style associated with the Gulf Coast and Chichén Itzá, such as paneled scenes with multiple individuals rather than a single paramount elite and images of "Mexican" deities such as Ehecatl, the wind god (e.g., Stela 9 at Ceibal; Chase 1985; Graham 1973; Kowalski 1989; Proskouriakoff 1950; Sabloff 1973; Thompson 1970, 41–42). The introduction of new "Mexican" calendars using squared day glyphs are evident on these Cycle 10 monuments and are thought to originate in the Gulf Coast (Rice 2004, 238). In addition, non-Classic styles of architecture including colonnaded and round structures have been linked with the Chontal-Itza of the Gulf Coast and Chichén Itzá (Andres 2009; Chase and Chase 1982; Harrison-Buck 2012a, 113; Harrison-Buck and McAnany 2013; Kowalski et al. 1994, 8; Pollock 1936). Examples of Terminal Classic circular shrine architecture have been found at the Chontal site of El Tigre on the Río Candelaria (Vargas 2001) and in Quintana Roo at sites such as Becan, Margarita, Lagartera, Uomuul, Dzibanché, and Yo'okop (Harrison 1979; Harrison, 1981, 281; Nalda 2005, Fig. 15.3; Shaw 2005, 151; Villamil and Sherman 2005, Figs. 13.2 and 13.4); at a few sites in Petén such as Nakum (Żrałka and Hermes 2012); and at numerous sites in the Chetumal Bay area and farther south in Belize (Chase and Chase 1982; Guderjan and Hanratty, this volume; Harrison-Buck 2007, 2012b). Additionally, examples of circular architecture with Terminal Classic components are found in northern Yucatan at Uxmal (Kowalski et al. 1994), Yaxuna, and at the Itza capital of Chichén Itzá, the location of the famous round Caracol shrine (Ruppert 1935; see also Harrison-Buck 2007, 2012b).

A Chontal-Itza Incursion in the Southern Maya Lowlands? Reevaluating the Model

The nature of the "Mexicanized Maya" influence stemming from the Gulf Coast and northern Yucatan is debated among scholars. Various models of Chontal-Itza incursions from the Gulf Coast and northern Yucatan have been proposed (Ball and Taschek 1989; Chase 1985; Harrison-Buck 2007; Harrison-Buck and McAnany 2013; Kowalski 1989; Sabloff and Willey 1967; Thompson 1970). To explain the depopulation in the ninth-century Terminal Classic period, George Cowgill (1964) proposed a "Mexican" invasion whereby southern lowland populations were forcibly resettled in northern Yucatan closer to Chichén Itzá. He suggested that some populations remained in the southern lowlands but that many others were forced into slavery. The Chontal-Itza were known for their slave trade, according to the ethnohistoric accounts (Scholes and Roys 1968, 29–30; Thompson 1970, 151). One of the biggest problems scholars had with Cowgill's theory was the timing of Chichén Itzá's florescence (Rice 2007, 148). For a long time, this site was thought to date largely to the Postclassic, reaching its apex later in the tenth century AD. However, a revised chronology for the northern lowlands now suggests greater overlap between the collapse of southern lowland cities and the rise of Chichén Itzá in the ninth century, making Cowgill's (1964) theory perhaps more plausible. Population increases during the transition from the Late to the Terminal Classic have been documented not only in the northern lowlands but also in other "peripheral" regions of the Maya area, including the Gulf lowlands of Mexico and the eastern Maya lowlands of Belize. Despite the revised chronology for Chichén Itzá, the notion of a Chontal-Itza invasion of the southern lowlands has largely fallen out of favor among scholars (Kristan-Graham and Kowalski 2007, 34–36; Tourtellot and Gonzalez 2004; but see Kepecs 2007). Thompson's (1970) suggestion of a Chontal invasion of Chichén Itzá in AD 918 is no longer tenable based on the available data, but the potential impact of Chontal-Itza migrations into the southern lowlands is still worth considering (see Cohodas 1989).

While the role the Chontal-Itza played in the Classic Maya "collapse" is far from clear, most scholars agree that the influx of non-Classic features in the southern lowlands was due to a gradual, outward movement of "Mexicanized-Maya" groups from the Chontalpa region during the eighth and ninth centuries (Kristan-Graham and Kowalski 2007, 35). The iconographic and epigraphic evidence suggests that if Chontal-Itza peoples were responsible for changes in warfare and for the demise of the Classic Maya centers, such an incursion did not happen overnight. The overthrow events documented at Palenque and Dos Pilas in the mid- to late eighth century may offer supporting evidence for earlier intrusions down the Usumacinta. This theory has been posited by a number of scholars. Jeremy Sabloff (1973, 123–124), for instance, noted that at Ceibal the first monuments in Group A that show influence from the Gulf lowlands date to AD 790. He and others have suggested that changes including population increase and a reduction of polychrome pottery at sites such as Ceibal and Altar de Sacrificios may have begun as early as AD 771 (Adams 1973a). Tatiana Proskouriakoff (1950) also noted numerous non-Classic features in the iconography at Yaxchilan and Piedras Negras as early as the mid-eighth century (see also Stone 1989). In the Usumacinta, there is evidence of a "Mexicanized" calendar as early as AD 767 that use squared cartouches, which likely originated from the Gulf Coast region (Rice 2004, 238). A Gulf Coast influence also is noted early on at Palenque farther downstream on the Usumacinta. Here, connections with the Chontal center of Comalcalco are seen in the eighth century and continue through AD 814, when the latest reference to Palenque is found on a clay brick at Comalcalco (Martin and Grube 2008, 175; see also Marken and Straight 2007, 292–294; Straight 2007, 181). Sabloff (1973, 124–125) notes that by AD 830 the changes first seen in the late eighth century were in full effect and may signal the control of Ceibal and the wider Usumacinta-Pasión Valley by "intruders" stemming from the Gulf Coast. If Sabloff is correct, earlier waves of Chontal-Itza warrior-merchants were responsible for raiding and overthrowing royal Maya centers in the period between AD 771–830, followed by a postconquest (AD 810–830) influx of Itza nobility who occupied places such as Ceibal and introduced non-Classic features characteristic of the ninth century, such as circular shrines, Pachuca Green obsidian, Pabellon Modeled-carved ceramics, and other imitation fine wares.

While sometimes found in termination contexts, higher frequencies of fine paste ceramics have been found in so-called postconquest occupations at sites such as Ceibal and Punta de Chimino (Foias 1996; Palka 1997; Sabloff 1973, 1975). Sites such as Aquateca and Dos Pilas with termination deposits but minimal Terminal Classic construction have yielded very few of these ninth-century diagnostics (Inomata 2008a, 281). Non-Classic traits generally appear to be restricted to a set of ritual objects, special-purpose pottery, ceremonial architecture, and specific iconographic motifs. Moreover, there is a general lack of significant changes in basic household ceramic assemblages in the southern Maya lowlands (Foias and Bishop 1997; Ringle et al. 1998, 215–216). Rather than a single, wholesale population replacement, it might be more productive to view these non-Classic features as the result of trading diasporas of elite warrior-merchants, particularly given what we know of the mercantile preoccupation of the Chontal-Itza

(Harrison-Buck et al. 2013; Ball and Taschek 1989; Kowalski 1989; Scholes and Roys 1968; Thompson 1970).

In trading diasporas, "some portion of one culture's people—usually merchants—settled as immigrants among a foreign population" (Cusick 1998, 4). Also defined as "circular" migrations, trading diasporas involve small-scale "regular population movements with an intention to return" and are often used to describe trading voyages and religious pilgrimages (Knapp 2008, 49). If trading diasporas occurred, Chontal-Itza groups may have entered places such as the Usumacinta-Pasión drainage, Petén, and/ or the Motagua River valley and become permanent or semi-permanent elite resident merchants, but they likely would have retained strong ties with their homeland (the Chontalpa and northern Yucatan). These professional, long-distance traveling merchants may have resembled the later Aztec *pochteca*, the special guild of warrior-merchants who ventured into enemy territory on behalf of the nobility. The *pochteca* often also served as spies for the state, and the trade these warrior-merchants conducted was a precursor to military conquest. For the Chontal-Itza, initial incursions in the mid- to late eighth century to places such as the Usumacinta-Pasión region may have involved both mercantile business for the Itza nobility and a mercenary component that involved subsequent military conquest, perhaps aimed at securing resources such as obsidian, jade, and slaves, as Cowgill (1964) suggests. If this was the case, it was not until ca. AD 830–889 that they gained their strongest foothold in this "enemy" territory, as this is when we see the most widespread distribution of non-Classic features and the sharpest decline of Maya population levels in the southern Maya lowlands.

Discussion

The phenomena documented across a broad area of the Maya lowlands at the end of the Classic period align well with Tainter's (1988, 2000) definition of "collapse," in which a steady decline of political, social, and economic systems occurred over just a few generations (cited in Dunning et al. 2012, 3652). There has been seemingly endless discussion of the various problems that may have contributed to the decline of the Classic Maya kingdoms (e.g., Demarest et al. 2004; Demarest 2006, 154–157; Iannone et al. this volume). In their attempts to explain the demise of Classic Maya aristocracy, most scholars agree that no single causal factor can explain the cultural and temporal variability of the "collapse" (Aimers 2007; Aimers 2012). While there seems to be little doubt that drought played an important role, scholars argue that multiple variables were likely at work, including ineffectual kingship and bankrupted state finance (Iannone et al. this volume; McAnany 2010, 302–303; McAnany and Gallareta Negrón 2010, 159). Yet very few speculate about *who* was actually responsible for ousting these ineffective kings, aside from vague references to "other political players" and "dissatisfied subjects." If Maya rulers in the Classic period were held responsible for their conduct and interrogated and publically sacrificed for "for failure of ritual knowledge," as some suggest (Freidel and Shaw 2000, 277, as quoted in Iannone et al. this volume), then in my mind the next question is *who* was doing the interrogating and killing of these royal individuals?

I suggest that it may have been the Itza nobility who were doing the interrogating. The Maya *Book of Chilam Balam of Chumayel* indicate that the Itza head chief tested local lords on their mastery of the esoteric ritual knowledge that was deemed necessary to rule, interrogating them in their ritual "Language of Zuyua" (Edmonson 1986; Roys 1967). Elsewhere I argue that the segment of the *Book of Chilam Balam of Chumayel* that mentions this formal interrogation, sometimes called the questionnaire (Roys 1967, 137), may date to as early as the transition from the Classic to the Postclassic, ca. AD 700–950 (Harrison-Buck 2014). Roys (1967, 91–92) details the violent removal and killing of local lords who failed the questionnaire and offers the following translation from the *Book of Chilam Balam of Chumayel*:

> If [the words] are not understood by the chiefs of the towns, ill-omened is the star adorning the night. Frightful is its house. Sad is the havoc in the courtyards of the nobles. Those who die are those who do not understand; those who live will understand it . . .

The pattern of terminal deposits at the end of the Late Classic period, which involved the targeted removal of the king, defacement of his monuments, and destruction of his royal elite compound, is intriguing when viewed in light of the questionnaire. Conceivably, the "havoc in the courtyards of the nobles" found archaeologically at sites across the southern Maya lowlands may be the remains of local rulers who did not pass the test of the Itza head chief and who failed to inherit positions of leadership in the midst of rising Yucatec Maya aristocracy during the transition from the Late to the Terminal Classic. Additional passages in the *Books of Chilam Balam* "tie the greed, immorality, profanity, and ritual ignorance of rulers to drought, pestilence, and famine" (Freidel and Shaw 2000, 277). Notably, ostentatious displays of royal wealth and long-term drought conditions both reached their peak in the southern lowlands around the end of the Classic period, suggesting the possibility that Itza incursions may have been concerned with securing both a moral and political economy.

Concluding Thoughts

Further testing is needed to determine whether Chontal-Itza groups were responsible for the fall of the Classic Maya kings or whether they simply took advantage of a power vacuum created by other forces. In either case, the presence of widespread termination rituals and the influx of non-Classic traits point to new kinds of warfare practices, substantial shifts in the economic organization, and dramatic changes in the political landscape. The strength of the trading diaspora model is that it considers multiple variables, such as local and long-distance trade, migration, and developments at multiple scales of interaction (at both local and regional levels).

While the evidence suggests that new ideas and people moved into the southern Maya lowlands during the Terminal Classic period, some Classic traditions clearly persevere. These groups shared the belief that monuments were active agents that interacted with other actors, both human and non-human. In ancient times, both monuments and the heads of royal personages were "wrapped" with cloth as a form of soul protection. Stuart (1996), who deciphered the *k'al* glyph as "to fasten" or "enclose," references hieroglyphic passages that use this term in the context of "fastening" or "wrapping" cloth on the heads of royal personages at accession ceremonies and also in the context of "binding stone" monuments (the *k'altuun* ritual). As the "essential identity" of a person, the head houses the animating essences of the soul and must be protected from soul loss (Duncan and Hofling 2011, 203; Houston et al. 2006, 61–72). Stuart (1996, 157) argues that "binding" and "wrapping" monuments and rulers (with cloth headbands) had a shared intent: "to contain some sacred essence held within" (see Houston et al. 2006, 61–62, 81–89 for further discussion). Notably, Plank (2004, 46) observed that the *k'al* glyph for "binding" and "wrapping" also frequently appears on lintels over the doorways of elite residences, specifically at the sites of Chichén Itzá and Xkalumkin. Duncan and Hofling (2011, 205) argue that stone lintels served as the "door's roof" and like the roof of house structures was equivalent to the human head and needed protection from soul loss

(Duncan and Hofling 2011, 204–205; Vogt 1998, 21–27). This might explain why lintels supported by piers (particularly those carved with royal portraits) were targets of purposeful destruction and were toppled, smashed, and in some cases physically removed from the royal buildings at sites such as Piedras Negras, Palenque, and Copan.

Both doorways and monuments appear to have been important thresholds where human and nonhuman agents came into contact and housed a vital essence that needed protection and was vulnerable to soul loss if damaged. Some ritual behavior, such as bloodletting, was "soul-connecting" and lent objects "a certain animate and precious quality" (Stuart 1998, 396), while other rituals, such as monument defacement and the toppling of roof structures, may have served to displace the soul and kill the animate co-essence within. Monuments were among the many receptacles for the king's soul parts, and these "kings of stone" were no doubt viewed as powerful agents who perhaps were dangerous if left standing following an enemy conquest. The same may be said for their masonry palaces and temples, which were perhaps targeted for destruction because they held powerful soul parts of the king. The purposeful destruction of the ruler's monuments and his ancestral houses or lineages was necessary so that unfit rulers "[could not] be born to rule again" (Mock 1998b, 119). The archaeological patterns of termination activity support Vogt's (1969, 371) observation that the most important interactions for the Maya were not between humans or between humans and objects but between the soul parts housed in these receptacle-bodies who interacted at important interstices. In Classic times, monuments and royal palace and temple contexts were among such liminal thresholds, where other-than-human persons battled it out at the end of the Classic period.

Concepts of Legitimacy and Social Dynamics

Termination Ritual and the Last King of Aguateca, Guatemala

TAKESHI INOMATA

In the introduction chapter of this volume, Iannone and colleagues advocate a focus on the cross-cultural comparison of divine rulership for a better understanding of Classic Maya politics. I strongly agree with them about the importance of this approach in general. Elsewhere I have suggested that the concept of divine kingship can be successfully applied to the Classic Maya case (Inomata 2001, 2006a, 2008b). My underlying view is that analyzing Maya rulers in this perspective would allow us to move away from the overly functionalist explanation of Maya politics, which attributes a strong managerial role to rulers as individuals or the ruling elite as a group and characterizes them as the main movers of political processes, resembling political players in modern Western societies. The perspective would help us pay closer attention to the symbolic aspect of rulership and the royal court, which may have been as much caught in the constraints of historical traditions as their subjects. As Iannone (chapter 2) notes, the symbolic representation of the ruler as an embodiment of the polity does not necessarily equate with the ruler's supreme power. The ruler may not have much say in the day-to-day management of the polity, which may be run largely by the officials, and the ruler's authority may be challenged by those elites. Iannone's excellent review of relevant cases from around the world advances this line of study substantially.

A more specific question that Iannone and colleagues ask (chapter 1) is whether this model is applicable to the explanation of what happened at the end of the Classic period. With regard to this specific issue, I am skeptical about the utility of the divine rulership model. We need to be aware of the limitations and weaknesses of this theory as addressed by Iannone et al. In their recent review of political anthropological theory, Hansen and Stepputat (2006, 298) note that the study of divine kingship, which followed the tradition of Frazer (1993 [1922]) and Hocart (1936) and culminated in the work of Evans-Pritchard and Fortes (1940), among others, was largely ahistorical and ultimately advanced a Durkheimian view of political authority because it was grounded in the idea of a collectively shared will. Because of these shortcomings, according to Hansen and Stepputat, this substantial body of work on kingship has contributed little to later studies of postcolonial and modern states. More important for our purpose, the ahistorical and Durkheimian nature of this tradition offers little utility in explaining changes in the system of divine kingship itself. The significant social transformation that occurred at the end of the Classic period presents such a challenge.

A related issue is the concept of legitimacy, which Iannone and colleagues also address in their chapter. Archaeologists often use the concept of legitimacy, explicitly or implicitly, following the original formulation developed by Weber. In my view, however, the uncritical adaption of Weber's concept leads to unrealistic or inappropriate understandings of premodern societies. Common archaeological narratives go like this: when a state or polity remains stable, it retains its legitimacy, and when it declines, its legitimacy is lost. In other words, the legitimacy of the king is challenged at the time of crisis. However, we need to question monolithic, one-dimensional views of legitimacy, following the intense critique and evaluation of Weber's theory raised in political philosophy, political science, and sociology. Various critics have noted that the fundamental problem of Weber's conceptualization derives from his formulation of legitimacy as people's belief: the regime is legitimate when the subjects express their belief in its legitimacy (Beetham 1991; Friedrich 1963, 186; Malešević 2002; Pitkin 1972, 280–286). Blau (1963), Schaar (1970), Grafstein (1981), and others have argued that in this conceptualization legitimacy is equated with acquiescence: as long as the regime remains stable and people do not express dissent, it is considered legitimate, although in reality people may covertly disapprove of the regime. This is a circular argument.

As alternatives to Weber's formulation, various scholars have proposed that legitimacy needs to be examined on the basis of normative measures, including the correctness and fairness of procedures (Beetham 1991;

Grafstein 1981; Schaar 1970). In a particularly influential work, Habermas (1975, 97–102) has suggested that Weber's conceptualization presents ethical and moral problems and that the study of legitimacy needs to question people's beliefs. The fundamental problem of Weber's conceptualization of legitimacy is that it affords little explanatory potential for social change. Various archaeologists still appear to assume implicitly or explicitly that social change ultimately derives from deterioration in material conditions and that the failure of legitimacy and associated ideologies is an end result of environmental or economic calamities. Habermas's central argument, however, is that we need to explore the possibility of social change emerging from the negotiation of ideologies. In his view, a legitimation crisis does not necessarily arise from factors external to society but is an endemic state to which modern states are subjected because of their internal processes. I should also add that it is not clear how applicable Habermas's notion of legitimation crisis, which was developed specifically for modern societies, is to the explanation of social dynamics in premodern contexts. In my view, the use of his concept as an explanatory model for the collapse of premodern states is a misapplication. If we are to gain inspiration from Habermas's work, we should focus on the reflexive aspect of his philosophy to critically evaluate researchers' conceptualizations. In other words, we need to problematize the notion of legitimacy by examining not only the time of political turmoil but also that of apparent stability of the regimes.

The problems related to applying Weber's version of legitimacy to archaeological contexts should be obvious. When written records are not available, archaeologists cannot directly access people's beliefs, and we should not simply equate the state of a polity or people's behavior, as estimated from the archaeological records, with common beliefs in legitimacy. Particularly suggestive in this regard is Scott's (1990) discussion of discrepancies between publicly visible behavior of conformity and internal or covert resistance waged by subjects. He contends that although in the public domains non-elites typically follow the "public transcripts" that conform to elites' views, they often express their "hidden transcripts" behind the scenes, demonstrating dissent with the authorities. Thus, legitimacy is not necessarily monolithic and coherent. It follows that a legitimation crisis may exist at the time of apparent political stability. We need to examine the multilayered, fragmentary, and inconsistent nature of legitimacy (Beetham 1991).

In examining multiple layers of legitimacy, we need to pay attention to the following points. First, we need to distinguish between the relevant conceptualizations regarding individual kings and the conceptualization about the entire political regime, including divine rulership. Discussion by some archaeologists may focus largely on the legitimacy of individual rulers. In my view, however, the central question, particularly in the study of social change at the end of the Classic Maya period, should be that of the overall regime. A divine king may be killed when his health or sexual potency declines. In this case, the king may be viewed unfit to rule, but the resulting regicide may not mean that the broader political regime is considered illegitimate. Acts of regicide are rooted in the very notion of divine rulership and serve to maintain the political system tied to this ideology. As Taylor (this volume) notes, the individual fortunes of specific kings may be ephemeral, but the ideology of sacred kingship can be more resistant to change. Second, the recognition of multiple layers of legitimacy implies that complex processes of negotiation exist. Instead of treating legitimacy as a monolithic entity, we need to ask what aspects of legitimacy may have been challenged at the end of Classic period and what aspects may have persisted by situating such changes against the dynamics of political negotiations during the time of seeming stability. It should be clear that most critics of Weber's conceptualization are not throwing away the concept of legitimacy altogether. Neither do they deny the presence of dominant forms of discourse and representation. Instead, they compel us to pay closer attention to how dominant discourses and public transcripts interact with subjugated discourses and hidden transcripts.

Historical Settings

I examine the nature of Maya rulership and the dynamics of its legitimacy through the analysis of termination ritual remains and other evidence of destruction at Aguateca. Evidence of termination rituals associated with settlement abandonment or military conflicts is now well demonstrated at various Maya sites (Freidel et al. 1998; Suhler and Freidel 2003). Typically, large buildings such as royal palaces and pyramidal temples were intentionally destroyed or burned, and in many cases numerous broken objects were deposited. The detailed analysis of such symbolic acts should provide important information about the nature of social relations, prevailing ideologies, and political strategies. Investigations at the Classic Maya center of Aguateca, Guatemala, provide a significant data set in this regard (figure 1.1). Following a military defeat at the end of the Late Classic period, large-scale termination rituals were conducted in the royal palace complex and in the main ceremonial plaza. Destructions were selective, focusing on the buildings tied to the last ruler of this center. This pattern probably reflects the importance of a ruler as an embodiment of communal identities and political power for both the community members and their antagonists.

Aguateca, located in the southwestern lowlands, was a subject of intensive archaeological investigations from 1990 through 2005. Various publications (Inomata and Triadan 2010, 2014; Inomata et al. 2001; Inomata et al. 2002; Inomata 2003) have reported the results of the initial mapping and excavations as part of the Petexbatun Regional Archaeological Project from 1990 through 1993 and of the large-scale excavations of the royal palace group and the adjacent elite residential area that were conducted as the Aguateca Archaeological Project First Phase. Here I summarize these data and discuss the results of excavations in the Main Plaza carried out as part of the Aguateca Restoration Project and the Aguateca Archaeological Project Second Phase from 2002 through 2005 (Inomata et al. 2009).

The primary focus of this chapter is the epicenter of Aguateca, which includes the royal Palace Group complex; the elite residential area along the Causeway south of the Palace Group; and the Main Plaza, which was most likely the primary stage for communal ceremonies (figure 4.1). To the south of the Main Plaza, outside the epicenter, an area in the middle of the steep escarpment that we called the Barranca Escondida was used for the placement of stelae and ritual activities. Our initial investigations demonstrated that the elite residential area was burned during an enemy attack that probably dates to around AD 810. These buildings contained numerous complete and reconstructible artifacts, ranging from such utilitarian items as storage jars, cooking vessels, and grinding stones to precious objects such as jade ornaments, elaborate polychrome vessels, and shell and bone ornaments carved with glyphic texts. Prior to this event, the residents of Aguateca probably felt the increasing threat of an outside attack.

The dynasty of this center appears to have suffered a military defeat in AD 761 (Houston 1993; Martin and Grube 2008). The royal family and the elite left their primary capital of Dos Pilas and moved to the secondary capital of Aguateca, which was in a more naturally defensible location. The last ruler, Tahn Te' K'inich, tried to regain the former glory of the dynasty through a series of military campaigns and the erection of large stelae. However, the political situation surrounding Aguateca continued to deteriorate. The residents of Aguateca suspended the ambitious construction of a pyramidal temple, L8-8, on the western side of the Main Plaza and began to build a series of concentric defensive walls to protect the

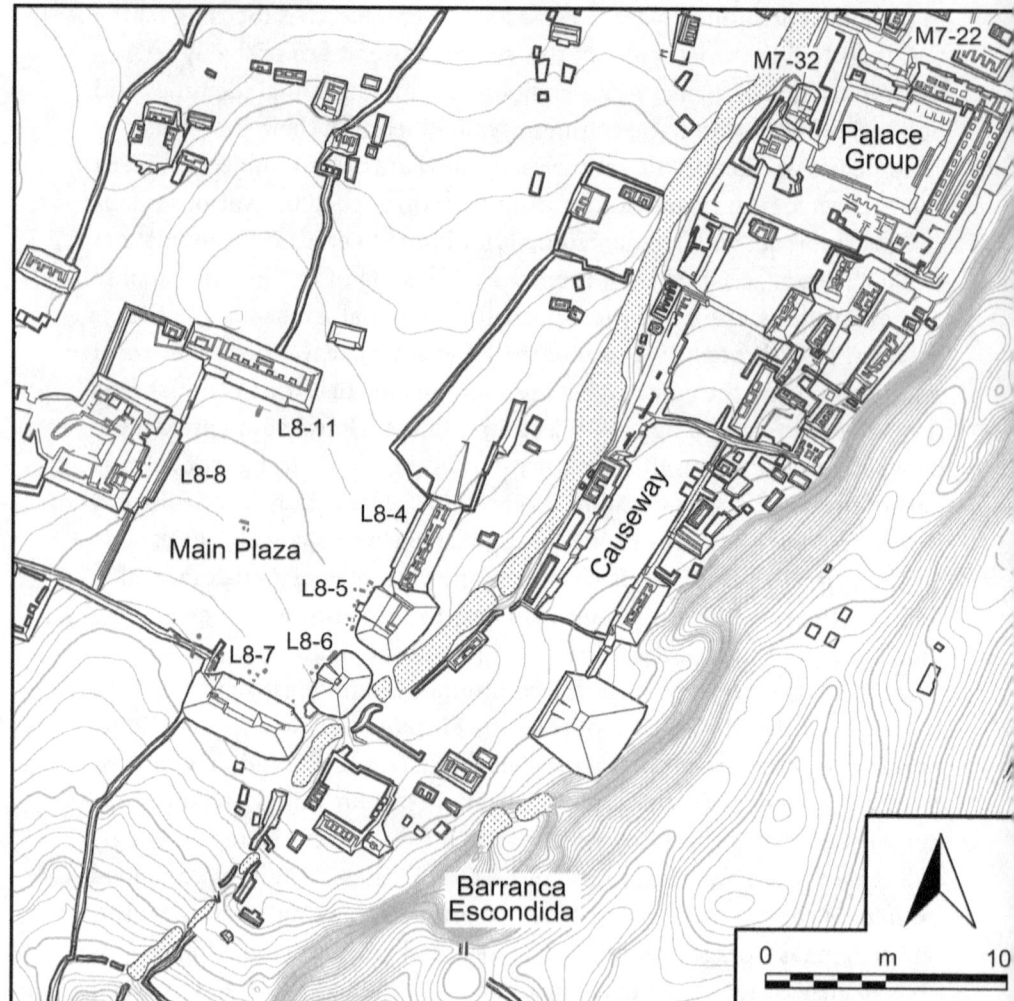

Figure 4.1. Map of the Aguateca epicenter.

center. The ruler and his family appear to have evacuated the center, nearly emptying the Palace Group and placing select royal possessions in a sealed storage room of this complex. The attack of the enemy came quickly. The remaining elite did not have time to carry away their possessions. The areas outside the epicenter were not burned, and inhabitants were able to empty their residences when the center was completely deserted soon after the attack.

Termination Deposits at Aguateca

Before the complete abandonment of the center, the victorious enemies appear to have conducted termination rituals in the royal palace complex and in the Main Plaza. The excavations of Structures M7-22 and M7-32, the main royal residences of the Palace Group, revealed clear evidence of such symbolic acts. The enemies probably found most rooms empty, but they opened the sealed storage room (the easternmost room of Structure M7-22) and intentionally broke some stored objects, scattering their fragments in the area in front of the room. During the termination ritual, the enemies deposited numerous broken objects around Structure M7-22, in the front room, in part of the central throne room of Structure M7-32, and in the areas on the sides of the building. In the central room of Structure M7-32, the capstone of the niche in the side wing of the throne was removed and part of the throne surface was damaged. Broken objects were thrown in the exposed niche and on the damaged part of the throne. Excavators found thin layers of white soil, possibly of limestone origin, which appear similar to the marl layers reported from some termination ritual deposits at other sites (Freidel 1986; Freidel and Schele 1989). These buildings and the associated deposits of artifacts were severely burned. The thick plaster layers in the sealed storage room turned gray and crumbled in many parts, suggesting that they were exposed to heat of 700 to 800°C (see Birbhushan et al. 1996). Participants in the ritual probably deposited a large amount of organic fuels in and around the buildings to make this substantial fire (Inomata 2014).

All major buildings around the Main Plaza have been at least partially excavated, and the results allow us to evaluate different treatments of these buildings at the time of abandonment. Structure L8-8, an unfinished temple, does not appear to have been subjected to ritual destruction. Structures L8-4, L8-5, and L8-11 were nearly completely excavated, but the excavators did not find unequivocal evidence of termination rituals (Valdés et al. 1999). The clearest evidence of termination rituals was found at Structures L8-6 and L8-7 (Ponciano et al. 2009). Some portions of their cut stones were dismantled and a large quantity of broken objects was deposited over and in front of them. From stratigraphic evidence alone it is impossible to determine the exact timing of the rituals; whether they were carried out by the residents of Aguateca before the center was attacked by the enemies or whether they were perpetrated by the victorious enemies after their successful attack on Aguateca is uncertain. Although we should continue to evaluate various possibilities, circumstantial evidence favors the latter interpretation.

Prior to the attack by enemies, the remaining elites of Aguateca, though feeling the threat of an imminent attack, were trying to maintain the traditional courtly culture with activities such as refurbishing royal headdresses and guarding ornaments carved with the ruler's name and the Aguateca emblem glyph. It is unlikely that the residents of Aguateca destroyed those temples. I should also note that important monumental buildings may have continued to receive ritual visits that resulted in an accumulation of dense deposits over a period of time (Navarro-Farr 2009; Navarro-Farr and Arroyave Prera 2014). This, however, was probably not the case at Aguateca, as various lines of evidence suggest that Aguateca was completely abandoned soon after the final attack (Inomata 2003; Inomata et al. 2004). The dense deposits at Structures L8-6 and L8-7 and those in the Palace Group were most likely placed immediately after the attack by the invading enemies.

Excavations at the base of Structure L8-6 revealed a dense deposit of broken artifacts similar to those found in the Palace Group (figure 4.2). In front of the stairway, the dense deposit was placed directly on the plaza floor, but in the area south of the stairway a layer of yellowish sandy soils was found between the plaza floor and the artifact deposit. This layer, which accumulated against the retaining walls of the pyramid and was up to sixty centimeters thick, did not contain artifacts or large pieces of cut limestone blocks. The origin of this soil presents a vexing problem. One possibility is that some of the cut blocks that covered the stairways and retaining walls were removed prior to the deposition of broken artifacts and that the yellow soil accumulated in this area during the process of dismantling or is attributable to subsequent erosion. The yellow soil appear to be identical to the material in construction fills found immediately behind veneer stones. In the excavation of the stairway, two courses of steps were found in situ, but blocks of the upper steps were absent, and both over the stairway and in the area south of it the number of cut blocks in the collapse layer was relatively small, supporting the interpretation that some portion of blocks was removed. Another possibility is that the enemies brought the yellow soil from other locations as part of the termination ritual. If so, this material may be comparable in function to the white powdery materials found in the Palace Group and the marls identified in termination rituals at other sites.

The deposits of artifacts found in front of Structure L8-7 were not as dense as those of Structure L8-6, but they still contained a considerable

Figure 4.2. Dense deposit of artifacts found south of the stairway of Structure L8-6.

quantity of broken objects. Unique features found during the excavation of this building included piles of irregular stones placed over and in front of the stairway. Underneath the stone pile found over the stairway excavators was a dense deposit of broken objects placed on the plaza floor directly in front of the stairway. We also noticed that in the area to the east of the pile the second and higher steps of the stairway had been removed, whereas the first step remained in its original position (figure 4.3). These observations suggest the following sequence of events. The invading enemies deposited numerous broken objects over and in front of the stairway during a termination ritual for this building. They then removed cut blocks in the eastern part of the wide stairway and piled irregular fill stones removed during this process in the central part of the stairway. However, they left intact blocks of the first step of the stairway that were embedded in the plaza floor. In addition, blocks covered by the piles of irregular stones were left untouched. It is not clear where they took the removed blocks.

Examining the specific contents of these deposits helps us understand their nature. Table 4.1 compares the quantities of ceramic types found in the deposits associated with the Palace Group, the Causeway area, Structures L8-6 and L8-7, and the Barranca Escondida. As to the deposits found in

Figure 4.3. Stairway of Structure L8-7 after removing the pile of stones viewed from the west. Note that in the eastern portion, the second and higher steps have been dismantled. A pile of irregular stones was placed over the preserved step, where a tree root is visible.

the Palace Group, they have close similarities to those found in the Causeway area. A large part of the Causeway area materials consist of complete and reconstructible vessels left in residences and associated buildings, thus representing common domestic assemblages, whereas those of the Palace Group derived substantially from the dense termination deposits. The close similarities between the materials from these areas accord with the hypothesis that domestic refuse materials were transported and deposited in the Palace Group during the termination rituals. In both areas the ratios of Encanto Striated, which mostly served as storage jars, are highest, and those of Pedregal Modeled, which were almost exclusively used as censors, are low. Those assemblages also show similar quantities of other common domestic types: Tinaja Red and Pantano Impressed, which were predominantly liquid-containing jars; Subin Red and Chaquiste Impressed bowls used for cooking and storage; and Saxche-Palmar Polychrome and other Petén Gloss types, largely representing serving vessels.

Table 4.1. Frequencies of ceramic sherds found in different areas of Aguateca

	Palace Group		Causeway Area		Barranca Escondida		L8-6		L8-7	
	Freq	%	Freq	%	Freq	%	Freq	%	Freq	%
Uaxactun Unslipped Ware										
Cambio Unslipped	400	0.8	1,471	1.6	8	0.5	11	0.1	0	0.0
Encanto Striated	25,080	48.0	35,388	37.3	17	1.0	3,722	39.0	1,615	39.0
Pedregal Modeled	0	0.0	10	0.0	145	8.5	0	0.0	1	0.0
Other Uaxactun Unslipped types	4,564	8.7	9,983	10.5	199	11.7	1,131	11.9	289	7.0
Petén Gloss Ware										
Tinaja and Pantano	9,389	18.0	24,686	26.0	312	18.3	1,956	20.5	995	24.0
Subin and Chaquiste	8,346	16.0	10,289	10.9	124	7.3	2,154	22.6	919	22.2
Saxche-Palmar Polychrome	2,866	5.5	8,090	8.5	336	19.7	344	3.6	244	5.9
Other Petén Gloss types	633	1.2	2,055	2.2	552	32.4	69	0.7	27	0.7
Other ware	983	1.9	2,807	3.0	10	0.6	150	1.6	48	1.2
Total identified	52,261	100	94,779	100	1,703	100	9,537	100	4,138	100
Eroded/Undetermined	45,627		2,4708		1,785		3,008		1,844	
Total	97,888		11,9487		3,488		22,082		10,120	

The main difference between the assemblages of the two areas is that a substantial portion of the ceramics from the Causeway area consisted of complete or reconstructible vessels, whereas most materials from the Palace Group could not be refitted. This observation adds further support to the view that a large portion of the Palace Group materials consist of secondary deposits taken from middens. The somewhat lower ratios of Tinaja and Pantano jars and Saxche-Palmar and other Petén Gloss serving vessels in the Palace Group assemblage suggest that these materials derived primarily from middens associated with food-preparation areas, whereas those of the Causeway area were found in residences, thus representing the vessel composition of food-consumption areas. Other objects found in the Palace Group deposits include numerous chert and obsidian tools, fragments of grinding stones, and animal bones that were probably transported from middens along with broken ceramics. These deposits, however, also contained items uncharacteristic of domestic middens, such as human skeletal remains and a substantial number of greenstone and shell ornaments. The deposition of such precious items during termination rituals is reported from other sites (Garber 1983), and in the Palace Group of Aguateca these items were probably added to the transported midden materials as part of the ritual.

The compositions of ceramics from Structures L8-6 and L8-7 are similar to those found in the Palace Group and in the Causeway area, indicating that these materials, like those of the Palace Group, originated from domestic middens. In this regard, the clear difference from the materials found in the Barranca Escondida is suggestive. The Barranca Escondida is a ritual location marked by stelae and a probable shrine that does not have common domestic structures (Inomata and Eberl 2010). The assemblage found there is characterized by the markedly low ratios of typical domestic types of Encanto Striated, Subin Red, and Chaquiste Impressed and by the high percentage of Pedregal Modeled censors and other possible ritual items. The pyramidal structures L8-6 and L8-7, which are associated with stelae, most likely served as temples, and we might expect that their original artifact assemblages would be characterized by an abundance of ritual items like those from the Barranca Escondida. The predominance of domestic objects on and around Structures L8-6 and L8-7, however, suggests that these deposits did not result from the original use of the buildings but are secondary (that is, transposed) deposits placed during a termination ritual. I should add that there are some differences in the composition of ceramics in the Palace Group, the Causeway area, and Structures L8-6 and L8-7. Such small variations are expected, as the use and discarding of specific vessels vary from one group to another and from one social context to another. But the percentages of ceramic types associated with Structures L8-6 and L8-7 are essentially identical. It is probable that the materials deposited at these temples were taken from the same middens.

As in the case of the Palace Group deposits, most ceramics from Structures L8-6 and L8-7 could not be refitted. In addition, the deposits at those temples contained numerous chert and obsidian tools, animal bones, and fragments of manos and metates, all of which most likely came from middens. Greenstone and shell ornaments and other elaborate art pieces are present (Figure 4.4), but their quantities are substantially smaller than those in the Palace Group deposits. It is not clear whether those ornaments were originally included in the middens or whether they were added during subsequent rituals.

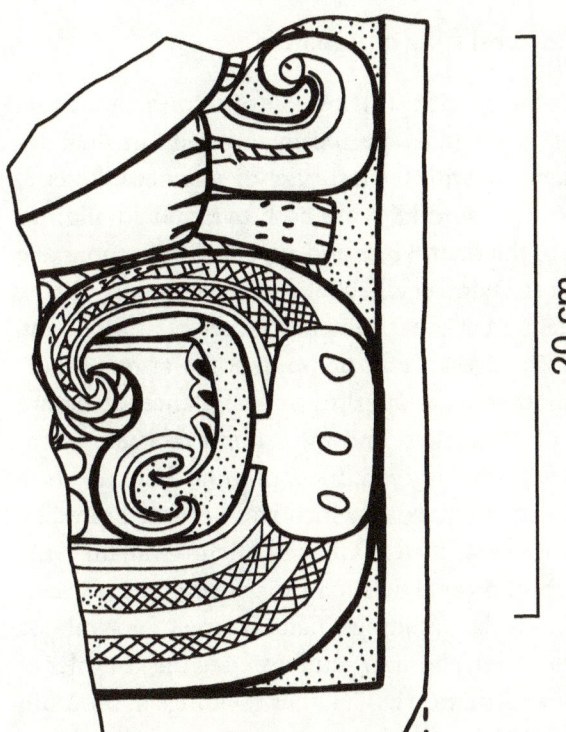

Figure 4.4. Fragment of a carved limestone object found in the deposit of Structure L8-6.

The ritual and secondary nature of the deposits in the Palace Group and at Structures L8-6 and L8-7 appears to be comparable to those found at Structure 3 at Blue Creek, Belize (see Guderjan and Hanratty this volume). Clayton et al. (2005) report that the dense deposits covering this pyramidal structure, which was located in a public plaza, also consisted mostly of sherds that could not be refitted. They argue that these materials were transported from middens, but unlike the Aguateca materials, they may have been taken from feasting refuse rather than from common household middens. The early literature on termination rituals emphasized the presence of reconstructible or partial vessels that were probably smashed and scattered as part of the ritual (Freidel 1986; Robertson 1983, 112; Walker 1998). The Aguateca and Blue Creek deposits reflect different activities from those examples, suggesting that variations existed in the practices associated with what we call termination rituals (see Houk this volume).

Termination Rituals and the Last King of Aguateca

A plausible explanation for the specific distribution of termination ritual deposits at Agauteca is that the enemies specifically targeted for ritual destruction the buildings associated with the last ruler of Aguateca, Ruler 5, Tahn Te' K'inich. Structures L8-5 and L8-6 are both pyramidal buildings located on the eastern side of the Main Plaza and appear to be comparable to Structure 3 at Blue Creek (Clayton et al. 2005) and other eastern shrine structures identified at Tikal and at other centers (Becker 1971; McAnany 1995; Navarro-Farr 2009). The presence of dense deposits at one building and their absence at another seem puzzling at first glance. Structure L8-5 must have been one of the earliest and most important temples at Aguateca. It was associated with the largest number of stone monuments—Stelae 1–5, and Altars A–E and S—many of which had been dedicated by Ruler 3 and his successor, Ruler 4, K'awiil Chan K'inich (Graham 1967; Houston 1993). Its importance in the dynastic history of Aguateca is evident, and that could have made this building a natural target for symbolic destruction. The enemies, however, chose structures tied to the last ruler of Aguateca and spared the older Structure L8-5. Other buildings in the Main Plaza, Structures L8-4 and L8-11, may have also been associated with the early kings, or as range structures they may not have had heavy symbolic value comparable to the temple-pyramids. Given the shared elite culture and close interaction, it would not be surprising that some outsiders had knowledge of specific temples.

Structures L8-6 and L8-7 were most likely closely connected to the last ruler. In front of Structure L8-6 were Stelae 6 and 19, both dedicated by Tahn Te' K'inich. Our excavation in front of this building revealed the base part of Stela 6 in situ, confirming the original placement of this monument. Stela 7, which was placed in front of Structure L8-7, is also the monument of the last king. The other three stelae found near Structure L8-7, Stelae 8, 9, and 10, are heavily eroded, but their large sizes suggest that the last ruler also erected them. The earlier kings, Ruler 3 and K'awiil Chan K'inich, dedicated relatively small monuments at the secondary capital of Aguateca while erecting larger stelae at their primary seat of power, Dos Pilas. After the probable military defeat of K'awiil Chan K'inich, his successor, Tahn Te' K'inich, reestablished Aguateca as the primary capital of this troubled dynasty and then began to erect large stelae that rivaled those at Dos Pilas. At the same time, Tahn Te' K'inich appears to have invested in substantial construction at Aguateca. Structures L8-6 and L8-7 were probably the main temples he commissioned and used as the primary stages of his ritual activity. Whereas the earlier temple, L8-5, had a superstructure made of perishable material (Inomata 2010), Structures L8-6 and L8-7 boasted vaulted temples. Although we did not directly confirm this by excavating the top of those buildings, our excavations at their bases revealed vault stones that originated from the masonry-roofed buildings that once stood on those pyramids. Tahn Te' K'inich apparently ordered the even more ambitious construction project of Structure L8-8, but it was suspended in the deteriorating political situation prior to the final attack.

The Palace Group may also have been associated primarily with Tahn Te' K'inich rather than with his predecessors. We can safely assume that the Palace Group of Aguateca was the main residential complex of Tahn Te' K'inich and his family (Inomata et al. 2001), but uncertainty remains about whether this palace complex was established during the reigns of his predecessors. Excavations into the basal platform of Structure M7-22 and the patio of the Palace Group showed that this structure (and possibly the entire compound) was built essentially in one construction episode directly on the bedrock (Inomata and Triadan 2010; Ponciano 2009). Likewise, most of the elite residences located along the Causeway appear to have been built in one construction stage. The fills of the Palace Group and residences along the Causeway contained a small quantity of Chablekal Fine Gray and volcanic ash–tempered ceramics that largely date to AD 760 to 810 (Foias 1996) mixed with a large quantity of less time-sensitive Late Classic types. These data point to the tantalizing possibility that much of the elite core of Aguateca was built after the probable military defeat of Dos Pilas in AD 761; that is, during the reign of Tahn Te' K'inich. At the same time, I need to note the possibility that some portion of Chablekal Fine Gray and volcanic ash–tempered wares dates earlier than has been commonly assumed. Even if the Palace Group was constructed earlier, Aguateca appears to have been considerably less important for the earlier kings than Dos Pilas; they probably spent little time at the secondary center. The Palace Group must have been strongly tied to the deeds and image of the last king, Tahn Te' K'inich.

These data suggest that the remains of termination rituals are concentrated at the buildings that were strongly associated with the last king, whereas the temples dedicated by the earlier rulers lack comparable traces. The destruction of important buildings probably represented a symbolic defeat of the enemy that is comparable to the Aztec practice of burning enemy temples (Berdan and Anawalt 1992). However, the concentration of termination ritual remains at the structures associated with the last ruler may tell us deeper stories about the nature of Maya rulership and communities. It appears that the dominant form of representation at Aguateca was the individual king rather than broader notions of dynasty or polity, and it was therefore the king who strongly defined the unity and identity of the community for both community members and opponents.

The importance of the individual king at Aguateca may have derived partly from the personality and charisma of Tahn Te' K'inich. This ruler brought a major transformation of the community for the local residents of Aguateca when he established it as the primary seat of dynastic power. Not only did he erect monuments significantly larger than earlier ones at this center but he also ordered ambitious construction projects, including vaulted temples of Structures L8-6 and L8-7. In particular, Structure L8-8, though it was never finished, was probably intended to be a large pyramid that would have far surpassed any existing buildings at Aguateca. Tahn Te' K'inich also appears to have been (or at least to have presented himself as) an active warrior. His preserved monuments, Stelae 6, 7, 13, 14, and 19, all depict him with war captives (Houston 1993; Martin and Grube 2008). As Iannone (this volume) notes, these activities may have represented his desperate attempts to reestablish the glory of the Aguateca polity under deteriorating circumstances. The grand construction projects and war campaigns may have fostered pride in the community centered on the ruler, but they may have at the same time strained the resources of the already weakened population and exacerbated antagonisms with other groups.

As significant as the personality of an individual is, I would like to emphasize the importance of the ruler's body and physical action in shaping the image of a community. This is a more general organizational property that was shared by various groups in the Maya lowlands. I have argued elsewhere that in Classic Maya society the abstract institution of polity as an object of loyalty and emotional attachment may have been relatively weak (Inomata 2006a, 2006b). Senses of belongingness were probably fostered to a substantial degree by physical interactions among social agents set in specific historical and spatial contexts. I suspect that under such conditions the bodily presence of the ruler and his physical actions strongly shaped community members' perceptions of their relationship to the political authority. The ruler was indeed an embodiment of a political community (see also Iannone this volume). People's senses of loyalty, affection, hatred, and fear were tied to the physicality of an individual ruler rather than the abstract notion of collectivity that modern scholars may variably term polity, state, or nation. In this sense, the destruction and rituals focused on the buildings associated with the last ruler of Aguateca were not carried out by chance; instead, they closely reflected the nature of Maya political organization. Defeating an individual ruler and destroying material symbols tied to that person must have been the primary way to weaken the unity and continuation of the community.

Conclusions

The events that happened in the final days of Aguateca were shaped by the historical settings of this short-lived center. Some of the monumental buildings at Aguateca, including Structures L8-6 and L8-7 and possibly also the Palace Group, appear to have been built during the reign of the last ruler, Tahn Te' K'inich. These buildings were probably tied strongly to the person and deeds of this king, in the minds of both community members and some outsiders. After the enemies attacked this center and destroyed its elite residential area, they conducted termination rituals specifically at the buildings associated with the last ruler. To seal their victory over Aguateca, the enemies focused their symbolic battle and destruction on the last king and his buildings. It appears that the unity and identity of the community hinged strongly on the physical presence and acts of an individual king.

I do not necessarily think that the political organization at Aguateca closely applies to other Maya centers. After all, communities are flexible and variable and present different forms and configurations across time and space. This variability may depend partly on how strongly the personality of an individual ruler affects the affairs of the political community. In addition, we need to keep in mind that the main occupation of Aguateca dates to a time of drastic social change in the Maya lowlands. With warfare intensifying and many centers declining, the traditional forms of rulership and political organization were challenged. In particular, the complete abandonment of Aguateca after its military defeat marked a major break from the Classic period tradition in which defeated groups typically maintained their own centers and dynasties.

Yet the events that happened at Aguateca probably reflect the common nature of Maya political communities of various groups in the lowlands. The integration of a community in the Maya lowlands during the Classic period was based significantly on physical interactions among social agents, and political authority was created and maintained through public events at which people could witness the body and act of the king and other elites. The durability of buildings associated with the ruler and his political authority probably complemented the fleeting nature of power relations that depended on physical interaction. These material symbols lent a sense of persistence to the unity of the community and the authority of the king and elites. This means that these buildings could be a target of destruction even after the battle was over.

I should note that the focus on the person of the king and on his buildings and monuments as extensions of his quality as targets of bellicose attacks was a common practice throughout the Classic period (e.g., Suhler and Freidel 2003). In this regard, we see certain similarities and differences in practices associated with divine rulership in the Maya area and Africa. Among the Classic Maya, kings were required to conduct auto-sacrifice in the form of bloodletting rituals and they were the ones who had to be sacrificed in the wake of military defeats. These practices reflect the nature of Maya rulers as embodiments of their respective polities, analogous to the ideologies associated with divine rulership of Africa and other parts of the world (as detailed by Iannone this volume). Nonetheless, in Classic Maya society there is no known case of regicide in the sense described by Frazer. In this sense, we see historical uniqueness of Maya rulership.

If the sacrifice of defeated kings by the victorious enemies was a common practice throughout the Classic period, such killings do not necessarily signal the loss of legitimacy for the institution of divine rulership or even for the defeated polities. Defeated polities may have endured humiliation and certain political meddling from their vanquishers, but the dynasties typically continued without surrendering their autonomy completely. The ideology and institution of divine rulership persisted through many episodes of victories and defeats. But if we accept the criticism of Weber raised by Habermas and others, we should not equate the persistence of rulership with coherent and universal beliefs in its legitimacy.

Most important, there is a fundamental difference between what happened at Aguateca in early ninth century and what went before. At the end of the Classic period, the dynasty at Aguateca died out and its center was completely abandoned following the military defeat. Similar disruption and decline occurred at many other centers at about the same time, as is documented in the various chapters in this volume. This pattern reflects a significant change in the nature of rulership and political ideologies beyond the fortunes of individual kings. The coexistence of old practices of sacrificing defeated kings and their key buildings with a new systemic change in political ideologies and regimes may fit the concept of the residual discussed by Williams (1977); certain elements of an old era persist through social transformations. After the abandonment of Aguateca, the nearby center of Seibal (aka Ceibal) prospered in an effort to revive its old dynasty. This residual element of the Classic period regime is reminiscent of the persistence of certain elements of sacred kingship in modern Rwanda that Taylor describes (this volume). However, the dynasty of Seibal did not survive for long. Although the institution of rulership continued in the Maya area in the Postclassic period, monumental representations of rulers as embodiments of their communities became far less common. There appears to have been a significant change in the nature of rulership and in associated ideologies and symbolism.

The theory of divine rulership that Iannone (chapter 2) explores presents an important perspective for the study of Classic Maya society. Nonetheless, its application to specific historical instances requires careful evaluation. In this regard, the question of legitimacy that Iannone and colleagues address (chapter 1) is critical. We need to distinguish the notion of fitness of individual kings to rule, the superficial conformity of subjects to the regime of rulership, and the attitudes of subjects toward rulers. These different layers and dimensions of legitimacy are mutually related but are not coterminous. Our task is to examine the interplay of their complex dynamics in specific historical contexts.

Acknowledgments

Archaeological investigations at Aguateca were carried out under a permit generously issued by the Instituto de Antropología e Historia de Guatemala. Support for the research was provided by the National Science Foundation (BCS-9707950, BCS-9910594, BCS-0414167); the Mitsubishi Foundation; the National Geographic Society (#5937-97, #6303-98); the Foundation for the Advancement of Mesoamerican Studies, Inc.; and the H. John Heinz III Charitable Trust.

5

The Life and Afterlife of the Classic Period Piedras Negras Kingdom

CHARLES GOLDEN, ANDREW K. SCHERER,
MELANIE KINGSLEY, STEPHEN D. HOUSTON,
AND HÉCTOR ESCOBEDO

The editors of this volume have challenged the contributors to consider the cross-cultural significance of the royal scapegoat as a model for understanding the failure of ancient Maya dynastic kingdoms. We are charged with examining what crises might bring about the transformation of paramount rulers from revered to despised figures, what the archaeological signs of such an abrupt loss of legitimacy might be, and if such a model may aid in the explanation of political failure and collapse in our case studies. We engage with these issues through the lens provided by three long-term research projects at the Classic period (AD 250–900) kingdom once centered on the archaeological site of Piedras Negras, Guatemala (see figure 1.1).

We argue that the collapse of dynastic rule at Piedras Negras was not a brief episode but a long-term process that extended over much of the Late Classic period (AD 600–900). There is little in the way of evidence for environmental or external crises at the end of the dynasty, although a particular episode of warfare may have brought long-simmering internal political strife to a tipping point. Further, despite the archaeological evidence for the destruction of royal buildings that encouraged earlier researchers to propose peasant revolts as a cause of Classic period collapse (Mason 1935, 562; Satterthwaite 1935, 1937, 1958), our interpretation of the data sees them as equivocal concerning the timing and explanation for such destruction. Ultimately, we do not rule out the possibility of scapegoating as one process at work in dynastic collapse at Piedras Negras, but we lack the data to clearly identify it as a causal explanation for the end of the Piedras Negras kingdom.

Now a mass of ruined buildings, Piedras Negras was for much of the first millennium AD a thriving city and the seat of a powerful dynasty. At its maximum extent, the territory encompassed by communities whose elites owed allegiance to the kings of Piedras Negras extended over at least 1,000 square kilometers. Though residents of the urban core may have numbered fewer than 5,000, the population throughout the kingdom at its height probably numbered in the tens of thousands (Anaya Hernandez 2001; Golden et al. 2008; Golden and Scherer 2013b; Nelson 2005). Military expeditions and marriage alliances with other dynasties further extended the hard and soft power of the rulers of Piedras Negras beyond the limits of what can reasonably be called its territorial limits, keeping open critical trade routes across the broken topography of the middle Usumacinta River valley (Anaya Hernandez 2001, 2005; Anaya Hernandez et al. 2003; Golden et al. 2012; Golden and Scherer 2013b).

But the dynasty took a fatal blow when the last securely attested ruler of Piedras Negras was captured by his rivals from the kingdom of Yaxchilan in AD 808 (Houston et al. 1999; Martin and Grube 2008, 153; Stuart 1998a). In the century following that defeat, the population of the kingdom shrank. Rural communities were slowly abandoned, and the residents of Piedras Negras filled in the rooms of their homes and once-royal buildings with debris, gradually reduced the number of room spaces used as living quarters, and departed for other regions. Thus, the political, economic, and ritual community of Piedras Negras dissipated with an initial loud military bang followed by a slow, wheezing population decline.

We can effectively speak of the architectural core of Piedras Negras as abandoned by AD 930. Masonry structures were no longer built, and any remaining occupants did not leave an archaeologically visible signature in the site epicenter. The forest overtook what had been a magnificent royal city, leaving it to the occasional visitor and later to Lacandón Maya, lumber camps, archaeologists, and guerillas.

Such is the standard narrative for a Classic period Maya kingdom—it rose, its capital center expanded with the reach of the power and authority of its dynasty, and the power of those rulers vanished and populations crashed during the Terminal Classic period (AD 810–900). Such a sequential history, however, does not tell the story of the community. It compresses history into simple chronology. Further, by locating the ninth century residents of Piedras Negras in the so-called Terminal Classic period, it inherently reduces them to the role of a remnant community of squatters and sad hangers-on; they become people living in the aftermath of greatness from which they are somehow disconnected. This linear narrative also calls for a crisis of rulership. It seeks a historical moment in which long-standing patterns of authority were called into question and monarchs—indeed a single and particular monarch who has lost his or her unique moral position—are overthrown, perhaps as scapegoats for the doom of their kingdom.

Collapse from such a perspective is an incident resulting from badly performed kingship and the disillusionment of a populace that had placed great faith in the powers of its suzerain for too long: the French or Russian Revolutions, in which monarchs were executed by mobs or insurrectionist armies; the rejection by some North American colonists of the right to taxes and property in the Western Atlantic of a once-revered British monarchy; the popular practice of dating the fall of the last Roman Empire to the abdication of Romulus Augustulus in AD 476 (see Iannone this volume; Taylor this volume). There is no doubt that such flash points offer dramatic historical narratives. The historical moment of failure that comes down through the ages, though, is a tale told by the victors (or, at the very least, the survivors) justifying revolution or collapse as necessary acts required to replace bankrupt administrations and perhaps rejuvenate society.

Further, to view collapse as a historical moment misses much of the story before and after such political failures. The sad truth is that the end of a kingdom is more often a long-term process, a drawn out whisper rather than a noisy flash. Any successful revolution or coup d'état is typically the last in a long series of failed attempts to bring down a ruling system. Romulus Augustulus was neither the first nor the last Roman emperor to be overthrown, and the Russian Revolution of 1917 was only the most successful of a series of uprisings that had wracked Imperial Russia for decades. The end of the Russian monarchy cannot be understood except within the context of wider trends leading to the decline of governing monarchies across Europe and the wider wars and economic and political struggles that shook the continent.

There is thus often not *a single* "legitimation crisis" that explains an episode of discontent and dissolution (Habermas 1975; Iannone this volume; Jameson 1981). Rather political life is *a series* of liminal crises both large (e.g., extended droughts, peasant uprisings, or defeat in warfare) and small (e.g., courtly intrigues or perceived slights against local political allies), requiring political work and ritual, during which rulership may be replicated, reformed, or extinguished (Hüsken 2007; Schieffelin 2007; Turner 1967, 93–111). Individual kings may indeed fail to fulfill their obligations or be called upon to sacrifice their lives to fulfill those obligations (see Taylor this volume). Yet as Christopher Taylor (personal communication, 2013) notes in distinguishing the Maya cases from his Rwandan data, the end of Classic period kingdoms in the waning decades of the first millennium forces us to consider not just the political decline and death of a single ruler but also the utter abandonment of a political system across a wide geographic area involving multiple states.

The loss of legitimacy in a failed or collapsed state is not the outcome of short-term pathologies but is rather the exacerbation of more general problems present in apparently "pre-crisis" healthy and strong states (Cowgill 1988; Zartman 1995, 7–8). The failure of a state requires the movement over time of most political actors, including so-called elites and non-elites, away from a commitment to the state as a serious political option. It also requires effort on the part of rulers to achieve failure, though that is rarely their intent. Failure can come even as political leaders make appropriately rational decisions that they may genuinely believe are to the benefit of the state, the results of which are nonetheless detrimental to the polity as a whole (Rotberg 2003, 23; Rotberg 2004, 14). Epigraphic data now make abundantly clear that individual royal bodies were regularly captured, killed, and tortured and their royal precincts battered over the many centuries of the Classic period, yet dynastic rule persisted.

Piedras Negras makes a particularly apt case study for these questions. In many ways, excavations during the 1930s at Piedras Negras provided the template for interpretations positing the violent overthrow of Maya kings and the end of the Classic period. Upon finding robust evidence for the destruction of monuments and the burning of buildings prior to site abandonment, J. Alden Mason and Linton Satterthwaite Jr. proposed that an invasion or peasant revolt had brought a dramatic end to the rulers of Piedras Negras (Holley 1983, 201; Mason 1935, 562; Satterthwaite 1935, 1937, 1958). This interpretation was itself revolutionary, raising the possibility of ancient violence and warfare among the Classic period Maya and suggesting that the ruling class might not have been a body of benevolent priests but rather an extractive and abusive elite who indeed may have been tempting scapegoats in times of crisis (see also Hamblin and Pitcher 1980; Thompson 1954).

More recent interpretations of the lead-up to abandonment at Piedras Negras have posited some connection between the burning of buildings and the destruction of monuments Satterthwaite and colleagues found and invasion by foreign forces (Holley 1983, 207–208). Indeed, data suggest that the capture of the last known ruler of Piedras Negras (typically called Ruler 7) by forces from neighboring Yaxchilan around AD 808 was roughly contemporary with the devastation wreaked on royal monuments and architecture around Piedras Negras (Houston et al. 1999, 2001; Houston, Escobeda, Child, et al. 2003, 228; Stuart 1998a).

Yet while epigraphy may provide graphic and textual records of violence, the archaeological record is typically opaque about distinct episodes of regicide or warfare. There are some uniquely robust data from a few sites such as Aguateca (Inomata this volume, 1997, 2003) and Cancuen (Demarest et al. this volume; Demarest et al. 2007) that provide us either with the human remains of a massacre or a Pompeii-like event in which doors were sealed, buildings were burned, and precious objects were abandoned by their fleeing owners. However, in the great majority of cases, what we are dealing with instead are contexts and objects that have suffered the slings and arrows of taphonomic processes and episodes of destruction, apparent desecration, and abandonment that are difficult or impossible to date with any certainty.

The latter is certainly the case at Piedras Negras, where the best we can hope for is a reasonable *terminus post quem*, acknowledging that we can say with certainty only that royal objects and spaces were damaged, demolished, and brought low sometime in the century after the failure of dynastic power. Whether that was within moments or decades of the death or dethronement of the final dynastic ruler we cannot say. Yet such questions of timing are critically important for understanding whether there was indeed a violent final rejection of sacred royal power or instead a gradual diminution and dissolution of authority. Whatever the role of foreign forces in damaging Piedras Negras, we can be sure that local inhabitants reshaped the once-royal spaces and imagery to suit the needs of a postdynastic world over the course of a century or more.

Instead, then, of focusing on the archaeologically invisible moment in which any final ruler is captured, killed, or faced with the loss of legitimacy, it may be useful to look at political collapse and the material remains of desecration and demolition as the results of process encompassing a period of decades or centuries during which the social stage is set for the dissolution of systems of rulership. The final monarch overthrown in such a process of dissolution may have been the particular target for the ire of the populace or former noble allies but may or may not be perceived as the cause of that dissolution (cf. Taylor this volume). Nor do the processes that lead to collapse end with the fall of a ruler and royal court. The decades following such a fall may be telling, revealing the social and political roles that rulers once played and that are conspicuous in their absence (Graffam 1992).

Piedras Negras in the Ninth Century: Transformation and Abandonment

Given the current archaeological and epigraphic data, it is reasonable to speak of the Terminal Classic at Piedras Negras as the period beginning with the collapse of dynastic rule around AD 810, in which the most obvious temporal archaeological indicator is the appearance of Fine Orange ceramics, that extends perhaps a century until the general abandonment of the site no later than AD 930. Such a chronological boundary, however, creates a false sense of social divide and injects the sense of immediate, absolute, and irrevocable change that would not necessarily have been evident to the people who lived through those years. While the final blow to the dynasty of Piedras Negras may indeed have come in the form of a spectacular and immediately felt military defeat and the capture of Ruler 7 by forces from neighboring Yaxchilan around AD 808 (Martin and Grube 2008, 153; Stuart 1998a), the failure of the polity must be seen as a long-term political problem extending back for many generations (Golden and Scherer 2013a, 2013b).

The loss of any single king need not have engendered dynastic collapse. Kings at Piedras Negras had been lost in battle during earlier centuries, and in neighboring kingdoms such as Palenque, Yaxchilan, and Santa Elena, kings had been captured, dethroned, and engaged in intra-dynastic struggles for succession in the Classic period as the institution of kingship and the polity as a whole carried on (see Martin and Grube 2008). Nor was the cessation of dynastic kingship necessarily a fait accompli in the immediate aftermath of Ruler 7's capture; a worn text on Altar 1 suggests the possibility of an otherwise unattested king on the throne as late as AD 810, and attempts to rebuild royal precincts may have continued, as we discuss below (Houston, Escobeda, Child, et al. 2003, 228).

At the beginning of the Terminal Classic period, population levels in what had recently been the dynastic capital were still significant, and they probably did not decline precipitously during the first decades of the ninth century. Occupation dating to the ninth century has been found in virtually

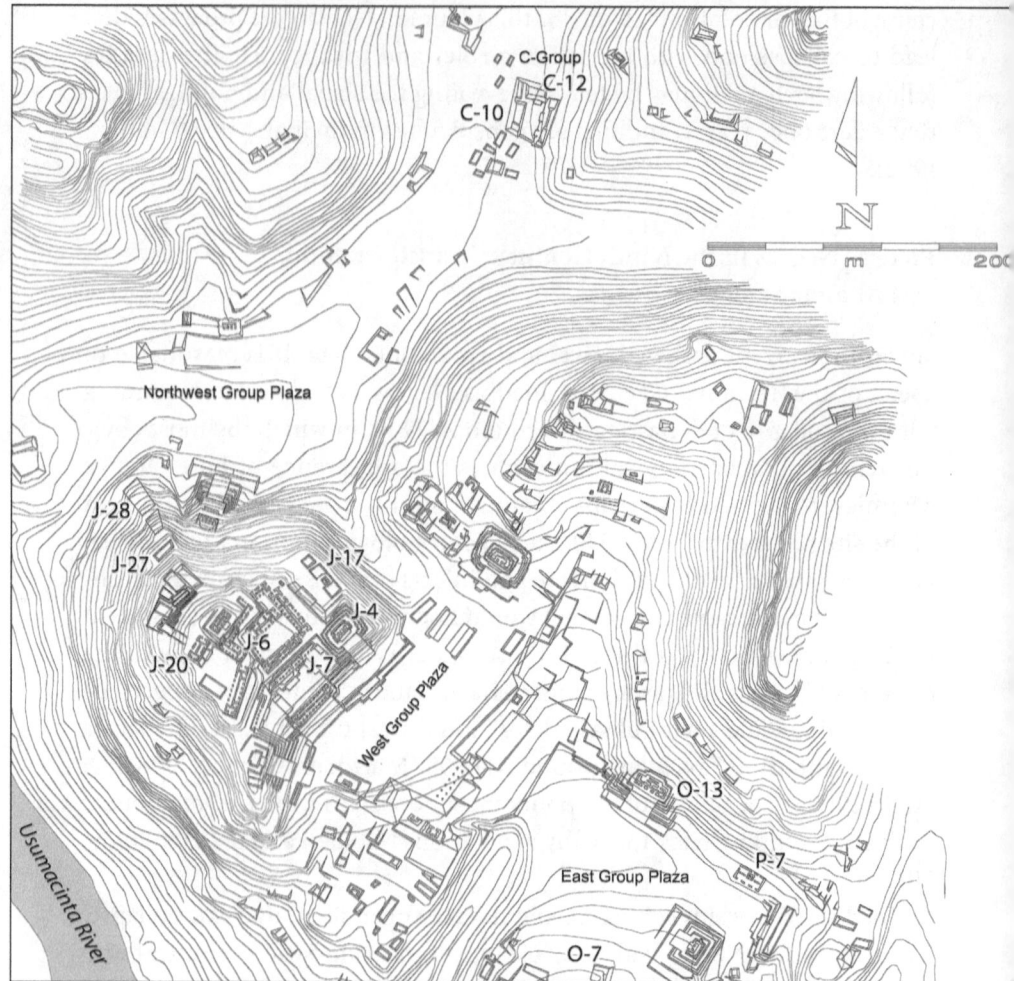

Figure 5.1. Map of the northern portion of the Piedras Negras epicenter with structures and areas mentioned in text. Digital map by Z. Nelson, N. Curritt, and T. Murtha with additions by C. Golden, based on original map by F. Parris and T. Proskouriakoff.

all sectors of Piedras Negras (Muñoz 2006, 168–169; Holley 1983, Table 33; Nelson 2005, Figure 7.6), suggesting an extensive resident population. However, few masonry buildings and no truly monumental construction episodes can be demonstrably assigned to the Terminal Classic period at Piedras Negras. In many cases Terminal Classic period deposits consist of surface scatters and humus layer debris or materials found immediately above the final architectural phases of buildings, apparently representing middens and ritual terminations of buildings immediately before abandonment.

The most vivid evidence for transformation of architecture following dynastic collapse at Piedras Negras comes from the apparent desecration and demolition of royal monuments, particularly in the Acropolis. Throne 1, literally the dynastic seat of Piedras Negras's Ruler 7, was smashed and scattered. Most of its pieces were thrown about inside Structure J-6, from where its royal occupants had once dominated the Acropolis (figures 5.1 and 5.2; see Inomata this volume, for a discussion of similar activities at

Figure 5.2. Throne 1 at Piedras Negras: (*top*) Fragments of Throne 1 as found smashed and scattered on the floor of Structure J-6. (*bottom*) Field reconstruction of the throne back, with faces missing from figures. Used by permission of the archives of the University of Pennsylvania Museum.

Figure 5.3. Fragment of modeled stucco head discovered in the collapse of Structure J-4 in the Acropolis of Piedras Negras. Used by permission of the archives of the University of Pennsylvania Museum.

Aguateca). While excavators in the 1930s were able to recover almost the entire throne, including fragments measuring just a few inches across, the faces of royal figures in the throne's back were never located and were either pulverized or carried off in antiquity (Houston 2014; Satterthwaite 2005 [1935], 68–72; see Harrison-Buck this volume for a discussion of similar examples).

Throne 1 was not the only monument defaced. The faces depicting royal personages on virtually all the stelae and panels at Piedras Negras were removed or mutilated. The massive stucco human figures that once graced the façades of the Acropolis were also torn down. Only fragments of limbs and digits that hint at the full scope of the original decoration remain to be found (figure 5.3; Golden 2002, 190–191; Satterthwaite 2005 [1935], 57; see

Schwake and Iannone this volume for similar destruction of stucco friezes at Minanha).

The collapse of the palace buildings of the Acropolis was accelerated by the loss of the lintels that once supported their doorways and roofs. Because no stone lintels have been found in the Acropolis, we strongly suspect that they were made of wood (Houston et al. 2001, 73). What we cannot determine archaeologically is whether the lintels simply rotted away with time or were instead burned or ripped out to bring down the masonry (e.g., Harrison-Buck this volume).

Beyond such destruction, the occupation of the Acropolis during this period does not reference the dynastic past of the place. Instead, garbage was heaped into the J-17 sweat bath, perhaps as an act of desecration to terminate the once-royal space or perhaps simply as a convenient dump for residents who no longer desired such elaborate architecture. In Court 4, residents built poorly constructed homes from blocks that had been ripped from or had fallen from monumental architecture, while middens grew over a meter deep in the alleyways separating structures. Some of the Terminal Classic residences in the Acropolis, as elsewhere at Piedras Negras, are so ephemeral that it is difficult to determine if they were ever finished or were instead abandoned in the middle of construction (Child and Golden 2008, 80–86; Golden 2002, 303–305; Houston et al. 2001; Houston, Escobeda, Child, et al. 2003).

In some cases, Terminal Classic materials were placed as offerings in collapsing dynastic-era buildings or new ritual uses were made of existing structures. The clearest example of such activity is the caching of two Silho Fine Orange plates, likely imports from Yucatan, together with organic objects on top of a pile of rubble in the corner of a room in Structure P-7, once a royal sweat bath. The building's outer rooms were already falling into ruin when the offering was made, making it perfectly clear that P-7 no longer warranted maintenance or at the very least that labor could not be organized to provide such maintenance (Child 2006, 388–489; Child and Golden 2008, 86–87; Houston et al. 2001, 108; Houston, Escobeda, Child, et al. 2003, 227–228; Muñoz 2006, 169–170, 349).

Complicating the picture of demolition and transformation of Classic period buildings during the ninth century is the simple truth that Piedras Negras, like any other city, was a perpetual work in progress for its inhabitants. Renovations, demolitions, and the abandonment of building programs were likely common. Some construction that was initiated during the height of dynastic power, well before political collapse, was simply never finished, and these hulking rubble piles might easily be mistaken for buildings that were demolished and desecrated in the aftermath of collapse, a problem that has been noted at many other Maya centers (e.g., Coe 1988, 72; Hammond 1999a; Hammond and Tourtellot 2004; Iannone 2005; Inomata et al. 2004; Jones 1996; Zaro and Houk 2012).

Some of these structures remained incomplete and apparently unused for the remainder of the dynastic occupation at Piedras Negras and beyond (e.g., Fitzsimmons 1999; Houston, Escobeda, Child, et al. 2000, 101; Houston, Escobeda, Terry, et al. 2000, 13). Other unfinished structures, however, were reborn and renovated in the ninth century. For example, below Court 4 in the Acropolis is Structure J-27, where building likely began as the foundation for a temple in the mid- to late seventh century AD, with Structure J-28 originally intended as a staircase (Child and Golden 2008, 82–84; Golden 2002, 303–305). The rubble fill was laid in place, but the façade of the building was never completed and the terraced fill was left exposed. Left unfinished for over a century, what began life as the foundation for a royal building became a modest house in the aftermath of dynastic collapse, probably about AD 830. This residence was in turn abandoned no later than the end of the ninth century.

Structure O-7 provides another (and particularly interesting) example of the ritual transformation of space during the Terminal Classic period. The building faces across the East Group Plaza toward the O-13 pyramid and is located between that late dynastic shrine and the South Group, which continued to be occupied into at least the tenth century AD (figure 5.4; Satterthwaite 2005 [1958], 332–342). Whatever the building's function in earlier periods, during the Terminal Classic period twenty-four column altars were brought from elsewhere at the site and placed in and around Structure O-7 (figure 5.5). In earlier periods, column altars at Piedras Negras were typically placed singly in niches in the interior room of temples and shrines. In Structure O-7, however, the postdynastic occupants variously aligned the altars in rows or bunched them into groups and placed at least one in the center of a masonry cist (see Satterthwaite 2005 [1958], Table 10.11).

Satterthwaite also found three obsidian eccentrics scattered around one of the column altars, and a fourth was found in debris on a stair tread. Finished obsidian eccentrics at Piedras Negras are otherwise almost exclusively found in formal caches associated with stela dedications or construction episodes of temple-pyramids, often arranged inside uniform

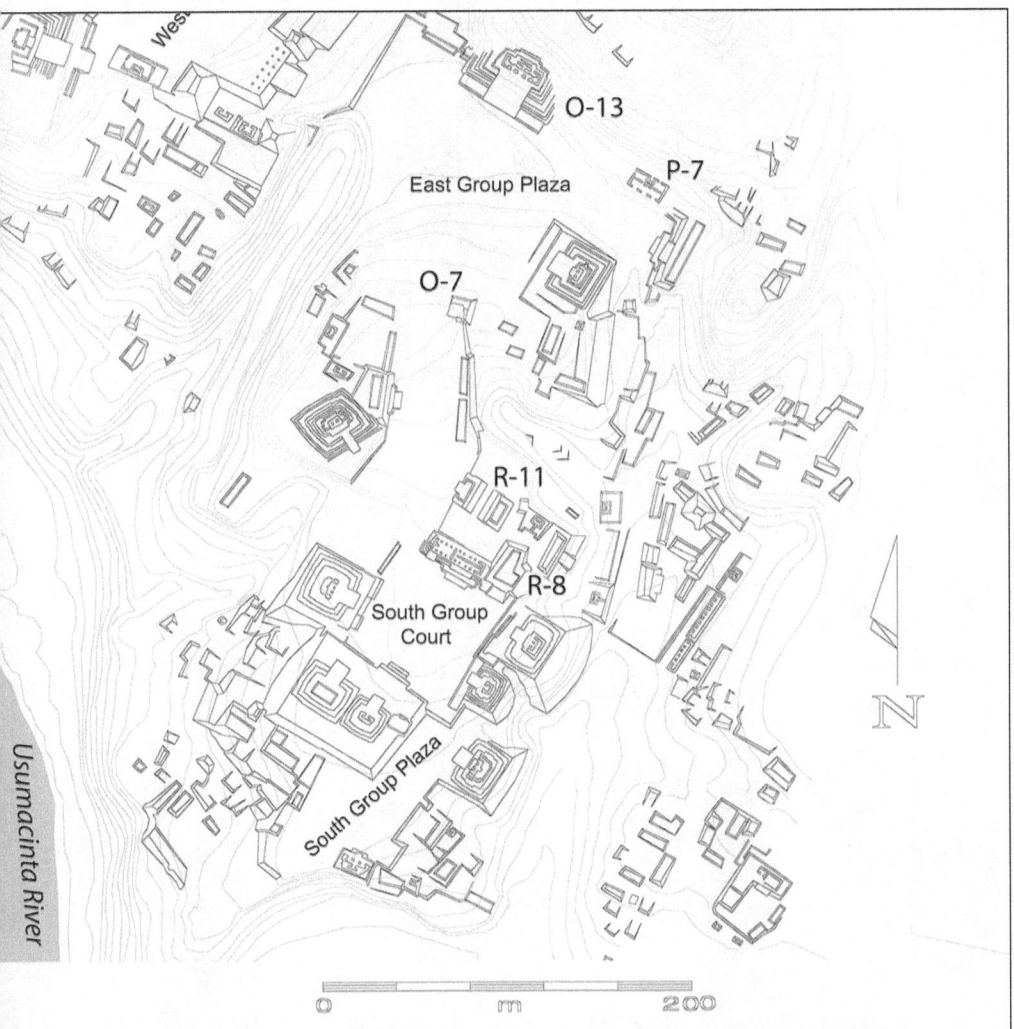

Figure 5.4. Map of the southern portion of the Piedras Negras epicenter with structures and areas mentioned in text. Digital map by Z. Nelson, N. Curritt, and T. Murtha with additions by C. Golden, based on original map by F. Parris and T. Proskouriakoff.

orange-slipped cache vessels (Coe 1959; Hruby 2006). Sattherthwaite concluded quite reasonably that the eccentrics were taken from earlier caches to be used in rituals and redeposited in association with the altars (Satterthwaite 2005 [1958], 338–339). The late residents of Piedras Negras finally heaped a poorly defined low earth and rubble mound over the top of some of the column altars, effectively ending the use life of Structure O-7.

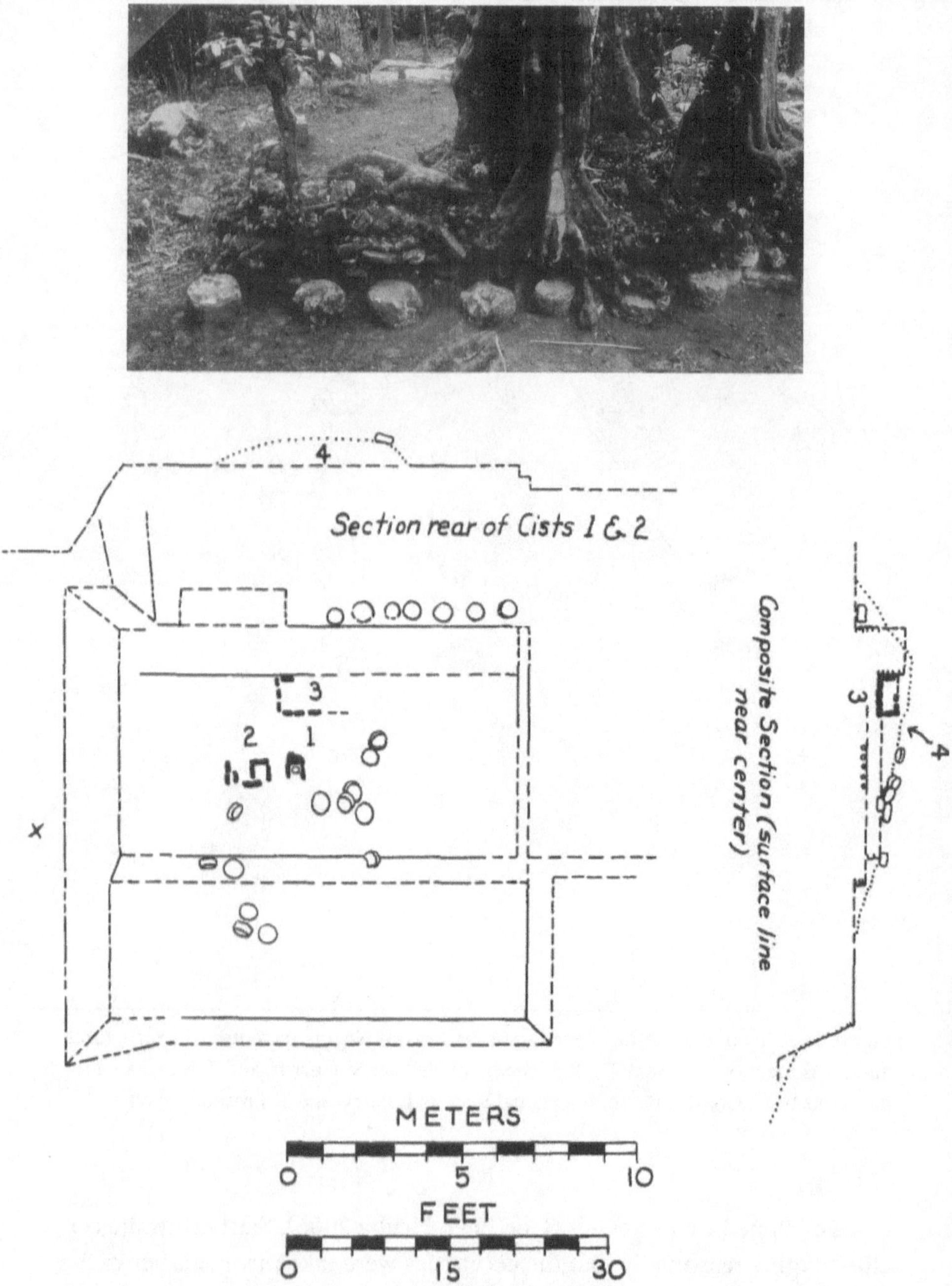

Figure 5.5. Structure O-7 at Piedras Negras: (*top*) Altars in front of Structure O-7 (Satterthwaite 2005 [1952], Figure 10.6). (*bottom*) Plan and section of Structure O-7 (Satterthwaite 2005 [1952], Figure 10.5).

Associated with this final deposition of material over Structure O-7 was an array of bone fragments and ash that Satterthwaite (2005 [1958], 338–339) believed to be a cremation burial, and similar deposits were found in other near-surface deposits across the site in the 1930s and in more recent work during the 1990s (Coe 1959; Golden 2002, 267; Houston and Arredondo Leiva 2000, 49; Houston et al. 1998, 51; Houston, Escobedo, and Scherer et al. 2003, 121; Houston and Urquizú 1998, 244). Satterthwaite interpreted this as the introduction of dramatically new burial practices in the aftermath of violent social upheaval indicative of a cultural disjunction with the community of the Classic period.

However, true cremation—represented by high temperature, prolonged burning of the body to reduce it to ash, and residual fragments of bone—has never been convincingly demonstrated for the Maya. The burned human remains of the Maya area lack the glassy and warped fragments of calcined human bone indicative of cremation in other parts of the world (e.g., Liston 2007; Symes et al. 2008; Ubelaker and Rife 2007). Thermal alteration of bone, however, by briefly burning fleshed bodies, body parts, or dry bone is a well-attested practice (e.g., Medina Martín and Mirna Sánchez Vargas 2007; Ruz Lhuillier 1991) and is occasionally mistaken for cremation.

Instead of new burial patterns introduced by an intrusive postdynastic occupation, the near-surface finds of burned human remains are more likely to be part of a pattern with a much deeper history at Piedras Negras and across the Maya area. Human bones were often used in rituals that we would not consider formal burials and that often incorporate human remains that had been curated for long periods or recovered during reentry into burials (Coe 1959; Houston, Escobedo and Scherer et al. 2003). In fact, two of the Late Classic period royal tombs at Piedras Negras, Burials 10 and 13, demonstrate both the removal of bone and the burning of human bone (Coe 1959; Escobedo 2004; Houston, Escobedo and Scherer et al. 2003), and such complicated post-funerary rituals are well attested in the epigraphic record (Fitzsimmons 1998; Stuart 1998b).

Despite the evidence of dramatic changes in the function and meaning of space and of gradual population decline, architectural signs of continued elite—and perhaps royal—life are found in several areas. Northeast of the Acropolis, in Structures C-10 and C-12, elite residences show continuity with earlier occupation in the same group, indicating that such elite life endured through much of the long abandonment of the site (Houston, Escobeda, Child, et al. 2003, 229; Jackson 2005, 550–574). More central to our arguments, there was an attempt to build a palace-type structure in the

South Group at Structure R-8 (Child and Golden 2008, 84–86; Houston, Escobeda, Child, et al. 2003, 229; Muñoz 2006, 167). Unlike the Terminal Classic period residential buildings elsewhere at Piedras Negras, Structure R-8-1st was kept clean of the sorts of debris found on the Acropolis. Its form, it lack of quotidian artifacts, and its location—built above an Early Classic pyramid housing a royal tomb and adjacent to the earliest ball court and sweat bath at Piedras Negras—suggest a failed attempt to rejuvenate royal activities at a locus that was intimately linked to the origins of dynastic authority. Such attempts to connect with ancestral locations are common to kingship globally, not just in times of crisis but as part of the basic "toolkit" used for legitimation (see Iannone this volume; Taylor, personal communication, 2013).

The South Group is also where the great majority of Terminal Classic Fine Orange and Fine Gray materials were found during the 1930s (Butler 2005 [1935]; Cresson 2005a [1939], 2005b [1939]; Holley 1983). But such materials have also been found in small numbers across Piedras Negras, including the Acropolis and further afield at the northern limits of suburban settlement of Piedras Negras at the site (or perhaps settlement cluster) known as El Porvenir. Altar group fine wares were found in small quantities at El Porvenir, as was Matillas Fine Orange imported from Yucatan (Brainerd 1958; Kingsley et al., 2012; Monterroso et al. 2009; Smith 1971). Small quantities of Plumbate ceramics at El Porvenir place some of the occupation there securely in the tenth century AD, if not later (Neff and Bishop 1988; Neff and Bove 1999; Neff et al. 1992; Shepard 1948). Whether the limited quantities, in comparison to nearby sites such as Yaxchilan (López Varela 1989, 2005), of diagnostic Terminal Classic trade wares reflects a particularly small population or a significant population with limited access to these trade wares is difficult to say, although, as we will discuss below, we feel that the latter option may be the case.

Piedras Negras in Historical and Regional Context

To understand the death of the political and economic community at Piedras Negras, we must turn back to the establishment of the royal dynasty. Epigraphic and archaeological data suggest the appearance of dynastic rule at Piedras Negras and neighboring Yaxchilan during the Early Classic period—probably no later than the mid-fourth century (Golden and Scherer 2013b; Golden et al. 2008; Martin and Grube 2008). These dynasties were likely established by the arrival of royal courts from areas outside the middle Usumacinta, and much of the regional population subsequently moved to these centers (Houston 2008, 5). Populations may have flowed into the new capitals to participate in the vibrant political, economic, and social communities that grew up around these dynasties (Houston, Escobedo, Child, et al. 2003), but they may also have congregated as a way of escaping the vicissitudes of a Preclassic countryside wracked by warfare (Golden et al. 2008, 265; Golden and Scherer 2006).

The dynasty at Piedras Negras established itself in the Preclassic period heart of the site in what would become the South Group (figure 5.4). The community that formed around the dynasty at Piedras Negras grew over the course of the Early Classic period, expanding around this monumental core. Its participants developed a unique material identity by which they distinguished themselves from members of the neighboring Yaxchilan-centered community. Such disparate practices included the production and consumption of distinct ceramic styles and technologies, settlement strategies, architectural styles, and burial practices (Golden et al. 2008). Construction of monumental architecture gradually moved away from the South Group, and by the fifth century AD royal architecture was increasingly focused on the area that became the Acropolis.

In the midst of this Early Classic expansion there was a political and architectural break that is important to the story of social life in the aftermath of dynastic collapse during the Terminal Classic period. Epigraphic data strongly suggest that Piedras Negras suffered a defeat in the mid-sixth century at the hands of the rulers of the Pomona kingdom, located some forty-eight kilometers to the northwest (Golden 2002, 358; Houston and Inomata 2009, 181–182; Houston, Escobeda, Child, et al. 2000, 101; Schele and Grube 1994). There is no archaeological or epigraphic evidence to suggest that the epicenter of Piedras Negras itself was invaded, but in the aftermath of defeat, the architecture of the Acropolis was ritually terminated (see Navarro-Farr this volume for a discussion of similar activities at the site of El Perú-Waká).

All archaeological data point to the involvement of local participants in these termination activities, perhaps initiating the demolition or instead cleaning up what remained after invasion (Golden 2002, 358–360). Excavations strongly suggest that these activities were part of a reverential performance. At least one of these structures, J-20-sub-1, was burned. As the ruins still smoldered, large fragments of elaborate ceramics—some probably made specifically for the feasting and deposition associated with this event—were deposited on the building's surface, accompanied by figurines, earspools, and jade. Some of these objects were placed carefully and some were smashed, sending sherds flying over several meters.

There is no evidence among these buried materials of "foreign" ceramics or other materials that might have been left by invading forces, as is the case at Yaxuna, Mexico, for instance (Ardren 1999). What is evident is a local ceramic inventory consistent in broad terms with a local late Naba Phase ceramic assemblage (ca. AD 550). However, this deposit contains ceramic types that are rare or unique in the overall site assemblage at Piedras Negras yet foreshadow technological and stylistic innovations of the subsequent Balche and Yaxche ceramic phases. René Muñoz and Charles Golden (2001) have argued elsewhere that such objects were unique pieces created by local artists specifically for such ritual events.

As the building smoldered, a cap of dark clay was placed over the burning remains, effectively extinguishing the fire and leaving a thin layer of ash and hardened clay at the interface. One can imagine that any one person with a torch could have accomplished the destruction of the structure, whose frame was constructed of poles and thatch. However, burying the burning hilltop building—and in fact much of the courtyard—with a layer of heavy clay would have involved a considerable group effort.

Other buildings in the Acropolis were similarly treated, but later construction has obscured many of the specific details evident in J-20-sub-1 (but see Houston and Arredondo Leiva 1999a, 1999b). When these performances were finished, though, every one of the structures of the Early Classic Acropolis had been destroyed and buried (Golden 2002). For nearly fifty years the Acropolis was abandoned to the elements, while royal activity was recentered on the South Group, the foundational heart of Piedras Negras that linked the pre-dynastic and dynastic histories of the site.

Golden (2002) has argued elsewhere that this demolition of the Acropolis and the move by the dynasty back to the South Group was done to rejuvenate royal authority and the attendant political community following the disgrace of defeat by refocusing royal ritual practice on the oldest section of the city. The South Group was the point of origin for political power at Piedras Negras; it was where dynastic rulership had been established in ritual spaces in a history that extended well back into the first millennium BC. Maya rulers of the Classic period, like their highland and lowland Postclassic counterparts (e.g., Christenson 2007; Roys 1967), certainly invoked the trope of "stranger kings" (see Iannone this volume) in substantiating their right to govern. Indeed, the monuments of Piedras Negras are famous for their depictions of kings and princes garbed in the regalia of Central Mexican authority (Stone 1989).

Claims of foreign origin, however, are a double-edged sword. They offer just the sort of vital difference for rulers that distinguishes them from other political leaders and kin structures within a society (see Iannone this volume; Taylor this volume) while at the same time they threaten to disconnect rulers from kin-based, territorially oriented, or other locally focused sources of authority that form the foundation of their capacity to rule (see also Schwake and Iannone this volume). Modern and historical Maya social-spatial groupings reveal the complex interweaving of place and lineage in defining political authority throughout the Maya region (e.g., Akkeren 2000, 24; Braswell 2001, 319–325; Braswell 2004, 133–136; Cancian 1996; Canuto and Fash 2004; Carmack 1981, 83; Landa 1978, 36, 38–39, 52; Hanks 2010, 283–314; Hill 1996, 64; Hill and Monaghan 1987, 74; Miles 1957; Mulhare 1996; Restall 1997; Restall 1998, 46–50; Vogt 1965b, 1969; cf. Roys 1957, 7). The social practices linking individuals, household, and larger corporate groups into political structures were cross-cut by lineage and descent groups that were themselves couched in and sometimes trumped by territorial and other concerns that created complex networks of social obligations. Ultimately it was the ties to local authority, local history, kinship, and local power that the monarchs of the Piedras Negras dynasty needed to cultivate to substantiate rulership (see also Schwake and Iannone this volume).

These maneuvers in the sixth and early seventh centuries apparently served the dynasty well, and the Piedras Negras kingdom thrived and expanded. By the seventh century, the countryside that had been largely abandoned at the close of the Preclassic period was once again filling in with settlements expanding outward from Piedras Negras and nearby kingdoms such as Yaxchilan and Palenque (Golden and Scherer 2006; Golden et al. 2008; Liendo Stuardo 2007).

Maintaining Community after the Collapse

It is only in light of this regional and local history that the destruction of royal architecture and the attempt to rebuild in the South Group at the close of dynastic history can be fully understood. The last securely dated ruler at Piedras Negras, Ruler 7, was captured in or around AD 808 by forces from Yaxchilan. Although a last attempt to dedicate a royal monument at Piedras

Negras may have been made in AD 810, the scribes of Piedras Negras fell silent thereafter (Houston et al. 2003, 228; Martin and Grube 2008, 153; Stuart 1998a).

As in the sixth century, in the ninth century, following defeat by forces from Pomona, the remnant nobility and royalty at Piedras Negras attempted to rejuvenate and salvage the dynasty with a move away from a disgraced history associated with the Acropolis and toward the ancient, foundational, and constructive history associated with the South Group. From this perspective, what might otherwise appear to be the desecration of the Acropolis was part of an active choice to erase dangerous associations with the defeated ruler and his court. Piedras Negras had already passed many decades of problematic succession; new patterns of accession had been created as kingship passed laterally among brothers rather than vertically from parent to child since the death of Ruler 4 in AD 757 (Houston, Escobeda, Child, et al. 2000, 107; Martin and Grube 2008, 151–152; Stuart 2004). The defeat in battle of Ruler 7 may very well have brought about yet another crisis in rulership (see Iannone this volume; Taylor this volume) if the royal court did not provide a single, uncontested successor and multiple candidates for kingship vied for the throne.

However, crises are also potential opportunities. By clearing the way for a rededication or other transformation of the royal palace, those who sought to stabilize the dynasty may have hoped to stave off collapse and return to the Acropolis and other royal precincts at some point in the future, just as the royal court had done at the beginning of the seventh century after defeat in the sixth century. The construction of the small palace R-8-1st over an Early Classic pyramid with a royal tomb in a Preclassic settlement, adjacent to the oldest sweat bath and ball court at the site (Child 2006, 213; Satterthwaite 2005 [1933], 30–47), similarly mirrors the actions of the late sixth-century rulers of Piedras Negras and their move away from the Acropolis.

Such actions can be seen as precisely the sort of "keep calm and carry on" processes of containment Gyles Iannone discussed in this volume. What had worked in the past, though, was no longer an effective political strategy. The future the remnants of the royal court of the Terminal Classic period sought to build never materialized.

Through all of this—the defeat of Ruler 7, the demolition of the Acropolis, and the reorganization of space throughout Piedras Negras—the community struggled on and apparently maintained its sense of an identity distinct from that of neighboring centers such as Yaxchilan (see Garcia

Moll 2003, 336–337), even as those dynasties were also in collapse and the boundaries between kingdoms were fraying. On the southern border of what had been Piedras Negras territory, Yaxchilan's garrison settlements such as Tecolote and La Pasadita were abandoned (Scherer and Golden 2009). Recent excavations by Golden and Andrew Scherer at the hinterland palace of Budsilha also suggest that this site, which was initially settled no earlier than AD 600 as a Piedras Negras outpost and formed part of the western borderland of the kingdom, was abandoned at the beginning of the Terminal Classic period (Scherer and Golden 2012). Hinterland communities with deeper histories in what had been the Piedras Negras kingdom such as El Cayo and El Porvenir were able to weather the storm a bit longer, and some people hung on into the tenth century.

Burial and architectural patterns maintained their distinctiveness on either side of the former border between these two rival polities. Ceramic styles and distribution patterns changed, but these changes maintained a sense of distinct community identities. In particular, the distribution of Altar Fine Orange and Tres Naciones Fine Gray ceramics are revealing about this divide. These materials were produced around Yaxchilan (Ron Bishop, personal communication, 2007, 2010) and probably made their first appearances in the closing years of dynastic history in both kingdoms. Altar and Tres Naciones fine wares are found in great abundance at Yaxchilan and in surrounding hinterland sites (Golden and Scherer 2006, 8; López-Varela 1989, 54–58; López-Varela 2005, 50) and made their way south into the Pasión River area, where they may also have been produced.

However, when compared with more distant sites in the Pasión, the quantity of such materials at El Cayo—a former Piedras Negras satellite—is much less than one would expect on the basis of its proximity to Yaxchilan (see ceramic analysis by Angela González Moreno in Mathews and Aliphat Fernandez 1997, 178–256). At Piedras Negras itself, the quantities of these wares found in twelve seasons of excavations is remarkably small, constituting far fewer than 100 sherds (Holley 1983; Muñoz 2006), and only a few additional examples were found at the outlying El Porvenir settlement cluster (Kingsley et al. 2012). By comparison, these materials are apparently more abundant at more distant Pomona and La Joyanca than at Piedras Negras and its outliers (Forné 2006, 206–208, 230; Garciá Moll 2005; López Varela 2005, 48–50).

Though this disjunctive distribution of Altar and Tres Naciones group materials might be the product of sampling error, it seems unlikely, given that Piedras Negras has been more extensively and intensively studied than either La Joyanca or Pomona. Further, this would not seem to be an issue of population size, as a reasonably healthy occupation persisted across Piedras Negras through most if not all of the ninth century AD. The presence of imported Matillas Fine Orange ceramics from Yucatan and Plumbate materials from the Pacific Coast of Guatemala at El Porvenir also suggests the maintenance of trade networks, despite the fall of the Piedras Negras dynasty (Kingsley et al. 2012).

The limited distribution of Altar and Tres Naciones group fine wares at Piedras Negras is best accounted for by social and economic reasons that discouraged the import of these wares to Piedras Negras and/or their consumption by members of that community. We suggest, again, that the selective use of particular ceramics—as in earlier centuries—was part of a broader practice by which the community at Piedras Negras fostered a distinct identity, even in the aftermath of dynastic collapse. Consumers chose not to use, display, and exchange these fine wares in Piedras Negras and in its slowly dwindling hinterland populations.

Why do all of these patterns of material distribution among postdynastic populations matter in a discussion of dynastic collapse? Because they hint that some of the fundamental ties that linked members of the Piedras Negras community together and connected them to wider social and economic networks were not immediately ruptured by the failure of dynastic power. Further, there is no clear sign from these patterns about what proximate cause might have existed for a people to abandon their commitment to the institution of dynastic rulership and their loyalty to any particular king. We have observed no material signs whatsoever of the sort of declining prosperity that might trigger a crisis of legitimacy for the rulers of Piedras Negras.

Other material signatures, however, suggest that the threads that constituted the social fabric of the community were indeed slowly unraveling, perhaps leading up to dynastic collapse. Evidence for the social atomization of community practices comes in part from the diet of the residents Piedras Negras (Scherer et al. 2007). At the height of dynastic power at Piedras Negras, from about AD 625 to 750, dietary stable isotope signatures indicate uniform patterns of maize and meat consumption among the royal, elite, and non-elite members of the polity capital. Though the quality of cuts and types of dishes may have differed, all members of society enjoyed access to similar foodstuffs. This suggests that some combination of redistributive mechanisms, including marketing, gifting, and feasting, were at work. By the second half of the eighth century and into the early ninth century, isotopic signatures diversified as dynastic power waned, suggesting a breakdown in the previously shared dietary patterns. Some residents consumed less maize and, most striking, other inhabitants shifted their consumption of protein resources to include greater amounts of fish rather than terrestrial meat resources.

Such changes may be linked to stresses in systems of resource production (agriculture and hunting) and redistribution; households seem to have had differential access to different foodstuffs. These patterns, however, also suggest that foodstuffs were not being shared in significant quantities between households—sharing that might have taken place in previous generations through marketing, gifting, and feasting.

There may have been attempts to counter this social fracturing. One of the hallmarks of ceramic change at Piedras Negras that began as early as the late eighth century AD is the abundance of feasting platters, dishes that are far larger than more standard-sized "plates" found in earlier periods, typically at Piedras Negras in association with the remains of feasting there (Muñoz 2006, 187–190).

However, such large platters are absent in excavations from the hinterlands, even in close proximity to the capital at El Porvenir (Kingsley et al. 2010). This material divide between center and hinterland suggests not simply distinct habitual choices and pottery preferences but fundamentally different practices of exchange and feasting that were critical components linking super-household units in political and social relationships that build trust (LeCount 1999, 2001). Such changes would be linked to and further encourage the decline in social interaction and trust between households and the super-household groups in which household members had previously participated. However, this process had begun in the century preceding the dynastic collapse and was not itself a result of the failure of the royal political system.

These data suggest a mixed story of gradual dissolution of community beginning probably in the eighth century (if not before) and continuing into the ninth century at least (Golden and Scherer 2013a, 2013b). Within these longer-term patterns, the failure of the royal dynasty to perpetuate itself, the demolition of the Acropolis, and the attempts to move courtly life back to its place of origin in the South Group are symptomatic of wider social patterns. With apologies to Ruler 7, who must certainly have felt that his end at the hands of his enemies at Yaxchilan was a dramatic blow, the dynasty and then the community at Piedras Negras went out with a whimper.

Conclusions

In summary, the period from the foundation of the Piedras Negras dynasty in the Early Classic period through its failure as a dynastic system by about 810 AD was an extended time of ongoing crisis, resolution, and reformation. Though previous rulers had suffered defeats, in retrospect, the capture of Ruler 7 in AD 808 was an insuperable blow. There is no evidence of environmental or economic crises that might prove to be immediate triggers for such failure. Instead, the failure must be seen as the final phase in long-term political processes of political fracture that were at work in the apparently healthy kingdom of the Late Classic period (Golden and Scherer 2013a, 2013b). From approximately AD 810 to 930, the population of Piedras Negras gradually dwindled, a decline that over the course of a few generations gave way to the nearly complete abandonment of the site. These ninth-century residents are best understood as a community that persisted from the dynastic period, maintaining and transforming an identity that grew up around the royal court and that the dynasty had helped engender.

We do not see in the remains of the postdynastic occupation, even in the evidence of burning and destruction of monuments first documented by Mason and Satterthwaite (Holley 1983, 201; Mason 1935, 562; Satterthwaite 1935, 1937, 1958), a complete break with the past indicating the arrival of a new population (cf. Manahan 2004; Manahan and Canuto 2009). Instead, conceptions of architectural space and the use life of that space and the transformations of ritual practice referred to the dynastic past even if the mode of making such references was inversion and erasure. Nor, in fact, can we securely attribute the demolition of monuments and buildings to the moment of dynastic collapse. Stratigraphy, ceramics, and other dating techniques allow us to say only that such acts against royal architecture and images took place in the aftermath of dynastic collapse. If thrones and stucco friezes were smashed years or decades after the dissolution of the royal court, they can hardly be attributed to violence directed at the court in a moment of crisis and aimed at a scapegoat king.

Though there is not sufficient space here to fully explore the topic, we must ask why the Piedras Negras dynasty was not able to recover from defeat in AD 808, as it had after a similar defeat in the sixth century. Moreover, why should local communities that had endured and thrived for centuries despite the challenges posed by environmental dynamics, warfare, and other threats wither away after a few generations without its royal court? There is currently no evidence to suggest environmental degradation or drought along the Usumacinta as a proximate cause for dynastic collapse (Golden and Scherer 2013a, 2013b; Scherer and Golden 2013). Indeed, although current data should never be unquestioningly applied to the past, it is important to note that current rainfall in the Usumacinta Basin during the dry season exceeds that of the rainy season in many parts of the Maya area and that the Middle Usumacinta region has one of the highest rainfall levels in the region, more than enough to support maize crops, even during many recent drought years that have plagued southeastern Mexico and Guatemala (Magaña et al. 1999, 1583; Magaña et al. 2003, 315; Seager et al. 2009; Stahle et al. 2009).

Further, while variation in the diet increased between individuals, the general health of the population remained relatively stable throughout all periods of occupation at the site (Scherer et al. 2007). The collapse of economic connections with the highlands (Demarest 2004b, 118; Demarest et al. this volume) due to warfare and political upheaval in the Pasión region does not offer a satisfactory explanation. The political community at Seibal was evidently able to overcome such difficulties and maintain a royal court through this same period. Moreover, the Pasión is not the only trade route from the highlands, and Piedras Negras was never a large-scale consumer of such highland prestige goods as jade, even at the height of the dynasty's powers (Golden et al. 2012; Houston, Escobeda, Scherer, et al. 2003, 122; Hruby 2006). Neither does endemic warfare as a cause of collapse account for collapse. The dynasty and the community had survived several centuries of relatively frequent war with neighbors near and distant.

We would suggest here, as we have elsewhere (e.g., Golden and Scherer 2012, 2013a, 2013b; Houston, Escobedo and Child et al. 2003; Scherer and Golden 2013), that the dynasty did not survive because its members had ceased to function as the heart of a political community. Their legitimacy had been lodged in their ritual, political, and ideological functions (see Iannone this volume; Taylor this volume). Founded as the center of a "moral" or "imagined" community that required the dynasty as an identifiable focus, over the course of almost five centuries, the rulers of Piedras Negras had increasingly divested their authority onto subordinate nobles and subject courts scattered across the countryside. In decentering its power, the dynasty also decentered its role as a focal point for the Piedras Negras community. The community no longer perceived sovereigns as a necessity, and the defeat of AD 808 was simply the final death blow of a kingdom that had been in long decline.

Thus, attempts by resident elites to revive dynastic pretensions through such material means as recentering the political life of Piedras Negras on the South Group and away from the Acropolis and restructuring ritual practice in buildings such as Structure O-7 could not draw on the real-world resources provided by a functioning moral community to rekindle dynastic rule. The result reveals the disjunction of different kinds of community markers. Local identity related to the political and economic community—perhaps glossed as ethnicity—persisted in some ways, including choices made about the kinds of ceramics and other quotidian materials consumed, and was maintained as one marker of communal life throughout the ninth century. However, why the political and economic community could not survive the loss of its dynastic center remains a critically important mystery that must be understood in light of the broader political changes sweeping across the Maya Lowlands.

In closing, we return to the questions posed by the editors in the first two chapters of this volume. Was the collapse of dynastic rule a brief event or a protracted process? At Piedras Negras, it was a centuries-long process. What seems like a moment of collapse from the perspective of the present may not have been such a clear-cut division for those who lived through the period.

Was there a crisis that might have caused the populace to see the king as a scapegoat? Ruler 7's loss in battle against forces from Yaxchilan may have put a final bitter note on things, and indeed it must have posed a crisis of confidence and succession. Yet in previous centuries similar crises had been overcome.

We have yet to identify any particular crisis in resources, prosperity, or the environment that might adequately explain why such a loss in AD 808 was different. Other political figures struggled to carry on in the aftermath of that defeat. These postdynastic attempts to revive the fortunes of Piedras Negras floundered, however, without the material support of a wider community that had entirely abandoned the political system.

Are the material correlates associated with the end of the dynasty and the postdynastic occupation consistent with the model of a scapegoat king? Quite possibly. People clearly targeted façades depicting rulers and nobles for destruction, demolished once-sacred precincts, and smashed royal monuments, including the very seat of power in the form of Ruler 7's throne. Yet we are faced with the simple and familiar archaeological problem of precision. We can securely say that such destruction occurred after the fall of Ruler 7, but we lack the stratigraphic context or other data to say whether such events occurred within days, years, or decades of that fall.

Finally, does the scapegoat king model have explanatory value for our case study? The archaeological and epigraphic data cannot resolve this issue at Piedras Negras. The trope of the scapegoat certainly exists in later Maya contexts. The *Books of Chilam Balam* are rife with accounts of political conflict and failures at Chichen Itza, Mayapan, and elsewhere, heaping the blame for widespread political chaos squarely on the shoulders of a few individuals (Roys 1967). Yet even in the Chilam Balam books, such blame serves as a retrospective assessment and a warning for future leaders rather than a contemporary explanation. For Piedras Negras, then, we can only be agnostic and say "perhaps."

Acknowledgments

The permit for work at Piedras Negras from 1997 to 2000 and in 2004 took place under the direction of Stephen Houston and Héctor Escobedo with permission from the Instituto de Antropología e Historia de Guatemala, and the division of Monumentos Prehispánicos. Investigations at Piedras Negras could not have been carried out without support provided by the generous donations of Ken Woolley and Spence Kirk of Salt Lake City and funds from a variety of foundations, including the National Geographic Society; the Ahau Foundation; the Heinz Foundation; Brigham Young University; the Foundation for the Advancement of Mesoamerican Studies, Inc.; the National Science Foundation (Dissertation Improvement Grant BCS-0000179); the Fulbright Fellowship; and the Fulbright-Hayes Fellowship. Regional data is drawn from the work of the Sierra del Lacandón Regional Archaeology Project, directed by Charles Golden, Andrew Scherer, Rosaura Vasquez, Ana Lucia Arroyave, and Luz Midilia Marroquin. That research has been generously funded by grants from the Foundation for the Advancement of Mesoamerican Studies, Inc. (grants 2020, 05027, and 07043); the National Geographic Society (grants 7575-04 and 7636-04); the National Science Foundation (SBE-BCS Archaeology Grants 0406472 and 075463); a Waitt Foundation–National Geographic Society grant (W90-10, awarded to Kingsley); Dumbarton Oaks Research Library; the H. John Heinz III Charitable Trust Grants for Latin American Archeology; the Kaplan Fund through the World Monuments Fund; Baylor University; the Norman Fund and the Jane's Fund at Brandeis University; and Brown University through Stephen Houston's professorial funds.

6

Destruction Events and Political Truncation at the Little Kingdom of Minanha, Belize

SONJA A. SCHWAKE AND GYLES IANNONE

The current volume explores the potential ritual and behavioral responses when it was perceived that Classic Maya kings were failing to uphold their role as guarantors of the prosperity for their kingdoms. The ensuing crisis of legitimacy was a dynamic moment in the history of many polities, and their constituent members engaged in a diverse array of reactions to the leadership crisis, often resulting in the scapegoating of both kings and the particular institution of governance associated with Classic period kingship. As Iannone (this volume) points out, although Maya kings were treated as if they were gods, it is unlikely that they were actually conceived as such, and this created an opportunity for polity members to exercise some agency when faced with declining prosperity and ineffective governance. By carefully examining contexts that are contemporaneous with times of leadership stress and legitimation crises for a particular kingdom, we can access the material correlates of the various actions community members undertook in light of these perceived failures. This chapter does this by assessing the significance of several interesting "destruction" events that occurred in key settings of the ancient Minanha royal court complex during the Late to Terminal Classic transition (AD 750–850). Our goal is to use careful description and interpretation of archaeological contexts and associations to elucidate the nuanced actions that both local community members and regional powers initiated in response to the shifting political landscape of the late eighth to early ninth centuries and to examine how these actions impacted the little kings who ruled from Minanha.

The Minanha Case Study

The remains of the ancient Maya kingdom of Minanha are located in the karst uplands of the Vaca Plateau in west-central Belize (figure 1.1). This area of the central Maya lowlands is characterized by steep-sided limestone slopes, deep-cut valleys, a lack of readily available surface water, and mixed tropical vegetation (Iannone 2005, 28; Iannone et al. 2014; Reeder et al. 1996; Schwake 2008, 87). The region is notable for its abundance of sinkholes and caves (Reeder et al. 1996, 121), features the ancient Maya considered to be particularly sacred parts of their landscape (e.g., Moyes et al. 2009).

Minanha is one of several centers dispersed across the Vaca Plateau (figure 6.1). In geopolitical terms, it was once home to a "little" kingdom that was bounded by the myriad similarly sized kingdoms that once flourished in the Belize River Valley to the north; the "great" kingdom of Naranjo, situated roughly twenty-five kilometers to the northwest; the densely settled waterways and interfluvial valleys of the southeastern Petén to the west and southwest; and the "great" kingdom of Caracol, situated approximately twenty-five kilometers to the south (Iannone 2005, 29; Iannone et al. 2014; Laporte and Mejía 2000). Its location vis-à-vis Naranjo and Caracol situates Minanha in an intermediate position in relation to some of the major political players in this part of the central Maya lowlands during the Late Classic period (AD 675–810).

Developmental History

The initial settlement of the Minanha region began as early as the Middle Preclassic period (600–400 BC), as evidenced by pottery sherds dating to that time period recovered from later mixed-fill deposits (Iannone 2005, 29, 2009, 4). The first evidence of concentrated settlement in the site epicenter (figure 6.2) dates to the Late to Terminal Preclassic transition (ca. 100 BC to AD 250). Adjacent valleys immediately surrounding the epicenter were also first settled at this time (Iannone 2009, 4; Longstaffe and Iannone 2011, 47; Macrae and Iannone 2011, 190; McCane et al. 2009). Research indicates that these early settlements were founded in close proximity to good agricultural lands and perennial springs. The springs were a particularly important attractor in a landscape devoid of readily available surface water (Iannone 2005, 29; Macrae and Iannone 2011, 190). Well-made but isolated agricultural terrace subsystems were first constructed by groups of smallholders during the Terminal Preclassic period (Macrae and Iannone

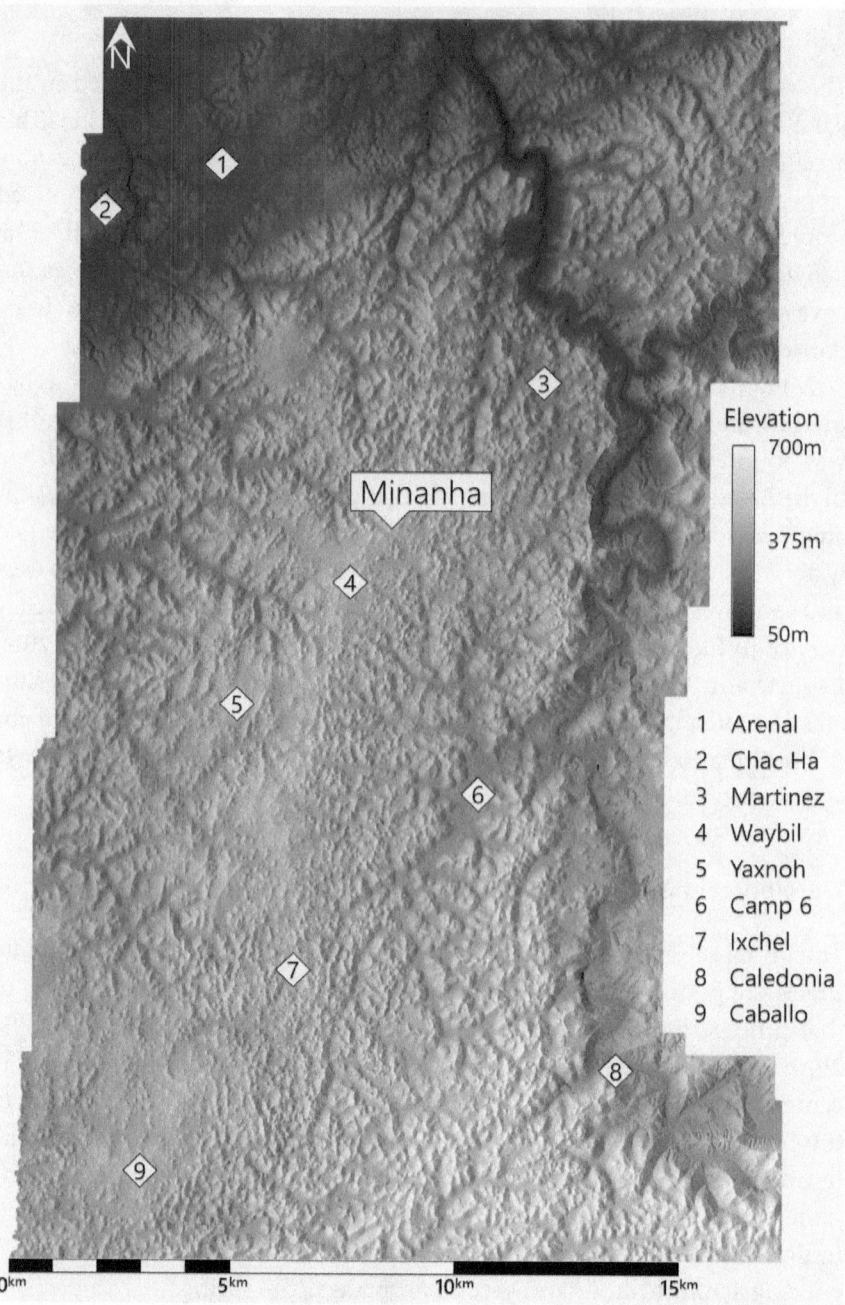

Figure 6.1. Map of the Vaca Plateau and adjacent areas showing the location of Minanha and other key centers in the region.

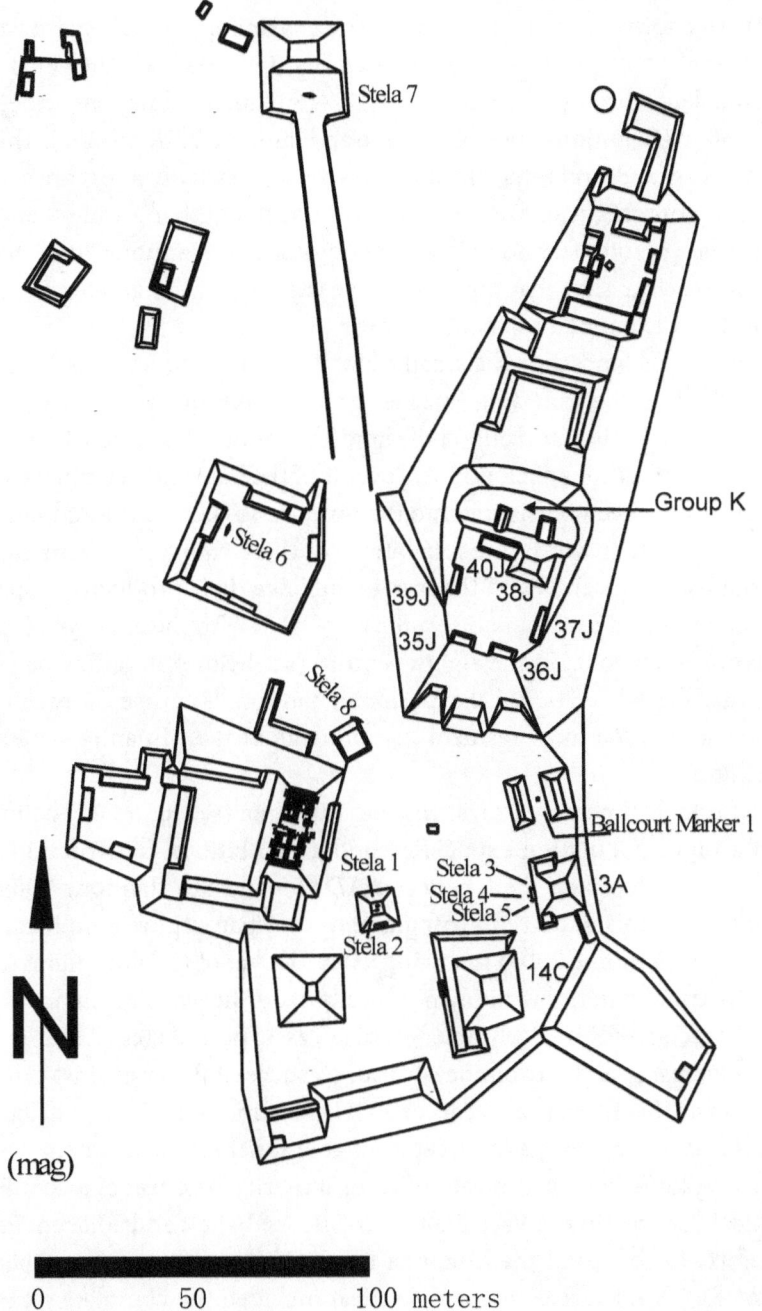

Figure 6.2. Rectified isometric plan of the Minanha epicentral court complex showing the location of key loci discussed in the text.

2011). This form of highly localized terrace farming gradually gave way to the formation of larger terrace systems that incorporated the previously isolated fields through the Early (AD 250–550) and Middle Classic periods (AD 550–675; Iannone 2009, 4; Macrae and Iannone 2011, 191–192). This increase in agricultural intensification was at least partially a response to the growing population size and density in both the outlying valleys and the Minanha epicenter (Iannone 2009, 4; Longstaffe and Iannone 2011, 48–49). It is also a clear sign that the productive capacity of the greater Minanha community expanded substantially over time.

Within this landscape the small number of larger courtyards originally established by the founding lineages grew in size and complexity to the point that they still stand out on the landscape today. These courtyards survived the tumultuous sociopolitical events of the Late and Terminal Classic periods, some even persisting into the Postclassic (Longstaffe and Iannone 2011, 53). In other words, the inhabitants of these courtyards were the first to establish themselves and the first to enhance their productive capacity, they experienced the dramatic events associated with the emergence of the Minanha royal court in the eighth century (see below), and they persisted after that short-lived political experiment had run its course. They can thus be considered *the* most resilient components of the Minanha settlement continuum.

The establishment of a royal court at Minanha (see figure 6.1) coincides with a rapid population expansion, and an ambitious construction program was undertaken there between AD 675 and 810 (Iannone 2009, 4). Significantly, this occurred during a period of pan-regional political balkanization (Iannone 2005) following Tikal's defeat of Calakmul in AD 695 and the concomitant breakdown of the broader hegemonic alliances that had characterized the Early and Middle Classic periods (ca. AD 250–675; see Demarest et al. this volume). Naranjo's successful war against Caracol, which occurred fifteen years earlier, in AD 680, may have been particularly significant for creating a landscape suitable for the establishment of new little kingdoms in west-central Belize, as it marks the onset of a century of political disorder in the Vaca Plateau, the Belize Valley, and adjacent Petén.

Efforts to construct the Minanha royal court concentrated on the creation of a 9.5-hectare court complex that included the complete set of architectural features—buildings with residential, ritual, civic-ceremonial, and service functions—required for a "full-service" center (Iannone 2005, 29–30). These structures framed a series of large public plazas and smaller, more restricted courtyards and patios. Ceramic microseriation and Bayesian probability analysis of radiocarbon dates suggest that the royal court complex was built sometime after AD 693 but before AD 775.

This construction program implies more than a rank-size increase in construction efforts; it signifies the appearance of a new type of sociopolitical organization at the center: a fully functioning Maya royal court (Iannone 2005, 30). The royal court complex constitutes the first physical manifestation of the institution of kingship at Minanha, and its rapid appearance has been interpreted as evidence that nonlocal elites moved into the sub-region, possibly disaffected nobles from an established royal court such as Caracol (Iannone 2005). The presumably nonlocal "stranger king" who established the Minanha royal court enacted an agenda that tapped into broader symbols and representations of Maya rulership, including the deliberate alignment of the center's central architecture to mimic the cosmological world view reflected in the site plans of larger centers such as Caracol and Naranjo (Iannone 2005, 30).

Crucial to identifying the presence of the institution of kingship at Maya centers is the ability to find the material correlates of kingship on the ground. At Minanha, the physical evidence of the institution of kingship initially included a highly restricted and elevated elite residential courtyard (Group J) containing a pyramidal shrine (Structure 38J-3rd), a formal vaulted entrance to the group with narrow wing rooms on either side (Structure 35J-2nd), a vaulted residential building (Structure 37J-2nd), and a large, brightly painted performance platform (Structure 39J-2nd; Iannone 2005, 30; Iannone and Longstaffe 2010, 72). Adjacent to this courtyard, to the north, was a small service patio (Group K). Other indicators of the existence of a royal court include a ball court, an E-Group/eastern ancestor shrine, vaulted administrative buildings, an intrasite causeway linking the epicenter with a small shrine, and at least eight stelae that were erected at different times during the court's existence.

These features, which were constructed during the early facet of the Late Classic period, constitute the physical seat of power for the first individuals at the center who set themselves above the rest of the resident Minanha population both by a factor of scale and by being distinctly different in kind. The way Maya kings engaged in a sacred covenant with the gods and represented themselves as intermediaries between the supernatural forces and the members of their kingdoms was fundamental to their legitimacy (see Iannone this volume). The rituals they enacted were likely intensified in times of warfare and/or declining productivity—whether the result of resource degradation or climate change (Freidel and Schele 1988a, 548; Freidel and Shaw 2000, 272)—as these were periods when prosperity was the most under threat. The new Minanha rulers undertook their role as the guarantor of prosperity for the community seriously, as evidenced in the grand construction program that marked the establishment of the royal court, especially the creation of key ritual edifices, such as the E-Group/eastern ancestor shrine and the ball court complexes. The terrace system in the Contreras Valley was also expanded during the reign of the first Minanha kings (Macrae and Iannone 2011), and a swampy area to the east of the epicenter was modified to create a large reservoir (Primrose 2003). The density of population among the rural supporters of the kingdom increased significantly (Macrae and Iannone 2011, 192). All of these factors are material signifiers of the legitimacy and prosperity of the fledgling kingdom.

One strategy the nonlocal entities who constituted the new Minanha royal court used to establish their dominance was to negotiate their legitimacy using long-established places of community power. One of these locations is the E-Group/eastern ancestor shrine complex situated in the epicenter's main, public plaza. The construction of a new shrine structure and placement of associated caches at this locus allowed Minanha's foreign rulers to physically link themselves to ritual offerings dating back to the Late to Terminal Preclassic community (Iannone 2005, 32; Schwake and Iannone 2010). In doing so they would have created a bond between themselves and the local community, an idea that is lent credence by the fact that community members must have played a role in helping establish the precise spatial connections manifest in the axially aligned caches that spanned centuries and multiple construction levels. This implies cooperation on the part of some key members of the Minanha community with respect to the establishment of the royal court.

In order to solidify the new claim to extant sacred space, a shrine room leading into a multiple-entry tomb (Burial 3A-B/1) was also constructed within the central pyramid of the E-Group (Structure 3A-2nd). An additional burial was placed beneath the floor of the shrine room (Burial 3A-B/3; Iannone and Longstaffe 2010, 72; Schwake 2001, 19, 2008, 134). This locus became one of the resting places for the ancestors of the new royal court. In other words, one of the pre-eighth century community's most significant symbolic spaces was repurposed, if only in terms of who controlled it. By co-opting loci at the center that had been previously sacralized through the ritual processes of the founding population and by controlling the newly created physical "place" of the royal court, Minanha's nonlocal kings were able to establish and legitimate their position as the center's premier power elites.

In summary, in the early facet of the Late Classic period, prior to AD 775, Minanha was apparently a reasonably successful kingdom, albeit small and comparatively weak. Iannone (2009) has discussed the utility of conceptualizing the kingdom of Minanha as part of a dynamic sociopolitical framework that includes the position of its "little" kings in relation to the more powerful "great" kings based at the centers of Caracol and Naranjo. The patron-client relationships in this shifting political landscape would mean that at times Minanha would have enjoyed a significant degree of autonomy—especially given its frontier setting between Naranjo and Caracol—but at other times its autonomy would have been more strongly contested, and it may have even been fully subjugated to the authority of one king or the other (Iannone 2006; Iannone 2009, 7–9; Iannone 2010b). Munson and Macri (2009, 428) have suggested that such shifting relationships between polities would have been similar to those described using network analysis, where centers are nodes that are relationally constituted vis-à-vis each other in asymmetrical, value-fluctuating ways. Minanha's developmental sequence clearly exhibits the types of growth and decline and shifts in the nature of rulership that one would expect in such a geopolitical landscape.

Regardless of its apparent success as a little kingdom, at least two significant destruction episodes mark challenges to the authority of the upstart Minanha royals. These have been dated through ceramic microseriation and Bayesian probability analysis of radiocarbon dates; one dates to approximately AD 775 and the other to around AD 800 (Iannone and Longstaffe 2010, 72). These two discrete destruction events were different in intent and severity, and they elicited different responses from the members of the Minanha royal court. Schortman and Urban (2011, 7) point out that archaeologists are well positioned to chart the actions of different factions because of the way that political landscapes are transformed through time. The transformations that the Minanha royal court underwent in the Late and Terminal Classic period are a perfect example of this competitive process of creating and erasing the material correlates of power.

The Ups and Downs of the Little Kingdom of Minanha

As is the case for most kingdoms, the growth trajectory of the Minanha royal court is not one of steady, gradual expansion over time, which would be interpreted as an indication of the relative stability and success of the political system. Instead, it is marked by a series of building episodes interspersed with destruction events that transformed the outward appearance of the physical places related to the institution of kingship. As early as the late facet of the Late Classic period, between AD 775 and 810, events at Minanha indicate that the rulership of the Minanha kings had become tenuous and that other political players were able to make some inroads into the subregion, resulting in the erosion of the position of the Minanha royals.

Destruction Event #1 (ca. AD 775)

Evidence from Group J, the royal residential courtyard, and Structure 3A, the central shrine structure in the center's E-Group/eastern ancestor shrine, indicates that the first destruction event occurred sometime in the late facet of the Late Classic period, likely after AD 775 but before AD 810 (Iannone and Longstaffe 2010, 72). At this time the pyramidal shrine on the northern side of the royal residential courtyard, Structure 38J-3rd, was razed down to its basal courses (see figure 6.3). A cache, 38J-F/1, and probably one other cache situated a few meters to the north—both of which had originally been placed in front of the shrine structure—were apparently reentered at this time and their contents removed (Iannone and Longstaffe 2010, 72). Various excavation units also uncovered evidence that the entire courtyard was subsequently subject to a massive burning episode (Iannone and Longstaffe 2010, 72).

Additional acts of destruction were also visited on the E-Group in Minanha's main plaza at this time. The shrine room and multiple-entry tomb (Structure 3A-B/1) in Structure 3A-2nd, the central pyramidal structure on the eastern side of the complex, were sealed off. The burial that had been placed in the floor of the shrine room (3A-B/3) at the time of its initial construction was also reentered and the majority of the contents removed, with the exception of the distal extremities of the individual interred in the chamber; these were likely left behind because they could not easily be reached from the reentry point (Schwake 2001, 19).

Figure 6.3. Remnants of the razed 38J-3rd shrine showing its basal courses, discovered beneath the penultimate courtyard surface associated with the 38J-2nd shrine (also shown).

Following destruction event #1, a new building program was initiated that reformulated the architecture of the Group J royal residential courtyard and the E-Group shrine in Group A. These rebuilding events followed shortly on the heels of the destruction activities (Iannone and Longstaffe 2010, 72). Within Group J, the entire courtyard was apparently swept clean. A new shrine structure, Structure 38J-2nd, was then built to a height of 8.5 meters. This shrine had rounded corners and at least one stucco frieze on its exterior (Iannone 2005, 30; Iannone 2010a, 270). A large dedicatory cache (38J-F/2) containing broken serving vessels, finger bowls, faunal remains, and charcoal—likely the results of a feast to celebrate the completion of a major construction component—was placed beneath the central landing of the axial stair, and an elaborate crypt (38J-B/1) was built beneath the shrine's summit (Iannone and Longstaffe 2010, 72). Modifications were also made to the 37J-2nd residential building. These modifications involved laying down a new plaster floor and the construction of an axially aligned throne that initially had two levels; only later would this throne be modified to have a single level. This modification was made at the same time that a cache (37J-F/1) was either cut through the original bilevel version (Iannone 2007, 8; Iannone and Longstaffe 2010, 72) or the contents of an earlier cache were removed. The 39J-2nd performance platform and the 35J-2nd vaulted entrance both appear to have been reused with little modification as part of the new courtyard (Iannone 2010a, 270). Finally, an additional building was added to the adjacent service patio (Group K).

At the same time that the royal residential courtyard was being remodeled, the now-sealed-off 3A-2nd shrine room and associated multiple-entry tomb in the E-Group were covered by the axial stair for a new pyramidal building, 3A-1st. Two uncarved compact limestone stelae (Stelae 3 and 5) flanking a central slate stela (Stela 4), which may have been carved in antiquity, were set in front of this new shrine. Two dedicatory caches (3A-F/1 and 3A-F/2) were placed in conjunction with these monuments (Schwake 1999). Finally, two miniature monuments (Stelae 1 and 2), both made of limestone, were erected on the western building of the E-Group at this time (Structure 9A).

In our view, the acts associated with destruction event #1 appear to fit quite well with what has been defined as a "desecratory termination" act (Navarro-Farr et al. 2008; Stanton et al. 2008; Suhler and Freidel 2003) that likely coincided with a shift in rulership (Freidel 1998, 191), as has been documented elsewhere, in particular at Aguateca (e.g., Inomata 2003). It appears that the original Minanha rulers must have had some knowledge that they and their kingdom were about to be attacked. Before fleeing, they emptied some of their most important caches and burials and carried the bones of their ancestors and other significant items with them when they left. The precision indicated in the ways these offerings and burials were "surgically" entered lends support to this interpretation. Marauding enemies would not have had the same knowledge of the precise location of many of these deposits. Eventually the conquerors arrived and focuses their efforts on symbolically "killing" Minanha's ruling lineage by dismantling the Group J shrine and burning the surrounding royal residential courtyard and by closing off, and hence erasing from memory (Schortman and Urban 2011), the shrine room and multiple-entry tomb associated with the Minanha E-Group, one of the most important ancestor veneration venues for the departed Minanha royal court.

Following the ritual destruction, the royal residential courtyard was apparently swept clean. In ancient Maya society, the act of sweeping a space clean was often related to ritual purification (McAnany 2010, 105; Stross 1998, 32), and it may have also had restorative health benefits for those who now sought to occupy the space (McAnany 2010, 63,139; Monaghan 2000, 32). Subsequently, a new royal residential courtyard was built that incorporated the original Group J stair, the formal vaulted entrance, the performance platform, and a newly built shrine with a stucco frieze. This shrine contained an elaborate crypt and a large dedicatory offering. As noted earlier, the first throne was also installed in the courtyard's principal residential building at this time. The fact that it had two levels suggests that some form of joint rule may have been formally established at the center, perhaps with one of the region's great kings (or their agents) sitting on the high side of the throne and the newly installed vassal sitting at a lower level appropriate to their station (Iannone and Longstaffe 2010, 69).

Elsewhere, the E-Group was modified to include an outset stair where the eastern shrine room used to be. As noted previously, three monuments were erected in association with this stair. The middle one was made of slate. Two additional monuments were also positioned on top of the western building of the E-Group. Significantly, this pattern of monument placement, including the prominent usage of a slate monument, also occurred at Caracol (Anderson 1959, 211; Chase and Chase 1987, 17; Grube 1994, 87) and Calakmul (Reese-Taylor 2003), which implies that the new rulers were attempting to tap into patterns of symbolic representation that had been established by these great powers (Iannone 2005).

In summary, we believe that there is strong evidence of a desecratory termination event at Minanha that likely occurred sometime around AD 775. This conquest coincided with a shift to joint rule that likely brought Minanha under the umbrella of a larger and more powerful hegemonic alliance centered on one of the great kingdoms in the region. Interestingly, textual evidence indicates that the great kingdom of Naranjo burned the little kingdom of Bital in AD 775 and again in 777 (Martin and Grube 2008, 80; Chase, Grube, and Chase 1991, 10). Although the precise location of Bital has yet to be determined, Minanha's location in the frontier between Naranjo and Caracol and the timing of destruction event #1 suggest that it is a strong candidate for this center (Iannone 2005; see also Martin and Grube 2008, 80). If it is indeed Bital, the destruction event may signify a shift in affiliation from Caracol to Naranjo in the late eighth century.

Destruction Event #2 (ca. AD 800)

Sometime around AD 800 and likely before AD 810 a second major destruction event occurred at Minanha, once again centered on the royal residential courtyard and the E-Group complex. The event included the careful infilling of the royal residential courtyard, with the exception of the upper 3.7 meters of the 38J-2nd shrine, which was reused as part of a much smaller and far less grandiose residential courtyard (Iannone 2005; Iannone 2010a, 270; see figure 6.4). The extreme care that was taken in the entombing of the buildings associated with Minanha's royal residential courtyard is what makes this particular destruction so significant (Iannone 2005; Iannone 2010a, 270).

The process of infilling started with sweeping all of the floors and surfaces clean and then covering them with a lens of very fine sediments ten to twenty centimeters thick. The stairs of the buildings were then carefully covered with slabs of stone that were laid against the risers and on the treads. Subsequently, the vaulted rooms of the courtyard were laboriously filled from the inside, apparently to protect and preserve them. It was only after these protective measures had been carried out that larger limestone boulders were brought in to form the bulk of the five-meter-thick layer of dry-stone fill that covered the majority of the features associated with the royal courtyard. This fill was contained by well-made construction pens, attesting to the degree of care, labor, and resources that were put into this construction effort. The top of this thick fill deposit served as the courtyard surface for a new residential group that was comparatively impoverished. The surface of this new courtyard coincided exactly with the top of the

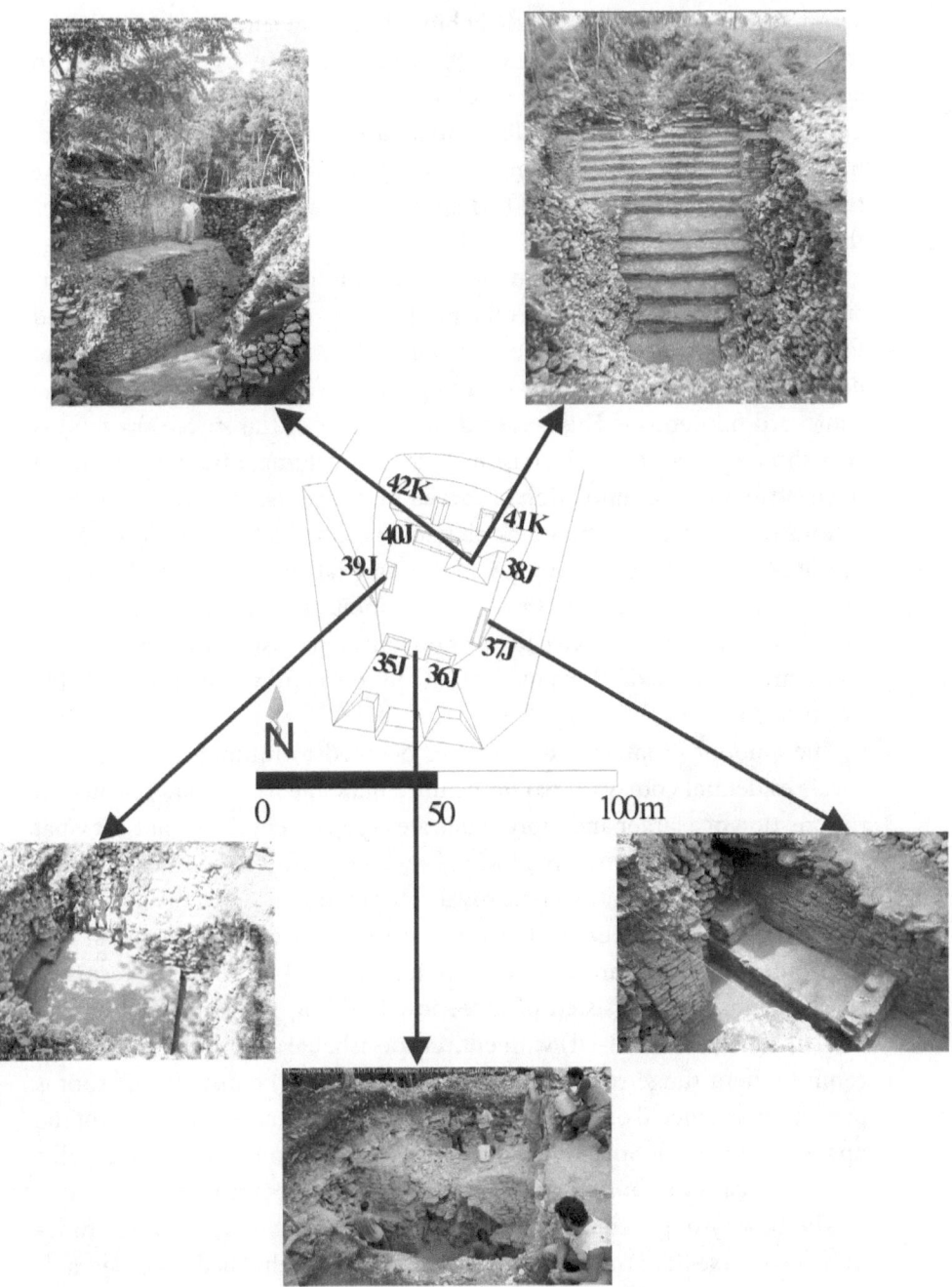

Figure 6.4. Components of the buried penultimate royal residential courtyard (*clockwise from the top left*: *a*) 38J-2nd, west side; *b*) 38J-2nd, front; *c*) 37J-2nd, final version of the throne; *d*) 35J-2nd, formal entrance; and, *e*) 39J-2nd, performance platform).

second terrace of the now partially buried 38J-2nd shrine, which allowed the reused portion of the shrine (38J-1st) to maintain its proportions. To achieve this, the very tops of *some* of the other buildings (37J-2nd and 39J-2nd) also had to be partially dismantled at the new courtyard level (Iannone 2005, 34). In combination, these construction choices imply that the termination of the infilling at this specific elevation was planned rather than accidental.

In contrast to the careful and methodical infilling, other features associated with the Minanha royal residential courtyard were directly targeted for destruction. Specifically, the stucco frieze(s) on Structure 38J-2nd were deliberately destroyed, and the resulting pieces were scattered about in the courtyard fill deposit. This targeted destruction of the stucco frieze(s) is very similar to the actions Harrison-Buck (this volume) discusses related to the destruction and mutilation of carved monuments. She posits that such actions represent a specific attack on known individuals. These destruction acts at Minanha contrast starkly with the care taken to preserve the buildings and rooms of the courtyard itself (Iannone and Longstaffe 2010, 72). Finally, the Group K service patio was no longer accessible after the Group J courtyard was buried, which meant that the courtyard was no longer usable by servants.

The amount of labor and resources devoted to infilling the Minanha royal residential courtyard would be unremarkable if they had resulted in the creation of a larger and more elaborate replacement. The reality of what the courtyard was transformed into, however, leads to the interpretation that the burial of the Late Classic royal court compound *was* the goal. Only very small and unelaborate structures were constructed and used at this locus after the courtyard infilling (Iannone 2005, 34). The new Terminal Classic courtyard consisted of three low building platforms (Structures 37J-1st, 39J-1st, and 40J-1st) with entirely perishable superstructures, a six-room tandem range structure (Structure 35/36J-1st) consisting of rooms partially constructed of perishable materials, and the reused portions of the upper 3.7 meters of Structure 38J-2nd (38J-1st; Iannone 2005, 34). Finally, a new staircase was built to access the now-higher courtyard level.

The new Group J courtyard was smaller, less elaborate, and less functionally diverse than the royal residential courtyard that had preceded it. It therefore contrasts clearly with the normal sequence of construction events one would expect, especially given all the labor involved in the infilling. The fact that the thick walls of the buried vaulted buildings were reused as the footings for the buildings of the new courtyard implies that there was

Figure 6.5. Butt of Stela 4 (slate).

little to no time gap between the infilling of the royal residential courtyard and the construction of its smaller successor. If there had been a gap, the builders would not have been aware of where the buried walls were actually located. Like the ending of the infilling at the level of the second terrace of the 38J-2nd shrine in order to maintain its proportions, the dismantling of some of the upper portions of vaulted buildings to bring them down to that same level, and the clear abandonment of the Group K service annex, the use of the buried walls as footings supports the idea that the ultimate goal of the infilling was the burial of the courtyard. These data are not suggestive of a construction event that was never completed.

Some focused destruction also occurred in front of the E-Group in Group A at the same time that the royal residential courtyard was infilled. The three stelae monuments in front of Structure 3A (Stelae 3, 4, and 5) were broken off; only the bases of these monuments were left in the ground (figure 6.5). Taken alone, this kind of decommissioning of monuments might be seen as a way of terminating the commemorative associations of the monuments. However, since this breakage occurred simultaneously with the other dramatic destruction events in the royal residential courtyard—especially the tearing down and scattering of the stucco frieze—it makes sense to see these actions as related. The target of these focused destruction events may have been the particular individuals depicted on these public monuments (assuming they were carved or painted), and the desecratory acts against them were likely meant to erase the personhood and memory of specific rulers (see Harrison-Buck this volume).

Another intriguing occurrence from Group A, also dating to the end of the Late Classic period, is the cessation of an unfinished construction project on Structure 7A, a large pyramidal structure just to the south of the E-Group. Today, the remnants of a crude ramplike feature extend from the courtyard surface to the level of the first terrace of the platform on the northwest corner of the building (Iannone 2005; Prince 1999, 72). This feature is thought to be the remains of a construction ramp, one that would normally have been dismantled at the termination of the construction episode for which it was built. The abrupt end to the construction efforts associated with Structure 7A speak to the frantic atmosphere at Minanha during the Late Classic to Terminal Classic transition. Perhaps the destruction event of AD 800 literally stopped the orders coming from the top to continue with site aggrandizement projects.

Finally, two of the center's administrative structures also appear to have been terminated, one by the deposition of artifacts in doorways and the undermining of roof supports (Structure 12A) and the other by complete burial and subsequent repurposing as a possible non-elite residential building with a number of primarily perishable rooms (Structure 14C; Seibert 2001).

In the end, the actions undertaken in association with destruction event #2 differ significantly from the earlier destruction event of AD 775. This time, the intention appears to have been to permanently erase any physical evidence of the existence of the Group J royal residential courtyard. The burial of the courtyard also coincided with the destruction of some of the key symbolic elements of the Minanha royal court—namely the stucco frieze on the 38J-2nd shrine, and the stelae in front of the E-Group—which suggests that a degree of desecratory behavior was involved. Nevertheless, the royal residential courtyard was not burned, and for the most part, its buildings were not dismantled. Similarly, there is no evidence of the types of termination rituals that were usually carried out to release the sacred *ch'ulel* that imbued the buildings with a life force in preparation for the construction and dedication of a new courtyard (Freidel et al. 1998; Inomata 2003; McGee 1998, 41–42; Mock 1998a, 5, 10–11; Stanton et al. 2008; Stross 1998, 37; Suhler and Freidel 2003). Instead, the courtyard was swept clean, likely in an effort to purify it (Stross 1998, 32; McAnany 2010, 105).

Subsequently, its vaulted rooms were filled from the inside to preserve them intact, and other than one possible informal offering of a small olla, a chipped-stone bipoint, and a large obsidian blade that were placed together, likely on the medial molding of the formal entrance to Structure 35J-2nd, no ritual activity appears to have been carried out as part of the infilling of the courtyard.

Significantly, the upper portion of the 38J-2nd shrine and the Late Classic burial chamber in its summit continued to be used into the Terminal Classic period (ca. AD 810–900). Elsewhere, offerings continued to be made in association with the E-Group into the early Postclassic period (AD 900–1200), and a burial was also placed within the deconsolidated rubble of the long-abandoned Group J courtyard even at that late date (Burial 42K-B/1). These activities imply that although efforts had been made to decommission—and even erase—these loci from collective memory, they still retained some ritual significance for community members who continued to live in and around them (Snetsinger 2012), as was the case for many of the defunct royal spaces discussed in this volume.

In summary, destruction event #2 was not a full-on desecratory termination event. The destruction was clearly focused on the friezes and monuments that would have contained key symbolic imagery and politically charged references to the late-eighth-century Minanha royal court, its rulers, and their actions. Although the obliteration of these sculptural or textual elements can be read as a direct attack on the legitimacy and/or divine-sponsored authority of the Minanha rulers and hence a shift in rulership at the center (Schwake 1999, 52), this destruction was apparently not ushered in by a burning event, as was the case in destruction event #1. It may, however, have coincided with the capture and physical removal of the Minanha rulers by a foreign power. Intriguingly, Caracol claims to have captured the rulers of both Ucanal and Bital at this same time (Martin and Grube 2008, 97). If Minanha is indeed Bital, this event may signify the shift back to an affiliation with Caracol after a brief association with its enemy, Naranjo, that lasted about twenty-five years. Intriguingly, unlike destruction event #1, which marked the onset of a period of power sharing, this new shift in political relations may be characterized as an effort on the part of the great kingdom to achieve complete dominance, given the move to eliminate all vestiges of the upper tier of the local Minanha political hierarchy.

Importantly, the courtyard infilling event that followed the small-scale destruction does not fit the model for a termination event associated with the construction of a new royal residential courtyard (Iannone 2005), which again suggests that what happened around AD 800 was more careful and reverential than what happened in and around AD 775. Finally, we would also argue that destruction event #2 does not fully square with Schortman and Urban's (2011, 6, 13) recent suggestion that actions of obliteration are often focused acts of "collective forgetting" that reconfigure the symbolic frameworks of politically imbued material culture. Clearly, the 38J shrine and the E-Group were not forgotten; instead, Minanha's community members continued to engage with them for generations to come. Iannone (2010b, 366) describes the scenario:

> On one hand, the burial of the royal residential compound beneath ca. five meters of rubble removed it visually from the community. However, its former position as the most symbolically charged, and politically important, settlement node within the Minanha realm meant that it was not so easily erased from the collective memory of the community. Similarly, the labor involved and the care taken to preserve the features associated with the royal residence also suggests that this was in some ways an unforgettable ritualized process, and that as a result of the infilling, the royal residential group itself was likely burned into the collective memory of the Minanha community for the long-term [sic].

Discussion

The two destruction events that we have isolated at Minanha fit a broader pattern of sociopolitical turmoil that characterized the southern Maya lowlands during the transition from the Late to the Terminal Classic (e.g., Webster 2000). Nevertheless, each episode is unique, and by focusing on them as individual historic events we gain a richer understanding of the types of processes that lead to the downfall of the institution of kingship and a shift to the new sociopolitical reality of the ninth century.

Destruction event #1 appears to represent an episode of desecratory termination associated with conquest. It involved the dismantling, burning, purification, and resanctification of portions of the Minanha royal residential courtyard, the closing off of the shrine room and multiple-entry tomb in the E-Group complex, and likely the move toward some form of joint rulership. In other words, although this appears to be a case of disruption, at the same time it reflects alliance building and a level of sociopolitical *continuity*. Similar shifts in rulership with comparable destruction of royal residential courtyards appear to have occurred at other centers in the region at this same time, such as Xunantunich (LeCount and Yaeger 2010), another little kingdom also situated between the competing great kingdoms of Naranjo and Caracol.

The crises that stimulated such destruction events may have been broad in scope. Specifically, such events may reflect the actions of great kings who, severely challenged by the changing environmental (e.g., droughts, resource degradation), economic (e.g., growing population, declining agricultural productivity, shifting trade networks), and political (e.g., increased competition and warfare) circumstances of the late eighth century, strove to demonstrate that they were still legitimate guarantors of prosperity by reasserting control over the domains of the little kingdoms that had emerged during the era of pan-regional balkanization initiated by Tikal's defeat of Calakmul in AD 695. The physical removal of little kings and their local governance structures and the desecration and deactivation of the spaces and powerfacts associated with their kingdoms was a necessary step in their reincorporation into the broader power structures of the overlords.

Destruction event #2 suggests that something very different occurred at kingdoms such as Minanha around the crucial time period of AD 800–810. Although the focus at Minanha was once again the royal residential courtyard and the E-Group/eastern ancestor shrine, this time the destructive episode was less dramatic, although it was probably more labor intensive. Even though this event may have again been associated with some form of conquest by a great king scrambling to maintain legitimacy by capturing Minanha's less powerful ruler, thereby acquiring a new tribute stream, it does not signify an episode of disruption in a period of sociopolitical continuity, as in destruction event #1. Rather, destruction event #2 appears to mark a time of significant sociopolitical *discontinuity* (Schortman and Urban 2011, 14). The actions associated with this complex event were marked, on one hand, by highly focused acts of desecration that were likely carried out by the agents of a great king who aimed to take control of the kingdom's resource base by physically removing the little king and erasing any texts and imagery that supported his claim that he was the legitimate local power (e.g., the destruction of the stelae and friezes). At the same time, it seems as if the fall of Minanha's last little king also involved community efforts to physically encapsulate the royal residential courtyard, thus reverentially "caching" rather than symbolically terminating it. These latter efforts were seemingly aimed at maintaining some ritual ties to the former seat of power of the local kingdom. The fact that small-scale offerings and burials continued to be made for centuries in association with both the buried courtyard and the remains of the E-Group/eastern ancestor shrine supports this interpretation.

Although difficult to interpret, the complex combination of desecratory and reverential actions associated with destruction event #2 clearly mark the appearance of a very different form of Terminal Classic community, one that was formed in the absence of a Minanha ruler, and did not replicate the earlier form of sociopolitical structure associated with the institution of kingship. The presence of the much smaller and less ostentatious buildings existing alongside derelict, yet still powerful edifices from the old regime suggests the possibility that a shared form of community decision making took hold, one that favored Minanha's traditional power brokers (the heads of the long-standing lineages who controlled improved land and water sources), in clear contrast to a governance structure centered on a single divine ruler who could no longer guarantee prosperity for anybody, with the exception of some possible deference to a much more distant overlord whose powers and legitimacy were also declining rapidly.

What crises were ultimately responsible for such sociopolitical disjunctions? In broader terms, destruction event #1 at Minanha and others like it suggest that competition, conflict, and shifting political alliances were the norm in the mid to late eighth century, as kings of all rank and order attempted to maintain their legitimacy as guarantors of prosperity in the face of changing trade networks, declining resources bases, climate change, population growth, competition, and diminishing returns on productive investments (see Iannone et al. this volume; Iannone this volume). The strategies they adopted included initiating wars to capture the rulers of other centers and/or establishing patron-client relationships with less powerful polities. Both of these strategies would have secured higher levels of tribute, promoted greater investment in intensive agriculture to increase production, enhanced the ability to construct larger temples and host more grandiose ceremonies and rituals in order to curry the favor of the gods and placate followers, and facilitated the manipulation of ideology to shore up the crumbling edifice of the institution of divine kingship. These responses to problems clearly attest to the dependencies that characterized most kingdoms of this time period. Unfortunately, it appears that in many instances the strategies of containment the ruling regimes of the mid- to late eighth century adopted simply compounded their problems (i.e., the sunk-cost effect took hold).

Destruction event #2 at Minanha and other similar episodes of ritual destruction noted elsewhere imply that a tipping point—an insurmountable crisis of legitimation that could not be contained (see Iannone this volume)—was reached at many kingdoms sometime between AD 800 and 830. This is what we have traditionally referred to as the Maya collapse. Divine kingship as an institution was highly vulnerable by this time precisely because it was grounded in the idea of prosperity for all, and prosperity could no longer be guaranteed given the many issues that Maya communities had to contend with.

What issues were specific to Minanha during the early ninth century? For one, although the chaos that occurred as a result of the era of balkanization that began in the late seventh century may have initially promoted the autonomy and prosperity of little kingdoms such as Minanha, the resulting increased competition for human and natural resources may have eventually contributed to their demise as well. Minanha's frontier location, between Caracol and Naranjo, would have made it particularly vulnerable to the machinations of the competing overlords who ruled these great kingdoms. The competition for human and natural resources was likely compounded by population growth.

In addition, it is evident that debilitating droughts occurred in the Vaca Plateau during the time in question. A particularly dry period began in the latter half of the eighth century and another persisted for roughly a century from AD 872 to AD 995 (Webster et al. 2007). Droughts would have been a challenge in the karstic environment of the Vaca Plateau because of the lack of surface water (e.g., rivers) and the porous nature of the limestone substrate, which promoted rapid percolation of water downward to the relatively deep water table (Polk et al. 2007). Nevertheless, droughts may not have been as harsh in the Vaca Plateau as they were in adjacent regions for four reasons. First, the prevailing easterly winds that carried much of the rain would have been affected by the higher elevations of the plateau (the orographic rainfall pattern), and more rain may have fallen in these uplands than in adjacent regions during the drier periods (Penn et al. 2004, 23). Second, the rugged nature of the topography may have inhibited surface drying as a result of wind action (the effect of surface roughness) (Griffin et al. 2014; Shaw 2003). Third, because good soils were found in pockets and terracing also seems to have been restricted to certain valleys, less forest may have been cleared in the plateau and thus it may have experienced less extreme droughts (Griffin et al. 2014; Polk et al. 2007).

Fourth, the overall population of the northern Vaca Plateau may have been less dense when compared to the subregions surrounding it, and thus there may have been less of a drain on available water sources during the dry periods of the eighth and ninth centuries. It is worth noting that a recent assessment of the impacts of various droughts on the populations of the Vaca Plateau concluded that the negative effects of the dry periods have been overestimated and that periodic droughts influenced communities quite differently (Iannone et al. 2014).

Still it is likely that seasonal water sources that relied completely on rainfall and runoff, such as *sartenjas* (low-lying areas that naturally collect water during the rainy season) and the large artificially modified reservoir adjacent to Minanha would have been impacted by the droughts. Whether perennial springs were negatively influenced by the drier conditions remains uncertain, although many are still active today during a relatively dry climate regime (suggesting they may have been present in past times of drought stress as well). Regardless of the precise impact of drought on the various components of Minanha's water management system, water likely became scarcer over time and contestation for that resource likely increased. Crop yields likely also declined because of diminishing rainfall and possibly as a result of centuries of intensive farming of select valleys.

All of these issues in combination, would have severely undermined the prosperity of the little kingdom of Minanha and eroded the legitimacy of its rulers. In contrast, the traditional, long-standing, and more stable power brokers (the lineage heads), who had more tangible control over the key land and water sources that were still viable, would have found their voices gaining more sway in the broader community, especially among their kin (the kingdom's principal workforce). In the end, although nonlocal agents were likely responsible for extinguishing the individual ruler, erasing all physical attestations to their pedigree (e.g., stelae and friezes) and exorcising the key "souls" enshrined in their monuments (see Harrison-Buck this volume), some of the more astute local agents likely fostered this change in governance in an effort to bolster their own standing in the community, and it was presumably these same local entities who eventually sponsored and organized the careful, even reverential, infilling that encased the royal residential courtyard, the center of the now-defunct kingdom. These actions, in effect, preserved this place of former glory and power for future generations to symbolically tap into when and how they desired. Such behavior is reminiscent, in some ways, of how Rwanda's last Hutu president was killed for perceived ineffectual behavior at the same time that his legacy became something to celebrate (see Taylor this volume).

Conclusions

In keeping with the ideas brought up in the introduction to this volume, we would combine the two destruction events at Minanha into a single, relatively short period of dramatic change (ca. 25–30 years) that culminated in the scapegoating of the institution of kingship itself rather than in the scapegoating of a single king. At Minanha, the crisis that led to this dramatic change in governance and community organization was complex and likely involved insurmountable environmental (droughts), economic (declining agricultural productivity), social (obstruction on the part of disaffected supporters, especially traditional power brokers), political (increasing competition between great kingdoms), and ultimately ideological (the kings were no longer seen to be fulfilling their role in the sacred covenant) problems.

In addition, it is interesting to consider that all of the kings at Minanha may have been essentially nonlocal "stranger kings," including the rulers who established and administered the first royal court prior to the AD 775 destruction event and the new kingly line that took over the center following that event. It is plausible that some of the long-established, yet far less powerful local lineages at Minanha (those we have referred to as the traditional power brokers for this community) never fully recognized the legitimacy of these strangers. Although some community members may have deliberately aligned themselves with the various stranger kings (as implied by the shared knowledge required to perfectly align the caches in front of the E-Group) because they perceived some benefit for themselves in doing so, by the end of the Late Classic, few in the Minanha community seem to have found the case for elite legitimacy to be strong enough for their continued support. Without supporters, the institution of kingship quickly disintegrates, as it appears to have done between AD 800 and 830 in many parts of the southern lowlands, including Minanha.

Following the physical removal of the ruler and those who suffered from guilt by association (the ruler's entourage) and destruction of the ruler's key powerfacts (stelae and friezes), presumably at the hands of competing great kings, the more resilient members of the Minanha community—the traditional power brokers who would see benefit in the removal of a demanding yet ineffectual overlord who had apparently lost the favor of the gods—apparently chose to reverentially "cache" the royal residential courtyard that was once the power center of the defunct little kingdom of Minanha. In doing so, they promoted a new form of sociopolitical and socioeconomic organization that was more fitting for the time and that was more consistent with the long-term organizational structures that had characterized highly successful socioecological systems in the Maya world for many centuries before the landscape of kings emerged. Nevertheless, as attested by various chapters in this volume, the sacred spaces associated with the great experiment in sociopolitical complexity were never fully deactivated by the destruction and infilling events of the early ninth century. For centuries to follow, these loci continued to serve as points of power, and they were periodically reactivated through new, albeit small-scale, ritual acts by members of the post-king world.

Acknowledgments

We are grateful for the ongoing support of the Institute of Archaeology in Belize. Funding for the Minanha excavations was provided by the Social Sciences and Humanities Research Council of Canada and Trent University. Finally, we appreciate all the hard work the numerous members of our research team have contributed over the years to our efforts to learn more about the little kingdom of Minanha.

7

The Collapses in the West and the Violent Ritual Termination of the Classic Maya Capital Center of Cancuen

Causes and Consequences

ARTHUR A. DEMAREST, CLAUDIA QUINTANILLA,
AND JOSÉ SAMUEL SUASNAVAR

At Cancuen about AD 800 a singular event occurred: one of the largest termination rituals recorded in the Maya lowlands. An entire site—a high *kaloomte'* royal capital of a rich riverine kingdom and the center of a sprawling economic exchange network—was ritually terminated. The entrances to the royal palace were buried in meters of clay and rubble, the monuments were carefully defaced, and much of the nobility—over fifty men, women (two of whom were pregnant), children, and the king and queen—were assassinated. Most were deposited in two sacred cisterns, one at the entrance to the palace and a second near the main plaza. But the king, Kan Maax, and his probable consort were simply buried under 60–80 centimeters of mud at the second entrance, without tombs or even cists. Strangely, these nobles and royalty were interred with fine offerings and dressed in full regalia. The Cancuen epicenter was then abandoned completely and never reoccupied.

This event also marked the complete disintegration of one of the great exchange routes of the western Petén and a signal event in the violent collapse of the Classic Maya kingdoms of the west. In terms of scale, details, and clarity of data, there are few more explicit examples of the violent ritual end of royal power in the Classic Maya lowlands.

Furthermore, the events at Cancuen provide the best-dated chronology for the late-eighth-century period of the crisis of divine authority that is discussed in this volume. In that period, Cancuen's contexts are very clearly divided into phases of 760–780 (Los Laureles), 780–790 (Early Chaman), and 790–800 (Late Chaman) based on historical texts, typological and modal ceramic microchronology based on midden deposits, interregional cross-dating of ample ceramic imports (sourced by instrumental neutron activation analysis), a six-stage palace construction sequence in which three reconstructions have in situ monuments with dedication dates, and a general architectural style sequence based on the palace and other well-dated architecture (e.g., Barrientos 2014).

But what happened at Cancuen? Who carried out this strange massacre? Why with such elaborate ritual? Why at that time? What does it tell us about the ideology of the eighth-century Maya states and the reasons for their disintegration? What does it tell us about the crisis of legitimacy described throughout this volume (see especially Iannone this volume)?

Seventh- to Eighth-Century Challenges to Centralization and Interregional Spheres of Hegemony

To understand the root causes of the disasters at Cancuen and elsewhere, we must go back at least a century. The crisis of legitimacy at the end of the Late Classic was not a sudden phenomenon; it was a culmination of a long process of fragmentation throughout the eighth century. This process involved challenges at even higher levels than royal power.

The period of maximum reach and power of royal authority might be seen in the epoch of the greatest *kaloomte's*, the "Middle Classic" kings of kings of the greatest centers such as Tikal and Calakmul. In the fifth and sixth centuries Tikal dominated much of the Petén (Martin and Grube 2008). While direct control of the administration of other kingdoms is unlikely, the placement of allied or related rulers, tribute in exotics and commodities, and labor are reflected in the archaeological and epigraphic record of Tikal and other lowland sites in this period.

If we look at the western Petén trade corridor of the Pasión River, Verapaz, and transversal valley land routes (figure 7.1), we see that Central Petén influence, monuments, and Tzakol-style ceramics have been found in both the highlands and Pasión River sites. Thousands of broken vessels of Tzakol-style ceramics that date to about AD 400 to 600 were found in the cave shrines that line the valley route from Cancuen at the southern frontier of

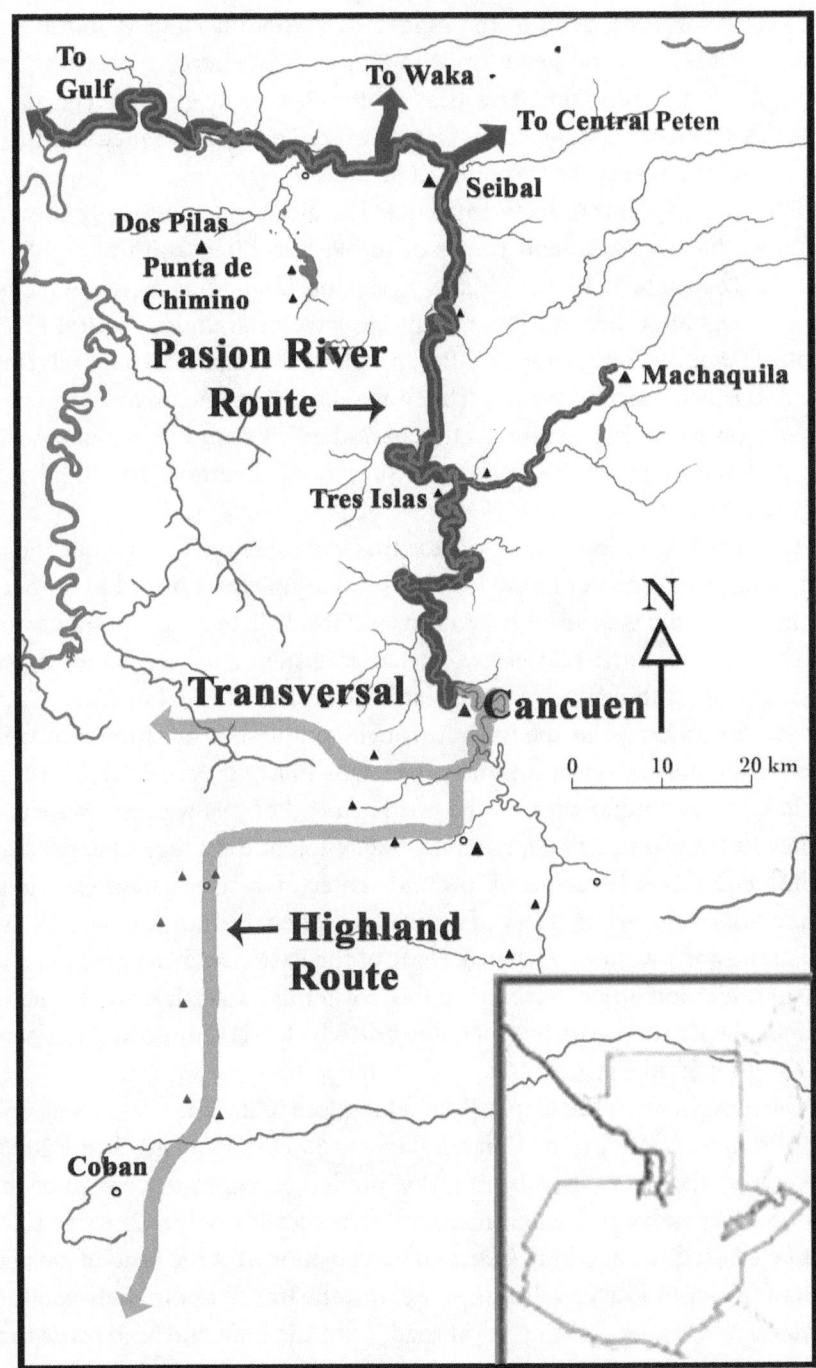

Figure 7.1. Map showing the principal western exchange routes of the Pasión, the highland route, and the "transversal." Illustration by Luis F. Luin.

the Petén lowlands, deep in the highlands (Woodfill 2010; Woodfill and Andrieu 2012). Central Petén–style monuments were erected at sites such as Punta de Chimino and Tres Islas on the Pasión River route (Bachand 2010). A Petén-style stone coffer was recovered even in the piedmont and highlands at Hun Nal Ye (Woodfill et al. 2012).

Evidence of Central Petén influence, therefore, was uniformly present on both the river and land routes of the Pasión River and the highland valleys. The route to highland jade, pyrite, obsidian, quetzal feathers, Pacific conch, and other exotics appeared to have been under Central Petén control (Woodfill and Andrieu 2012), probably through merchant pilgrimage and other peaceful means. This was reflected in the great abundance of jade, obsidian, and exotics in this period at Tikal and its region and in the Tzakol presence at the trade route sites in the piedmont and highlands (figure 7.2a).

The very beginning of the process that eventually led to the decline of centralized royal power in the lowlands can arguably be traced as far back as the rise of the Calakmul hegemony and its challenges to the status quo on the Tikal-dominated western exchange system and elsewhere. In the sixth and seventh centuries, the great hegemonies of Calakmul and Tikal battled for influence in the west. Through conquest or asymmetrical alliance, Calakmul asserted authority over Dos Pilas, El Perú-Waka', La Corona, Uxul, and other sites on the northern end of this western route and routes further west, using a complex but systematic strategy of expansion of influence. This sequence of lowland centers, which began at Cancuen, formed the major trade artery of the western Petén, including what we have called the great western exchange route of the Pasión and Usumacinta and what Freidel and others have called the "royal road" to Calakmul, the latter half via the Pasión River, but then due north by land (Canuto and Barrientos Q. 2013; Freidel et al. 2007).

The movement of the Upper Pasión kingdom to its Late Classic seat and its founding at Cancuen by Calakmul in AD 656 (Martin and Grube 2008) was a key element in establishing this unified access to or control of the Pasión River valley and the entire route. The accession of the Cancuen ruler was celebrated at Calakmul. Cancuen was positioned at the head of navigation of the Pasión River valley (figure 7.2b), the transfer point between this lowland river route and the "royal road" with the highland land route that led south through the Verapaz to many resources (Barrientos and Demarest 2007; Demarest et al. 2008, 2009). Also note that figure 7.2b shows only half of the Calakmul sphere of influence; its political machinations were also being carried out in the east in interactions with Caracol, Naranjo, and other sites (e.g., Martin and Grube 2008).

The beginning of the gradual process of decentralization of power through the lowlands might be traced to AD 695, when Calakmul and its allies suffered a devastating defeat by Tikal (Martin and Grube 2008). While that led to a decline at Calakmul, it did not lead to reunification of the western exchange route under Tikal. Instead, political relations on the land routes became quite complex and were characterized by greater regional autonomy. Neither the Tikal nor the Calakmul superpowers regained control of the system. However, the Middle Pasión Petexbatun kingdom of Dos Pilas began a campaign of conquest and alliance in an attempt to control or at least assure access to the southwestern Petén and the Pasión River half of the route (figure 7.2c). Conquest and control of other Petexbatun sites was followed by further expansion on the river (Demarest 2006). A celebrated royal marriage alliance with Cancuen brought that site into the Dos Pilas sphere of dominance (Martin and Grube 2008, 60).

It is clear that this Petexbatun Pasión hegemony represented a great reduction in the area of hegemonic control as early as the end of the seventh century. Neither as extensive nor as active as the earlier hegemonies, Dos Pilas unified only the Pasión River portion of the trade route, despite ample evidence (discussed below) of exchange south via the gateway center of Cancuen. By the eighth century the highland Verapaz land portion of the route no longer registered Petén influence in material culture (Woodfill 2010). The Dos Pilas hegemony was limited to the Pasión River valley and did not extend, as it had previously, to the north or east on the Petén land routes to El Perú-Waka', Calakmul, Tikal and other sites. Furthermore, unlike the Early Classic, during the seventh- and eighth-century period of Cancuen's role as a gateway center, there is little lowland influence in the piedmont and highland Verapaz sites. In contrast, elaborate highland-oriented ritual settings were created within Cancuen itself. We can assume that control of access to those routes was in the hands of independent highland political entities.

The size and centralization of hegemonies shrank even further after Tikal defeated El Perú-Waka' in AD 743 (and defeated Naranjo in the east in AD 744). After that, the last Dos Pilas ruler, K'awiil Chan K'inich, struggled to maintain the Petexbatun alliance. In AD 761, Dos Pilas was violently attacked, besieged, and destroyed (e.g., Demarest 2006; Demarest et al. 1997). These events were documented in many primary contexts at Dos Pilas and in other texts. The Pasión region balkanized into battling independent

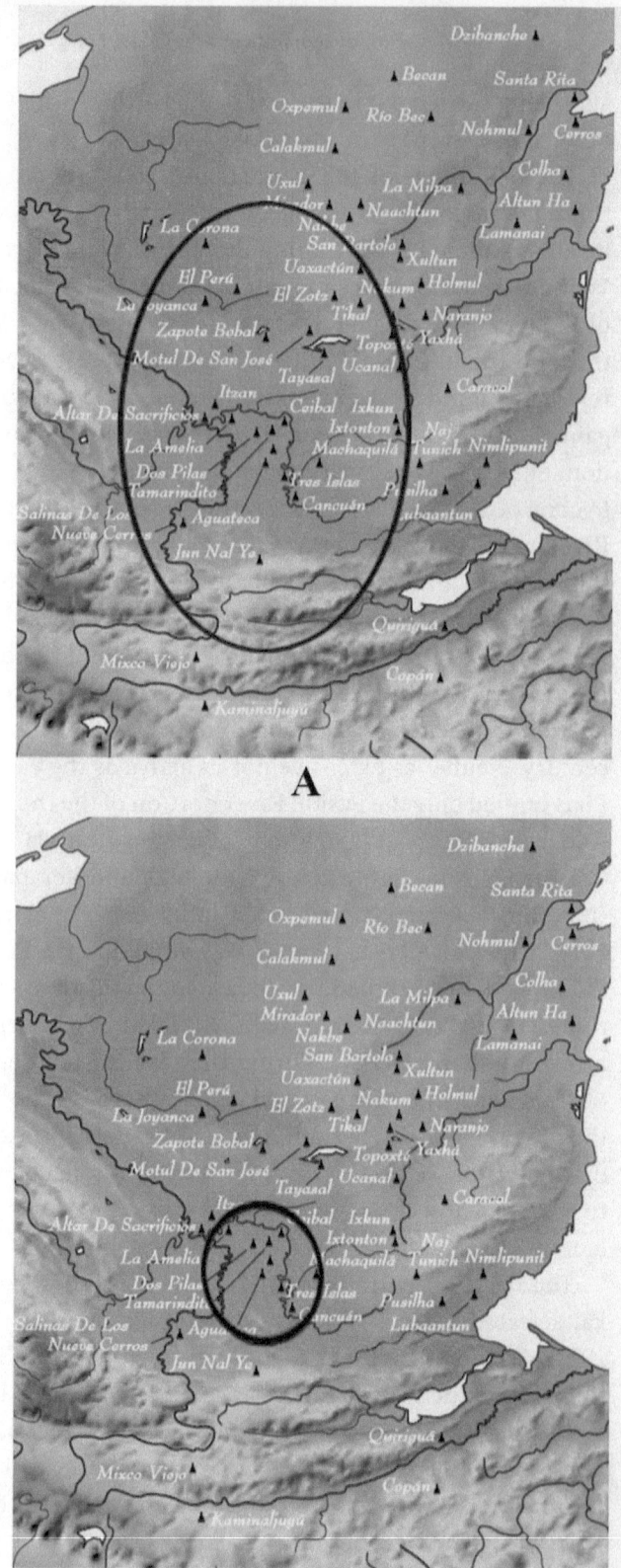

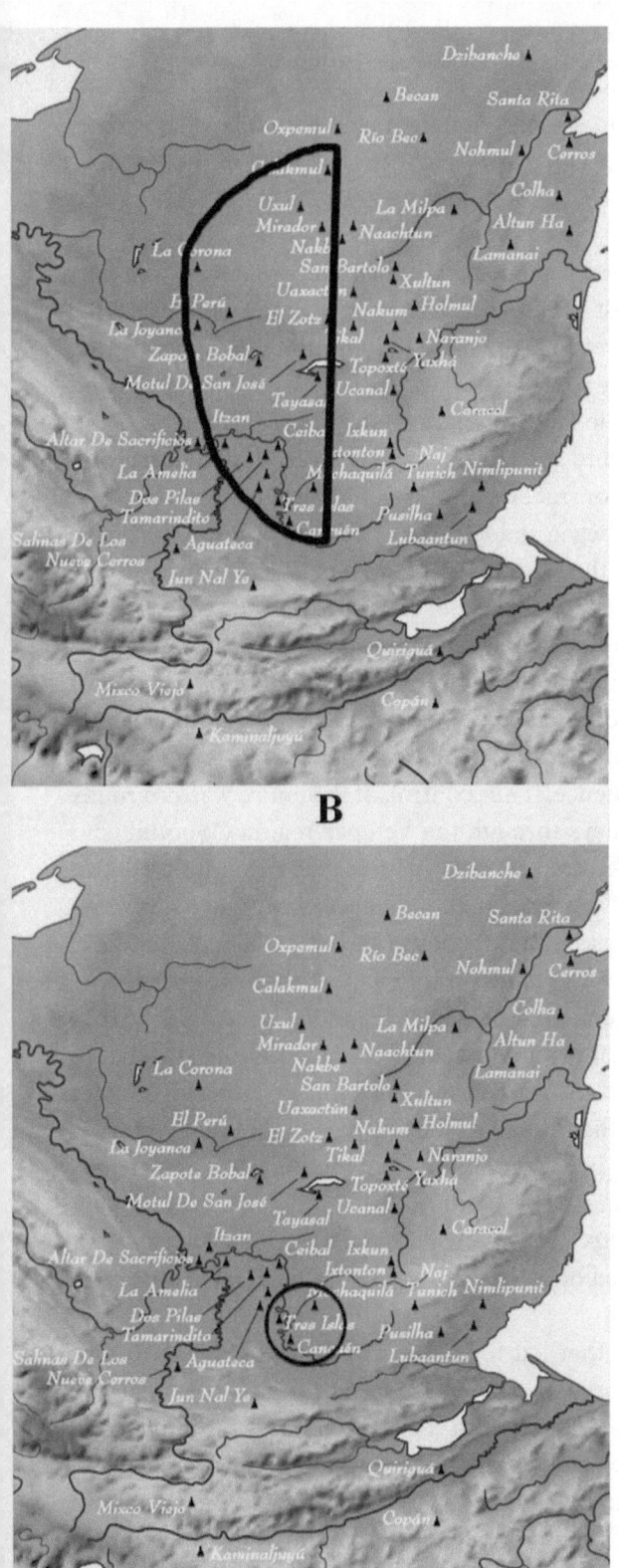

Figure 7.2. *A*) General area of fifth- to mid-seventh century Tikal hegemony over the western exchange route (note that only the western route sites are circled in each map); *B*) General area of mid-seventh- to eighth-century area of Calakmul hegemony over sites on the western exchange route; *C*) Area of early eighth-century Dos Pilas hegemony over the Pasion river exchange route; *D*) Area of late eighth-century Cancuen hegemony over the Upper Pasión exchange route. Illustrations by Luis F. Luin.

powers such as Tamarindito, Ceibal, Aguateca, and Santa Amelia, each of which had their own emblem glyph or fought to claim that of the Petexbatun (e.g., Demarest 1997, 2004, 2006; Inomata 1997, 2008c; O'Mansky and Dunning 2004).

At this point, AD 760–800 Cancuen was fully independent and was entering its period of greatest florescence (Barrientos and Demarest 2007; Demarest et al. 2008). However, the Cancuen dominion was only over the Upper Pasión portion of the route, as shown in figure 7.2d (Barrientos and Demarest 2007). The Middle Pasión remained in chaos, and the highland valleys were independent (and apparently not very interested in borrowing elements of lowland ritual or material culture). In the late eighth century, Cancuen's ruler and elites began to look to the far west and the northeast for alternative routes, since the Middle Pasión was so disrupted by endemic warfare (Demarest et al. 2009; Demarest et al. 2014).

Thus, viewed in chronological order and transregional perspective, there was a sequential reduction during the Classic period in the scale of hegemonies and the area of alliance networks under the great *kaloomtes* (compare figures 7.2a, 7.2b, 7.2c, and 7.2d). First (figure 7.2a), the Tikal hegemony had extensive influence, if not control, of the entire western route, including the highland valleys through the Verapaz region (Woodfill and Andrieu 2012) and a parallel strategic control in Belize to Honduras (Bell et al. 2004). After that, the subsequent Calakmul hegemony (figure 7.2b) covered much of the same territory, but its power ended at Cancuen and did not register influence in the highland Verapaz valleys to the south, despite confirmed large-scale movement of resources from that zone. Its influence also did not extend southeast to the Motagua. Subsequently, the Petexbatun kingdom (fig. 3c) extended its boundaries, but only to control a smaller portion of the route from the middle to the upper Pasión. Finally, the destruction of Dos Pilas and the Petexbatun hegemony led to the disintegration of its alliance and a period of battling city-states (Demarest 2004b; O'Mansky and Dunning 2004), each with a limited range of authority. That of Cancuen (fig. 3d) covered only the upper Pasión River (Demarest et al. 2008).

Thus, the later changes that led to the demise of the kings at a local or subregional level must be seen against the backdrop of a transregional balkanization and a general reduction in the size and scale of influence of larger political units. These changes would have resulted in a more limited range of power, tribute, and patronage of the *k'uhul ajaw* of the respective capital centers. The rise of many individual polities and smaller zones of power was a factor at the highest level of decentralization of power. It also led to an intensification of all forms of status rivalry, from monuments to warfare, as the reduced subregional elites vied for power. Therein lay the seeds of the late-eighth-century crisis of legitimacy (Iannone this volume; Iannone et al. this volume).

Challenges to Royal Authority: The Rise and Proliferation of Subroyal Elites

By the end of the seventh century, at the same time that these changes were under way at the interregional level, each individual polity was beginning to experience a dispersion of power because of internal changes. Particularly in the west there was a simultaneous proliferation of individual emblem glyphs and an increase in and diversification of subroyal titles and offices. Beginning in the late eighth century, the number of such titles increased significantly. From 9.11.0.0.0 (AD 652) to 9.15.0.0.0 (AD 731) in the Maya Long Count, the number of inscribed subroyal titles increased sevenfold (Jackson 2005, Fig. 3.9). *Sajal, ajk'uhuun, yajaw-k'ahk', bach'ok, ti-sak-hu'n* were among the many designations for high-ranking but nonroyal lords (Houston and Inomata 2009, 173). By the eighth century, such lords had their own palaces, thrones, rich burials, and in some cases even their own courts as leaders of smaller petty kingdoms (e.g., Iannone 2005; Schwake and Iannone this volume). Bureaucratic involution, royal and high-elite polygamy, and general growth led to a dynamic in which larger courts intensified the local influence of the state, but they did so at the cost of greater internal divisions of power and probable internal status rivalry in addition to the interstate competition already present between the growing number of polities of many sizes.

The proliferation of elites was even more intense in the Usumacinta and Pasión regions of the western exchange and transport route than in other regions (Jackson 2005). There and elsewhere this reflected a balkanization of power. A similar process has been observed in more detail at sites such as Copan, where rich iconographic and epigraphic evidence has survived. Rulers such as Yax Pasaj were pressured to divide their authority with other nobles, some of whom probably controlled subsectors of the Copan Valley (Fash et al. 2004). Leadership was then coordinated and negotiated at *popolna*, or mat houses (Fash et al. 1992). Smaller palaces with thrones were associated with nobles with specific titles. It has even been suggested that such a division of power was an element in the internal aspects of collapse in the Copan Valley, as the central power of the *k'uhul ajaw* was weakened (Fash and Stuart 1991; Fash et al. 2004).

At Cancuen, this process of the internal rise of nobles is manifested in multiple lines of evidence (e.g., Demarest et al. 2014). This shift occurred even as the site experienced its apogee in the late eighth century. Elite complexes were found at various strategic locations in the site, and each of Cancuen's three most studied port areas was associated with such range structures (e.g., Demarest et al. 2014). Some of the site's noble complexes had impressive three-dimensional stucco sculptures similar to ones in the royal palace itself (Barrientos 2014; Demarest et al. 2014; Demarest 2013). Monuments indicate a sharing of power between the ruler and high elites. Panel 3 at Cancuen (figure 7.3a) displays the king as a water lord, but he shares that scene with an *ajk'uhuun* and a *sajal* noble. Meanwhile, although altars set as ball court markers celebrate military victories (Fahsen and Barrientos 2006), they were proxy wars, and Altars 2 (figure 7.3b) and 3 show the *k'uhul ajaw* with another companion *ajaw*. In one case, the other ballplayer is identified as the captor of a lord from a site of Sac Witz and later as the captor of the lord of the great site of Machaquila (e.g., Fahsen and Barrientos 2006). In many ways the ballgame monuments celebrate the victories of subordinate lords more than the power of the Cancuen *k'uhul ajaw*. Thus, the roles of *k'uhul ajaw* as both master of the ports (the economic raison d'être of Cancuen) and war leader seem to have been relegated to nobles, and other roles may have been reassigned as well.

The division of power is also apparent in the central royal palace of Cancuen in its final stages in the late eighth century (figure 7.4). It reflects changes in the nature of governance. Over a decade of detailed study, excavation, and comparative analysis Barrientos and his colleagues (e.g., Barrientos 2014; Barrientos, Arriaza, et al. 2006) have shown that the huge palace served only minimally as a royal residence and was more of an administrative and ritual complex that was also used by the many nobles at the site (Barrientos 2014; Demarest 2013). The architecture consists of many small nonresidential audience chambers, likely receiving rooms with benches for subroyal officials (figure 7.4). These may have served as the offices for the nobles living elsewhere in the other range structures at the site or even some may have been audience chambers of leaders whose residences were not located at Cancuen but in satellite centers. Only two courtyards of eleven in the palace have been shown to have a residential function. These were strikingly different in size, privacy, and form from the many *audiencias*. This shift in central architecture at Cancuen parallels that of other

Figure 7.3. Panel 3 (*A*) and Altar 2 (*B*) of Cancuen. Illustrations by Luis F. Luin.

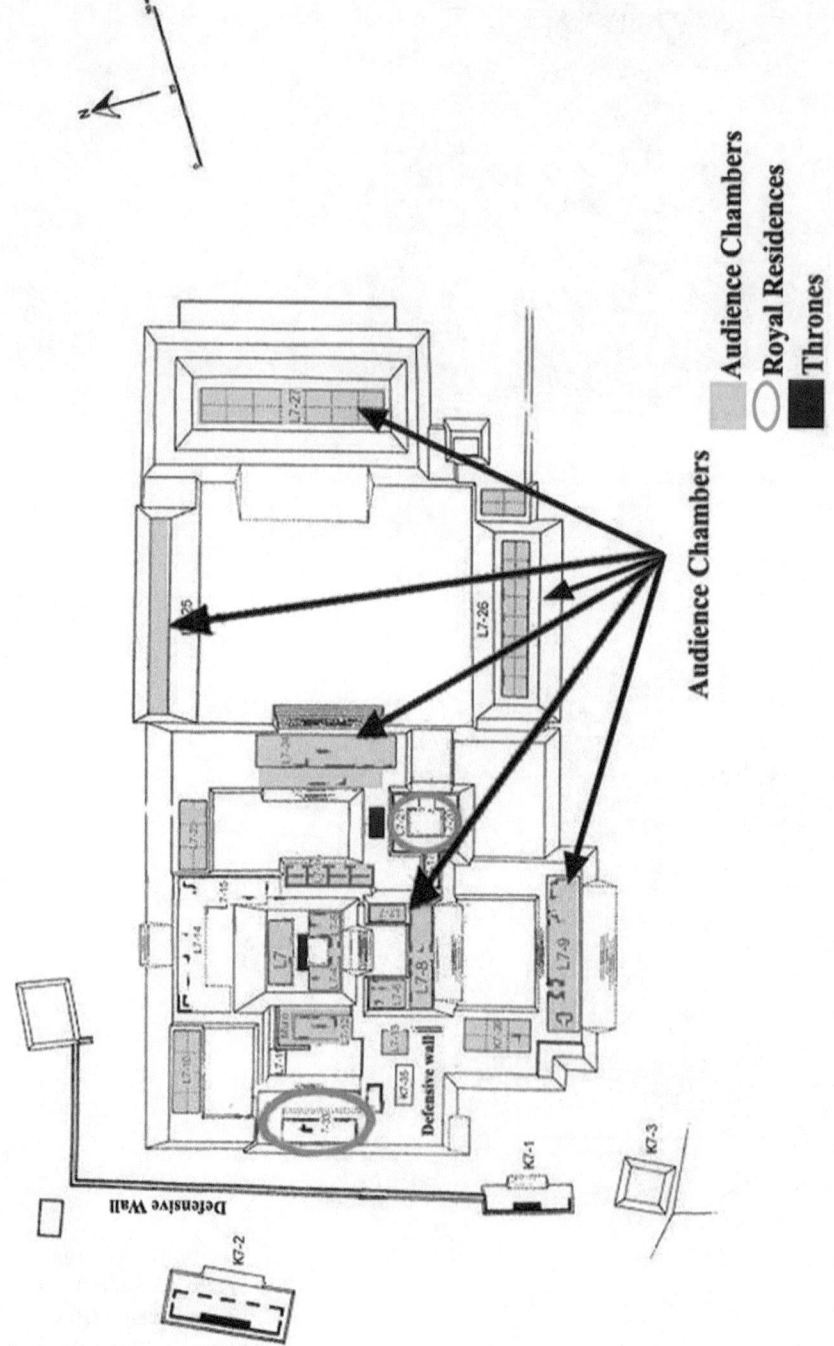

Figure 7.4. Plan view of the royal palace at Cancuen showing many audience chambers, especially in outermost areas. Illustration by Luis F. Luin.

centers with administrative palaces, including those at Nakum, Caracol, Calakmul, Ednza, and other late-eighth-century and Terminal Classic sites (Barrientos 2014). At Cancuen the association of these patterns with shifts in economy and foreign influence is notable (Demarest 2013; Demarest et al. 2014).

All of these changes indicate another level of challenges to centralized authority. Intrapolity division of power would have led to the type of unstable political dynamics observed in most regions in the late eighth century as rivalry between nobles (and potential rulers) intensified, threatening and weakening the *k'uhul ajaw*.

Challenges to State Regional Authority

There is much evidence that on the level of sites within states there were also significant challenges to the central power of the states dominated by *k'uhul ajaw*. Increasing autonomy was already present in the rise of more centers. The number of sites with emblem glyphs spiked at the end of the eighth century, but many of these were new small satellite sites that were expressing heightened local status and degrees of authority. Some sites registered a great degree of autonomy from the *k'uhul ajaw* and were ruled only by *sajals*. The situation in areas of extreme competition between larger centers may have allowed minor centers to negotiate for greater autonomy. Numerous smaller centers arose in the zone of conflict between Piedras Negras and Yaxchilan, some of which were fortified and were located in strategic positions (Golden and Scherer 2006; Golden et al. 2008). Similarly, in Belize, the rise of petty kingdoms such as Minanha and Xunantunich have been interpreted as reflecting the decentralization of power of larger polities such as Caracol and Naranjo (Iannone 2005). This proliferation of little kingdoms is also reflected in the increase in the number of sites that erected monuments that celebrated the endings of *k'atun* periods; the number of such monuments peaked in AD 790 (Sharer and Traxler 2006, 504).

Challenges at the Community Level

Even at the level of local non-elite communities, an increase in autonomy can be observed. Eberl (2007, 2014) has shown that in the Petexbatun region in the early eighth century, small communities began to develop internal hierarchies among family groups and adopt symbols of militarism and social differentiation in common ceramics (Eberl 2007). Even these more autonomous small communities were often fortified in the militarized landscape of endemic warfare in the Petexbatun (O'Mansky and Dunning 2004). Indeed, recent fine-grained chronologies indicate that some communities simply chose to leave or to move to defensible locations well before the 761 fall of Dos Pilas, leaving the major sites in a less-populated region (Eberl 2007, 2014; Eberl and Monroy 2007). Conversely, at Dos Pilas the elite abandoned the site after military defeat. Some of the non-elite local population lingered for a brief period, but as a dramatically reduced, comparatively simple community without any public architecture or evidence of elites (Palka 1995).

The degree of community autonomy in the zone of Cancuen may have been even more pronounced. The local populations in surrounding communities used local and Verapaz ceramics with minimal Petén influence or polychromes and, with a few exceptions, only earthen and cobble architecture. Many aspects of material culture in most of the surrounding communities are more similar to those of the highlands, and Cancuen can be regarded as truly defining the isolated frontier of lowland Maya civilization. Significantly, the highland trade corridor registered very little lowland influence in material culture in the late eighth century, despite the fact that it was a period of intensified exchange in jade, obsidian, shell, pyrite, and other exotics that came into Cancuen from the Verapaz route (Woodfill 2010). The mechanisms for that exchange do not appear to have involved direct control from Cancuen or even the presence of leaders from there or the use of coercive force in the highlands. As discussed below, the increased autonomy of the piedmont and highland communities may have been a crucial factor in the final demise of Cancuen.

Site-Level Differentiation and Challenges

In addition to the proliferation of subroyal elites, other indications of factionalism were present at Cancuen. A possible weakening of royal authority may be indicated by the distribution of foreign ceramics there (Forné et al. 2009, 2010). The apogee of Cancuen is in part attributable to the establishment of alternative exchange routes going west along the base of the highlands to Tabasco and Veracruz. This "transversal" exchange route is clearly marked at Cancuen by the presence, in significant quantities, of western ceramics, including variants of Chablekal Fine Grey that have been sourced by neutron activation to southern Chiapas or Tabasco (Bishop et al. 2005) and even Campamento Fine Orange from Veracruz (Forné et al. 2010). In this same period of AD 760 to 800, Zaragoza obsidian from Puebla appeared at Cancuen in quantities more characteristic of Terminal Classic to Postclassic sites (Andrieu and Quiñonez 2010; Andrieu et al. 2011a). However, all of these influences are registered near the ports and/or in some complexes in the northern zone of the epicenter. Even more striking are distinct zones of highland influence such as that surrounding a highland-style ball court (discussed below). Thus, the epicenter of the site appears to be segmented in terms of influences, and this might have led to less centralized royal control.

Meanwhile, the royal palace and adjacent compounds have little to no Tabasco or Veracruz material culture and few highland materials (Forné et al. 2009). This pattern might indicate further internal differentiation and increasing division within the general Cancuen community at the same time that subroyal elite power and status was growing, as evidenced by the patterns referred to earlier. At all levels, then, the centralized authority of the *k'uhul ajaw* appears to have faced new challenges.

Another sign of internal differentiation and challenges at Cancuen can be seen in its ball courts. Extensive settlement pattern studies in Chiapas and the Petén (Montmollin 1997) have linked a high number of ball courts in a single site to internal differentiation and the increased presence of elites who were asserting their identity and competing for power within a center. Comparative studies of nearly 100 ball courts in Chiapas found a correlation between the number of ball courts in a polity and the degree political decentralization (Montmollin 1997). It is significant, then, that at Cancuen, which was not a huge center, three contemporaneous ball courts were located within 200 meters of each other in the epicenter at the end of the Classic period. The trend toward more ball courts in the Terminal Classic and Postclassic might also strengthen the indications that Cancuen experienced a "premature Terminal Classic" in the eighth century, as is also signified by its administrative palace, nobles' palaces, and fine paste ceramics (e.g., Demarest and Martínez 2010). Differences in style and even orientation in Cancuen's ball courts may also reflect divided identities at Cancuen.

Royal Responses to Waning Power

Divisions of authority are also indicated by attempts by the *k'uhul ajaw* to hold onto waning power. These changes fit into royal strategies of containment seen at other sites in crisis at the end of the eighth century (Iannone this volume). As discussed above, such concessions at Cancuen include the facts that the administrative palace served the needs of local lords and that nobles shared the stage on monuments. These may have been indicators of royal attempts to mollify increasingly threatening elites. Other mechanisms to hold onto authority might have included military coercion. However, as noted above, such actions may not have been directly taken by rulers; they may have been relegated to other nobles.

Efforts to further impress the general populace were manifested in the exterior palace at Cancuen, which had enormous three-dimensional stucco sculptures. These projected royal power without the need for literacy in written texts (Demarest 2013). The ritual water system running through the site reinforced the imagery on monuments such as Panel 3 (fig. 3.3a), which show the ruler's definition as a water lord (Alvarado 2011; Barrientos, Demarest, et al. 2006; Demarest 2013; Fernández Aguilar 2010). Such associations of Classic Maya rulers with water (and with blood and other liquids) have been noted generally (Lucero 2006), but at Cancuen may have specifically linked the king with his power over the river. Claims of royal control over the river, ports, and the head of navigation may have been the goal of that symbolism. As an aside, note the remarkably parallel association of rivers with the corporal essence of both ancient and modern divine African rulers (Iannone this volume; Taylor 2010). As in Rwanda, such associations also placed much responsibility on the holy king. Nonetheless, at Cancuen in even the most explicit presentations of a water lord, such as Panel 3, the scene is shared with named and titled nobles and the direct presence at ports was that of nobles' palaces.

The most obvious attempt to consolidate weakening state power was Cancuen's northern ball court (Torres 2011). There, close relations with piedmont and highland neighbors were clearly being solicited. The northern ball court is unlike any yet found in the Maya lowlands. It is a 24-meter-long sprawling highland-style court (figure 7.5). Between its low mounds the playing alley was defined by sloping unworked stone slabs like those found in ball courts in the highland Verapaz and Quiche regions, which were the source zones of many of Cancuen's imports, including jade. Surrounding the ball court were massive middens that included pieces of serving vessels in local piedmont styles. It appears to have been a true feasting ball court like those found in the highlands and southern periphery (Fox 1996; Torres 2011). The most probable interpretation is that Cancuen's late-eighth-century rulers were hosting highland caciques and elites as part of a

Figure 7.5. Purely highland-style feasting ball court at Cancuen. Illustration by Luis F. Luin.

ritualized exchange relationship, even though in the highlands themselves lowland influence was no longer registered at sites or cave shrines in the Late Classic period.

Thus, Cancuen's access to highland resources and jade, which is so clearly manifested in its material culture, depended not on coercion or physical presence but on consensual and ritualized mechanisms. These were elaborate steps on the part of the state to maintain access to the piedmont and highland Verapaz Valley trade route.

The Sequence of Collapse in the West

The collapse of Maya kingdoms began earliest in the west, in the Middle Pasión River Valley, between AD 695 and 760. This process appears to have begun prior to major drought, deforestation, or the other factors that are often proposed as causes of the end of Classic period society. In the west, as throughout the southern lowlands, the kingdoms were destabilized by problems created by the very success of Classic Maya civilization and the growth of its ritual/religious/political state structure. That political system generated and reinforced power with massive ceremonies in the architectural theaters in which elites performed in beautiful and semiotically loaded costumes and props for these Negara-like spectacles (Geertz 1980). However, the very successes of the system led to tremendous pressures because of the proliferation of elites through polygamy, alliance, and bureaucratic involution, leading to greater demands on all aspects of the western exotics and commodities exchange systems.

Meanwhile, population growth, ecological stress, drought, and all of the various manifestations of proximate (final, immediate) causes of collapse, decline, or transformation developed in other forms in different regions. In any of these cases of regional or subregional crises, counterproductive strategies of containment such as those described above only added to the costs of maintaining states. Furthermore, such strategies of legitimation at Cancuen and elsewhere only increased further the linkage between the ruler and the increasingly difficult state of affairs—economic, ecological, political, and ideological—in the kingdom.

Specifically, the splendor and royal legitimacy of western cities such as Cancuen, Dos Pilas, Waka', Piedras Negras, Altar de Sacrificios, Yaxchilan, and Ceibal, was due in large part to their strategic positions on the great western routes of exchange and transport of precious exotics (jade, pyrite, Pacific shell, quetzal feathers, etc.) and commodities such obsidian and (surely) cacao, cotton, and salt (e.g., Demarest et al. 2014). As elite populations, centers, palaces, hegemonies, titles, and patronage increased in the Petén, warfare on the exchange route intensified, in part driven by the increasing demands for the goods imported on that route, which were needed for greater legitimation efforts, patronage, and status rivalry.

In the Petexbatun and Middle Pasión, the frequency and intensity of conflicts increased, culminating in the abandonment of some landscapes and crowding into fortified or defensible centers in others. Sixty years of intensive archaeology and ceramic studies that span from Gordon Willey's work in the 1950s through the Petexbatun project of the 1980s and 1990s to Markus Eberl's ceramic microchronology in the 2010s (e.g., Sabloff 1975; Foias and Bishop 1997; Eberl and Monroy 2007; Eberl 2014) have provided specific information about the history of this process. In the period AD 700 to 750, some Petexbatun village populations began to move into defensible locations or simply left the region. By the mid-eighth century, the settlement strategy in many western regions had been reduced to a single variable: defensibility (O'Mansky and Dunning 2004). The exchange system broke under the strain of its success and the increasing demand for exotics and the value of the route that supplied them. Sites were fortified (even villages) and centers were destroyed. Some centers such as Dos Pilas were abandoned or were left with scattered populations at 5 to 10 percent of previous levels (Palka 1995). Like dominoes falling, other centers in the greater Pasión Valley were destroyed or abandoned. In the end only a few sites remained, such as Seibal, Punta de Chimino, and Altar de Sacrificios, which were Terminal Classic highly defensible enclaves that represented a very different variant of lowland Classic Maya culture (e.g., Demarest 2004b, 2006; Tourtellot and Gonzalez 2004).

There was remarkably little ritual associated with the dramatic collapse of some Middle Pasión states. They score very high on two of the three variables emphasized in this volume—violence and collapse—but not so high on ritual. At Dos Pilas, there was were some resetting of monuments at the very end and a pit with a dozen decapitated skulls of adult males, undoubtedly warriors, adjacent to the breached defensive walls (Johnson et al. 1989). This deposit seems to be captive sacrifice. More significant termination rituals were found at the rapidly abandoned site of Aguateca (Inomata 2008c; Inomata this volume). However, at Cancuen, excavations recovered far more ritual activity associated with its abrupt ending. During the period of the Petexbatun and Middle Pasión collapse, the kingdom of Cancuen to the south (located at the head of navigation of the upper Pasión River) boomed, creating detours around the crisis zones to the north and access to three separate and important western routes (see figures 7.1 and 7.2d): 1) the river trade route on the Pasión to Tres Islas and El Raudal and then via Machaquila to the central Petén and east; 2) access to the Verapaz valley route through the highlands to the jade sources in the Quiche, past the sources of quetzal feathers and pyrite, and then south to the source of obsidian at El Chayal, then on to Kaminaljuyu and the Pacific Coast; and 3) the east-west transversal route that runs along the sharply defined base of the southern highlands into Chiapas and then northwest, keeping along the base of the hill ranges toward Tabasco, Veracruz, and beyond (Demarest et al. 2009, 2014; Forné et al. 2010). From its strategic position at the head of navigation of the Pasión, Cancuen could monitor or even control the movement of exotics such as jade, quetzal feathers, and pyrite and transversal commodities such as salt, cacao, and cotton. In addition to the importance of these routes and the changing economic and political patterns they point to, this exchange system also identifies some possible suspects for the royal mass assassination and the elaborate site termination ritual that ended Cancuen.

The Violent Termination at Cancuen

The most dramatic evidence of the Cancuen termination ritual comes from excavation of the southern palace cistern of the site (figure 7.6). A beautiful plaster-lined red-painted cistern of eight meters by ten meters and over two meters deep was located at the entrance of the royal palace. Fed by the ritual water system of the epicenter (e.g., Barrientos, Demarest, et al. 2006) and by a subterranean spring, it would have been a highly sacred location. Stone steps lead into it, and it might have functioned for ablutions prior to ascending the great staircase and passing the audience chambers to enter the royal palace itself. Excavations of the cistern in 2004 to 2005 recovered an enormous skeletal sample, over 600 bones that had been deposited there at the time of the ritual destruction of the site in about AD 800 (a date confirmed by the artifactual microchronology of Cancuen, texts, ceramic cross-dating, the palace architecture sequence, etc.).

The renowned team of the Forensic Anthropology Foundation of Guatemala (FAFG) conducted the field excavations and analysis of the system. The team normally works for the World Court and the Guatemalan Truth

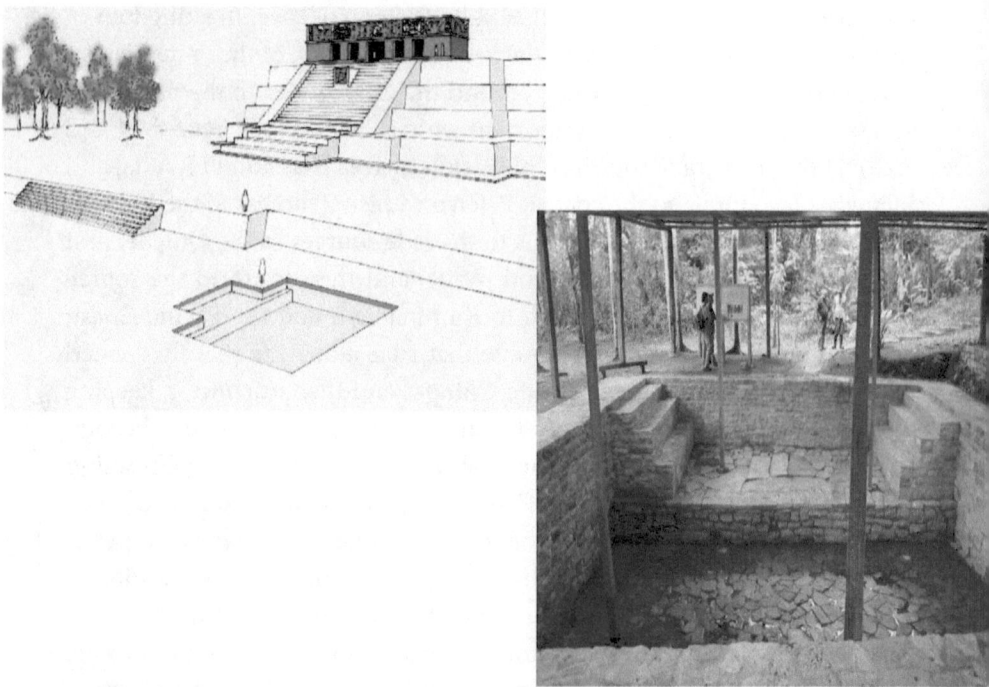

Figure 7.6. Southern cistern in front of the entrance to the royal palace, scene of the mass sacrifice. Illustration by Luis F. Luin.

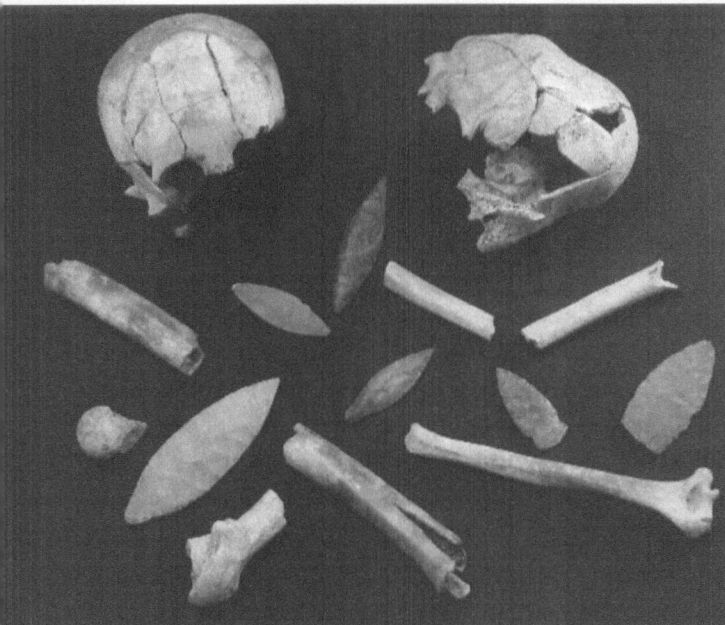
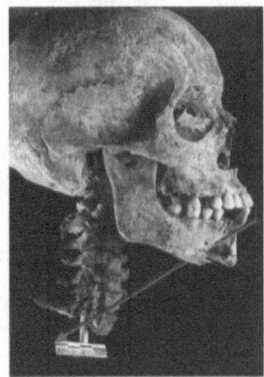

Figure 7.7. Some of the palace cistern deposits and one example of a perimortem wound from the large-scale sacrifice of nobles.

Commission in the difficult study and forensic analysis of war crimes and modern massacres. For a year, it studied this singular termination ritual at Cancuen, in their terms "an ancient war crime." The forensic team did an osteological study of the sacred cistern at the southern palace and its thirty-one skeletons (identified as the minimal number of individuals); other Cancuen subprojects also did complete artifactual studies and osteological and isotope studies continue (e.g. Quintanilla 2013; Winburn et al. 2014) (figure 7.7).

Some conclusions of the FAFG team were clear, consistent, and specific and provide clear evidence about this singular event (Suasnavar et al. 2007; Quintanilla 2013; Quintanilla and Demarest 2013). The individuals in the pool were in good health; they had strong, well-preserved bones and exhibited little pathology. Their elite status was marked by fine artifacts (most were probably elements of dress and adornment), by the most sacred location of their watery interment, and by aspects of their physical remains. Analyses of many more conventional burials (110 of 118 studied to date [Quintanilla 2013]) in Cancuen have identified the presence of paraphernalia made of shell and conch and finely made obsidian and chert artifacts as indicators of elite status (e.g., Andrieu and Quiñonez 2010; Andrieu et al. 2011a, 2011b; Quintanilla 2013). Furthermore, the individuals deposited here had various forms of dental alteration and decoration and cranial deformation consistent with a more elite status (Whittington and Reed 1997; Harrison-Buck et al. 2007; Tiesler and Romano 2008, 24; Quintanilla 2013). At Cancuen, the ceramics, artifacts, and architecture, all indicate a multiregional population, and preliminary results and isotopic analyses (Winburn et al. 2014) of the victims in the cistern confirm that they were members of the politically and economically dominant Central Petén elites, as the associated artifacts suggest.

The range of individuals was that of a living population, not one with the age profile of natural deaths. Context indicated the deposition of all of the bodies at the same time. Individuals included adults of both sexes, adolescents, children, infants, and remains in a good state of preservation of two fetuses. One FAFG study sampled bones from superior and inferior extremities, ribs, and vertebrae from the southern cistern that bore evidence consistent with blunt-force trauma and sharp trauma, such as stabbing, slashing, and puncturing (e.g., Suasnavar et al. 2007; Quintanilla and Demarest 2013). Of course, the cause of death could not be precisely specified for much of the sample studied if osteological evidence was not present (wounds are usually made to soft tissue). It is clear, however, that for much of the studied sample, the cause of death does not appear to be natural or illness and that some bones had clear evidence of perimortem trauma that was apparently inflicted by different types of weapons (e.g., Quintanilla 2013; Suasnavar et al. 2007). Bone trauma and scars on osteological samples were generally consistent with modern evidence the FAFG has recovered worldwide of execution with bayonets, clubs, or machetes (Suasnavar et al. 2007). In the pre-Hispanic period, this would have indicated wounds by spears, clubs, and axes; this is supported by the artifacts present. One individual was decapitated.

Note that the evidence is not that of an execution of adult male warriors, as at Dos Pilas and other contemporary sites (e.g., Wright 1990). Instead, it is a cross-section of the population; eight were identified as male, six as female, eleven as undetermined adults, and six as subadults. Given the presence of the two fetuses, it is probable that two of the women were pregnant.

Where the killing of these individuals took place is uncertain: at the cistern? in the adjacent palace? at various points in the site from which their remains might have been carried? Around the east port of the epicenter's peninsula, about 300 meters north, was a probable battle scene; two adult male skeletons were left unburied there, adjacent to a defensive wall around the east port and the subroyal elite palace group there (e.g., Alvarado et al. 2006; Berryman and Novotny 2004). Deposits of skeletal material and artifacts were discovered in the east port and of over twenty individuals in another ritual cistern that lies between that east port and the royal palace.

In addition to ceramics and context, the date of the event at AD 800 can be estimated by the last monument dates at Cancuen and by other contemporary textual references to the site. One inscription on a shell dated to AD 810 in a private collection refers to the last king, Kan Maax, but in a reference to the historical past. Recovered ceramic offerings can be securely placed in AD 790–800, in the Late Chaman phase.

One remarkable factor in this mass assassination of Cancuen nobility was that their precious elements of costume were interred in the sacred waters with them. Objects recovered in the southern cistern may have been personal adornments rather than deposited offerings, except for a capping sample of broken vessels that included polychromes—a probable termination deposit. The objects in the cistern included carved artifacts of jade, mother of pearl, and (especially) shell. Similarly, the shallow burial of the king and probable queen also held precious grave goods (see below). Strange as it seems to western thinking, it might have been a respectful, highly ceremonial, mass killing: a religious termination of the dynasty. Nonetheless, it was a *thorough* termination in terms of people, monuments, and architecture. Consistent with the demise of divine kingship discussed throughout this volume, this event was a religious and political act, not merely a war massacre. Again, the nature of the deposits contrasts with evidence of captive sacrifice or massacres elsewhere (e.g., the deposits at Colha [Mock 1998b; Buttles and Valdez this volume] and Dos Pilas [Wright 1990]).

Nearby, in the royal palace, in an entrance buried by massive earth and rubble fill (possibly a termination deposit), the last ruler, Kan Maax, and his consort apparently were also victims of the mass assassination of royals and nobles. They were hastily buried under only sixty centimeters of earth and without a tomb or even a haphazard cist (Barrientos, Arriaza, et al. 2006, Quintanilla 2013). The context and date indicates that the rulers were assassinated, although poor bone preservation in this context (unlike the context of the mud-filled cistern) made clear forensic confirmation impossible. Despite their apparent assassination and rapid burial in this mud fill, the royal pair also were laid to rest with great respect. Both burials were accompanied by fine imported vessels. The ruler had an engraved mother-of-pearl necklace that identified him as "*Kan Maax*, Holy Lord of Cancuen, Holy Lord of Machaquila" (Barrientos, Arriaza, et al. 2006). His elaborate headdress of cloth, feathers, and shell was stained into the mud above and at the sides of the skeleton, running from his head down to his lower legs. In the headdress, mother-of-pearl and carved coral fishes and water lilies matched the aquatic-themed headdresses shown in the carved monuments and stucco sculptures of the Cancuen rulers.

Again, the contradiction to modern sensibilities is striking: a mass assassination, but with respect and awe given the dead. In that paradox we believe lies some of the evidence concerning the perpetrators of the assassination.

The palace evidence could be consistent with the architectural termination rituals described throughout this volume (see Iannone 2005; Schwake and Iannone this volume). At Cancuen, deposits in the two palace entrances were so thick and massive that they buried parts of entire entrance structures. We had previously suggested an alternative hypothesis that it might have been the beginning of a new stage of reconstruction of the palace (e.g., Barrientos 2014). In the light of subsequent comparative study, these are more likely to have been termination ritual deposits sealing the structures most associated with the ruler, as described at other sites in the chapters in this volume. The rubble and dirt covered both major entrances to the palace, the spectacular monumental royal entrance in the southwest, and the more accessible open entrance to the palace in the east. The major royal entrance in the west, Structure L7-9, was covered with many tons of earth, clay, and loose rock, sealing and entombing the entrance under several meters of deposits. Its doorways over three meters high and its entire wide and high monumental stairway entrance were buried. A similar massive deposit of clay and rubble buried the eastern entrance structure, L7-27. It was in the fill over this second entrance that we found the shallow burials of the last king and his probable consort.

At the royal ball court specifically dedicated to the last two kings, Taj Chan Ahk and Kan Maax, there was more evidence of termination similar to those of the crises of legitimation at other sites. There, four monuments, three altars, and one finely carved panel were carefully defaced to remove just the faces of the rulers a *yajaw*, a *sajal*, and an *ajk'uhuun*. Similarly, the site's stelae were carefully defaced. This treatment is diagnostic of termination ritual treatment of monuments throughout the lowlands (e.g., Harrison-Buck this volume).

Elsewhere at the site, all evidence points to a rapid termination. There were defensive walls and unfinished defensive walls in and around the palace and around the east port. These were identical to the many kilometers of such walls that have been intensively investigated for two decades at the sites of the Petexbatun region (e.g., Inomata 1997, 2008c; O'Mansky and Dunning 2004; Demarest 2004a, 2006). The unburied male skeletons near one of these walls, the great cistern deposits, the probable termination rituals at the palace and elsewhere in the site, and, above all, the placement of decaying bodies in water sources all suggest a rapid end and a rapid abandonment. There was no occupation at this site after the Late Chaman phase (AD 790–800), so it was not conquered and absorbed into a new kingdom. It was ritually terminated and abandoned. The only subsequent occupation in the epicenter peninsula of Cancuen consists of one Terminal Classic residence and a few handfuls of scattered Postclassic sherds (not unlike Minanha; see Schwake and Iannone this volume). In the greater site area, no Postclassic material has been found to date.

Discussion and Speculations: Causes and Culprits?

Many questions surround the extraordinary events that took place at Cancuen. Above all, why was it terminated and why was it not reoccupied? Why were the nobles and rulers assassinated and yet treated with such respect and ritual and interred with precious artifacts? And who carried out those actions and why? These are questions that move us into the realm of speculation and alternative hypotheses.

It is not surprising that Cancuen was a target for military conquest. Its strategic location at the interface between highland and lowland transport routes and at the head of navigation of the great Pasión-Usumacinta exchange route through the lowlands and the "royal road" route to Calakmul and the north was highly desirable (Canuto and Barrientos Q. 2013; Freidel et al. 2007). Cancuen would thus have been a target for conquest and acquisition, not for destruction and abandonment. Furthermore, rival lowland kingdoms, such as the suspect Machaquila, would have celebrated the conquest of a center such as Cancuen in their many stelae that have been dated to the following forty years (AD 800–840). Yet none report such a conquest there, or at Seibal, or anywhere. Thus, suspicions turn to the highland and piedmont communities that surrounded Cancuen, lined its trade routes, and constituted its closest trading partners.

While the end of Cancuen remains an enigma for further investigation, the answers to its particular legitimation crisis and mysterious end surely relate to its role as an international exchange center. By AD 800, Cancuen had undergone many transformations. These included intense exchange with distant regions to the west from which ceramics, including Chablekal Fine Grey and Campamento Fine Orange, were imported from Tabasco and Veracruz and Zaragoza obsidian was imported from Puebla. Meanwhile, the control of Machaquila opened up routes to the north and east while avoiding the maelstrom of warfare in the Middle Pasión region (Demarest 2004b; O'Mansky and Dunning 2004).

Most significantly, exchange with the highlands to the south was critical to the florescence of Cancuen in the late eighth century. From that region (or through its valleys) came the jade, shell, quetzal plumage, pyrite, and other materials that were critical to the tribute, ritual, and patronage networks of the lowlands (e.g., McAnany 2013) and central to the role of Cancuen as a nexus of their exchange. Furthermore, more recent evidence indicates intensive trade with the adjacent highlands in commodities, including quantities of obsidian that were unprecedented in the lowlands and, in all probability, cacao, cotton, annatto, and vanilla from the transversal ten to fifteen kilometers south, an area identified by recent studies as a major zone of production of cacao, cotton, and condiments in the Contact and Colonial periods (e.g., Caso and Aliphat Fernández 2006, 2012; Akkeren 2012). Cancuen's connections to the highlands are emphasized by its highland-style ball court and other features in the center of the site. It would appear that Cancuen's rulers and elites were providing feasting rituals for their highland neighbors and trading partners at this ball court. Additional evidence of these ties is found in highland ceramics near the ball court and even in royal burials. The burial of even the probable consort of the last ruler had highland ceramics, hinting of a possible marriage alliance (Barrientos, Arriaza, et al. 2006).

The nature of Cancuen's "ideological solicitation" of highlanders through many ritual devices (Demarest 2013) contrasts sharply with the situation in the highlands themselves. Despite the evidence at Cancuen of massive exchange of both exotics and commodities in the Late Classic, the period of that center's apogee, Petén influence of any kind is virtually absent from the Alta Verapaz highland trade routes in this period. Both the areas that were the sources of precious ritual goods and the valleys along which they were transported lack lowland imports. The material culture of Verapaz, in all respects, from ceramics to architecture, is distinctly highland in nature. Thus, after the seventh century founding of Cancuen, there seems to have been a radical reassertion of identity by the highland and piedmont neighbors, who not only controlled the trade routes but were also the population surrounding Cancuen and probably served as its agricultural support and labor.

Thus, the situation of Cancuen might be broadly similar to that posited in Rathje's (1971, 1973) hypotheses regarding the relations of the highland and periphery with the lowlands, but in this case at a subregional level and with both sacred highland goods (see Blanton and Feinman 1984) and transversal commodities. In the Late Classic, as Cancuen reached the height of its splendor and its international role in exchange, the adjacent piedmont and highlands may have asserted their autonomy. The "periphery" became independent, if not controlling, as in Rathje's model. The sites and assemblages of the Verapaz reflect this reinforcement of independence and identity. Meanwhile, Cancuen was even more invested in mechanisms of creation and support of alliance with the highlands. For highland exchange relations it seems to have relied heavily, perhaps almost exclusively, on the ideological mechanisms of legitimation found in its architecture, monuments, and artifacts (Demarest 2013).

In the late eighth century, the many factors that weakened the *k'uhul ajaw* may have led highland populations to lose faith in the Cancuen divine kingship. Even during its apogee, Cancuen confronted such challenges. Together, highland autonomy and the internal division of power would have weakened the position of the Cancuen rulers. As at many of the other sites described in this volume, the stage was set for a legitimation crisis (Iannone this volume). Meanwhile, downriver in the middle Pasión, the route to Cancuen was torn by endemic warfare and collapse, striking numerous centers and smaller communities. Furthermore, Cancuen may have overextended its network of relations, which included ties to the more vigorous economies of Tabasco and Veracruz. Like later Terminal Classic polities in the northern lowlands, those zones had more well-developed interregional exchange systems that included the long-distance movement of commodities such as cotton, textiles, cacao, and salt. In contrast, the Cancuen region relied entirely on the adjacent highlands and piedmont for such products.

By the end of the eight century, Cancuen's reliance on ritual mechanisms for power may not have been enough. Indeed, maintaining the expense of such legitimation may have become increasingly difficult. As economic and military crises spread through the lowlands, the wealth from exchange that had funded such monumental display and the feting of highland elites at Cancuen may have been greatly reduced. Perhaps the highland neighbors, once awed by Cancuen's majesty, began to lose faith in the *k'uhul ajaws* of that revered center. The center may have even come to be regarded as parasitic because of its need for external subsistence support and massive labor for its construction projects. All of these factors might have led to its ritualized destruction.

But the question remains as to why the termination of Cancuen was so respectful. Why were the ruler and elites interred after assassination with rich costumes and grave goods? Several answers are possible. One is that regardless of disappointment or conflicts, the rulers and nobles of Cancuen might still have been regarded as holy lords and the kings perhaps as divine or semi-divine. Thus, in death they served as holy ritual scapegoats (Iannone this volume; Taylor 2010; Taylor this volume). This may be why the aspects of the built environment most associated with the divine king were the targets for ritual termination: palace entrances, audience structures, and sculpted monuments that displayed the royal personage. Yet even in death the holy lords would need to be respected and propitiated.

An additional reason for the elaborate termination might be that the highland caciques and lowland nobles and kings may have been allied via marriage and thus were relatives. The presence of highland residents at Cancuen was notable in many aspects of material culture and burials. Thus, these two worlds of the Classic Maya in the southwest, the highlands and the lowlands, may have had close ritual and kinship ties that were honored even in the destruction of the site.

Despite such connections, however, the end came to Cancuen rather abruptly. A defensive wall was left half-finished. Adult male bodies were left on the causeway entering the site. The deposition of probable nobles in the sacred cisterns and elsewhere, however respectful and religious it would have been, would have left the site polluted and uninhabitable. However, chert points were recovered amid the bodies of the slain nobles made from chert exogenous to the site yet still from the general region (Andrieu and Quiñonez 2010), again casting suspicion on Cancuen's highland and transversal piedmont neighbors.

Thus, the close allies and neighbors of Cancuen may have brought the center to its end. All activity ceased at its bustling ports, busy palace, and three ball courts. The sweeping processes of the ending of Classic Maya civilization that were beginning or under way elsewhere may have brought this kingdom and its divine dynasty to an early and dramatic end.

8

Social-Political Manifestations of the Terminal Classic

Colha, Northern Belize, as a Case Study

PALMA J. BUTTLES AND FRED VALDEZ JR.

During the Terminal Classic of the Maya lowlands, numerous centers experienced turbulent times, and many regions experienced significant population declines. The process often referred to as the "collapse" or demise of Classic Maya civilization has long been a subject of intense study and interest. Over the course of their history, the prehistoric Maya of northern Belize experienced and adapted to various disruptions that included growing populations, deforestation, droughts, and political shifts. The focus of this chapter is the interpretation of a decapitation and flaying event at the site of Colha, situated in northern Belize, around AD 800 (Mock 1998b; Buttles and Valdez 2007). The destructive and violent nature of the final events of the Classic period at Colha may reflect the removal of a ruling power the populace of the site deemed ineffectual (see Iannone et al. this volume). The Terminal Classic actions undertaken at Colha have implications for neighboring and distant regions, which are herein given some consideration.

The often-reviewed "causes" of the Classic Maya collapse include internal and external factors, and these are then divided into natural, economic, or sociopolitical elements (see Adams 1973a; Sabloff 1973). Gill (2000) found a direct correlation between northern European climatic fluctuations and rainfall on the Yucatan Peninsula. Both Gill's work and recent data suggest that the Terminal Classic period was characterized by a series of droughts that would not have been particularly devastating as individual occurrences (Valdez and Scarborough 2014). When a system has taxed resources and population is high, minor droughts occurring yearly or at close intervals add tremendous stress, encourage disease, and possibly spark dissension.

Many of these aspects of the Terminal Classic are discussed in detail elsewhere (see Iannone this volume). We begin with the premise that a concatenation of elements were at work in the Maya Classic decline. The result is archaeological expressions or manifestations of the troubled period in different geographic areas that occurred at varying rates and can be defined in multiple ways. The role of leadership clearly comes into play in many instances, especially in difficult times, as both Iannone and Taylor discuss in this volume.

Iannone (this volume) has proposed that during prosperous times, kings can take great advantage of a society's positive growth to increase their popularity. When these positive times turn negative, however, it is often the ruler(s) who carry the blame for the difficult circumstances. When difficult times arrive, the king/queen may be viewed as having failed as an intermediary between the populace and their gods. When the rulers are viewed as failing, the doors open for direct challenge and confrontation of those rulers.

Broader considerations related to these concerns and actions apply to many complex societies. Taylor has provided an analysis that compares Maya rulers and Rwandan kings. It seems that the longevity and depth of power of Rwandan kings was tied to ritual activity and the delivering of positive outcomes. Any difficulty, whether natural or political, could be interpreted as the king losing favor with the supernatural and could cost the king his life. Just as kings could order the death of subjects, so too could the king be removed if he was perceived to have lost his connection with the supernatural forces that had the power to bring prosperity to the kingdom. "Both Maya and early Rwandans appeared to have had a great deal of psycho-social ambivalence toward their sacred kings, as awe could quickly turn into hate in the event of political or ecological catastrophe," Taylor notes (personal communication, 2013).

Terminal Classic northern Belize, the focus of this chapter, is a broad region where a large population was supported for significant periods, agriculture was manipulated both extensively and intensively, and many Maya societies were likely pushed in to produce more goods. Each of these aspects can make any society vulnerable (Me-Bar and Valdez 2004).

Colha is one of the most important Terminal Classic sites that demonstrates both the stresses and the turmoil of the period. Valdez and

Scarborough (2014, 261) suggest that "three tracks seem to have been followed at the end of the Classic period by ancient Maya communities. Some places were 'simply' abandoned, others faced termination/violent activities, and a few manage to survive into a new political realm."

Relevant data of the Terminal Classic period in the southern lowland region of the Maya area is briefly presented here as a general backdrop to the Colha event. We provide general points of reference from the Pasión, Petexbatun, Petén, and Río Bec areas before discussing Colha and presenting a reconstruction of the Terminal Classic as a process with similar signatures in many locations.

Pasión, Petexbatun, Petén, and Río Bec

Early archaeological research at the sites of Altar de Sacrificios and Ceibal provide some of the best information about the Terminal Classic in the Pasión area. Adams (1973a) and Sabloff (1973) both use ceramic analyses and other interpretations to postulate a hypothesis that the Pasión sites were invaded by Mexicanized Maya from the Gulf Coast (see Harrison-Buck this volume). Excavations at Altar de Sacrificios found large amounts of fired adobe from burned wattle-and-daub architecture (Adams 1973a, 143). Perishable structures were placed on top of stone-faced platforms at Altar de Sacrificios. The context indicates that these perishable structures were elite residences that were burned at the end of the Classic period. Interpretations of this site from the Late Classic to the Terminal Classis raises the question of whether the residences were burned deliberately by disgruntled residents or by external forces (Adams 1973a; Buttles and Valdez 2010).

From the available data, it seems that the Pasión area's demise was likely a result of the actions of a foreign group or groups. Some evidence also implies that the "collapse" at Altar de Sacrificios may have been a violent termination; this issue will be revisited when we discuss the Colha data.

Similarly, the Petexbatun saw its share of difficulties during the Terminal Classic period. Explanations for inter- and intrasite conflict and abandonment have been reviewed elsewhere (Demarest et al. this volume). Of particular interest here is the reporting of documented action at several sites. Inomata (this volume) notes that "evidence of termination rituals associated with settlement abandonment or military conflicts is now well demonstrated at various Maya sites. . . . Typically, large buildings including royal palaces and pyramidal temples were intentionally destroyed or burned, and in many cases numerous broken objects were deposited." Inomata further indicates that the importance of rulers as representatives of communal identities became the focus during destructive activities at the end of the Classic period and that the large-scale termination rituals that included the burning and destruction of elite residential structures were likely tied to the last ruler and his family.

The burning of "elite" structures implies the removal of the current power holders. The sacking of a center, the burning of an elite building, and the abandonment of a site seems to be a recurring pattern. At other sites further west, including Tonina, elite structures were burned before abandonment of the site in general (Ayala 1994).

Less dramatic events took place in the Petén region, specifically Tikal, during the Terminal Classic than those noted for the Pasión. It presently seems that the Petén may have declined (or collapsed) without external force. While this certainly seems to be the case for Tikal, where a delicate balance between ecological, social, and political situations must have been maintained at all times, it also seems to hold for neighboring sites (Navarro-Farr this volume). Culbert (1973, 91–92), for example, concludes that Tikal fell too early and too fast to have been the target of external incursions; instead, he postulates, it declined due to some internal mechanism. We concur that much of the Petén region, using the Tikal area as an example, most likely deteriorated as a result of internal events.

Analysis of the Terminal Classic Period from the Río Bec region is also quite informative. Architecture and ceramics there were both influenced by interactions north and south, indicating that this region was actively trading in both directions. Rovner (1975) found material indicating the burning out of inhabitants at Structure IV there, indicating that the Classic Maya of Becan met a violent end.

Evidence for violent activity is provided from both sites, although the source or reason of this action remains uncertain. At Altar de Sacrificios, the destruction of the elite-class residences may have resulted from invasion, from internal strife, as ritual, or from some combination of these. The burning of Structure IV at Becan, as in the Altar de Sacrificios case, does not provide direct evidence of either external or internal instigation.

Colha, Belize

The archaeological site of Colha is located along the old Northern Highway of northern Belize, about forty-seven miles north of Belize City (figures 1.1, 8.1). The site is estimated to be at least eight square kilometers in size, and

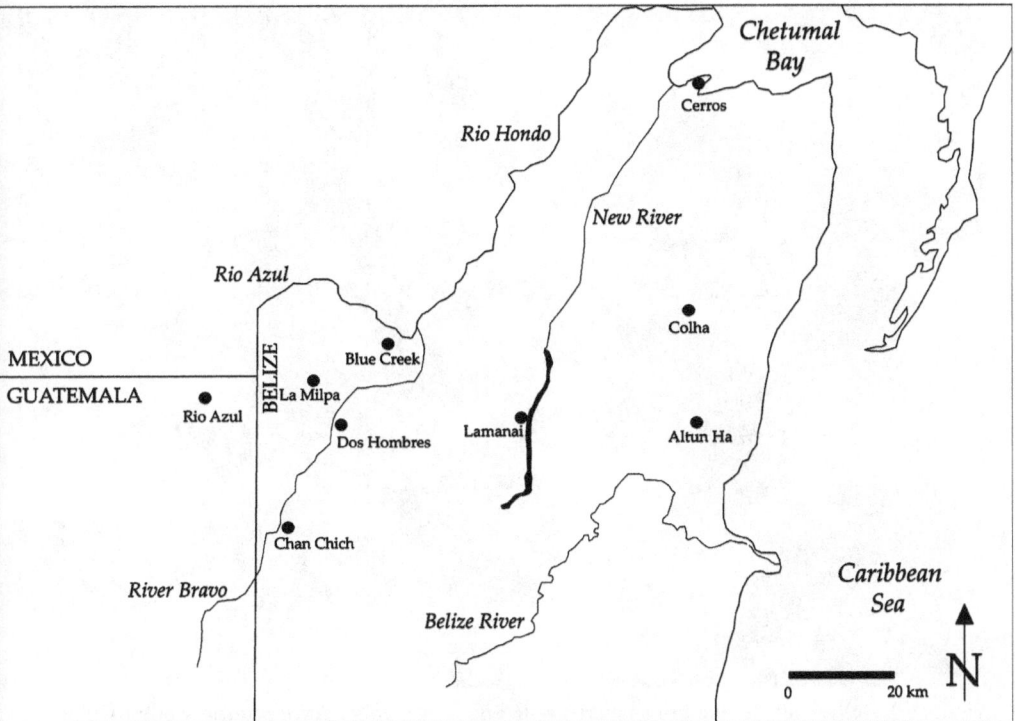

Figure 8.1. Map of northern Belize. Courtesy of the Colha Project.

the ceremonial center is located toward the northern edge of the settlement, near Cobweb Swamp.

Colha is best known for its vast deposits of chert and chert workshops that produced many different tools throughout its occupation. The site was initially settled about 1000 BC and was occupied through the Terminal Classic (ca. AD 850) before being abandoned.

By the Terminal Classic period, the dispersed population of Colha had begun to contract toward the central core area of the site. Hester (1985, 12) theorizes that the "congregated occupation of this sort might represent the desire to settle in more secure and restricted areas." During this period, the stemmed blade became the focus of lithic production in a smaller form than its earlier counterpart, suggesting that the blades may have functioned as atlatl spear tips (Masson 1989). It has been suggested that this reduction in size probably was made to meet consumer demands for implements of war (Masson 1989).

Archaeological excavations in 1980 produced an intriguing find within the main plaza of the monumental center. When a Terminal Classic (ca.

Figure 8.2. Colha skull pit and fire-shattered wall. Photo by Fred Valdez Jr., courtesy of the Colha Project.

AD 800) building that is believed to have been an elite residential structure (as represented by a long linear mound on the south side of the plaza) was partially excavated, a skull pit 80 × 110 centimeters was revealed. The pit feature was located in a corner area between the central staircase and the wall of the structure (Eaton 1980). The limestone blocks that formed a wall above the skull pit were extensively fire shattered (figure 8.2). The shattering and destruction of the wall were the result of the burning of the elite residential house. When the perishable structure, which was situated on a masonry platform, was burned, it fell in front of the wall and over the skull pit. Although the heat from the fire shattered the limestone blocks, the burned debris covered and helped preserve the skulls in the pit (figures 8.3 and 8.4).

A population of thirty individuals, including adult men and women and young children, is represented in the Colha skull pit feature. The skull pit does not seem to contain the remains of a nuclear family, as older children and teenagers (seven to eighteen years of age) are not represented in the pit. Analysis of the teeth of both children and adults identified many

Figure 8.3. Colha skull pit. Photo by Fred Valdez Jr., courtesy of the Colha Project.

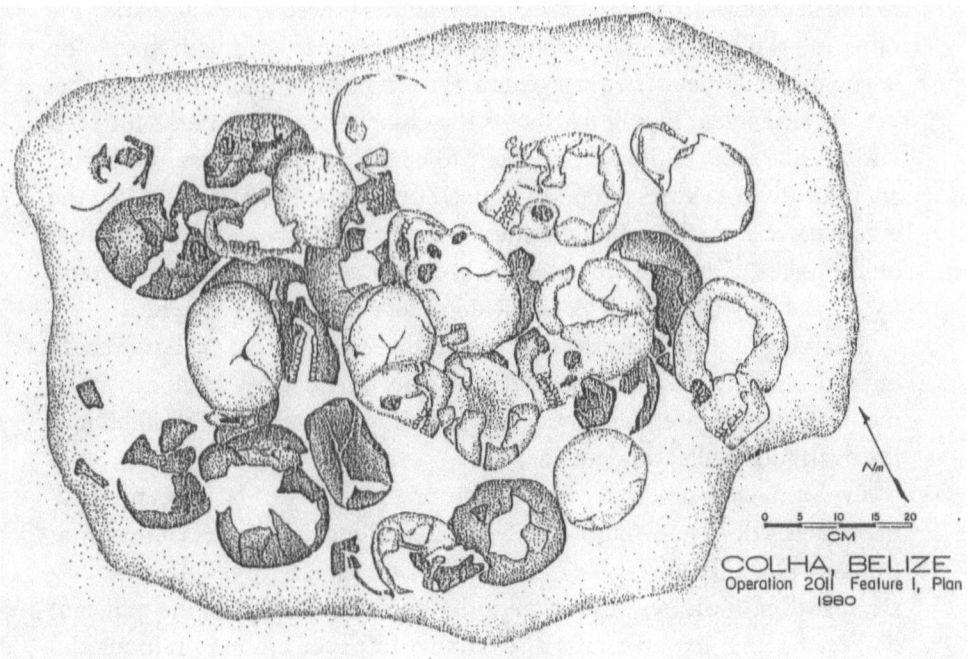

Figure 8.4. Colha skull pit illustration/drawing. Illustration by Kathy Bareiss, courtesy of the Colha Project.

pathologies, including calculus deposits, caries, antemortem tooth loss, enamel hypoplasia, alveolar abscesses, and periodontal disease (Massey 1989). The most common dental pathology noted for the adults is calculus deposits (found in nineteen of twenty adults), followed by severe caries (found in fifteen adult individuals). Seven of the adults showed markings of enamel hypoplasia, while eleven had lost teeth prior to death. The most common problem observed in the children's teeth was dental caries. Enamel hypoplasia and unusual notching of the incisors were other dental pathologies found in the children's teeth.

Infection of the bone, joint deformation, cribra orbitalia, and an unusual roughness of the palate were among the bone pathologies in the adult population. However, the only bone pathology found in the children was cribra orbitalia (Massey 1989). Culture modifications to bone and teeth were also observed in the Colha skull pit sample. Both cranial shaping (in at least eight individuals) and teeth filing (in nine adults) are present. Please note that we here have chosen to follow a recommendation from Julie and Frank Saul (personal communication 2004) and use the term cranial shaping, as it is not likely that the Maya saw this as cranial deformation.

Among the most intriguing feature of the skulls is the presence of numerous cut marks. Twenty of the thirty skulls showed clear cut marks; the other ten skulls were either too damaged or too encrusted with marl to be adequately analyzed. The average number of cut marks (per skull) in frontal view is seventeen. Figure 8.5 shows the composite of cut marks for each view. While most of the cuts are likely to be the result of flaying, some cuts are indicative of efforts to remove muscle or other soft tissue, including the eyes (cuts around the orbit) and the tongue (cut marks inside the mouth or on the palate). Unsuccessful attempts at decapitation were also observed on two of the cervical vertebrae, where deep cuts did not sever the head.

Charring of the bone was observed on three skulls. One skull was badly burned, and two are slightly charred. The burning occurred prior to interment, as all three were excavated from the lower level of the skull pit and the overlying skulls were not charred.

Even though numerous dental and bone pathologies have been noted, the analysis does not indicate widespread serious disease or malnutrition (Massey 1989). The presence of these diseases, especially enamel hypoplasia, however, indicates at least periodic nutritional stress of a significant degree. Enamel hypoplasia is also known to occur among preindustrial populations due to the stresses of weaning.

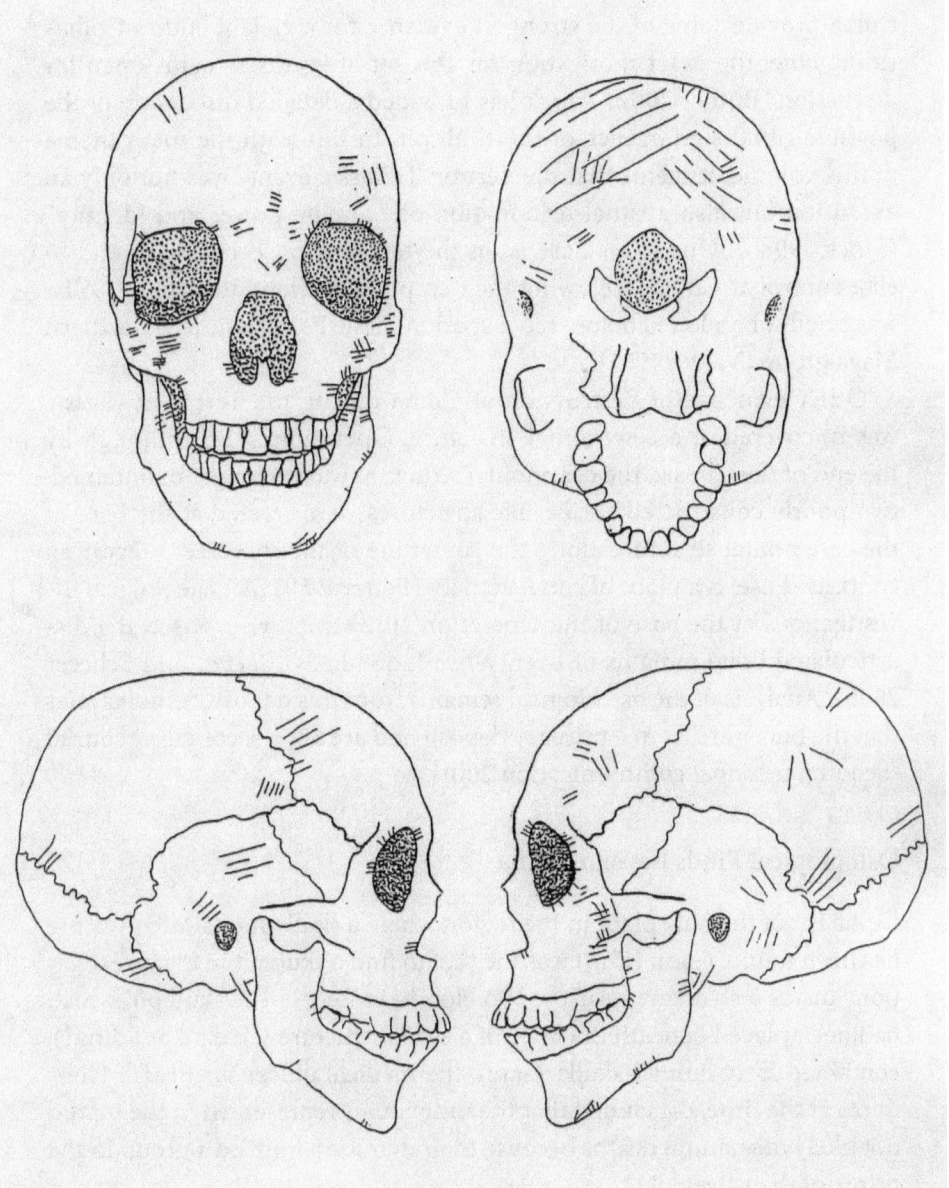

Figure 8.5. Composite of skull cut marks. After Massey 1989, Figures 9–12. Courtesy of the Colha Project.

While the pit of decapitated skulls and the burned elite structure at Colha provide some of the strongest evidence for a violent end to Colha's ruling elite, the exact motivation for this set of events remains open for discussion (Buttles 2002). Mock has provided a detailed discussion of the possible ritual significance of the skull pit. In line with the main theme of this volume, it seems that the Terminal Classic event "was not only an execution but also a ritual termination of . . . elite power and identity" (Mock 1998b). Our focus here is on the termination event as an end to elite control at Colha. Following the decapitation event, the site of Colha was briefly abandoned before reoccupation in the Postclassic by a northern Maya group (Valdez 1987).

Other evidence of destruction at Colha during the Terminal Classic was uncovered at a ceremonial structure, Operation 2012. Although by the end of the Classic, the ceremonial structure was no longer maintained, two poorly constructed shrine-like structures were erected at the base of the ceremonial structure along the centerline of the staircase, suggesting continued use as a place of ritual activity (Potter 1980). Archaeological investigations at the base of the Operation 2012 structure exposed the disarticulated bone remains of twenty-five individuals (Barrett and Scherer 2005). Analysis of the osteological remains from this deposit demonstrates that the bones are from a primary deposit and are not a secondary reburial (Scherer, personal communication 2001).

Osteological Finds beyond Colha

Colha is not the only place in the region where a skull pit or similar feature has been found. Gann (1918) was the first to find a skull pit in his investigations inside a structure near the Río Hondo in Belize. The skull pit, which had been placed beneath the floor of a stone structure (an elite building?), contained forty human skulls. Gann, the medical officer for British Honduras at the time, concluded that the individuals represented in the pit did not likely die natural deaths because their dentition implied a group in the prime of their lives.

Another find of decapitated skulls is reported by Stirling (1941) from excavations at Cerro de las Mesas, Veracruz, Mexico. Like Gann's find, the finds at the Stirling excavation resemble the decapitated skulls at Colha in several respects; the cache of skulls included cranial shaping and filed teeth.

Other Terminal Classic Data

Valdez and Mock (1991) have identified the Northern River Lagoon (NRL), a marginal area, as having been occupied during the Terminal Classic. The NRL site was occupied primarily in the Terminal Classic Period and is interpreted as having as its primary purpose (perhaps its reason for founding) activities related to salt making. The salt produced was used to prepare fish and other marine resources for transport into the interior lowlands. We believe that the NRL site was an attempt, perhaps by struggling elites, to increase food availability by exploiting marginal areas. When Classic Maya society fell apart, however, the NRL site was abandoned just as many interior sites were.

Summary and Conclusions

In this review of the Terminal Classic period, we have discussed relevant findings concerning the Classic Maya decline at selected sites. The osteological data (Massey 1989), climatic information (Gill 2000; Valdez and Scarborough 2014), and interpretation of the NRL site's function (Valdez and Mock 1991) all indicate hard times in northern Belize, and likely in the lowland area. Both the burned structure at Colha and the skull pit feature indicate a violent end to the Classic period. It is interesting, and we believe critically important, that the burned structure was an elite-associated residence; the burning of an elite structure at the end of the Classic period seems to be a common event at many sites in the central Maya lowlands. .

The skulls from the Colha feature seem to be representative of an elite group, given the cultural modifications observed on the skulls and the location of the pit in front of an elite residential structure. We base our theory that the individuals from the skull pit were a group of elites on the context of the pit and the sudden abandonment of the site and not simply on the cultural modifications to the skulls, as these are believed to have been more widespread. If the skull pit does represent an elite group, the various physical conditions evident in the osteological evidence (dental and bone disease) of that assemblage suggests that Colha's mass population was probably in even poorer physical condition. Health and disease concerns among the commoner population must have been widespread and more serious than those of the elite who, at least theoretically, would have had greater access to food, water, and medicine.

While much of the data from the Colha site could be interpreted in several ways, we propose a scenario that seems most consistent with the available information. First, there was a large Terminal Classic period population that was pushed to its limits in terms of productive ability. Second, a series of droughts likely decreased productivity, leading to crop failures and a decrease in available water and food that lead to malnutrition and disease. These seem to be evidenced in the Colha skull pit and have been reported for other sites (Saul 1973). Third, the decline in food production forced "colonies" into marginal areas in order to procure supplemental foodstuffs, as evidenced at the Northern River Lagoon site. Fourth, if the skull pit represents an elite group, as has been consistently interpreted, the general Maya population at Colha must have been in dire straits in terms of disease and hunger. These various strings of evidence, when tied together, provide a picture of a Maya civilization in which many places and situations became very difficult to tolerate. These conditions were likely severe enough to lead to an internal uprising.

The notion of an internal revolt is not new. J. E. S. Thompson (1954) suggested this, but only in popular writings, given the limited evidence available at the time. A. V. Kidder (in Smith 1950) suggested that elite demands may have sparked an internal revolt. Altschuler (1958) also saw social dissension as an issue in the Maya "collapse." He suggested that the aristocratic society of the Classic Maya might have been too weak to put down a revolution. Demarest (this volume) interestingly states that "population growth, ecological stress, and all of the various manifestations of proximate (final, immediate) causes of collapse, decline, or transformation developed in other forms in different regions." However, the possible connection of this scenario to an internal disintegration had not been recognized.

Here we contend that although different events occurred in different units or polities, we must remember, or emphasize, the probable interdependence between the various polities, particularly at the elite level, as it was the latter who likely came to be despised during times of extreme stress (as discussed in Iannone, and Taylor this volume). As Valdez and Scarborough (2014, 262) have commented, "The treatment of the individuals sacrificed, either at death or shortly afterwards, indicates serious, deliberate, and very strong abhorrence for those killed."

The various physical concerns (environmental, health, etc.) would have compounded the various social and political problems (cf. Hamblin and Pitcher 1980). Thus, the idea of an internal collapse at Colha supports

Hamblin and Pitcher's class-conflict hypothesis. They argue that "the precondition of class conflict is the existence of a well-defined structure of socioeconomic classes" (Hamblin and Pitcher 1980, 248). The existence of a class structure is supported by artifactual evidence at numerous sites in the Maya lowlands (see Culbert 1974; Chase and Chase 1992; Lohse and Valdez 2004). Evidence for class conflict can be difficult to determine archaeologically, given similar signatures from other forms of conflict (Valdez 1987). When considering all of the evidence as interpreted from the Colha research, the interpretation of an internal demise seems more probable. A class conflict model for the end of the Terminal Classic at Colha and many other sites across the lowlands should receive significant attention as part of the explanation for events ending the Classic Maya period. As Hamblin and Pitcher (1980) suggest, what seems to be a systematic mutilation of the faces of elites on Classic monumental art may be evidence of rebellion (see also Harrison-Buck this volume). It appears that elites gained in both material wealth and access to healthy nutrition throughout the Classic period. As populations increased, resources at all levels diminished, causing additional internal stresses.

The Colha data clearly fit Haviland's (1969) findings of general population degeneration, as these have been analyzed by Saul (1973). The increased wealth seen at Barton Ramie as evidenced by wide access to polychrome pottery is also a feature of the Colha settlement. It seems every humble household there had a jade bead or two and a fair amount of polychrome pottery (Buttles 2002). While the polychromes at these humble (non-elite) locations are in the form of large platters and are not the high-quality wares seen in elite contexts, it is nonetheless polychrome. However, as at most Maya sites, the Colha king or elite were failing the support population. Colha's inhabitants could no longer sustain their society and terminated their power structure. A similar interpretation, although with external antagonists, has been posited for Aguateca. Inomata (1997, 337) states that "Aguateca was finally attacked by enemies probably at the beginning of the ninth century." The elite residential area in the epicenter was burned and elites left or were taken away, leaving a large number of their possessions behind. Inomata (1997, 348) suggests that the primary target of the enemies was the elite and that they intended to terminate Aguateca as a political and economic power.

In reviewing various theories of the Classic Maya collapse, Hamblin and Pitcher (1980) indicate that there is much to consider when postulating about the causes of the termination of the Classic period kings and societies. At the least, the various types of stresses all contributed to the demise of Classic kings. There does not seem to be a single theory that can explain the termination of the Classic period. However, the various data seem to support or "favor the class conflict theory as the general explanation" (Hamblin and Pitcher 1980, 262).

This particular scenario also explains why the violent Terminal Classic activity occurs at elite structures and elite residential structures; such acts literally remove an ineffectual authority. Taylor (this volume) speculates that a similar dynamic for the Classic Maya and Rwanda may have been at work. "Resentful subjects either destroyed their kings and all that was associated with them, including the accompanying ideological and symbolic elements supporting kingship as a politico-religious system, or more respectful ones merely killed the king while attempting to treat many of the symbolic accoutrements of kingship with reverence" (Taylor, personal communication, 2013).

Not all lowlands sites saw a violent end to the Classic Period. One example is Tikal, where there presently is no evidence for a violent end to the site's population or settlement. While Tikal provides an alternate explanation for effects of Terminal Classic events, it nonetheless represents another version of an internal demise. As a counter to the destruction of a site, presently there is no evidence for this kind of violent end at Tikal. Because of the various conditions or problems that seemed to have occurred in Tikal's neighboring areas, the large center became an isolated entity. We are additionally much more in line with Culbert's (1973) analysis that the Maya decline is attributable to an internal mechanism that varied from site to site. Where external forces appear, they seem to do so after the decline had already begun; Mexicanized Maya and other opportunistic groups moved in on an already self-defeated Maya (see Harrison-Buck this volume).

At several sites, such as Dos Hombres and Chan Chich in northwestern Belize, termination deposits are found at or near elite buildings. Houk (2000; Houk this volume) and Harrison-Buck (this volume) provide fascinating data concerning the materials resulting from termination rituals. For our purposes, the destruction of ritual and/or elite items and their disposal at particular locations is perhaps telling evidence of a system rejected. These features likely reflect of what must have been tumultuous last days at each site (Houk 2011).

While several interpretations are available for the various data sets we have discussed, we contend that the larger picture seems to point to internal conflicts for the Terminal Classic Maya. Elson and Covey (2006, 9), who have reviewed the relationship between intermediate elites and power in pre-Columbian states, found that "conflict commonly occurs between members of the ruling family" and that "conflict in premodern states may be more likely to occur between elite groups that have more contact with one another than between social strata." Although internal uprisings and peasant revolts are often presented as grassroots actions, these activities are usually organized and financed by a disgruntled elite (see also Iannone this volume). Among the Classic Maya there surely existed many conflicting elite families just waiting for the seated king to stumble so they could initiate a move of destabilization, perhaps even the removal and usurping of power.

A modern case for consideration is the recent "Arab Spring," in which several nations in a particular geographic region removed and replaced their political leadership (whatever form that may have been). In some cases imprisonment occurred, while in others the killing of the former ruler was the end result, but both had the same desired effect: the removal of the power structure that had failed the society at large. In the case of the Terminal Classic Maya, we find that many centers share a common signature, at least archaeologically: an elite area is destroyed and the central power falls apart (or is removed). Maya society was always vulnerable to various threats, as are all political entities (Me-Bar and Valdez 2004). The exact nature of the vulnerability and threat to the Terminal Classic societies, or what sparked conflict and dissension, remains a topic open for discussion. We posit here a particular scenario that incorporates several lines of analysis, and that fits with the archaeological pattern observed. Some have asked why the cities were not reoccupied. One issue may be the quality of life by the end of the Terminal Classic. The criteria that must be present for a region or site to be reoccupied are varied (see Me-Bar and Valdez 2003), and in several cases, such as at Altar de Sacrificios or Colha, cities were occupied only briefly after the Terminal Classic, only to be abandoned again, this time forever.

Clearly some sites or areas were not abandoned after the Terminal Classic. These sites were located close to water. The Petén Lakes sites in Guatemala, Lamanai in Belize (Pendergast 1981), and Copan in Honduras (Webster and Gonlin 1988) are among those that continued to be occupied through the Terminal Classic and into the Postclassic. The failures of many and the success of the few make the Terminal Classic events difficult to interpret. Each kingdom had its methods of dealing with difficulties, whether that involved engaging in combat with neighbors, producing foodstuffs, or maintaining social order, among other things. All we can see today is that most failed and a few succeeded.

9

Signs of the Times

Terminal Classic Surface Deposits and the Fates of Maya Kingdoms in Northwestern Belize

BRETT A. HOUK

This chapter describes examples of Terminal Classic surface deposits from Dos Hombres, Chan Chich, and La Milpa, three medium to large Maya sites in northwestern Belize (see figure 9.1). These examples highlight the variability of abandonment and post-abandonment behavior in this corner of the Maya world at the end of the Classic period, but they do not provide direct evidence of the fates of the rulers of these sites. Rather, they fall into the implicit theme of "guilt by association" that pervades many of the case studies in this volume. In this part of the Maya world, only one king is known by name from the Late Classic period, and the iconographic record is silent—either eroded or absent—after AD 780. Furthermore, many surface deposits related to site abandonment are poorly dated, and we have only a vague notion of exactly when the Maya abandoned their major centers. However, the contexts of the deposits described here make it clear that they are related to the abandonment of Dos Hombres, Chan Chich, and La Milpa, even if we cannot anchor the exact abandonment dates in time.

The goal of this chapter is neither to support the scapegoat king model nor to refute it. Rather, the intent is to present three different data sets that are linked by time and proximity and highlight the similarities and differences among them. The nuanced distinctions among the archaeological deposits suggest that the forces responsible for their creation involved different actors and events at these sites in northwestern Belize.

Although these features share contextual and assemblage-level similarities, they resist simple classification and universal interpretation. There is

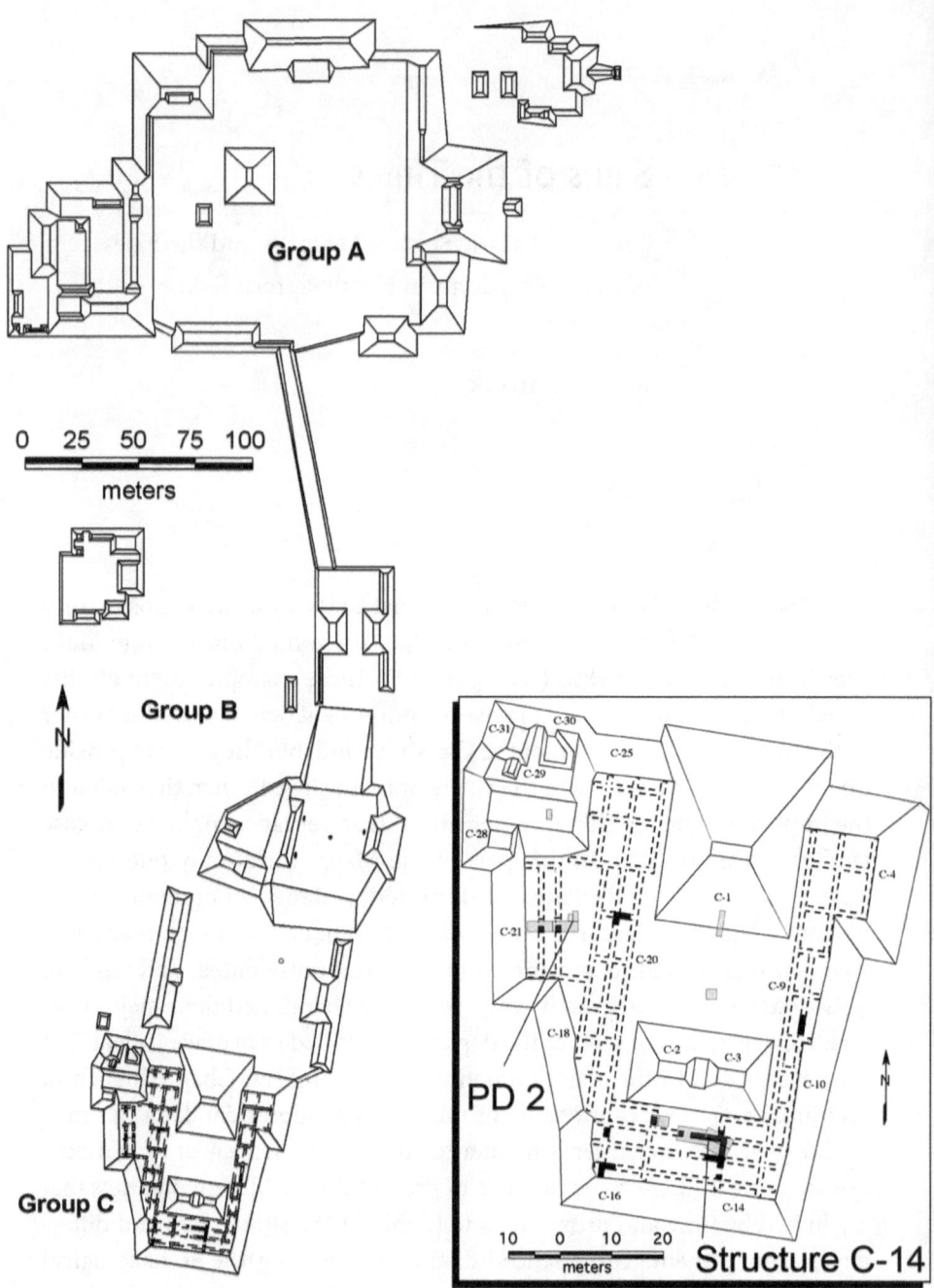

Figure 9.1. Map of Dos Hombres, with inset map of Acropolis showing locations of PD 2 and Structure C-14. After Houk 1996, Figures 1.4 and 5.36.

a much larger corpus of data from the site core of La Milpa than from the combined cores of the other two sites. As a result, it is possible to contextualize the La Milpa deposit more fully with aspects of the built environment that reflect abandonment and post-abandonment activities and behaviors.

Terminal Classic Surface Deposits

The types of features described here are examples of the class of Late to Terminal Classic (ca. AD 800–850) surface deposits that defy simple placement into common archaeological categories in terms of content and context. As a class, these deposits resemble middens with high percentages of broken ceramics, many of which do not refit, but they usually lack faunal material and they include types of artifacts commonly termed exotic or elite. They also frequently include fragments of human bone (Navarro-Farr 2009, 96; Navarro-Farr this volume). In terms of context, they are found not on the backs of structures, where middens would be expected, but on steps to palaces and temples, covering shrines, and blocking access ways to elite space (Navarro-Farr 2009, 96). Archaeologists have applied labels such as problematic or special deposit to them or have interpreted them as termination deposits. Harrison-Buck (2012a, 103) includes the Dos Hombres and Chan Chich examples in her recent study of termination deposits at nearly two dozen Lowland Maya sites. She avoids using the word ritual in her category, as in "termination ritual" or "ritual termination deposit," noting, however, that the use of "termination" and "terminal" *are* appropriate because the deposits mark the abandonment of the sites where they are found (Harrison-Buck 2012a, 115).

Methodologically, these surface deposits present several challenges. First, they are frequently encountered while investigating some completely unrelated research question. Second, because they are surface deposits, they could represent palimpsests of material, potentially the result of multiple events that spanned days or decades. Perhaps it is because of both of these issues that several decades ago these deposits were commonly chalked up to the work of squatters. A third problem is that the label applied to them in the field tends to color the description, analysis, and interpretation of them. Using the "problematic deposit" category that was popularized by the Tikal Project to classify, at least temporarily, confusing artifact deposits can avoid attaching a function or interpretation to them in the field and may lead to more critical evaluation later. As Olivia Navarro-Farr (2009, 437) has noted, "When an assemblage defies categorization first we must ask why." Such an approach is bound to lead down fruitful avenues of inquiry.

Because they resist simple classification, these deposits are at times controversial. In the late 1990s, researchers at Blue Creek excavated Special Deposit 1, a dense concentration of sherds and dark matrix on the centerline of the stairway of Structure 3 that extended into the plaza and up the slope of the mound and covered a small stairway shrine (Clayton et al. 2005; Guderjan and Hanratty this volume). The Blue Creek deposit is interesting because it highlights the difficulties that arise when trying to contextualize these Terminal Classic deposits. The project director referred to the feature as a "large-scale termination ritual" (Guderjan 2004, 239), but the excavators and ceramicists concluded that it represented a secondary deposit composed of broken vessels resulting from "long-term feasting-refuse discard behaviors" (Clayton et al. 2005, 128), what Garber et al. (1998, 130) called "transposed ritual middens." In large part this latter conclusion was based on the lack of refits in the assemblage—Clayton and colleagues (2005, 124) argued such refits would be expected in an in situ termination deposit—and the high ratio of serving vessels to storage vessels the recovered sherds represented (Clayton et al. 2005, 124, 128). Missing, however, from this redeposited midden, the original location of which has not been discovered, are faunal remains and ground stone artifacts (Clayton et al. 2005, 128).

Navarro-Farr (2009) excavated much more extensive and varied Terminal Classic deposits at Structure M13-1 at El Perú-Waka' in Guatemala. Her study makes several important contributions to the growing literature on these surface deposits. First, Navarro-Farr demonstrates a great deal of variability in these features at a single structure. Second, she concludes that instead of representing "a single destructive event on a massive scale" the M13-1 deposits represent "a more diverse set of ritual activities including interments, sacrifices, ritual terminations, dedications and votive offerings throughout the Terminal Classic" involving commoners and elites (Navarro-Farr 2009, 433). These activities took place after the structure had been abandoned but while the site was still occupied and the power of the royal court was waning.

Although the Dos Hombres and Chan Chich deposits were excavated in the 1990s, the La Milpa example was discovered more recently. Each is described below and then considered in a regional context. As witnesses to the final days of once-successful and vibrant centers, these surface deposits have much to say about the abandonment of the cities in northwestern

Belize. Because no written account of the deeds of the kings or elite who presided over the final days of the kingdoms in northwestern Belize has survived, these surface deposits are important features of the built environment and barometers of the political landscape of the region.

The Setting

Northwestern Belize is part of the Three Rivers adaptive region (Dunning et al. 1998; Garrison and Dunning 2009). The boundaries of the region include the watersheds of the Río Bravo, Booth's River, and Río Azul/Río Hondo; this covers parts of Mexico, northeastern Guatemala, and northwestern Belize and encompasses more than a dozen medium to large Maya cities, including Xultun, San Bartolo, La Honradez, and Río Azul in Guatemala, and Chan Chich, Punta de Cacao, Dos Hombres, Blue Creek, Gran Cacao, and La Milpa in Belize.

The three cities discussed here occupy different topographic settings. La Milpa, like Blue Creek to its east, is in the La Lucha uplands, west of the highest of three stair-stepped escarpments that dominate the area. Chan Chich, to the south, is in the hilly terrace lowlands of the Río Bravo. Dos Hombres, which is located approximately midway between La Milpa and Chan Chich but farther east, is on a low hill in the low-lying Río Bravo embayment, about one kilometer east of the Río Bravo Escarpment.

La Milpa is the largest of the three sites; its monumental architecture covers approximately 8.2 hectares. Chan Chich's core encompasses 6.85 hectares, and Dos Hombres' core measures 4.7 hectares. At La Milpa, there is strong evidence that the site was ruled by a dynasty of divine kings throughout the Classic period (see Hammond and Tourtellot 2004). Twenty stelae are found at the site center, and three minor centers within 3.5 kilometers of the site core also have one stela each. Although Chan Chich and Dos Hombres are smaller than La Milpa, they, too, may have been largely independent kingdoms by the end of the Late Classic, as they have most of the trappings of capital cities, such as large plazas, multiple courtyards, ball courts, multiple monumental buildings, and at least one stela (see Garrison and Dunning 2009, 532). While La Milpa is known to have had an emblem glyph during the Late Classic period, no emblem glyphs have been discovered at Chan Chich or Dos Hombres. Thus, we do not know whether the two smaller cities were independent polities headed by their own dynasties or vassal kingdoms of some larger polity.

The Dos Hombres Examples

The site core of Dos Hombres is oriented in a distinctive north-south line with a large public plaza at the north end and an elevated acropolis group at the south end. The visible form of the site plan took shape in the Late Classic period, although excavations have encountered Late Preclassic and Early Classic construction at the north end of the site. In the mid-1990s, archaeologists excavated two above-floor deposits in the Acropolis (Houk 1996); one is associated with the abandonment of that complex and the other appears to be an example of post-abandonment activities.

Excavators discovered Dos Hombres Problematic Deposit 2 (PD 2) in a test pit in a small courtyard at the entrance to the Acropolis at the site (Houk 1996). The Acropolis was built during the Late Classic and consists of a complex of small courtyards, palace-like rooms, and temples surrounding the smallest plaza at the site. Access to the Acropolis was through the northern end of Courtyard C-7, where excavators encountered PD 2 in the course of digging a test pit to establish the chronology and construction history of the Acropolis. Based on ceramic data, the entire sequence, with the exception of the deposition of PD 2, took place in the Late Classic, ca. AD 700 to 810.

The earliest construction at Courtyard C-7 was a hard-packed dirt floor surface built directly on bedrock approximately 2.75 meters below the modern ground surface. This floor surface was covered by twenty-five centimeters of dry-stone core rubble fill, which was capped by an extremely well preserved plaster floor surface twenty centimeters thick. This courtyard surface was buried as part of a ritual, during which a thin layer of marl and smashed artifacts were spread across its surface. This event, which presaged PD 2, preceded a major expansion of Courtyard C-7 that elevated its surface by approximately one meter and likely represented the height of the Dos Hombres ruling family's power. The final floor of the courtyard consisted of packed earth and marl over a thin layer of earth and cobble fill (Houk 1996, 202–209). This rather humble renovation of the entrance to the royal compound suggests that the royal family was suffering declining prosperity immediately before their ultimate demise, as described below.

During the Terminal Classic, the last episode in the occupational history of the courtyard took place. A layer of artifacts fifty centimeters thick, designated PD 2, was deposited on the floor. It contained some of the most exotic artifacts excavated at the site, including numerous partially reconstructable vessels; an eccentric biface of imported chert; a ceramic roller stamp; a figurine head with an elaborate bird headdress; a ceramic animal face; a drilled (jaguar or dog) canine tooth; an obsidian biface; pieces of turtle carapace, which could be part of a musical instrument; and an anthropomorphic whistle. Also included in the deposit were five human cranial fragments. Although most of the ceramics were utilitarian (striated or unslipped), exotic ceramics, including a Cubeta Incised sherd with hieroglyphs, Daylight Orange plate fragments, and Palmar Orange Polychrome vessel sherds, were also recovered (Houk 1996, 209–217). The total number of ceramics recovered from the estimated four-cubic-meter excavated section of the deposit exceeded 6,700 sherds (1,675 sherds/square meter). If the materials extend across the entire courtyard, then the sample represents less than 7 percent of the deposit, which could include over 100,000 sherds (Houk 1996, 211). The Terminal Classic age of the deposit is based on the presence of Daylight Orange ceramics, which are traditionally considered late arrivals in northwestern Belize and are temporally diagnostic of the Terminal Classic period, ca. AD 800–850 or so.

Though PD 2 resembles a midden in many ways, aspects of its composition and context suggest it is something else. It lacks much faunal material, it includes human skeletal material and numerous exotic wares and artifacts, and it blocks access to the entire Acropolis (Houk 2000). In many ways it resembles a ritual termination deposit, one that ended the use of the Acropolis at the site but may have been more of a secular act aimed at the ruling elite. This feature has been described as a "destructive event deposit" (Houk 2000, 144) and is very similar to what others have called "desecratory termination ritual deposits" (Pagliaro et al. 2003, 77).

PD 2 and the earlier ritual deposit briefly described above are interesting when considered together. Both deposits occupy the same horizontal space at the site but are separated vertically by two construction episodes. While that could be coincidental, the context of the two finds in the entrance to the Acropolis suggests that the relationship may be significant.

The two deposits are bookends to the glory days of the Dos Hombres ruling family and may be interpreted as examples of collective or cultural memory. The memory of the earlier ceremony, which was a reverential act and preceded a massive expansion of the Acropolis, may have lingered in the minds of the people responsible for PD 2, which was desecratory in nature because it blocked access to the Acropolis.

There are archaeological correlates at Minanha, Belize, where Schwake and Iannone (2010, 336) have documented an astonishing example of cultural memory: three caches separated by over 150 centimeters of construction and 425 to 750 years were similarly aligned in plan view. The Minanha example comes from the eastern shrine in a public plaza at the site (Schwake and Iannone 2010, 334), a location from which the community at large could have viewed the rituals associated with the placement of the caches. The Minanha caches span a period of dramatic political change at the site during which a group of outsiders replaced the local ruling elite. Schwake and Iannone (2010, 336) argue that these new rulers placed the upper two caches to tap "into the traditions and long-term social memory of the Minanha community."

In the Dos Hombres example, the group participating in the ritual associated with the expansion of the Acropolis would have been small, perhaps restricted to members and guests of the royal court. Thus, the people responsible for the desecratory PD 2 deposit in the Terminal Classic may have been from the same restricted group that shared the cultural memory of the original event. Of course the list of suspects is long (members of the royal family, nonroyal elites, retainers, visitors, etc.), but it does not include all members of the Dos Hombres community. Whereas the Minanha examples represent the use of cultural memory to create a tie to the past, the Dos Hombres example demonstrates how cultural memory can be used to create a break with the past.

The second example from Dos Hombres was also recovered in the mid-1990s. Limited excavations targeted some of the collapsed rooms in the Acropolis, focusing on Structures C-21 on the western side of Courtyard C-7 and Structure C-14 on the southern end of the Acropolis. Of interest here are the excavations in Structure C-14, which partially cleared the interior of a once-vaulted room. The floor, which still retained its original red color, was covered in a layer of dark sediment five to ten centimeters thick that had probably accumulated after the structure was abandoned and before it collapsed. Near the entrance into the room, at the base of an interior wall, excavators recovered two granite manos, a bark beater, an obsidian blade, three ceramic figurines, and several human bone fragments (Houk 1996, 217–230). Although originally interpreted as material left in the room at the time of abandonment (Houk 1996, 226), the fact that the floor in the rest of the room and other floors in the Acropolis had no artifacts on them suggests that the concentration of items near the door may be significant.

The only identifiable fragment of human bone was part of a femur, and a number of researchers have pointed out that long bones and crania were commonly removed from primary burials and included in secondary burials in ancestor shrines (McAnany 1995, 1998; Navarro-Farr 2009, 113–118,

434). Navarro-Farr (2009; this volume) encountered both human crania and long bones in several of the above-floor Terminal Classic deposits at El Perú-Waka'.

The presence of human bone is reason to believe the artifacts do not represent things left behind when the structure was abandoned. Rather, the figurines, manos, other artifacts, and human bones represent post-abandonment activities very different from the behavior responsible for the creation of PD 2 in the nearby courtyard. The Structure C-14 deposit is analogous to ones Navarro-Farr (2009) excavated at El Perú-Waka' and likely represents veneration of either the monument itself or the ruling ancestors who once resided there. The artifacts left in the room and the more extensive surface deposit in Courtyard C-7 may represent different ends of the spectrum from reverential to desecratory and were likely created at different times and by different people.

The Chan Chich Examples

The Main Plaza at Chan Chich was constructed on a broad hill at an elevation of 119 meters above sea level (Houk 2015, 190). The La Lucha Escarpment is visible approximately 3.75 kilometers to the west, rising abruptly just inside the border with Guatemala. Eighteen kilometers to the south, the Yalbac Hills divide the Río Hondo and Belize River watersheds and mark the southern limit of the Three Rivers adaptive region, according to Garrison and Dunning (2009). Chan Chich is the southernmost city in the Belizean portion of the region, and it is geographically closer to some of the major sites in the Belize River Valley and the large site of La Honradez in Guatemala than it is to La Milpa.

The site core is dominated by a 350-meter-long series of contiguous plazas and courtyards dominated by the Main Plaza and the elevated Upper Plaza acropolis. Two wide causeways enter the Main Plaza from the east and west. Smaller courtyards dot the surrounding countryside. In the western half of the site, the two largest courtyards are the Western Plaza and Norman's Temple courtyard. The former is a Plaza Plan 2 group with a large range structure that forms its southern edge. The latter is a smaller courtyard group built on the summit of a heavily modified hill and surrounded by a low wall.

During the initial season of excavations in 1997, the Chan Chich Archaeological Project (CCAP) conducted limited excavations at the Western Plaza and Norman's Temple courtyard (figure 9.2). Excavations at the base

Figure 9.2. Map of Chan Chich, showing locations of Terminal Classic surface deposits. After Houk et al. 2010, Figure 2. Courtesy of the Chan Chich Archaeological Project.

of one of the platforms facing Norman Temple's courtyard encountered a dense accumulation of artifacts on the courtyard floor. These materials included imitation Fine Orange pottery, a fragment of a thin biface, part of a figurine, and fragments from a ceramic whistle (Meadows 1998, 62–64).

Guided by this discovery, over the next three seasons the CCAP targeted excavations on the steps to range buildings in the two western groups and found similar concentrations of artifacts. The concentrations contained numerous partially reconstructable vessels, figurine fragments, shell artifacts, obsidian blades, manos, incised bone, a jaguar canine, a large fragment of a tenoned stone artifact, and scattered human skeletal material (Harrison 2000; Houk 2000, 2015). Faunal remains other than the jaguar tooth were absent. Among the partially reconstructable vessels was a fragment of a Pabellon Modeled-carved Fine Orange bowl. This find, along with the imitation Fine Orange sherd from the 1997 excavations, date these deposits to the Terminal Classic period, ca. AD 850.

Importantly, when excavating the building on the summit of Structure C-6, Harrison (2000, 79–80) observed that the highest concentration of artifacts was recovered in the collapse debris above the plaster floor outside the building. This concentration rested on less than five centimeters of fine collapse debris and included debitage, chipped-stone tools, several fragments of worked marine shell, and several partially reconstructable vessels. Because the room itself lacked artifacts on its floor and benches, Harrison (2000, 80) speculated that the material outside the room represented "the result of a later clean-up activity," which took place sometime after abandonment.

In general terms, the content of these deposits is comparable to the surface deposits at Dos Hombres, but the density and location of the features are very different. Another key difference is that excavators encountered evidence for Terminal Classic occupation of one of the structures associated with these deposits at Chan Chich. Structure C-6, which is the largest building in the Western Plaza, showed evidence of continued use and modification during the Terminal Classic, including the creation of a crude dividing wall made of vault stones robbed from elsewhere and the placement of a simple burial on the centerline of the structure beneath a bench (Harrison 2000). The burial ritual involved burning something on the bench, which discolored the plaster on the surface of the bench and on the face of a higher bench behind it. The bench was then broken through at the spot of the burning, and an adult male was placed into the hole below the bench along with a small Terminal Classic vessel and two shell disks. The body was covered with rubble fill, including the pieces of burned plaster from the broken bench, and then the hole in the bench was replastered with noticeably inferior stucco (Harrison 2000). Exactly who was using the structure at this time is unclear, but the crude wall built in the back of the central room points to a diminished capacity of the occupants to marshal the kinds of resources the elite at the site had access to during the Late Classic period.

It is not possible to refine the sequence of events any better than to say the crude wall, the burial cut into the bench, and the artifacts deposited on the steps and outside the structure all date to the Terminal Classic. The material on the steps of the structure is truly broken and scattered. While it may be hard to identify the remains of individual ceramic vessels, particularly during excavations, the tenoned stone artifact is a good example of the nature of the deposit. Once the artifact was discovered near the base of the stairs, the excavations were expanded with the goal of finding the rest of the artifact. Despite more than doubling our excavation area, the excavations failed to find any more fragments of the artifact. Either the other piece or pieces were taken from the site or it or they were scattered fairly far from the known piece.

The deposit on the steps to Structure C-6 may represent multiple events and visitations to the site, and it is even possible that the burial is related not to the occupation of the structure but to post-abandonment behavior just after the structure and site were abandoned. The artifacts outside the room, which Harrison (2000, 80) attributed to later clean-up activities, could represent another post-abandonment deposit that was created after the building had begun to collapse.

La Milpa: The Structure 104 Deposit

Although the Dos Hombres, Chan Chich, and Blue Creek surface deposits were excavated in the 1990s, nothing like them was found at La Milpa until recently. As the largest site in the eastern part of the Three Rivers region during the Late Classic, the apparent absence of Terminal Classic surface deposits in comparable contexts there was an important consideration for researchers wrestling with the nature of site abandonment across northwestern Belize during the Terminal Classic period. Both the La Milpa Archaeological Project in the 1990s, which worked in the Acropolis, and renewed investigations at the site by the Programme for Belize Archaeological Project (PfBAP), which worked in Plazas A and B, consistently found clean stairways and clean rooms with no signs of violence (see Hammond and Tourtellot 2004; Zaro and Houk 2012). All evidence suggested that La Milpa did not experience the kinds of events that led to the creation of surface deposits at other centers in the region.

However, there are multiple indications that the ruling dynasty of La Milpa began to lose power at the time its city reached its zenith in the late eighth century. The rulers of La Milpa launched a number of major construction projects, including an expansion of the Southern Acropolis—which was the home of the royal court (Hammond et al. 2000)—and a complete renovation of Structure 21, the fifth largest temple-pyramid at the site, neither of which were ever completed (Zaro and Houk 2012). These grand and resource-intensive construction projects might have been a response by the elite to worsening economic or social conditions as a way to appease the gods and restore equilibrium. At a minimum, the unfinished projects indicate rulers out of touch with the severity of the crisis in their kingdom.

Aside from these other unfinished construction projects, evidence related to the collapse of the ruling dynasty and the abandonment of the city was lacking (see Hammond and Tourtellot 2004) until recently, when the La Milpa Core Project (LMCP), operating as a component of the PfBAP, excavated an extensive surface deposit in a small courtyard attached to the northeastern corner of Plaza B (Moats et al. 2012). Contextually, this feature differs from the others in the region; it was found draped against the inside and outside of a low masonry wall that formed the eastern edge of Courtyard 100, not on the steps to a palace or shrine and not blocking access to an elite residential area (figure 9.3).

From 2009 to 2011, the LMCP excavated approximately nineteen cubic meters of the surface deposit on the inside and outside of Structure 104. In 2011, over 28,000 sherds were recovered from the deposit, for an average density of 2,080 sherds/cubic meter. In addition to ceramics, the Structure 104 deposit contained nearly 300 pieces of animal bone, a few marine and terrestrial shells, fragments of ground stone, over 150 pieces of obsidian, dozens of chipped-stone tools and tool fragments, and over two dozen whistle, ocarina, or figurine fragments (Moats et al. 2012, 44). The ceramics included fragments of a drum and nearly two dozen Fine Orange or imitation Fine Orange sherds (Sullivan 2012, Table 2).

In terms of composition and density of material, the Structure 104 deposit is comparable to PD 2 from Dos Hombres. It is unique, however, among the examples from the region (including Blue Creek Special Deposit

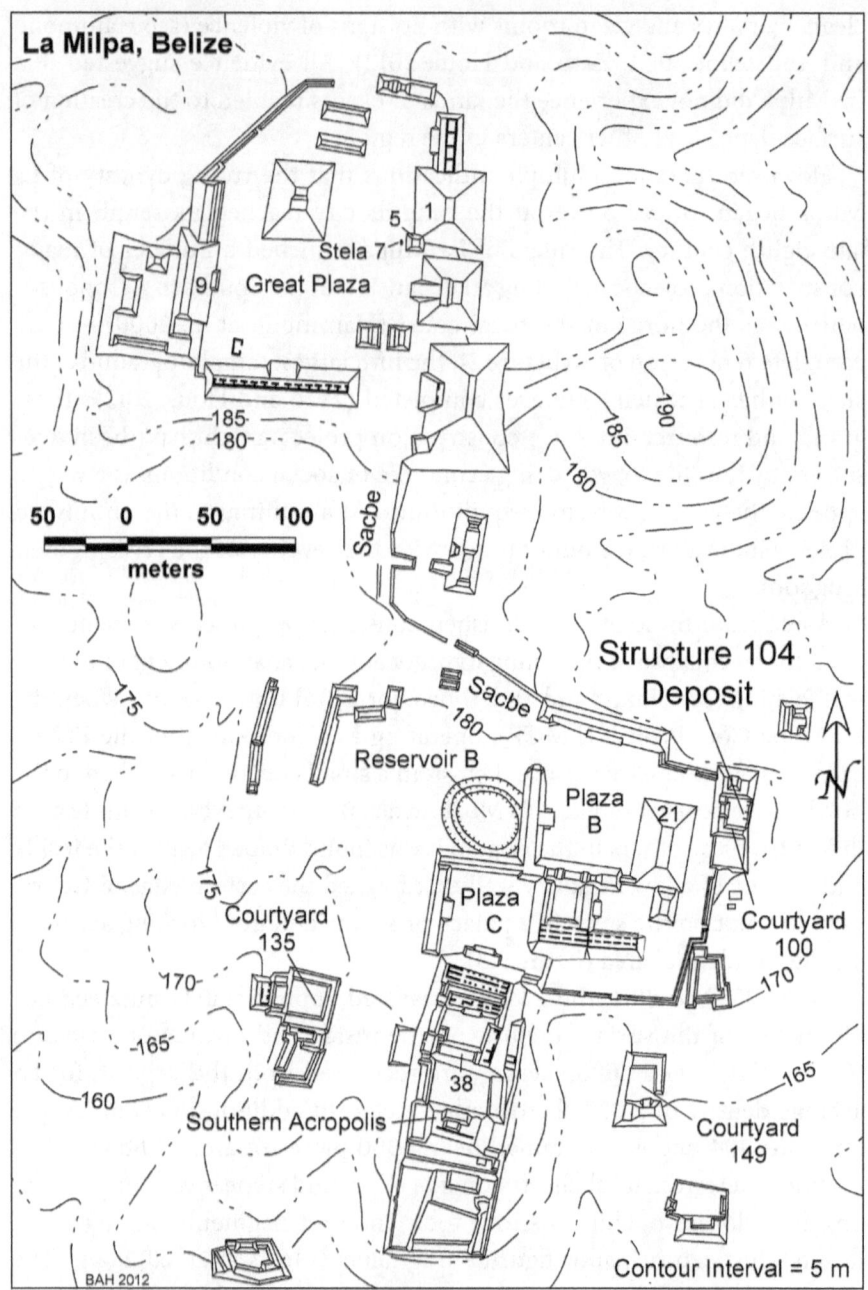

Figure 9.3. Map of La Milpa, showing location of Structure 104 surface deposit. Courtesy of La Milpa Core Project.

1) in its context, which is what makes it so curious. Instead of being located on a prominent shrine or elite palace structure, it is piled up on either side of a rather unremarkable wall in an auxiliary courtyard. The ceramic analysis suggests that the deposit is not a collection of vessels smashed in situ; rather, it is composed of sherds and fragmented vessels brought to the location already broken (Sullivan 2012, 79–80). Sullivan (2012, 80) speculates the deposit represents "an elite domestic midden or a transposed elite domestic midden." The high quantity of animal bone stands in stark contrast to PD 2 and argues in favor of a midden interpretation, whether primary or transposed.

It is quite possible that the deposit began as a midden against the outer wall of Courtyard 100 near the end of the Late Classic or the beginning of the Terminal Classic but transformed in function shortly thereafter. Not only was there human bone in the deposit, which is reminiscent of PD 2 at Dos Hombres, but the Structure 104 deposit formed over the course of several centuries; it was still being visited long after the site had been abandoned. The ceramic analysis found Terminal Classic diagnostic types (including Fine Orange, Tumba Black-on-orange, and Buyuk Striated sherds) located vertically throughout the deposit (Sullivan 2012), and excavators noted that the artifacts were mixed with collapse debris, which means that the deposit accumulated over a long period of time as people continued to place artifacts in the deposit while the wall of the courtyard gradually collapsed (Zaro and Houk 2012, 153). Radiocarbon dates suggest some internal stratification even if the ceramics do not and confirm the long depositional history of the deposit. A piece of animal bone from the base of the deposit yielded a firm 2-sigma Late Classic date of cal. AD 678–776, and two charcoal dates from near the top of the deposit returned Postclassic dates: 2-sigma cal. AD 1268–1294 and cal. AD 1309–1361/1386–1406 (Moats et al. 2012, Table 3).

Because there is no other evidence for occupation at the site after the Terminal Classic, the continued formation of the deposit, concurrent with the gradual collapse of the Structure 104 wall, suggests that either the deposit was never a primary midden or that it ceased to be a midden and became a spot for some other kind of activity, such as visits by pilgrims venerating their ancestors or the particular place on the landscape, sometime during or after the Terminal Classic period. Evidence for Postclassic monument veneration at La Milpa has been documented in the Great Plaza, where offerings spanning the Late Postclassic to Historic periods were placed at the base of stelae (Hammond and Bobo 1994) and *incensarios* and other artifacts were placed, apparently during the Postclassic period, on the stairs and landing of Structure 3 (Trein 2011, 49). While the Structure 104 case may be part of this larger pattern of Postclassic visitation and veneration in the region (e.g., Houk et al. 2008), it is still puzzling because of its setting and apparent lack of importance in the overall cityscape of La Milpa. For some unknowable reason, this small courtyard in the shadow of an unfinished renovation project became another spot on the landscape for veneration and another example of cultural memory.

Discussion

The Dos Hombres, Chan Chich, and La Milpa Terminal Classic surface deposits are signs of the times; they are the remains of some of the final activities to occur at the cities of the Three Rivers region. When considered alongside Special Deposit 1 from Blue Creek, they highlight not only the striking variability of surface deposits but also the apparent range of responses to the events associated with the failure of political leadership and the abandonment of the cities in the region.

Navarro-Farr (2009, 437) makes a compelling argument for avoiding the categories of "reverential" and "desecratory" to describe the nature of these surface deposits because they often represent multiple events forming a complicated palimpsest of material. In some cases, however, context, content, and association favor one interpretation over the other possible explanations. For example, in the Dos Hombres examples, PD 2 in Courtyard C-7 appears to represent a desecratory act, whether ritual or profane. The creation of the surface deposit blocking the entrance to the Acropolis effectively terminated the use of that elite space. As a cultural memory event, this act of desecration created a deliberate break with the past and may have accompanied the violent fall of the royal family. It certainly suggests the ruling family was no longer using the Acropolis, although their ultimate fate is unknown. PD 2 is a prototypical "termination deposit" following Harrison-Buck's (2012a, 107–112) criteria and is very similar to deposits at Aguateca Inomata has described (this volume).

On the other end of the spectrum, the artifacts and human bone fragments placed in Structure C-14 almost certainly represent a reverential act. They were likely placed sometime after PD 2 was deposited but before the building's vaulted ceiling collapsed. The actors in this case may have been members of displaced royal family who returned to perform this reverential act or some other member of the community who recognized the royal acropolis as a sacred spot on the landscape.

The Chan Chich examples are contextually and compositionally different from PD 2 at Dos Hombres. They are light to moderate scatters of artifacts on the steps to elite palaces at the site. They range from utilitarian ceramics and ground stone implements to more elite items like the jaguar tooth, the tenoned artifact, and the partial Pabellon modeled-carved bowl. The Chan Chich surface deposits may be reverential offerings, possibly left by commoners and elite alike, as is discussed below, over the course of many different visits to the site. If so, it is interesting to consider the possibility that the Structure C-6 burial may be part of this same pattern of reverential offering after the structure had been abandoned. It is worth noting that while the Chan Chich surface deposits are dissimilar from PD 2, they are similar in composition to the deposit of artifacts found on the floor in Dos Hombres Structure C-14.

Alternatively, the Chan Chich examples may be evidence of non-elite resistance to increasingly ineffective elite rule, if not outright repudiation of their authority (e.g., Joyce and Weller 2007; McAnany 2010, 197). McAnany (2010, 197) notes that "efforts to terminate the authority of a court may appear only as subtle signs in excavated deposits," and the Chan Chich surface deposits are certainly subtler than the massive event hinted at by PD 2 at Dos Hombres.

The Structure 104 deposit from La Milpa is similar to PD 2 in composition (other than its higher quantity of faunal material) and density, but dissimilar in terms of location. It stands out in stark contrast to these other examples and to the remarkably clean state of rooms and stairways elsewhere in the La Milpa site core. It is clear that the deposit formed over a long period of time. As the courtyard crumbled into ruin, Maya visitors continued to place ceramics, obsidian, animal remains, stone tools, and even human bone along the eastern wall of Courtyard 100. It is possible that the deposit was actually a midden throughout its use, but that would suggest that people were living at La Milpa for much longer than suspected and while the buildings were falling apart (see Zaro and Houk [2012] for a discussion of La Milpa's abandonment), and there is no evidence of construction, renovation, or occupation in the courtyard after the Terminal Classic period (see Moats et al. 2012). Were it not for the collapse debris mixed with the artifacts in the surface deposit, the Structure 104 deposit would be classified as a midden, given its low percentages of ceramic refits

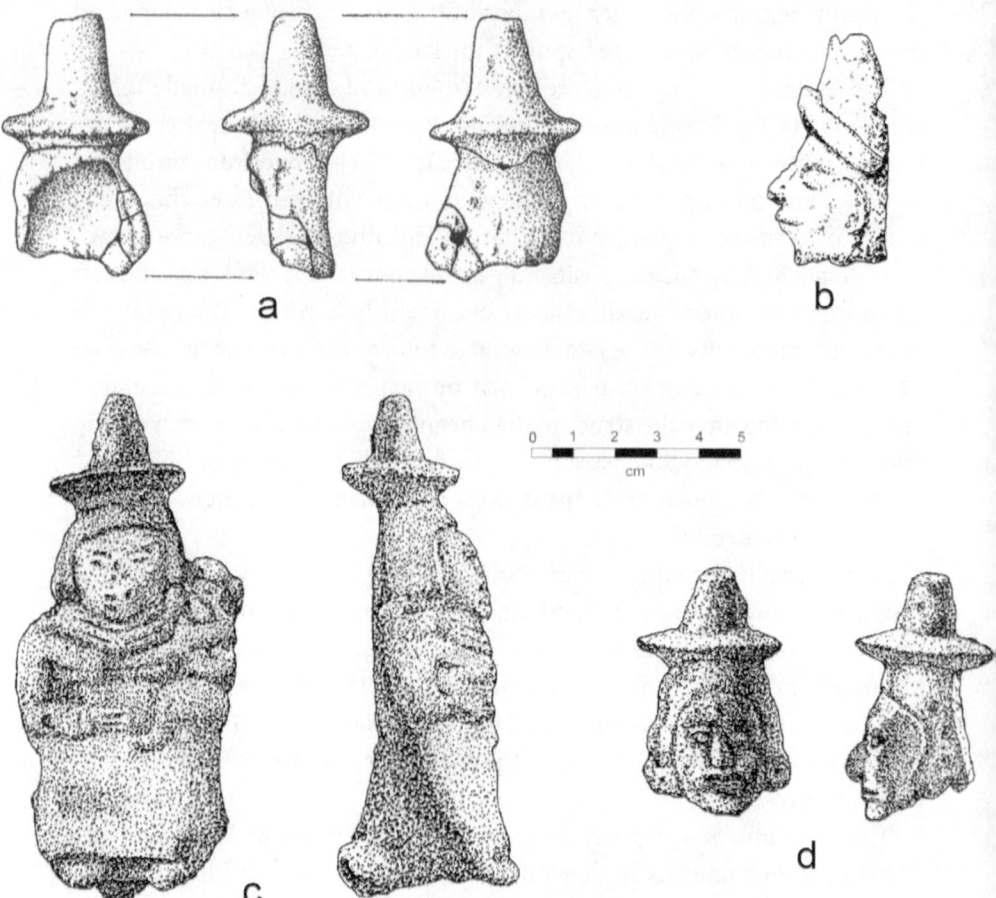

Figure 9.4. Figurine and whistle fragments from Terminal Classic surface deposits: *a*) figurine from Chan Chich, illustration by Ashlyn Madden, after Meadows (1998, Figure 7.6); *b*) whistle from La Milpa, Structure 104 deposit, illustration by Jennifer Bryan; *c* and *d*) figurines from Dos Hombres, Structure C-14 deposit, illustrations by Patrick Peterson after Houk (1996, Figure 5.57).

and higher concentration of faunal material compared to the other deposits described here.

An interesting aspect of Navarro-Farr's (2009, 105; this volume) study of the complex surface deposits at El Perú-Waka' is her questioning of the assumptions that non-elites were not engaged in rituals at monumental architecture. Navarro-Farr classified the artifacts from the Structure M13-1 deposits into the categories of ceremonial (i.e., the types of artifacts found in sealed ritual deposits, such as caches and burials) and domestic in order to test the hypothesis that multiple levels of society were involved in the creation of the surface deposits, not just the elite. An important component of her study was the recognition that a variety of artifacts can be both ceremonial and domestic, including figurines, spindle whorls, and chert tools (Navarro-Farr 2009, 11, 452). Those types of artifacts might be indicative of non-elite involvement in the creation of surface deposits such as those at El Perú-Waka'.

Applying her approach to the Chan Chich examples, the Dos Hombres Structure C-14 deposit, and the La Milpa Structure 104 deposit suggests that non-elites may have been partially, if not solely, responsible for the deposits. While these three cases differ from one another in many ways, they share two important features: they include very similar figurines and figurine fragments (and the fragments are almost always human heads; see figure 9.4) and they lack greenstone or jade artifacts. In other words, while the deposits contain artifacts that bridge the ceremonial/domestic categories, they lack markers of high status such as personal adornments made of jade (including beads and earspools). At La Milpa, the deposit contained a rather crude ceramic earspool, perhaps a piece of non-elite jewelry, and a number of spindle whorls and chert tools (Moats et al. 2012).

Apparent non-elite involvement in the creation of these deposits suggests that the monumental cores of the sites and the physical residences of the elite were powerful symbols to the non-elites who were tied to each city. The curious context of the Structure 104 deposit at La Milpa stands, again, in stark contrast. It serves as an excellent reminder of the complex nature of the abandonment and post-abandonment activities that took place at these sites.

Conclusions

In general, the approach to studying Terminal Classic surface deposits has matured greatly in the past fifteen years with the recognition that they could be something other than just trash left behind by poorly documented squatters. As elements of the abandonment and memorialization of the Maya cities of the lowlands, surface deposits such as the ones described here are one key to understanding the complicated social and political processes that befell many Classic Maya kingdoms. Interpreting these surface deposits, however, requires an understanding of the timing and circumstances of their depositions.

William Sanders and David Webster (1998; see also Fox 1977) have called Maya cities regal-ritual centers to stress the strong linkage between the place and the ruling family. The link between a Maya king or queen and his or her city is intrinsic (Webster 2002a, 154). This link is perhaps no stronger than with the dynastic architectural assemblages of the ruling family, and while we do not know who was ruling the three centers discussed here, these surface deposits and their related rituals or activities are clearly associated with elite and/or royal architecture, with the exception of the La Milpa example, which is nonetheless in the heart of the site's epicenter. In the case of Dos Hombres PD 2, a strong case can be made that the ruling family was the target and that the symbolic termination of their royal acropolis was the projectile fired at that target. At Chan Chich it is not clear if the scatters of broken artifacts on the steps to elite palaces represent abandonment-related acts of resistance or aggression directed at the rulers (or at their guilty-by-association nonroyal elite relatives) or if they represent post-abandonment reverential ritual behavior, as the Dos Hombres Structure C-14 artifacts apparently do. Finally, the long-lived surface deposit at La Milpa is the most difficult to interpret because of its context, but it too is a sign of the times.

10

Events and Processes Leading to the Abandonment of the Maya City of Blue Creek, Belize

THOMAS H. GUDERJAN AND C. COLLEEN HANRATTY

Whether or not the event is referred to as a "collapse," there was clearly a significant depopulation and unraveling of infrastructure at the end of the Classic period in the Maya lowlands, and there has never been a lack of theory about the reasons for the demise of Maya complex society (Culbert 1973; Demarest et al. 2004; McAnany and Yoffee 2010; Morley 1946). In this volume, we are interested in the role of kings and their failures or successes in leading their kingdoms during a time that saw most of them fail. In this chapter, we present information from the site of Blue Creek (see figure 1.1) in northwestern Belize, which has been the focus of annual investigations since 1992 (Guderjan et al. 1993; Guderjan 2004, 2005, 2007; Guderjan et al. 2009; Guderjan et al. 2010). This effort has produced a massive and important database that offers an increasingly detailed and nuanced perspective on the events and processes that preceded the abandonment of Blue Creek at the end of the Classic period.

The most simplistic arguments regarding the disintegration of social and political complexity in the southern Maya lowlands have long ago been shown to be inadequate (Adams 1973b; Culbert 1973; Brenner et al. 2002), and most recent discussions have focused on environmental issues (Brenner et al. 2002; Butzer and Endfield 2012; Curtis et al. 1996; Diamond 2005; Dunning et al. 2012; Emery 2008; Gill 2000; Gunn and Adams 1982; Gunn et al. 2002; Hanratty and Guderjan 2007; Marcus 2003; McAnany and Yoffee 2010; McKillop 2002; McNeeley 1994; Turner and Sabloff 2012;

Webster 2002a; Yaeger and Hodell 2009). The most sophisticated of these studies recognize that disjunctures in human-environment relationships result in complex sets of choices and alternatives from which kings may choose. In some cases, the kings chose well; in other cases, they chose poorly. The outcomes of leaders' choices produced measurable archaeological data that we can examine to understand the challenges they faced, the options that were available to them, and the actions they chose.

While it is clear that the Classic Maya faced large-scale and important environmental issues by AD 810, it is also clear that the responses to these issues were variable and had regionally differing consequences. Few suggest that human responses to climate change have easily predictable outcomes (see Weiss and Bradley 2001). Hamblin and Pitcher (1980) argue that class conflict may have been a factor in the end of the Classic period. More recently, Houk (2001, this volume) has suggested that artifact deposits from rituals found at sites such as Dos Hombres and Blue Creek in Belize may have resulted from class conflict. While this may seem to harken back to Eric Thompson's (1954) early thinking about the collapse, Houk incorporates a much more detailed, nuanced, and complete model of the Classic Maya that goes far beyond Thompson's "peasant uprising." In some places, kings may have lost control of critical resources such as water (Lucero 2002). In the Petexbatun region, and very likely in other areas, interpolity warfare increased during the Late Classic and may have transformed into wars of conquest in order to capture fertile agricultural lands and sources of tribute as a response to declining agricultural productivity (Demarest 2004a; Demarest et al. 2004; Emery 2008). However, Wright and White (1996) have shown that Maya diets were relatively stable throughout the Classic period, and they reject generalized ecological models that emphasize diet and health. Further, recent evidence from Copan indicates that large-scale deforestation had occurred centuries prior to abandonment and was not a factor in Copan's collapse (McNeil et al. 2010), undermining the idea that environmental stress at the end of the Classic period was causative.

While such factors likely played some role in the large-scale Late Classic depopulation that occurred in the southern lowlands, they impacted individual communities differently, and some polities survived better than others. The rulers at Lamanai, for example, continued to construct large public buildings (Pendergast 1986, 1990), and the idea of the *ahau* (king) as an institution of leadership and rule continued to thrive there. Although this was in part due to Lamanai's strategic location on the New River lagoon, where it could take advantage of the increasingly secular riverine and coastal trade system, it was also surely due to the choices its kings and principal agents made.

There is a great deal of regional variation in the complex situation of the Late Classic, just as there is variability in the actions and responses of individual polities (Aimers 2007; Demarest et al. 2004; McKillop 2002). Many years ago, Kent Flannery (1972) warned against searching for single prime movers in understanding the origins of civilization. That thinking can be extended to understanding the collapse of civilization. Further, despite efforts such as those of Aimers (2007), and Demarest et al. (2004), detailed data regarding the abandonment of Maya centers are still lacking.

What was the role of kings in these events? That is the question Iannone, Houk, and Schwake pose in this volume. Most agree that divine kings were central to the origins of Maya complexity. But what are the roles of scapegoat kings in the demise of complexity? As we review the Blue Creek database, we question whether only a king negotiated power, legitimacy, and authority. In this chapter, we review what we know of Blue Creek and then attempt to address some of our editors' questions and test implications for the scapegoat king model.

The Site of Blue Creek, Belize

Multidisciplinary and ongoing research has been conducted at Blue Creek for two decades (Guderjan et al. 1993; Guderjan 2007; Guderjan et al. 2009; Guderjan et al. 2010; Guderjan and Hanratty 2012). Public buildings as tall as fifteen meters surround Blue Creek's main plaza (Figure 10.1). At least two stelae were once present: one was stolen and another has been reburied. There is also an Early Classic ball court, albeit a very small one. This medium-sized Maya center was occupied from approximately 600 BC until approximately AD 800–900, then partially reoccupied about 200 years later (Guderjan 2004, 2007). The hinterland and sustaining area of Blue Creek covers approximately 100–150 square kilometers (Guderjan 2007; Lichtenstein 2000). In that area, nearly 500 buildings have been documented, and approximately 100 have been excavated in the 20 percent of this area that has been intensively studied.

By the Terminal Preclassic period (AD 100–250) and through the Early Classic period (ca. AD 250–550), Blue Creek became a wealthy city (Guderjan 1998, 2000, 2004, 2005, 2007). The clearest proxy for wealth is jade or, more properly, jadeite and nephrite, the most precious stones in the Maya

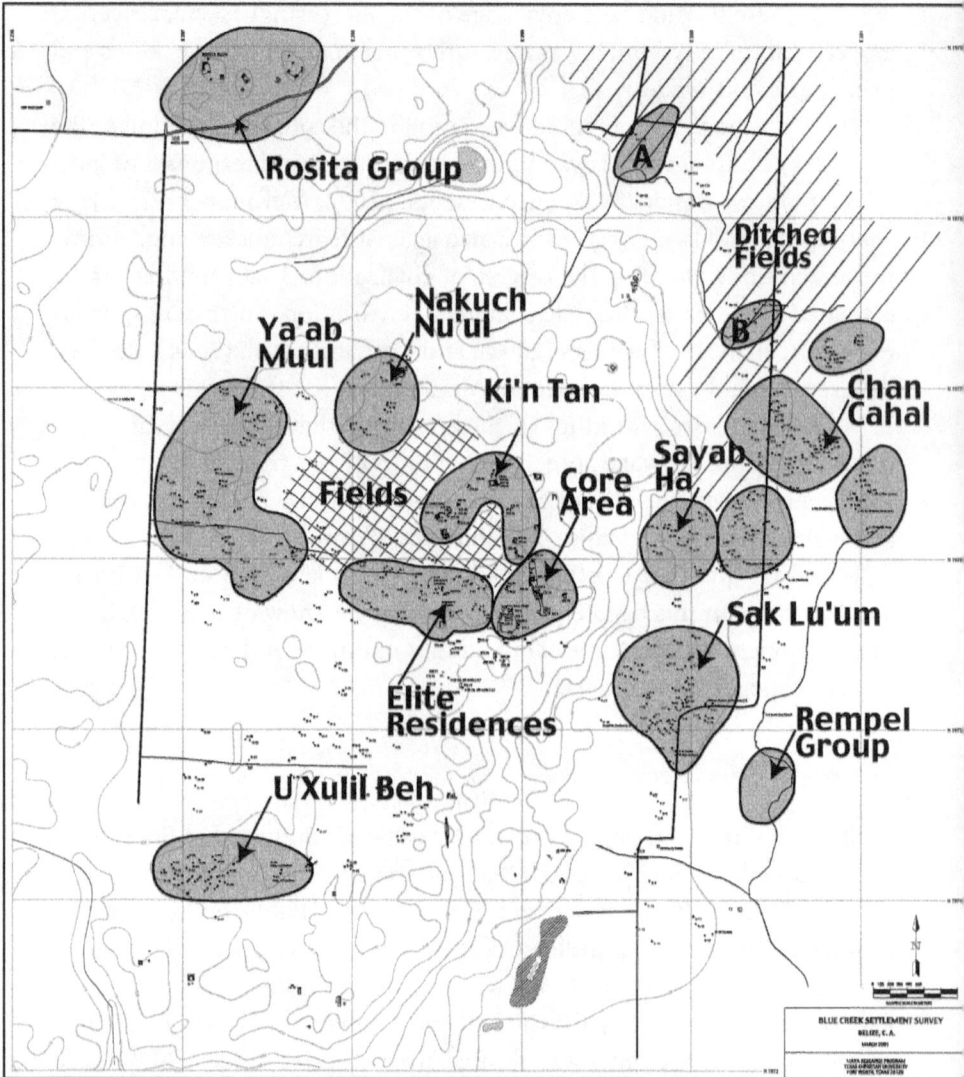

Figure 10.1. The central twenty square kilometers of Blue Creek showing known residential groups.

world; jade was worn only by royal elites and was occasionally gifted to non-elites. Approximately 1,500 jade ornaments have been recovered from Blue Creek. In addition to jade, Blue Creek had access to many other exotic goods, including grinding stones made of metamorphic rocks, obsidian tools, and sponges from the Caribbean coast. These elite-reinforcing goods are an exhibition of surprising wealth that surpasses anything we have seen at the nearby sites we have been investigating for the past several years.

Blue Creek's prosperity derived from three equally important economic factors. The first is the presence of some of the richest and most extensive agricultural soils in Central America (Beach et al. 2009; Guderjan 2007; Guderjan et al. 2003). More than half of the area around Blue Creek was used for agriculture. Agricultural systems range in size and importance from small household kitchen gardens to expansive production systems, such as large-scale upland non-irrigated farming and lowland drained-field farming (Guderjan 2007). It is clear that Blue Creek was an exporter of agricultural products.

The central precinct of Blue Creek straddles an escarpment 100–150 meters long that divides the low coastal plain from the karstic hills of the uplands. Above and west of the escarpment the terrain is a mixture of eroded limestone hills separated by large expanses of clayey soils that today are prized by modern large-scale farmers. These *bajos* and *bajitos* range in size from one to forty square kilometers. While we lack direct evidence for their use prehistorically, the facts that no Maya homes have been found in them and the Maya went to extraordinary lengths to expand these fields by building terraces and check dams on adjacent hillsides suggest that the *bajos* were fully under cultivation (Guderjan 2007).

In addition, below the escarpment are equally rich soils, but these were subject to seasonal inundation that could easily lead to complete crop losses. To prevent this, the Blue Creek Maya dug hundreds of kilometers of ditches to drain these fields (Baker 2003; Beach et al. 2009; Luzzadder-Beach and Beach 2009; Guderjan 2007; Guderjan et al. 2009; Guderjan and Krause 2011). Our ongoing studies of these fields indicate that they were dug in the Early Classic period and maintained until the abandonment of Blue Creek, which began around AD 810 (Beach et al. 2009; Guderjan et al. 2009).

The second factor in Blue Creek's economic success was its strategic setting at the headwaters of the Río Hondo, which provided access to other key markets (Barrett and Guderjan 2006; Guderjan 2007). Coastal trade in elite-reinforcing exotic goods was active throughout the Classic period. We now believe that Maya trade canoes filled with food and other commodities virtually circumnavigated the Yucatan Peninsula and penetrated into the interior via rivers (Andrews 1983, 1990; Andrews and Mock 2002; Guderjan 1995; Hammond 1972; McKillop 1996; McKillop and Healy 1989; Sabloff 1977; Sabloff and Rathje 1975). Blue Creek is located at the terminus of the Río Hondo, and canoes filled with goods could reach the Caribbean in just three days. Equally important, canoes coming from the Caribbean into the interior would have had to stop at Blue Creek to offload goods or continue up the Río Bravo. From Blue Creek, these goods would have been taken overland into Petén sites. Thus, Blue Creek's economic success was enhanced by its critical location on the trade network. Blue Creek's gateway setting also facilitated the distribution of its own agricultural products. Confirmation of this is the discovery of a dock (Barrett and Guderjan 2006) and related facilities at Blue Creek similar to features found downstream at the site of Nohmul (Pring and Hammond 1975).

However, power and authority are not merely functions of resources and trade. In the case of the Maya, we can see how human agency played out through the multigenerational interactions of leaders (Guderjan 2007; Guderjan and Hanratty 2006, 2007). It was the choices Blue Creek's kings and other leaders made that enabled them to take advantage of these resources and become prosperous.

The king's power, authority, and legitimacy were symbolically displayed and played out in Blue Creek's *k'ui'k*, or central precinct, which included large open plazas, graceful yet massive temples, at least one carved stela that proclaimed royal accomplishments, and a ball court where the Maya origin myth was ritually reenacted. Blue Creek's central precinct also includes innovative architecture that was constructed during the Early Classic period, indicating the strength of its early kings. For example, by AD 350, Structure 1 had a columned superstructure that supported a perishable roof (Driver 2002; Guderjan 2004). On the south side of Plaza A, a stone-lined shaft surrounded by caches was integrated into Structure 4 at the same time. This shaft marked Structure 4 as a symbolic axis mundi, or center of the world, and may have supported a banner on a pole in front of the superstructure (Guderjan 1998, 2005, 2007). It may also have been the symbolic portal to the founding king's tomb. Near Plaza B, the façade of another temple, Structure 9, was decorated with the image of a ruler, king, or *ahau* (Grube et al. 1995). Also dating to the Early Classic period, this unusual stucco mask marked the power and authority of Blue Creek's ruler. Finally, Blue Creek's ball court is the only one in the region that was constructed during the Early Classic period (Guderjan 2004).

These symbols of power are not seen in the Late and Terminal Classic periods (ca. AD 550–810). However, Blue Creek's late kings commissioned new construction, such as the addition of a pseudo-E-Group, a nonfunctioning but symbolic solstice marker of the kind that is widely seen earlier at other sites (Guderjan 2006). The building features a small, open stela shrine and a dedicatory cache with symbolic materials related to the sun god, or God K (Driver and Wanyerka 2002; Guderjan 2004, 2007), which likely marks it as a symbolic re-creation of the Maya cosmos and links it to associated creation myths (Bozarth and Guderjan 2004).

However, to understand the nature of power and authority in Maya cities, we need to look beyond the central precinct into the surrounding settlement zone. At Blue Creek, broad expanses of agricultural lands separate outlying residential neighborhoods, or barrios, giving us the opportunity to study each separately and compare them with each other. Only 1 kilometer west of the central precinct is Kín Tan, which consists of a group of nonroyal elite residences built throughout the Classic period (see figure 10.1). These were important families in the political fabric of Blue Creek who buried their lineage founder around AD 150–250 and then built a shrine over him. Not long afterward, another important male, perhaps the founder's son or grandson, was buried in front of the shrine and the shrine was expanded to incorporate his tomb. This was home to a family of apparently increasing political and economic strength at Blue Creek for another 600 years (Guderjan and Hanratty 2006; Guderjan et al. 2003; Hanratty 2002). Their power and authority was created and maintained by their multigenerational interactions with the ruling lineage.

Other lineages never attained such power and authority. Examples include the residents of Sayap Ha and Chan Cahal, located east of the central precinct and surrounded by ditched agricultural fields (Guderjan 2007; Popson 2000). Most people lived in humble thatch-roofed wooden-pole homes and had little in the way of valuable and exotic possessions, with one exception. At about the same time that the founder was buried at Kín Tan, a male founder was buried under a house floor at Sayap Ha with "knock-off" goods, such as a royal bib head carved from bone rather than jade (Guderjan 2007). But he was also buried with a pair of shell ornaments inlaid with exotic stones and coral inscribed with images of Teotihuacán-style scribes. Despite whatever he did to attain such prestige, he did not originate a lineage that could inherit and build upon his power. For the next six centuries, his descendants would be workers in the agricultural fields, not their owners. Thus, we argue that power and authority in a Maya city were based on the complex interactions between powerful lineages (see also Schwake and Iannone this volume), such as the rulers in the central precinct and the residents of Kín Tan. Further, once a lineage was excluded, such as the residents of Sayap Ha, they remained excluded.

Our understanding of Blue Creek through the Classic period provides a contextual platform for the events and processes that preceded, defined, and followed the large-scale population decline and unraveling of infrastructure that occurred in the ninth century. Further, it helps us understand how Maya rulers acquired wealth, power, and authority; how trade and economics were the glue the held together disparate and distant Maya kingdoms; and how the Maya structured their unique form of urban life and built a complex society through human agency and interaction.

Late Classic Processes

In the Late Classic period (AD 550–810), the Blue Creek population grew and expanded into locations with low agricultural potential, such as U Xulil Beh (Guderjan 2007; Guderjan et al. 2010; Lichtenstein 2000; see Figure 10.1). At the same time, we have evidence at Blue Creek and elsewhere in the region of soil erosion (Binford et al. 1983; Dunning et al. 2009) and declining productivity. Such evidence of an increasing population and increasing demands on agricultural production systems clearly points to increasing stress during this period.

Population Expansion into Low Resource Areas

Throughout Blue Creek, we see increasing numbers of residential structures in the Late Classic period (Guderjan 2007) and interpret this as the consequence of increasing population size. This is not surprising given the ample evidence in the region for increasing population sizes in the Late Classic (Culbert and Rice 1990). Immediately southwest of Blue Creek, estimates indicate that populations at their Late Classic maximum were three to eight times as high as in the Early Classic (Adams et al. 2004). While there are methodological problems with that likely led to underestimation of Early Classic populations (Sagebiel 2005), it is still clear that Late Classic populations were significantly higher.

An example of such population increase is found at U Xulil Beh, a small, informally clustered group of twenty-two visible house mounds with no monumental architecture or larger residential structures (figure 10.2) located approximately 2.5 kilometers southwest of Blue Creek's central precinct (Lichtenstein 2000; Guderjan et al. 2003; Guderjan 2007). The group is bounded on three sides by erosional cuts more than ten meters deep and has no access to the high-quality agricultural soils. The residences did not exhibit the multiple floors, refurbishing, or Early Classic burials so commonly seen elsewhere (Lichtenstein 2000), and all datable ceramics were

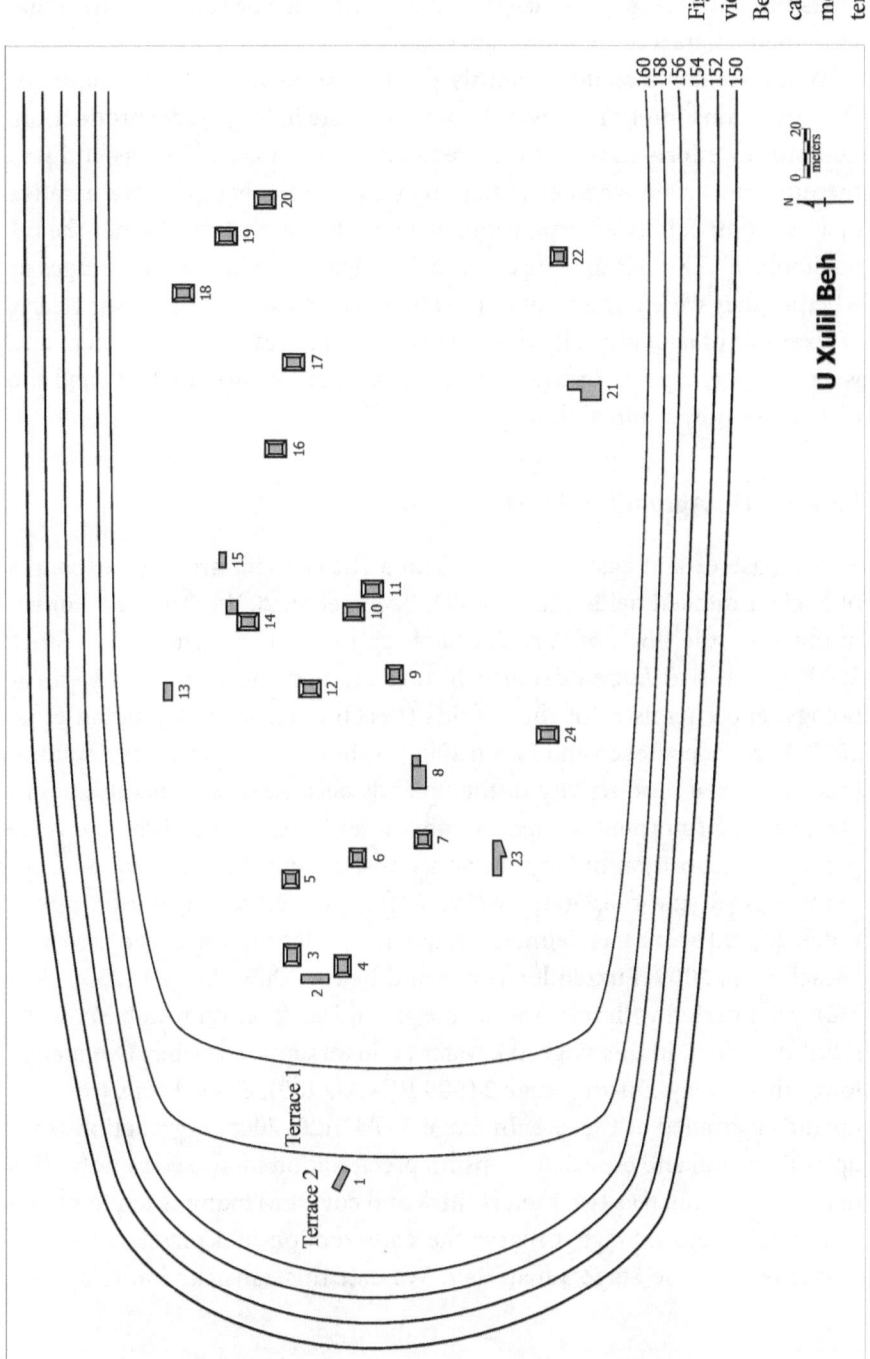

Figure 10.2. Plan view of U Xulil Beh showing locations of house mounds and terraces.

Late Classic. Although excavations in 2008 confirmed the presence of artificial agricultural terraces, they clearly had very limited agricultural potential; the depth of the soil would have been ten or fewer centimeters above limestone bedrock, as contrasted with the highly fertile soils elsewhere that were many meters deep (Guderjan et al. 2009).

While residents could obviously produce some agricultural goods for their own consumption, they did not participate in large-scale production. Our survey efforts have not often extended into marginal areas and it is therefore uncertain whether U Xulil Beh is an anomaly or is representative of a common pattern of expansion. Further, it is uncertain whether the inhabitants of U Xulil Beh were derived from existing Blue Creek lineages or whether they were immigrants from elsewhere. Nevertheless, this is clearly an example of later arrivals who were relegated to resource-poor areas and were not participants in the interaction among lineages that defined the creation of power and authority.

Processes in Agricultural Systems

At the base of and east of the Río Bravo Escarpment are large expanses of ancient ditched fields (Baker 2003; Beach et al. 2009). The best known of these are the Birds of Paradise fields and the Chan Cahal fields. Since 2003, Beach and Luzzadder-Beach have studied the stratigraphy, chronology, and chemistry of these fields (Beach et al. 2009; Guderjan et al. 2009; Luzzadder-Beach and Beach 2009). While Classic period agricultural practices taxed productivity in the uplands because of erosion and possibly because of nutrient depletion, the lowlands experienced the converse problem—deposition of large amounts of sediment that had eroded from the watershed and evaporate formation from the extremely hard groundwater. Recent work has defined a sequence of deposition in the lowlands (Beach et al. 2009; Luzzadder-Beach and Beach 2009). Stage 1 (2500–600 BC) was a period with relatively stable ground surfaces on which Maya agriculture began. In this stage, the water table was approximately two meters lower than today. During Stage 2 (600 BC–AD 100), eroded soils from the uplands aggraded at the site. In Stage 3 (AD 120–700), aggradation from upland erosion and especially gypsum precipitation increased rapidly. This material is as much as two meters thick and covers as many as ten to fifteen square kilometers. Stage 4 marks the construction of a massive network of ditches into the Stage 3 materials. We date this construction to a more recent time than the sediments it intruded into (300 BC–AD 700) and later than the earliest dates from the sedimentary infilling of these ditches (Stage 5, AD 870–1010).

The construction of the network of agricultural ditches, which extends 1–2 kilometers eastward from the base of the Río Bravo Escarpment and for many kilometers along the escarpment, was most likely not driven by intensification of agriculture but by a desire to reclaim what were probably preexisting agricultural lands. These had been buried by alluvial aggradation as the water table rose. The rising water table would have the effect of keeping these wetlands wet. The drainage ditches were dug to control the moisture levels in the root zones of agricultural plants. Again, we see the construction of these as human responses to declining productivity and the environmental stresses of excessive gypsum and soil burial.

In summary, it appears that large-scale agriculture began well before the Late Classic and that forest clearing, perhaps as early as the Preclassic period (600 BC–AD 100), caused significant upland erosion and aggradation in the low-lying wetlands. In response to this change, the Blue Creek Maya dug a vast network of ditches in order to control the negative impacts of waterlogged soils and poor groundwater.

These data, while important in themselves, are also proxies for related processes. As at Copan, it appears that forest clearing probably occurred long before the Late Classic and possibly before the Early Classic period. The conversion of upland areas to agricultural land began a process of significant erosion that, in turn, buried long-used lowland agricultural lands, creating the need to dig vast networks of ditches to control soil moisture. This also supports the idea that upland (dry or nonditched) agricultural lands were being eroded and losing potential productivity, a view supported by numerous previous studies (Binford et al. 1983; Beach et al. 2002) and contemporary observations. For example, we have seen incidents of very rapid erosion when today's upland fields are plowed at the end of the dry season, and early rains can erode large quantities of soil in a single event.

Despite the attention given to wetland agricultural systems because of their tremendous research potential, at Blue Creek upland agricultural systems actually covered larger areas (Guderjan 2007). The karstic uplands are composed of limestone hills with little or no extant soil. Between these hills are upland low-lying areas, or *bajitos*, that have deep, rich, clayey soils that often covers a square kilometer or more. In many cases, these *bajitos* have drainages that lead to the wetlands below, and they were the sources of the alluvium that eroded onto those wetland agricultural areas during the Classic period.

Our view that these were intensively cultivated is based on the nearly complete absence of residential architecture in them, the construction of agricultural terraces on hillsides sloping to them, and additional agricultural and water control features at their base. While the need or desire to optimize productivity in marginally productive areas is not surprising, we did not expect to find such a quantity and range of variability of such features because soil resources were so abundant at Blue Creek. It appears that these features would not have been constructed unless the adjacent *bajitos* were being cultivated. While the presence of such features reflects the scale of agriculture at Blue Creek and elsewhere, when they were constructed is most critical here, and these features are notoriously difficult to date. While most cross-channel features such as check dams at Blue Creek are believed to date to the Late Classic period (Guderjan 2007), recent information from the Minanha site in central Belize contradicts this view of the larger pattern. There, several contour terraces were sealed by the construction of Early Classic residences and date to either the Terminal Preclassic or Early Classic (Macrae and Iannone 2011; see also Schwake and Iannone this volume), though other such features at Minanha do apparently date to the Late Classic period (Iannone, personal communication).

While stress and the reduction of agricultural potential were both likely by the end of the Classic period, this does not necessarily mean that Blue Creek was unable to produce ample food for sustenance. Blue Creek had a relatively low population density and access to large expanses of agricultural soils. Therefore it is reasonable that agricultural goods were the source of Blue Creek's wealth. These changes would have affected the means of producing wealth, power, and authority, not the fundamental ability to produce enough food to survive.

Late and Terminal Classic Abandonment Events

By the Terminal Classic, Blue Creek's sociopolitical landscape had dramatically transformed. Abandonment took place first in the central precinct (*k'ui'k*) and the nearby elite residences of Kín Tan at the end of the Late Classic period, which we estimate to around AD 810. In Plaza A, the front of Structure 3 was buried by thousands of ceramic sherds and other portable objects (Clayton et al. 2005; Driver 2008). Another such deposit was found in front of and inside the doorway of Structure 13, an elite residence adjacent to Plaza B, and smaller deposits were recovered from the floor of the Structure 19 Courtyard. At approximately the same time, even larger termination deposits were placed at several elite residences and shrines in Kín Tan.

As discussed earlier, Kín Tan was the home of a powerful and wealthy but nonroyal multigenerational lineage (Guderjan 2007; Guderjan and Hanratty 2006, 2007). Nevertheless, the Terminal Classic ritual deposits at Kín Tan were similar to those in the central precinct (Guderjan 2004; Guderjan et al. 2009; Guderjan et al. 2010; Hanratty 2002). Such ritual deposits were recovered from an ancestor shrine, Structure 34, and two residential structures (Structures 31 and 36) in the Structure 37 Plazuela, the largest residential group at Kín Tan. The final event at Structure 37 involved placement of a black trickle-ware ceramic vessel above the floor of Room B.

Special deposits were also recovered from the frontal facades of Structures 31, 34, and 36. These deposits consist of dense concentrations of rapidly deposited broken vessels and portable objects. While only one complete vessel was recovered, numerous partially reconstructable vessels were identified (contrary to Clayton et al. 2005). In all, 22,179 sherds (391.6 kilograms) were recovered from the plazuela's deposits. Nearly a fifth (19 percent; n = 5,304) of the identifiable sherds were unslipped striated sherds of jar bodies. Most rims were from Cayo Unslipped jars (15 percent). The remainder included serving vessels such as Achote Black bowls (7 percent), Tinaja bowls and jars (11.4 percent), and Garbutt Creek Red interior bolstered bowls (4 percent). In this assemblage, 1,302 (36 percent) rim sherds were too eroded to assign a type designation.

In addition, 428 pieces of lithic debitage and 203 small finds were recovered. Of the small finds, 36 percent were chert biface fragments, 35 percent were obsidian blades, 8 percent were chert cores, and 7 percent were metate fragments. The remaining 32 percent were ceramic appliqués, figurines, beads, stamps, whistles, mano fragments, armatures, spindle whorls, hammerstones, projectile point knives, scrapers, and counterweights.

Another special deposit was found at Structure 50 in the Structure 46 courtyard at Kín Tan (Figures 10.3 and 10.4). The courtyard consists of seven buildings, Structures 46–52. In 2007, Structure 50, a central ancestor shrine similar to Structure 34, was stripped to define the nature of a deposit known to exist there (Guderjan et al. 2010). Special Deposit 11 consisted of a dense concentration of rapidly deposited broken vessels (40 centimeters thick, encompassing nine cubic meters) on the floor and against the

Figure 10.3. Elevated view of Structure 50 after excavation.

Figure 10.4. Detail view of Termination Deposit at Structure 50.

northwest corner of the shrine. Again, no complete vessels were recovered, but numerous partially reconstructable vessels were. In all, 7,850 sherds (243.9 kilograms) were recovered. The majority (60 percent; n = 4,702) of the sherds were unslipped striated sherds of jar bodies. The majority of the rims were Cayo Unslipped jars (19 percent). The remainder included serving vessels such as Tres Mujeres bowls (10.5 percent), Achote Black bowls (10 percent), Garbutt Creek Red interior bolstered bowls (6 percent), monochrome cream bowls (6 percent), and Tinaja Red restricted-orifice jars (5 percent). Ninety-four (31 percent) rim sherds were too eroded or too small to assign a type designation.

Numerous small finds were also scattered throughout the deposit, including thirteen chert biface fragments, two obsidian blade fragments, a slate blank, a chert hammer stone, and a granite metate fragment. Additional small finds were recovered at the base of the deposit, lying directly on the floor, including two granite mano fragments, a chert mano fragment, four obsidian blade fragments, a chert biface fragment, a hammerstone, an intact coral bead, and a mother-of-pearl bead fragment.

Special Deposit 11 was quickly sealed and preservation was very good. However, no zooarchaeological or archaeobotanical remains were found within the deposit (Phil Dering, personal communication 2010). The absence of such materials indicates that the deposit was not a midden or redeposited midden or redeposited materials from a feasting event. Instead, it is the material remains of a ritual event marking the abandonment of the shrine, the courtyard, and the central sector of Blue Creek.

Another deposit was recovered 250 meters south of Kín Tan at the J-14 Courtyard. This deposit contained 7,734 sherds (199.9 kilograms) and was intermixed with broken bifaces, manos, metates, and obsidian blades. A significant amount (29 percent; n = 2008) of the identifiable sherds were unslipped striated jar body sherds. The majority of the rims were Cayo Unslipped jars (14.5 percent). The remainder included Tinaja Red restricted-orifice jars (6.5 percent), Achote Black bowls, (5 percent), and Garbutt Creek Red bowls (4.3 percent). An additional 416 (33 percent) rim sherds were too eroded to assign a type designation. Numerous broken small finds, such as chert bifaces, granite manos and metates, and obsidian blades, were also found throughout the deposit.

There has been debate about the behavior that resulted in the accumulation of these deposits (see also Houk this volume). We have termed them "termination deposits" and view them as the result of intentional smashing of cultural material as part of ritual activity that marked the abandonment of structures. They conform to events documented at numerous other sites that have been reported by various scholars (e.g., Garber 1986; Inomata 2003, this volume; Inomata and Webb 2003; Stanton and Brown 2003). Artifacts recovered from similar deposits at Blackman Eddy, Cerros, and Yaxuna are also only partially reconstructable, and it has been repeatedly emphasized that these deposits "can encompass an entire structure or extend across an entire site" (Brown and Stanton 2003, 82). Further, no faunal remains, macrobotanical materials, pollen, or phytoliths from consumable plants have been recovered from these deposits (Stephen Bozarth, personal communication, 2012). The matrix consists almost entirely of smashed pottery, often with a number of other domestic objects such as figurines, intentionally broken grinding stones, bifaces, and obsidian blades. We argue that these deposits are not the material outcomes of feasting activities. Regardless, the most pertinent points are that no human activity occurred in these areas after these events, the deposits thus date the abandonment of the associated buildings, and the deposits occur not only in the residences and public places associated with the king but also those associated with the shrines and residences of nonroyal elites.

Terminal Classic Revitalization at the Rosita Group

We anticipated that the broad pattern of abandonment would be repeated at the Rosita Group but were surprised by a radically different situation. Rosita was an elite residential group located approximately 2.5 kilometers northwest of the central precinct (Preston 2007). It consists of several complexes of large-scale masonry residences on the tops of large hills. Like Kín Tan, Rosita almost surely controlled the high-quality agricultural lands of the surrounding upland *bajito* zones.

This is best seen at Structure RS5, an elite patio group with two shrines and a large masonry residential building built in the Early Classic period that was occupied through the Late Classic Period. Unlike elsewhere, occupation continued after AD 810 into the Terminal Classic. On the north side of the patio group, a small residential building, R21, was razed in the Terminal Classic and replaced with a round Yucatecan-style shrine (Figure 10.5). The round shrine is similar to another building downstream from Blue Creek at Nohmul (Chase and Chase 1982). Another was found on Ambergris Caye, not far from the mouth of the Río Hondo (Guderjan and Garber 1995), and three others were recently found along the Sibun River by Harrison-Buck and McAnany (2006). The latter two researchers interpret

Figure 10.5. Photo of round Yucatecan-style shrine at the Rosita Group.

the proliferation of round shrines in the eastern Maya lowlands as being connected to contact with northern Yucatec trade groups, as these shrines are restricted to coastal zones and areas linked to the coast by navigable river systems (see also Harrison-Buck, this volume).

Rosita is located immediately south of the terminus of the navigable portion of the Río Bravo (Barrett and Guderjan 2006). Thus, as the southern lowland polities were crumbling, the polities of the northern lowlands, probably Chichen Itza, were extending their influence into distant lands via water routes (Andrews 1990; Barrett and Guderjan 2006; Guderjan and Garber 1995; Sabloff 1977). As central authority at Blue Creek failed, the survivors realigned themselves with these external powers and were thus able to thrive.

Furthermore, new Terminal Classic dedicatory caches with Daylight Orange ceramics were placed on the summit of Structure RS5. In the nearby R9 Patio Group, a Terminal Classic cache with another Daylight Orange vessel and a jade bead was placed inside a newly constructed bench

(Preston 2008). Daylight Orange ceramics are generally viewed as a temporal marker for the Terminal Classic period and they are rarely found in the Termination Deposits in the central precinct and Kín Tan.

In summary, after the central precinct and Kín Tan were abandoned, the Rosita Group was undergoing revitalization activities. We do not know how long Rosita was occupied after the general abandonment, but it does not appear to have been more than fifty or seventy-five years. By ca. AD 875–900, the residents of Rosita abandoned their homes as the macro-scale changes affecting the Maya world engulfed them.

We find no evidence of continued occupation after Rosita was abandoned. After at least 200 years, by AD 1100, some Maya people returned to Blue Creek. This is indicated by a small midden on top of Structure U-5 in the Chan Cahal residential group. They also reinhabited the Rempel Group on the margin of wetlands and near a watercourse leading to the Río Hondo (Padilla 2007), where they left their remains on top of the rubble collapse of the principal shrine for the group (Preston and Guderjan 2012). At the same time, some groups began to reuse the Birds of Paradise fields, constructing a pole-and-thatch structure adjacent to one of the infilled ditches. But for all intents and purposes, the end of Blue Creek's complexity came with the abandonment of Rosita.

Conclusions

Were there divine kings at Blue Creek during the Early Classic? Almost certainly. But they did not operate alone. They cleverly interacted with (manipulated?) the leaders of other important lineages to mutually build wealth, power, and authority. These leaders controlled Blue Creek's agricultural wealth and excluded members of lower-class lineages. They also rewarded some members of these lower classes with material symbols of power and recognition for their contributions to the kingdom. These people were not, however, rewarded with the prestige and power the controlling lineages kept to themselves.

Were there Terminal Classic scapegoat kings at Blue Creek? This is a much more difficult question to answer. Nevertheless, to paraphrase Alexander Hamilton, it does appear that the multigenerational lineages that controlled Blue Creek for 600 years hung together . . . and were hung together. Nothing is more telling than the many large-scale termination deposits in Plaza A and in the homes of both the king and several of his allied multigenerational lineages. Regardless of the specific events that resulted in these deposits or even who conducted the rituals, the king and his allies were all treated the same. And for a short time, at least one lineage that was apparently not allied with the *ahau*/king persisted by realigning with an outside power. But it, too, was nearing the end of its days.

We cannot address all of the questions posed by our volume editors, but we can address some. They ask, for example, what are the correlates that link legitimacy and prosperity. At Blue Creek, it is quite clear that the king and his allied lineages controlled large scale, important land and agriculture resources and excluded others via their multigenerational interactions. This is seen today in small Texas cities, where lineages descended from original large landowners control banks, hotels, and other institutions that require significant startup capital.

Our editors also ask us if this power and legitimacy is vested only in the king or in a larger cadre. In the case of Blue Creek, at least, the answer is the latter. The settlement pattern reflects an exclusionary economic structure, and those who were included had been included since the founding of the kingdom. As a result, when the kingdom was terminated, by whatever means, so were they.

The crisis that caused the end of the rule of the king's lineage and his interacting lineages must have been rooted in the source of their power, the economics of Blue Creek's agricultural base. For centuries the wealth created by production, export, and trade enabled these people to control their city. Their interactions excluded others from wealth and power. We have seen no evidence of "new" wealth in which a newly founded residential group was home to a lineage that later matched the status of those founded in the very beginning of the Early Classic. Thus, we believe that the cause of their undoing was that which had been previously the basis of their success. Precisely what events occurred we likely will not know. However, we can document processes that were sources of stress, such as increasing population and somewhat declining productivity, and macroprocesses such as losing control of the trade system.

Finally, our editors ask what could cause the removal of a king aside from declining prosperity. Well, we do not know. But we do know that declining prosperity seems to be the cause of removal and nonreplacement of the king of Blue Creek. And we do know that when he was removed, so were a large cadre of allied lineages.

Acknowledgments

Thanks to Gyles Iannone, Brett Houk, and Sonja Schwake for inviting us to participate in this effort and for their patience during the various stages of manuscript production. Many thanks also to the staff of the Institute of Archaeology of Belize for their support of this project and their collegiality. In recent years, Dr. John Morris has been our lead point of contact with Institute of Archaeology and has been helpful and supportive on multiple levels. His input into this work cannot be underestimated. We are also grateful to colleagues whose work has directly contributed to this paper. The project staff during the 2006–2012 field seasons include Tim Beach, Bill Brown, Steve Bozarth, Kim Cox, Bruce Dickson, Pieta Greaves, Sheryl Luzzadder-Beach, and Tim Preston. Funding for the project during 2006–2012 came from the Maya Research Program, the National Geographic Society, the National Science Foundation, the Denver Foundation, and the Estate of Alberto Pena. As always, we thank today's community of Blue Creek for accepting us into their lives for twenty-one years of their fifty-five-year history

Dynamic Transitions at El Perú-Waka'

Late Terminal Classic Ritual Repurposing of a Monumental Shrine

OLIVIA C. NAVARRO-FARR

For centuries, the concept of divine kingship was a hallmark of Classic Maya civilization. This divine authority was quite literally built into an entire worldview or cosmovision in which prosperity, sociopolitical and economic order, and the very balance of the cosmos were directly associated with this kind of divine authority. In the introduction to this volume, the authors pose a number of questions that challenge contributors to evaluate various aspects of divine kingship and the scapegoat model in the context of their specific data sets. Calls for consideration of violence, royal legitimacy, collapse crises, dominant ideologies, prosperity and decline in terms of politics, economies, environment, and other elements are central in these questions.

Evidence dating to the years that marked the Late Terminal Classic transition (ca. AD 750–850) at the lowland Maya city of El Perú-Waka' (henceforth Waka'; see figures 1.1, 11.1) indicates that these strong associations of prosperity with divine rulership were not discarded entirely by inhabitants of this major political and economic center. The strongest evidence thus far for postroyal continuity and transition at Waka' is seen at the city's primary public civic-ceremonial shrine, Structure M13-1. Artifact-rich and heavily and patchily burned offerings blanketed the northern and southern side of this structure's final central staircase at the plaza level and throughout various areas atop the superstructure (Navarro-Farr 2009; Navarro-Farr et al. 2013; see figure 11.2). We also noted numerous instances of reaggregated stelae (some of which had been broken in earlier periods) that had been

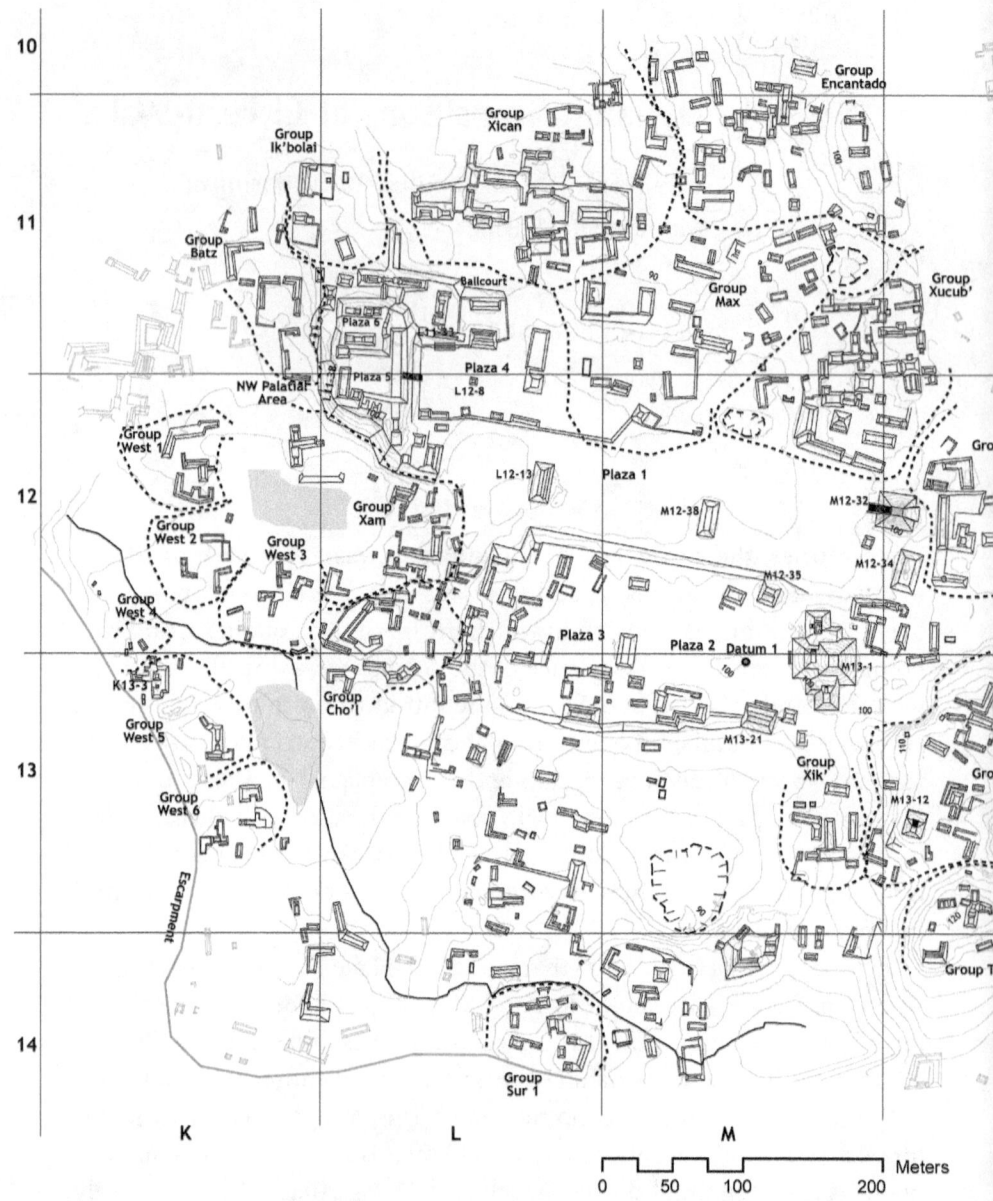

The City Center at El Perú-Waka'
(2003-2006, 2011-2012)

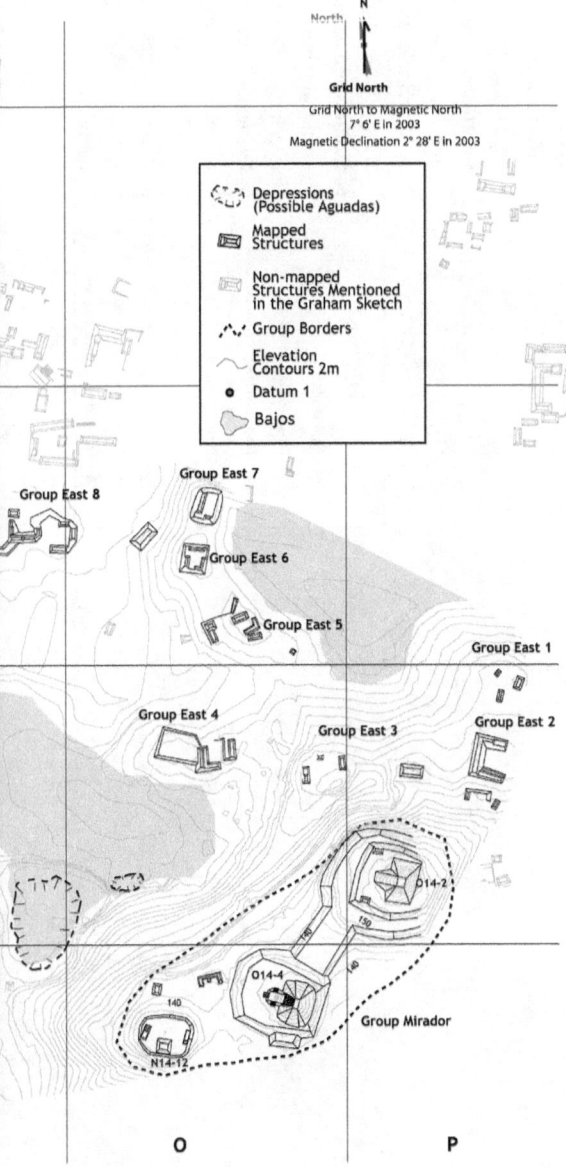

Figure 11.1. Central Zone at Waka'. Map compiled by Evangelia Tsesmeli. Data collected by Evangelia Tsesmeli, Damien Marken, Edwin Román, Melissa Knight, and J. C. Meléndez. Courtesy of the El Perú-Waka' Regional Archaeological Project.

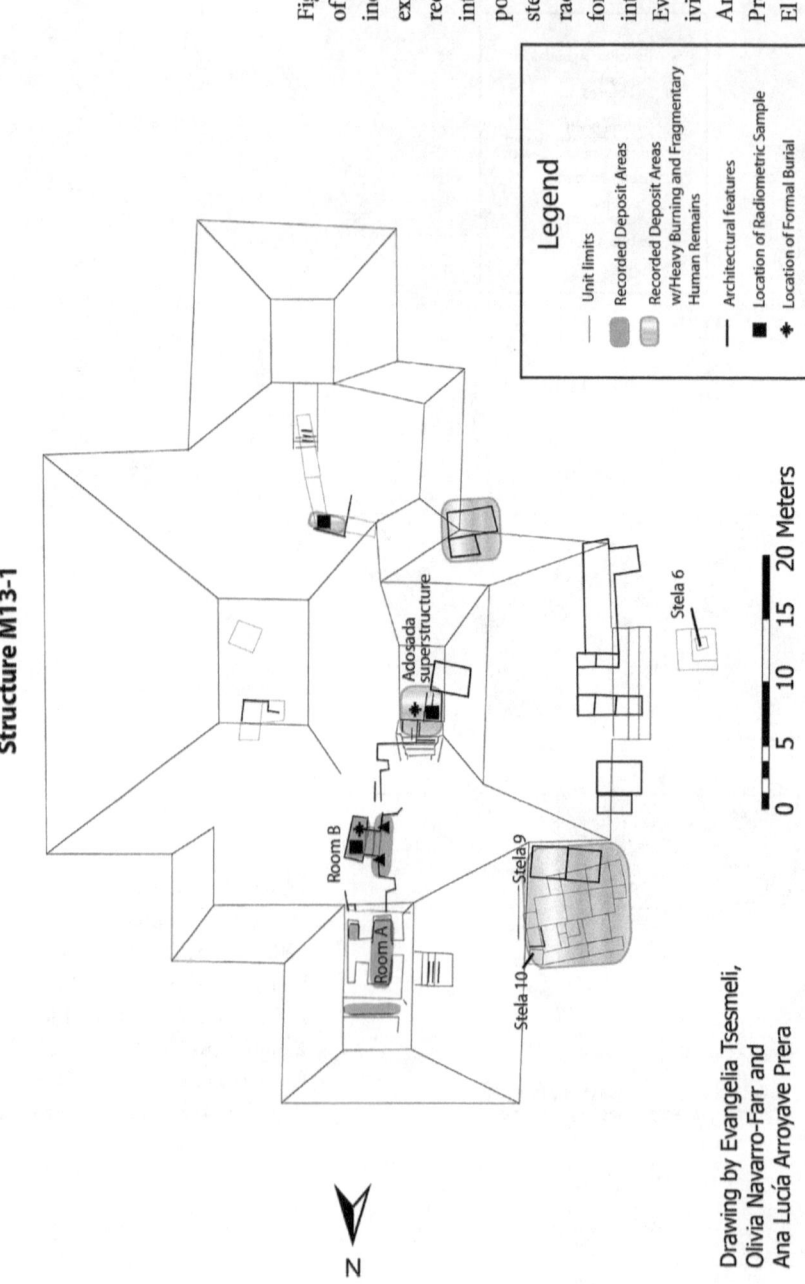

Figure 11.2. Plan view of Structure M13-1 indicating locations of exposed architecture, recorded deposit areas, intensely burned deposit areas, locations of stelae, areas sampled for radiocarbon dates, and formal and informal interments. Drawing by Evangelia Tsesmeli, Olivia Navarro-Farr and Ana Lucia Arroyave Prera. Courtesy of the El Perú-Waka' Regional Archaeological Project.

relocated to this building and were directly associated with these deposits. These activities demonstrate an understanding and deliberate manipulation of the material symbol systems associated with divine kingship that appears to have endured into the Late to Terminal Classic (ca. AD 750–950) at Waka'. Thus, instead of a strictly violent end-of-site occupation followed by rapid abandonment, as has been noted at other sites (e.g., Aguateca; see Inomata 2003, 2006a), what we see at this civic-ceremonial building is more indicative of cumulative and diverse ritual acts of votive behaviors that underscore the endurance of social memory (e.g. see Mills and Walker 2008; Van Dyke and Alcock 2003; see also Houk this volume).

Arguments for the specifically ritual and episodic nature of the deposits that blanket Structure M13-1 have been elaborated elsewhere and are not the primary focus of this chapter (see Navarro-Farr et al. 2008; Navarro-Farr and Arroyave Prera 2014). That said, as I consider evidence of ritual activity at M13-1, I think it is important to make clear how I view ritual theoretically. I frame ritual as a dynamic process that can simultaneously guide human actions, order society, and serve as a unifying point for diverse groups while also engendering innovative societal constructs that stimulate innovations and change. The Waka' data underscore the complex nature of ceremonial activity seen throughout a period associated with the decline of the institution of divine kingship, and this at least partially addresses some of the questions posed by the editors of this volume. Before I engage with the elements of the editors' questions that I see most germane to the Waka' case study, I will discuss the context of the deposits, chronology, mortuary evidence, and the reassembled carved stelae in more detail.

Background

Waka' is located within the southern Maya lowlands in the heart of the Laguna del Tigre National Park and Biosphere Reserve. This park is located within the municipality of San Andrés in the northwestern part of the department of Petén. The site is situated geographically east of the San Juan River and six kilometers north of the San Pedro Mártir River. Ceramic evidence indicates the site was initially settled during the Preclassic period (Pérez Robles et al. 2008), although we are still in the early stages of understanding the full extent and nature of the early settlement at Waka' (but see Pérez Robles 2004). Specifically, the site's occupational history spans the late Preclassic (approximately 400 BC to AD 250) to the Terminal Classic (AD 830 to AD 1000; Pérez Robles et al. 2008; see also Eppich 2011). The

Table 11.1. Ceramic sequence for El Perú-Waka'

Kaq Complex[a]	Q'an Complex[b]	Saq Complex[c]	Q'eq Complex[d]	Morai Complex[e]	Rax Complex[f]
			Palmar: orange ground Codex style		
			Palmar: Saxche variety		Miseria Appliqué
			Palmar Orange Polychrome: cream ground Codex style		
			Zacatel Cream Polychrome		
			Palmar Orange Polychrome		
			Tinaja Red		
	Sacluc Black-on-orange		Infierno Black		
	Picoleros Red-on-orange		Carmelita Incised		
	Flor Cream		Undesignated waxy redware		
Sierra Red			Undesignated waxy blackware		
Polvero Black				Anonal Orange Polychrome	
	Aguila Orange			Lombriz Orange Polychrome	
		Lucha Incised		Altar Orange	
		Caribal Red		Chablekal Grey	
		Iberia Orange		Chicxulub Incised	
		Balanza Black		Trapiche Incised	
		San Blas Red-on-orange		Torro-Gouged Incised	
		Boltco Black-on-orange		Undesignated red-on-cream bichrome	
		Dos Arroyos Orange Polychrome			Poite Incised
		Caldero Buff Polychrome			Pabellon Modeled-carved
					Cameron Incised
					Kilikan Composite
					Cholul Fluted

Source: Adapted from Eppich et al. (2005, Figure 1).
Notes: a. Late Preclassic.
b. Protoclassic.
c. Early Classic.
d. Late Classic.
e. Late Terminal Transition.
f. Terminal Classic.

site is situated in a geographically strategic position along extensive river routes and at the crossroads of powerful polities. It was occupied steadily throughout the Classic period and was abandoned gradually during the Terminal Classic period, although some level of occupation persisted until AD 1000 (Eppich 2011; see also table 11.1.).

Waka's epicentral plan illustrates the ritual significance of Structure M13-1. The architectural focal point is the vast palace complex situated atop an escarpment that overlooks a populous town below (figure 11.1). From this northwest royal palace, the prominent Mirador complex, built atop a natural promontory and visible to the southeast, would have been seen rising high above the surrounding countryside, although it is not likely to have been routinely visited by a majority of Wakeños because access to it was limited. Structure M13-1, as Waka's principal *public* shrine, occupies a pivotal place in Waka's central zone, between the westerly palace and the spatially restricted Mirador complex. M13-1's prominent position on the eastern periphery of one of the city's largest plazas designates the place and space as performative and highly accessible, suggesting that it was well situated in the collective social memory of all Wakeños.

Waka's Political History: Epigraphic Evidence

Epigraphic evidence dating to the Early Classic at Waka' is elusive. Texts and monuments dating to the earliest part of this period are few and those that exist tend to be badly eroded. What we do have from the latter part of the Early Classic that refers to even earlier centuries suggests the founder of the dynasty likely ruled during the first or second century AD (Guenter 2014). Monuments dating to the fourth century feature rulers bearing Teotihuacán-affiliated accouterments. Among the most informative monuments vis-à-vis Waka's Early Classic political history are Stelae 16 and 15. Stela 16 bears the only known representation of Siyah K'ahk', who was affiliated with Teotihuacán. Dedicated in 470 AD, it was commissioned nearly a century after the events surrounding Siyah K'ahk's entrada into Waka' and, subsequently, Tikal (Guenter 2014). Stela 16 also bears an early reference to Waka's three patron gods, the Drunken Death-God Akan, a badly damaged unknown god with a jaguar ear, and Ixik Uh, or "Lady Moon," an apparent moon goddess (Guenter 2014).

Waka's Stela 15 records the arrival of Siyah K'ahk' in January 378, only eight days before his arrival at Tikal, which he took control of. It is important to point out that although Waka' and Tikal share general Early Classic inclusion of Teotihuacán-affiliated royal insignia and experienced closely overlapping epigraphic hiatuses during the Middle Classic, Tikal abandoned much of this imagery in the late fifth century while Waka' appears to have emphasized it (Guenter 2014). Additionally, Guenter (2014) notes numerous stylistic differentiations suggesting divergent political paths and Waka's likely independence from Tikal. In the Late Classic, Waka' became a vassal of the Snake Kingdom (Calakmul), and its monumental inscriptions bear witness to this strong political alliance. Moreover, the fact that we found many of the Early Classic monuments deliberately fragmented (many of which had been reassembled) at some point(s) during the Late Terminal Classic leads Guenter (2014) to suspect that Waka's Late Classic political alliance with the Snake Kingdom may have played a role in the deliberate destruction of its earlier monuments. The eighth-century political history is quite difficult to make sense of, as many of the monuments and dates are either looted or eroded, resulting in a highly dubious and fragmentary record. In any case, we know that the site's monumental history ends sometime in the late eighth or early ninth centuries (Guenter 2014). This same Late Terminal Classic era is also the period when we see the extensive accumulative activities at Structure M13-1.

Structure M13-1: Context and Meaning in Materiality

Structure M13-1 spans the width of Plaza 2 along its eastern periphery (see figure 11.1). The building faces due west and features a high central pyramid with a large attached platform and two flanking constructions on its north and south sides. The northern terrace features a series of small rooms and is entirely asymmetrical with the southern flank, which includes a pyramidal superstructure with a staircase to its north. This south flank is still largely unexcavated and its construction history and relationship to the entire building is not yet understood. The building's continued importance is underscored by the extensive degree to which it was subjected to Late Terminal Classic period refurbishments along its northern terrace, which were recorded during the 2005 and 2006 field seasons (Navarro-Farr and Arroyave Prera 2014). Specifically, excavations on the final-phase architecture on the building's northern and central terraces and to a limited degree on the southern terraces revealed a complex series of poorly executed construction additions, abutting walls, and varied refurbishments. Many of these modifications were undertaken with inferior resources and cut stones robbed from nearby buildings.

Although surface deposits are seen in some isolated locations atop the superstructure, they are most densely accumulated immediately north and south of the building's final central staircase (Navarro-Farr 2009; Navarro-Farr et al. 2013; see figure 11.2). Materials deposited in these locales included varied quantities of ceramics, worked chert, obsidian and shell, fragments of human crania and long bones, painted and modeled stucco, and a suite of other worked and unworked materials, including some pyrite, jade, shell, speleothem, loofah, and other unidentified source materials. There are additional deposits signaling diverse ritual episodes throughout the superstructure in association with the Late Terminal phase architectural modifications mentioned above. The central staircase is part of the final construction episode of the attached platform, or *adosada* (Spanish for attached). The extensive range of worked and unworked materials present in nearly each level of these deposits in their various locales, both atop and at the base of the building, the diverse mortuary assemblages, and the differential patches of in situ burning suggests both diversity of activity and ceremonial purpose (Navarro-Farr et al. 2008; see Figure 11.2). Diversity is also underscored by the dating of the materials in the deposits themselves, which is discussed below.

Dating the Deposits: Ceramic Evidence

The exhaustive excavation, analysis, and interpretation of the behaviors that resulted in these deposits have provided a far more nuanced understanding of the ceremonial dynamics marking the Late to Terminal Classic transition at Waka'. In terms of the recorded history, this time frame is coeval with the placement of the site's last stela in the late eighth century. The depositional episodes that resulted in these accumulated materials correspond with the decline of the site's royal court. If Waka's royal court authority was dissolved, it appears this did not entirely inhibit continued occupation through the next century (as the dated deposit materials evince). Life did indeed go on at Waka'; we are still in the incipient stages of understanding, on a site-wide level, how Waka's governing body—previously in the form of a court surrounding a divine ruler—transformed into one without royal authority, but with some kind of organized political hierarchy.

Keith Eppich's (2010) analysis of ceramic samples from each in situ deposit indicates a relative span for the related activities from approximately AD 700 to 900. This chronology is corroborated by three radiometric dates (Navarro-Farr and Arroyave Prera 2014). However, we have also been able to isolate discrete events from various locales, permitting the outline of a rough sequence of activities, which further underscores their episodic nature. Eppich's (2011) ceramic data indicate deposits on the superstructure's northernmost room, atop the northern terrace, date to the Late Classic (ca. AD 700–820). Others along the center of this northern terrace, and at the far northern end, date, according to a recently identified transitional ceramic complex termed Morai (Eppich 2011), to between the Late and Terminal Classic (ca. AD 770–820). Finally, the deposit area at the base of the structure, to the north of the stair side dates to the early facet of the Terminal Classic (ca. AD 800–900). This indicates that, in general, the deposits atop the superstructure preceded those at the base in the northwest corner.

As mentioned, these deposits also include varying quantities of other artifacts, including broken chert projectile points and biface fragments, obsidian blade fragments, figurine heads (see Houk this volume, for more on figurine heads in similar contexts), worked and unworked fragments of shell, hematite, and jade, fragmented human remains, broken grinding stones, pieces of modeled stucco, broken stela fragments, and an array of other miscellaneous items. The quantities of these items vary by stratigraphic layer and horizontal position (see Navarro-Farr 2009). Within these dense artifact accumulations there is evidence of a variety of ritual patterns and technologies (Walker 1995), including patches of extensive burning, isolated small-scale ritual terminations, votive offerings, and a diverse array of mortuary assemblages embedded within certain depositional areas.

Mortuary Patterns

The varied mortuary assemblages incorporated in the deposits to the north of the central staircase and atop the northern terrace convey patterns of scattering and some isolated evidence suggesting dismemberment. At the base of the structure, deposits include numerous instances of scattered, desiccated, and fragmentary human remains consisting primarily of cranial and long-bone elements. There are also two isolated incidents of likely dismemberment; one consists of a severed foot within the deposits at the base of the building. The other is a decapitated cranium atop the superstructure. The severed foot included anatomically articulated metatarsals and phalanges and the connecting sesamoid bones (Navarro-Farr 2009, 173). In subsequent analyses, Piehl (2010, 192) noted that "the articulated left foot of an adolescent from level 3, strata 2 (18-3-65-NE-A, B) was associated with the distal end of the left tibia and fibula (18-3-65-NE-A, B, D)." The severed cranium included only the skull and at least three articulated cervical vertebrae. Although these vertebrae were present in anatomical position, no cut marks were observed. However, the cut marks were simply no longer visible due to severe cortical erosion and other taphonomic factors (Piehl 2008, 178–179).

Additionally, there are two rather distinct interments atop the northern terrace. One of these represents the repurposing of a small room opportunistically converted into a burial chamber, complete with a small vault. We designated this space Room B as it constituted the second terminal phase–era enclosed room discovered atop the building's northern terrace. The other interment was an individual who was deposited without formal burial architecture or furniture with burned materials on top of the torso. These diverse arrangements are all embedded in the extensive deposits at M13-1. Elsewhere, these varied overlapping ritual episodes and accumulations have been likened to a palimpsest (Navarro-Farr and Arroyave Prera 2014).

Jennifer Piehl (2010) noted a total MNI of nine from the skeletal material deposited at the base of the building alone. This includes one subadult and an unspecified number of infant remains. Based on the skeletal inventory, Piehl also suggests that some individuals who were deposited nearly complete, while selected elements of others were deposited. A minimum number of seven individuals is represented by the various mortuary patterns recorded atop the superstructure along the northern terrace (Piehl 2008). No MNI was noted for the south sector deposit, though heavy burning was recorded.

It is also important to address patterns exhibited in the deposits at the northwest base of the building, where Piehl's (2010) analyses revealed that crania and long bones were the most frequent elements present. In fact, she states that crania and dentition are present in every deposit layer there. The ancestor bundle is a principal form of votive offering that incorporates human remains. These often included the deposition of long bones and crania, as they were the preferred skeletal elements for removal from primary burials for secondary placement as dedication deposits in ancestor shrines (McAnany 1995, 1998; Schele and Freidel 1990; Schele and Mathews 1998). Ancestor veneration was apparently a common practice among the ancient Maya (Gillespie 2000; Kunen et al. 2002; McAnany 1995, 1998) and was usually linked to establishing ties to a legitimate ancestral line or house (Gillespie 2000).

The remains here are highly fragmentary and many have been exposed in various areas of the deposit to burning and modification. Some of the human remains in each level and stratum in the deposits recorded at the northwest base of the plaza floor level (north of the fronting platform) have been burned. Piehl (2010) notes the burning ranges from regular and total blackening of skeletal fragments to mere black smudging on some specimens. This suggests that there were varying intensities of burning episodes.

In terms of visible pathologies, the overall lack of cortical erosion and the better preservation of dental remains meant that dental health was more consistently determinable. However, this was also limited at times by enamel erosion. Caries are present on only about 4 percent of the entire assemblage of dental information corresponding to the deposit areas north of the central staircase atop the plaza floor. Calculus deposits are also present on 65 percent (26 of 40) of teeth. Dental hypoplasias, indicating health issues during childhood, were observed on 56 percent (18 of 32) of observable teeth in this assemblage. At least two individuals in this deposit had teeth that were filed (Piehl 2010, 195). In her concluding statements on pathologies from the skeletal assemblage recovered from deposits north of the staircase, Piehl (2010, 5) observes that the pathologies are consistent with those of the entire range of the Waka' population thus far known. This information cannot tell us who these individuals were or where they came from. The pathology and health information indicates that they fall well within the average range of Waka's general population. While this may not indicate that these are the remains of scattered ancestor bundles or who may have been responsible for their inclusion in these deposits, the pattern of their deposition and the associated context suggest that they may be tertiary depositions of once-bundled ancestors. Again, which socioeconomic sector(s) of the population these remains may pertain to remains uncertain.

I argue that the inclusion of fragmentary remains that may represent ancestral bundles does not necessarily suggest a profane act. Again, this would presuppose that the ancient Maya made these kinds of esoteric distinctions, which are neither supported clearly by archaeological data (see table 11.2) nor in evidence in contemporary Maya worldviews (Tedlock 1982). Of particular interest is the overlap in patterns Piehl (2008, 2010) identified in skeletal analysis with the chronological evidence Eppich (2011) analyzed. Specifically, along the central northern terrace, Piehl and Eppich note patterns in the skeletal and ceramic materials respectively, suggesting closely related activities, and a discrete area of behaviors distinct from other

Table 11.2. Categories of evidence for desecratory, reverential, and/or both forms of ritual termination

Reverential Termination[a, b]	Desecratory Termination[c]	Reverential or Desecratory Termination[d]
Broken shell adornments	Scattered and disarticulated human bone	Broken and displaced or reset stelae
Halved grinding stones and *manos*	Broken chert and obsidian spear and projectile points	Widespread burning
Fragmented jades		Widespread marl
Inclusion of "secular" or utilitarian items (possibly of domestic utility)		Scattered broken (reconstructible) vessel fragments
		Broken pieces of modeled and/or painted stucco

Notes: a. Note overlaps in observed phenomena and resultant interpretations.
b. Mock (1998); Freidel et al. (1993); Garber et al. (1998); Piehl (2005).
c. Ambrosino (1998, 2003, 2007); Inomata (2003); Pagliaro et al. (2003); Stanton et al. (2008); Suhler (1996).
d. Ambrosino (1998, 2003, 2007); Duncan (2005); Freidel and Schele (1989); Freidel et al. (1993); Garber (1983, 1986); Lucero (2003, 2006); Mock (1998); Pagliaro et al. (2003); Piehl (2005); Stanton et al. (2008).

activity areas both on top of and below the superstructure. By contrast, the deposit locales adjacent to the rear of the fronting platform's superstructure wall near the centerline, at the southern sector, and at the structure base, exhibit different patterns of inclusion and treatment of certain skeletal materials (see figure 11.2). Overall, the evidence underscores previous interpretations (Navarro-Farr 2009; Navarro-Farr and Arroyave Prera 2014) for a range of diverse activities carried out over time rather than a single large-scale event. The evidence thus points to long-term ritual revisitations and active engagement with this building.

It seems clear that the memory of M13-1 was alive and that its significance and continued potency as a vehicle for ceremonialism and communication with powerful ancestors was well understood by Late to Terminal Classic era Wakeños acting throughout a much longer period of time than single-event-driven ritual terminations would suggest. In other words, these long-term patterns point to enduring social memories and a determination to reside at Waka' much longer and with greater deliberation than might otherwise be expected when considering that these deposits represent not single episodes of massive ritual termination (as previously hypothesized by Navarro-Farr et al. 2008) but rather multiple, long-term, and varied ceremonial acts (see also Houk this volume; Schwake and Iannone this volume).

These acts contradict the traditional image of a declining polity on the brink of the Maya collapse; populations at Waka' did not appear to have diminished, as was the case in many of the case studies discussed in this volume. Moreover, at M13-1 we have evidence of a diverse body of artifacts and contextual arrangements that hint at a diverse body of social actors. These actors are not only actively engaged over a century after the demise of royal kingship but were organized in some fashion to execute feats of incredible labor and energy channeled toward the movement and reaggregation of massive stela fragments to this location, all with few and inferior resources. These acts, discussed below, likely were meant to invoke memories of times of greater prosperity.

Patterns in Stone: The Stelae at M13-1

In reviewing the evidence of multiple suites of ritual activity carried out over time at Structure M13-1—through the end of the Late Classic and into the Terminal Classic—it is important to discuss the implications for ritual activities involving the deposition of widely varied artifact classes and patterns carried out at a major public center at a time when the royal court authority was seriously waning. Commissioned stelae constitute one of the primary markers of authority, and many archaeologists take the absence of them to signal the fading of royal courts. Guenter (2014) indicates that at least one monument may have been dedicated as late as AD 801, though there is some uncertainty because of its highly eroded state; the decipherment of this date rests largely on stylistic attributes. Whether or not the site's final commissioned stela dates to 801 or earlier during the late eighth century, there is abundant evidence of the continued movement and reassembling of existing stelae that had been broken or defaced in previous centuries. Among the many instances of stela reassemblage are Stelae 9 and 10 (figure 11.3), both of which were discovered in direct association with the M13-1 deposits. They both feature prominent Early Classic style and figures. Stela 6 (figure 11.4) features a Late Classic ruler and was recovered face down in front of the building along the centerline axis.

Stela 9 is a monument from the fifth century (see figure 11.3). Excavations from 2003–2006 revealed three fragments of the monument's base embedded in the dense deposits north of the building's staircase. The fragments include some of the finest examples of Early Classic stone carving seen anywhere at the site. All were associated with these deposits on the north side of the front stair side, clearly having been placed there in temporal

Figure 11.3. *From left to right*, Waka' Stela 9, bottom section (photo by Patrick Aventurier) and Stela 10 (photo by David Freidel). Images compiled by Mary Jane Acuña. Courtesy of the El Perú-Waka' Regional Archaeological Project. The photographs of Stela 9 (left) and Stela 10 (right) are reproduced with the permission of Guatemala's Ministry of Culture and Sports.

association with those activities (Navarro-Farr 2009) sometime during the Late to Terminal Classic. The base of the monument features a *witz* monster with serpents emerging from the creature's mouth. There are also fine-line incisions surrounding the feet of the unknown ruler standing atop the *witz* monster. These texts make reference to a *wite' naah*, which some interpret as a fire shrine and a locus for new fire ceremonialism closely associated with Teotihuacán (Fash et al. 2009; Freidel et al. 2007; Stuart 2000; Taube 2004). Although the identity of the ruler depicted on Stela 9 is uncertain (only his/her feet remain), we do know that there is a reference in the fine-line incision text to the name K'inich Bahlam. Because of the style of the renderings on this monument (both iconographically and epigraphically), Guenter (2005) feels confident about dating it to approximately AD 500.

Stela 10 was found standing with a crudely constructed and collapsed platform surrounding it (see figure 11.3). Given the evidence of Terminal Classic period stone robbing from the adjacent structure M12-35 (see Escobedo and Acuña 2004; Acuña 2014), we hypothesized that this platform was likely constructed with cut stones that had been removed from other

Figure 11.4. *From left to right*, Waka' Stela 6 (photo by Francisco Castañeda) and Stela 34 Images compiled by Mary Jane Acuña, courtesy of the El Perú-Waka' Regional Archaeological Project. The photograph of Stela 6 (*left*) is reproduced with the permission of Guatemala's Ministry of Culture and Sports. The photograph of Stela 34 (*right*) is reproduced with the permission of the Cleveland Museum of Art: *Front Face of a Stela (Freestanding Stone with Relief)* Mesoamerica, Guatemala, Department of the Petén, El Perú (also known as Waka'), Maya people ((AD 250–900), Classic Period (AD 200–1000). Limestone, 274.4 × 182.3 cm. Purchase from the J. H. Wade Fund 1967.29.

buildings. This reuse of carved stones further underscores the lack of resources one would expect during a period of dynastic decline. The collapsed material of this crude platform was also found intermixed with the deposit materials (Navarro-Farr 2009). A test excavation associated with this monument not only revealed deposit materials in direct association with Stela 10 but also that the monument had been reset during the Late to Terminal Classic (thus, M13-1 was not its original location). Stela 10 is severely defaced on the carved surface; the face of the individual depicted has clearly been deliberately gouged out, leaving a concave depression where the face and identity of the individual would have otherwise been. However, what remains is distinctive enough iconographically to relate the individual and style to the late fourth through the fifth century. Teotihuacán's influence in lowland Maya art is distinguishable in the garb the figure is wearing (Guenter 2005). In his left arm, the individual holds a rectangular shield, a shape that contrasts with the typical round Maya shield. There are other examples of similarly shaped rectangular shields, specifically those seen being held by Teotihuacáno warriors on either side of King Siyaj Chan K'awiil on Stela 31 at Tikal.

Excavations were begun in front of Structure M13-1's central staircase in the 2004 season (Navarro-Farr 2005, 2009) to uncover Stela 6 (see figure 11.4), which appeared to have fallen or been pushed face forward in antiquity and was visible from the surface. This stela's position on the centerline of the building and the fact that it appeared, at least initially, to have been brought down intentionally were important reasons to excavate, examine, and restore it.

Once the monument was completely exposed and removed, the carved side revealed some interesting information. Although the face of the monument had sustained some erosion damage due to groundwater percolation, the carvings had clearly not been defaced in any way. The image depicted a female figure rendered in a Late Classic style analogous to that of Stela 34 at Waka', which features Lady K'ab'el and is on display at the Cleveland Museum of Art. David Freidel (personal communication, 2004) has speculated that the image rendered on Stela 6 might also represent Lady K'ab'el (see figure 11.4).

The Stela 6 excavations also revealed the base of a previously unrecorded and uncarved stela fragment adjacent to a circular altar. There was no evidence of any dedication activity associated with the fallen Stela 6. Although we did not recover evidence of deposit activity in this area, we noted the familiar pattern of resetting monuments. This behavior draws clear parallels with the deposition of other previously destroyed and/or defaced monuments that are also associated with deposits situated in close proximity and date to this later period.

In another context (Navarro-Farr et al. 2008), I have referred to Shirley Boteler Mock's (1998a) discussion of the manipulation of stelae in her volume on termination and dedication rituals, in which she says that such reuse and placement of fragments often form part of termination activities. However, I have moved away from interpretations of the activities at M13-1 as wholesale ritual termination, although there are identifiable episodes of such behaviors within the deposits. Mock's work certainly draws attention to the ritual potency of carved monuments, and she notes that their reuse is integral to harnessing such potency (see also Harrison-Buck this volume). Clearly there was a need to manipulate both Early and Late Classic stelae in the context of the intense ritual activities carried out for at least a century under the auspices of some as-yet-undefined authority. Although this authority remains undefined, we can argue that it is *not* a divine ruler, given the dates of related activities coeval with and following the erection of the site's last stela.

Preliminarily, I suggest those engaging M13-1 were referencing the role this building had during an earlier period. Considering its significant monumentality, its centrality in the site, and the locus of a great many repositioned defaced and/or fragmentary stelae, I posit that Structure M13-1 was viewed during this time as an instrumental element of the ritual cycle for the invocation of rains, the continued path of the sun, and the prosperity of the fragile ecosystem. State rituals carried out here may have been largely conducted in the interest of continued agricultural prosperity (see Iannone this volume) among other state matters. If this was the case and such prosperity had been successfully achieved in earlier periods, it would have made sense to continue to invoke Waka's principal ancestors (at their principal public shrine) for continued support, in whatever and as many ways as could be sought. In other words, the relocation of these monuments to M13-1 at this time may constitute evidence of attempts to focus the sociopolitical memory of the site's inhabitants to recollections of more prosperous times for the specific purpose of seeking to realign a cosmic imbalance.

It might seem inconsistent or counterintuitive to argue that Waka's residents besought the emblems of divine kingship if this institution is known to have been defunct. But it is actually quite understandable if these actions are considered from a Classic Maya worldview. While divine ancestors who took human form and thereby empowered themselves with the authority to carry out an institutionalized form of rule may no longer have been viable, their existence as transcendent beyond this particular form cannot have been questioned. In other words, as my friend Francisco noted in the field, "You can change the kings . . . not the gods."

Houston and Stuart (1998) and Houston, Stuart, and Taube (2006) have made significant contributions to the idea of manipulating fragments of portraits and rulers in their exploration of the concept of personhood and ancient Maya understandings of self. They do so by investigating the ancient Maya word *bah*. They point out the "semantic domains" of *bah*, which means "self" or "person," are also closely related to the words for "head" and "face" and are conveyed through representations of a head or a face (Houston and Stuart 1998). "The self extends visibly to other representations, yet essence transfers along with resemblance; the surface, the 'face,' does not so much mimic aspects of identity as realize them. In terms of being, an image embodies more than a clever artifice that simulates identity; it both resembles and *is* the entity it reproduces" (Houston and Stuart 1998, 77). To this end, ruined or defaced aspects of portraiture do more than mar a visual representation; they undermine the very identity and personhood or self that was represented therein and thus ritually kill the *chulel* of the individual (see also Harrison-Buck this volume). The stelae seen at M13-1 were either defaced or broken in earlier periods. This likely occurred as a result of changing alliances and shifting political affiliations. The *chulel* of the monuments was forcibly removed, their embodied figures were ritually dismembered, and those pieces were summarily scattered (as may have also occurred in the case of the friezes and stele at Minanha, as discussed by Schwake and Iannone this volume). That they were subsequently, at great physical cost and through significant organization of some labor forces, reaggregated and reset with crude yet earnest efforts to build incorporating enclosures around them and embed them in a highly charged ritual tableau of dense ceremonial accumulations at M13-1 indicates the lengths Wakeños went during Late to Terminal Classic periods to reengage with these pieces, the figures represented on them, and the memory of the place where they were resituated. I suggest that in so doing, they sought out the monuments and reset them here as enduring emblems of fecundity and prosperity and that in this way the monuments were ultimately honored and healed.

Addressing the Scapegoat King Model

In the introduction to this volume, the editors posed a number of questions challenging contributors to evaluate whether elements of the scapegoat model pertain to the collapse of institutional divine kingship in the Maya area in light of their specific data sets. These questions ask researchers to reconsider evidence of violence, royal legitimacy, collapse crises, dominant ideologies, prosperity and decline in the context of politics, economies, environment, and other elements. I believe the Waka' data set can contribute to discussions of some elements of these complex questions. They include the following (from Iannone et al. this volume):

> "Do ritual terminations and/or violence always accompany the removal of a king, and if so, why are such acts a necessary part of the process of deactivating divine authority?"
>
> "Are there other events or processes that coincide with the demise of kingly authority?"

These questions deal with the issue of ritual termination and its association with deactivation of kingly authority. The short answers to these questions are "not necessarily" and "yes, other events can coincide with the demise of kingly authority," respectively. I would also add to these discussion points that I do not believe correlates for ritual termination associated with possible "deactivation" or "demise of kingly authority" are necessarily always demonstrative of violence per se.

I think the challenge here lies in distinguishing termination rituals from a suite of other differentially motivated ritual acts that may on the surface look a lot like ritual termination. Making the distinction requires painstaking excavation and recording to tease out nuances in such patterns. Early in my own excavations, I was convinced the evidence at M13-1 constituted wholesale ritual termination (see Navarro-Farr et al. 2008). Ultimately, the noted parameters for ritual termination Freidel and colleagues (1993) and Shirley Mock (1998a) advanced and a number of Freidel's students (Ambrosino 2007; Garber 1983; Pagliaro et al. 2003; Suhler 1996) detailed materially, which include the ability to reconstruct in situ smashing of vessels and other preciosities, the blanketing of liminal spaces (such as doors and stairways), and the deliberate layering of marl and defaced building elements, the evidence at M13-1 simply did not fit materially with these patterns upon closer inspection. If not termination, what then did this evidence mean? This is a question I have and will continue to grapple with.

What I contend is that rather than constituting a mass ritual termination, the evidence indicates multiple acts layered on top of each other, each representative of different groups and intentions. The following elements can be bound together in this seeming disparity of ritual material and purpose: 1) selection of the same place (M13-1) as the locus for deposition; 2) the generally votive aspect of the layering and selective burning of objects, much like material votive accumulations associated with contemporary shrine sites across the Maya area (e.g., see Brown 2004); and 3) the fact that many of the items (particularly those encountered in the deposits at either end of the building's base) are more diverse in terms of artifact types than in any other analogous deposit yet found dating to the same period at the site.

Another element to these two questions relates to termination and violence. A point to consider is one I have elaborated elsewhere but that bears mentioning here. Attempts to differentiate between interpretations of intentional desecrating violence and reverential behavior in ancient Maya contexts are fraught with challenges (Navarro-Farr 2009; Navarro-Farr and Arroyave Prera 2014). From an indigenous worldview, these are not necessarily mutually exclusive domains. In other words, the sacred and the profane are not bifurcated as they are in Judeo-Christian traditions (Tedlock 1982). However, that complexity should not be understood to suggest that the ancient Maya did not practice votive ceremony, as this is what I believe most appropriately characterizes the nature of activities enacted at structure M13-1, particularly those at the base of the structure. Perhaps such complex intentional behaviors might be best understood as a responses to notions of personhood and essence or "soul force" (Freidel and Schele 1989; Freidel et al. 1993; Houston and Stuart 1996, 292 [after Vogt 1969]; Schele and Mathews 1998), which are embodied by both organic and inorganic matter in Maya worldviews.

Although there are instances that can be interpreted as violent, including the two examples of dismemberment discussed above, I do not believe that the evidence at M13-1 is indicative of reactionary violence or that it constitutes wholesale termination ritual. What I think these deposits do convey is more suggestive of votive deposition of diverse offerings, including fragments of what may have been once bundled ancestor remains. My answers to the questions of whether or not termination always follows the demise of divine kingship and whether or not it is always violent in nature would be "no, not always."

Other questions posed by the editors relate to the explanatory potential of the scapegoat model:

"Was the collapse of the kingly governance structure a protracted process (e.g., AD 750–1050), or do the key events suggest a comparatively short period of demise (e.g., AD 810–830)?"
"What specific events (and material correlates) mark the dissolution of kingly governance?"

"At whom were the events, and the actions that constituted these events, aimed (i.e., just the king? Or a broader range of political agents, spaces, and symbols)?"

"Do these events reflect the types of activities one would expect given the tenets of the scapegoat king model?"

It is difficult to speak directly to the process of decline of kingship at Waka' with the date I present here. However, if we consider the case at M13-1 to be an indirect index of reactions to declining kingship, I think the evidence definitely favors protracted responses at M13-1 (see discussion on deposit dates below). We know that occupation at the site definitely continued throughout the Late Terminal Classic (see site chronology discussion below).

Regarding the second question above, the commissioning of the site's final stelae in the late eighth or early ninth century (Guenter 2005) is considered to be an indicator of the decline of Waka's royal court. We know epigraphically that prior to that period Waka' suffered a political defeat when its ruler, Bahlam Tz'am, was defeated by Tikal's ruler, Yik'in Chan K'awiil, in AD 743 (Guenter 2014). Guenter surmises this was likely a major military defeat, as the history was recorded on the innermost lintel of Temple IV at Tikal. However, in spite of this defeat, we know the royal court was not immediately vanquished and likely limped forward at least some decades longer. If the activity at M13-1 was a response organized by members of Waka's populace during and after the decline of divine kings, then the activity was not limited to the site's elite. Indeed, this activity did not even take place at the palace; it took place at the site's most public and open civic-ceremonial structures and may have included, as I have suggested, a broad range of social actors. The actions at M13-1 are inconsistent with expectations of violence and attack on royal insignias as set forth by the tenets of the scapegoat model.

Discussion

While the data here may not be able to speak to the full range of complexity each of these questions presents, I may be able to address some related issues in the future. The evidence may be seen as indirect because it derives not from the context of a royal palace or other elite residence but rather from a civic-ceremonial temple. The evidence dates to a period during and after the decline of royal rule at Waka'. Thus, it does not constitute evidence that can be considered causal for such decline. I do not believe that the evidence conveys retaliatory violence in reaction to the gradual decline of Waka's royal court. Rather, Structure M13-1 was the locus for ritualized attempts to restore soul force through the various multilayered ceremonies and to reaggregate and reset stelae that had been broken and in some cases defaced in previous periods.

The limitations of the current data make it difficult to identify the multiple social actors (including participants, organizers, and sponsors) involved in these multiple depositions in terms of their socioeconomic status or their identities. However, I suggest that the players were a diverse group, based on the assemblage of materials, which includes a range of non-elite items such as abundant utilitarian plain ceramic wares (for more information detailing these arguments, see Navarro-Farr and Arroyave Prera 2014). In addition, ceramic and radiometric chronologies suggest cumulative deposition (Navarro-Farr and Arroyave Prera 2014) rather than in situ termination activity (see Freidel et al. 1993; Suhler 1996; Pagliaro et al. 2003). These deposits also incorporate secondary and/or tertiary deposition of a range of objects (discussed below). This and the location of their deposition flanking the north (Navarro-Farr 2009) and south sides (Navarro-Farr et al. 2013) of the final fronting platform while they are nearly absent on the fronting staircase (Navarro-Farr 2009; Navarro-Farr et al. 2013) is more consistent with patterns observed at contemporary Maya shrine sites (Brown 2004; Tedlock 1982) than those observed in association with ritual termination (e.g., placement on stairways or liminal areas; Mock 1998a).

Because these events spanned the end of the Late Classic through the early part of the Terminal Classic, the same time as the demise of Waka's royal court, they provide an intriguing view of what may have been a kind of ritualized social reorganizing or adaptation to processes of great political and socioeconomic change and distress.

These events correspond directly to the life span of this shrine, which is the locus of collective social memories and a dominant representation of royal ceremonies carried out over the course of its own life history and that of the royal court. These acts mark the tail end of this use life and were undertaken by some organized authority that suggests nonroyal sponsorship, particularly given that the period is coeval with and follows the decline of Waka's royal court. (For more on arguments for the nonroyal and multifaceted nature of the deposit activities marking the Late Terminal Classic use life of M13-1, see Navarro-Farr and Arroyave Prera 2014). This evidence raises new questions not only about how order and governance was restructured during postroyal periods at cities such as Waka' but also about how people perceived the significance of royal governing authorities even as their ability to maintain cosmic balance was waning (see Iannone, Houk this volume). In this light, we can see how people acting at M13-1 may have been working to harness the *chulel* associated with royal prosperity, particularly as it related to agricultural yields through restorative ritual processes meant to balance cosmic cycles and order. One possibility outlined below is the idea that the building was understood in antiquity to have served as a *wite' naah*, or fire shrine.

Remembering the Symbolic: M13-1 as Fire Shrine

Ultimately the evidence is greatly suggestive of diverse acts that appear to have been related to the invocation of memory because the motivations, however varied, were centered on engaging this particular building. I propose that the reason for the abundant Late to Terminal Classic activity at M13-1 has as much to do with the events of that period as with remembering the events that marked the building's earlier use life. I have proposed elsewhere (Navarro-Farr 2009; Navarro-Farr and Arroyave Prera 2014) that in earlier times, this building may have been the location of a lowland Maya *wite' naah*. That is, it might have been one of several Early Classic new fire shrines of highland origin that were established for conducting fire rituals, perhaps associated with prosperity in war or agriculture, which are not mutually exclusive ends (see Taube 2004).

In order to address the question of a *wite' naah*, it is necessary to re-examine what we know about such buildings. The new fire ceremony as practiced by the Aztecs was carried out after the passing of cycles or sheaves of fifty-two years called *tonalpohualli*. This is probably the best documented and latest manifestation of a ceremony that has deep Mesoamerican roots (Fash et al. 2009). The practice, as seen in the Codex Borbonicus, shows four priests holding bundled firewood (see Fash et al. 2009; Figure 3). The bundles were placed over the sacrificed individual's chest and set aflame. For the Aztecs, this act venerated the sun god for its continued presence (Fash et al. 2009). Fash and colleagues (2009) have noted that these bundles closely resemble the T600 Maya glyph from Thompson's catalog. They make a compelling case not only for identifying the earlier iterations of this ceremony at Teotihuacán but also that these ceremonies occurred in association with the attached west-facing frontal platform of the city's famed Pyramid of the Sun. They point to sculptural elements from the shrine on that platform that represent the twisted-cord fire drill of the new fire ceremonies. Fash and his colleagues have therefore identified this attached frontal platform, or *adosada,* as the setting for the inauguration of the Teotihuacán new fire ceremony; they identify it as the original *wite' naah.*

Fash and colleagues (2009, 201–214) make a case for the identification of one such *wite' naah* in the Maya area in the heart of Copan at Structure 10L-16, the seat of that dynasty's kingdom and founder, Teotihuacán-affiliated K'inich Yax K'uk Mo (after Taube 2004). There is much that is compelling about identifying this building as a *wite' naah* and the probable location for a Maya-area new fire ceremony. However, one architectural component is missing from the 10L-16 *wite' naah*: the attached *adosada* platform. In pointing this out, I do not mean to imply disagreement with the identification of 10L-16 as a *wite' naah.* Based on the arguments of Fash and colleagues, I see compelling and slightly distinct evidence at Waka's M13-1 that suggests it may be one such building: Stelae 9 (which refers to a *wite' naah*) and 10 (which features a figure wearing Teotihuacán-style garb) and the central architectural feature noted at Teotihuacán, an *adosada* that constitutes the western front of M13-1.

Concluding Thoughts: M13-1—Royal Monument of the People

The Late to Terminal Classic period at Waka' was a time of intense transition. This cannot have been experienced by Wakeños without some forms of violence. (Certainly economic and social hardships are a violence all their own.) The deterioration of the royal court's authority likely affected royals and the nobility the most. I have noted elsewhere (Navarro-Farr 2009) that the deposits at M13-1 are dominated by decidedly nonroyal items, which suggests that those responsible for the deposits were either no longer in possession of wealth items and therefore discarded what they could or were members of Waka's peasantry who never owned abundant preciosities. The evidence at M13-1 indicates not violence against authority but rather sacred memory of earlier rulers, under whose guidance times at Waka' were more prosperous and favorable. It appears that it was those times and those rulers whose sacred memory was being revered. This evidence allows for at least some reconsideration of a period otherwise known as "the collapse."

As the complexity of these deposits defies existing interpretations such as post-occupational squatter refuse and large-scale ritual termination, it has been challenging to approach this and related contexts interpretively. However, I have been able to reconstruct layered evidence suggesting that

Late to Terminal Classic Waka' experienced a turbulent political transition in ways that are not easily defined by or attributable to singular causal explanations, such as warfare or environmental stress. The decline in installation of royally sponsored public monuments, architectural projects, and hieroglyphic inscriptions was symptomatic of deeper problems that commoners and elites alike would have noticed. It seems likely that Maya people would have actively responded to the uncertainty of the period. I argue that a focus on public ritual performance would have been one such response, a search for order and guidance in tumultuous times. The evidence of active engagement and response throughout this period might then represent what some would call coping.

The picture seen at M13-1 speaks more to a deliberate reassembling and reuse of symbols most emblematic of the institution of divine kingship than it does to the end of that institution. From the deposit evidence we also surmise that the building was continuously revisited throughout this period in varied ways by multiple practitioners. The resulting tapestry of offerings and ritual acts and the location of their practice strongly suggest that members of the populace associated deeply rooted social memories (Mills and Walker 2008) with this building. Given the directed focus on the reuse and repositioning of numerous carved stela fragments, I suggest that the memories dealt specifically with an understanding of the building as a shrine to powerful ancestors.

I have argued elsewhere (Navarro-Farr and Arroyave Prera 2014) that the effects of the politico-economic decline nonroyal Maya citizens of large polities such as Waka' experienced do not tend to be a focus of discussions about why and how state collapse occurs. However, we are becoming increasingly aware of strategies of adaptation and attempted continuity at places such as Waka'. This leads me to question how state collapse narratives are framed. I look beyond the macro-scales and structural decline represented in those discussions toward the micro "on-the-ground" experiences of people who were carrying on in spite of the violence and tumult of declining political systems.

It is important to state a rather simple yet compelling bit of information this research has clearly demonstrated. Intense ritual activity and some form of organized labor were being carried out for at least a century after the decline of the city's royal court. Based on evidence from ceramic contexts dating to this period from across the site (Eppich 2011), population levels also appear to have been stable throughout the Late to Terminal Classic. Scholars frequently note widespread and rather rapid demographic decline as symptomatic of collapse in the southern Maya lowlands (Culbert 1973, 1988; Webster 2002a; Demarest et al. 2004). While this may be true of some major sites, this does not appear to be the situation at Waka' or indeed at many of the other centers discussed in this volume. While the site was ultimately abandoned, this did not occur immediately. Rather, the process was gradual; it took place over the course of at least a century, and probably more. The site-wide ceramic evidence points to the continuity of traditions associated with non-elite utilitarian wares rather than with royal polychrome and elite-centered potting traditions (Eppich 2011). If demographic decline continues to be associated with the decline of the institution of divine kingship, then Waka' represents an inconsistency with that expected pattern.

12

Lords of the Life Force and Their People

Reflections on Ritual Violence and Reverence in the Maya Archaeological Record

DAVID FREIDEL

When it comes to power and its material forms, what can be made can be unmade. As I have noted elsewhere, "Maya Kings were regarded as the instruments, objects, and sacrifices of their constituencies. They were the human stuff of power and like stone, wood, clay, fiber and food, they were the prosaic materials that could be made luminous, crowned resplendent, and transformed through acts of devotion, skill and courage" (Freidel 1992, 129). So it would seem to be with Maya divine kingship. One of our editors, Gyles Iannone, has taken on the daunting task of proposing an explanatory frame of reference for the demise of this institution in the Classic Maya world (chapter 2). Touching on an early effort to think about this prospect in the Maya case (Freidel and Shaw 2000), he has boldly put forward a universal analogy in the divine scapegoat king. He suggests that we can connect the sacrifice of individual kings to a more general, if metaphorical, murder of the institution itself by people who were victimized by the social chaos of the ninth century AD in the Terminal Classic southern lowlands. As a devotee of Maya divine kingship, I am very happy to see this detailed summary appraisal of the utility of the divine rulership hypothesis that presages his discussion of the scapegoat king. In the formative phases of this hypothesis (e.g., Schele and Miller 1986, 103), it was never a sure thing that Maya archaeologists working outside the area containing substantial numbers of public glyphic inscriptions would embrace it as a way of understanding their contexts. I would like to begin my discussion by offering some commentary and encouragement to Gyles Iannone and those who would explore such a challenging path.

First of all, I think we do have some fairly convincing instances of sacrificial murder of some Classic Period kings and queens, although I find that epigraphers of the ancient Maya tend to be quite cautious about identifying royalty in tombs that lack clear glyphic evidence to that effect. Arthur Demarest and his colleagues in the Cancuen research program have discovered what appear to be the remains of the murdered king Kan Maax in a shallow grave there (chapter 7), and the Colha massacre (chapter 8) likely represents another royal court. So while the issue of political action against the institution may still be under scrutiny, action against individual rulers may be documented in the record. I would like to expand this discussion to include two archaeological instances of likely regicide, one in the midst of the textually attested history of the Petén, the second in the northern lowlands, where such history is rare.

Juan Pedro Laporte and Vilma Fialko of the Proyecto Nacional Tikal (1990, 1995) identified the body interred in PNT 019 as plausibly that of a murdered ruler. The evidence included the larger context, which involved the careful preparation of other sepulchers in flanking structures in the old eastern range of the Lost World Pyramid E Group and the placement in those tombs of the corpses of men, women, and children. While the upper body of the individual in PNT 019 was fairly well articulated, it was significantly disturbed in the midsection. As the tomb showed no signs of reentry, it is reasonable in my view to suspect that this disturbance of the body dated from the time of interment or before. Circumstantial evidence, specifically the lack of lower spinal vertebrae in articulation, suggests to me that the individual may have been cut in half. As a form of dismemberment sacrifice this is depicted in several Early Classic scenes, including the Hauberg Stela (Schele and Miller 1986, Plate 66) and a remarkable bowl lid from Becan, Mexico (Finamore and Houston 2010, Plate 82). There are also monumental stucco images ornamenting a version of the North Acropolis of the upper torsos of such victims wearing trefoil crowns that date to this time period (Coe 1990).

Laporte and Fialko identify this individual as royal, based upon artifact evidence in the tomb that includes royal belt plaques typical of kingly regalia and a large tubular jade carved with the mat symbol. I can add that the tomb contained a curved piece of carved and polished conch shell that was pierced so it could be attached to a cloth headband. That artifact is quite like pieces of white polished shell pierced so it could be sewn onto cloth that formed the "white headbands" or royal crowns discovered in Burial 24, a late fourth- or early fifth-century tomb at Yaxuna in Yucatan (Ardren 2002; Freidel and Suhler 1998; Stanton et al. 2010; Suhler 1996). Virginia Fields and Dorie Reents-Budet (2005, 121, plate 25) provide an illustration of a Copan-area jade carving of an Early Classic king wearing such a crown made of rectilinear segments. Historically, the individual in the PNT 019 is quite possibly the king we now know as Chak Tok Ich'aak I, and Laporte and Fialko do propose this identification. They note that the lower half of a deliberately cut stela depicting this king, Tikal Stela 39, was reinstalled in a Late Classic temple room above the tomb. Based on the concentration of Manik II ceramics in the plaza fronting the building, they suggest that the stela may have been originally set in that location in the fourth century AD. Finally, the death of King Chak Tok Ich'aak I in 378 AD is recorded on Stela 31, which dates to the mid-fifth century, with a distinctive glyph depicting the lower half of a person in profile with large liquid scrolls emerging from the midriff.

Elsewhere, in 1993 archaeologists of the Selz Foundation Yaxuna Project discovered Burial 24 in Structure 6F-4, a royal sacrificial tableau macabre ceramically dated to the end of the fourth century or beginning of the fifth century AD (Stanton et al. 2010). Ten men, women, and children were carefully arranged around the decapitated corpse of the central adult male; the head was thrown in at the end of the ritual performance. A young woman flanking this central individual on the western side was still wearing a segmented shell crown with a northern lowland Early Classic style "jester god" jade diadem in the center (Stanton et al. 2010, 197, Figures 5.236 and 5.237). Ardren (2002) suggests that this is evidence that the young woman was the queen. Whether or not she was queen or princess she was surely of *ajaw* status, as designated by the *sak huunal* crown, to my knowledge the only one ever discovered in situ on the head of an ancient Maya person (although the king in El Perú-Waka' Burial 37 had the three crown jewels in position over the crushed fragments of his skull; see Freidel et al. 2013). A girl flanking the central figure on the east in Yaxuna Burial 24 had three jades on her chest in a field of olive shells carved as skulls. One of these is a northern lowland-style trefoil and a second is a profile of a deity with a motif shaped like a St. Andrew's Cross in the headdress. These women were evidently arranged to symbolize the Maize God resurrection of the man in the middle, a scene that is well attested in later Classic iconography. Whatever the interpretation of the tableau, it is clearly a royal one. In the

Early Classic period there is a clear and pervasive association of the trefoil diadem with royal status.

Three shell segments of a second crown were located at the foot of the decapitated central individual, the person I take to be the king. These segments were partially burned and lay in the middle of a 20-centimeter-diameter concentration of blackened material containing fragments of burned bone. Evidently the ritualists burned this crown in this place. This symbolic act of killing the crown of the king was matched by a cache jar of royal jewels placed in construction fill above the tomb and to the east of it. That cache of crown diadems, earflares, and collar beads was symbolically chopped with a black stone axe that was jammed into the neck of the jar.

The rituals marking the transition from one king and court to another at Yaxuna left elaborate traces involving other features and artifacts. But this is enough to show that it is likely another case of regicide in the context of a material symbol system, suggesting that the kings in question shared the ideas and regalia of divine status found among kings in lowland realms to the south. In this regard, it is one more case among many showing that the Classic Maya adhered to divine kingship throughout the lowlands. Whether or not there is textual evidence in a given archaeological setting, it is possible to identify regicide as a ritually charged aspect of the institution. In some cases, as discussed in the preceding chapters, it would appear that the institution itself was killed in the time of chaos, while in others it would appear to have been revered in memory. Either way, kings as sacrifices (and potentially as scapegoats) can have discernable material entailments.

On the Royal Path

The contributors to this valuable monograph may not have realized it during the process of presenting, writing, and rewriting, but through the quality of their expositions (and no doubt the judicious efforts of the editors) they have collectively sustained the proposition that it is possible to detect and trace the relationships between divine kings and their followers in the archaeological record of the pre-Columbian lowland Maya, whether or not that record includes glyphic texts. It has been very gratifying for me to see the enthusiastic pursuit of divine kingship in the Maya record and the emergence of new leadership in this arena, including the authors in this volume. Gyles Iannone's chapter on the scapegoat king hypothesis and Eleanor Harrison-Buck's review of stelae as royal persons (2012, this volume) are particularly outstanding in this regard. Harrison-Buck's focus on synthesizing the subject of the archaeology of divine kingship as reflective of cosmology and religion is already influential and is cited in several chapters.

Heinrich Berlin (1958) started us on the path to divine kings with his study of "emblem glyphs." Maya archaeologists have been talking about Classic kings since Tatiana Proskouriakoff's (1960, 1963, 1964) landmark studies of the royal stelae of Piedras Negras and Yaxchilan, which were soon followed by Berlin's (1968) identification of kings at Palenque. Peter Mathews (1985) did the definitive work on the "water group" prefix of emblem glyphs, which reads *k'ul*, holy or divine, and which has cognates in contemporary Tzotzil (e.g., *ch'ulel*; see Vogt 1969), among other living Mayan languages. In an iconographically related effort, David Stuart (1984, 1988) did breakthrough work on the flowing scrolls descending from offering hands and surrounding the "water group" prefix. He identified these as blood, a reading so enthusiastically embraced by epigraphers and iconographers that it helped inspire *Blood of Kings* as the title of the landmark exhibition and catalogue (Schele and Miller 1986).

Working independently with the Preclassic facades of Structure 5C-2nd at Cerros (Freidel 1985), I made the case for such scrollwork as transformations of blood and fire (red) and smoke and water (black), relating to sacrifice and rain making. As a student of Evon Vogt, I was quick to see the implications of such enduring cultural perceptions as embedded in the concept of *ch'ulel* (Freidel et al. 1993, 182–183), and collaboration with Linda Schele and her remarkable cadre of colleagues and students aided the identification of Maya kings, *K'uhul Ajawob*, in the orthography and spelling of the moment as "Lords of the Life Force" (Freidel et al. 1993, 182). Indeed I published a chapter in an homage volume for the great linguist Marshall Durbin (Freidel 1988) that proposed that stelae embodied the active essence of divine kings that was released to communion with observers by reading the texts on the stelae. By the end of the 1980s, divine kingship was a well-established principle (Freidel and Schele 1990; Sharer and Traxler 2006).

From the Late Preclassic forward, the divinity of Maya rulers was contingent upon their absorption of the power of gods through covenantal means, principally sacrifice (Freidel 2008; Freidel et al. 1993; Saturno 2009; Schele and Miller 1986; Taube 1985; Taube et al. 2010). What this means is that the human rulers represented and spoke for the gods. But those gods were local manifestations of widely known deities. The loyalty of people to the rulers was perforce a surrogate for their devotion to those particular gods. If the rulers failed, it was not necessarily the gods that failed (Navarro-Farr this volume) but rather their human emissaries. Gods could fail, be captured, even die (Freidel et al. 1993), but that was a distinct phenomenon. Even in failure, however, Maya rulers could sustain the status of hero. As Navarro-Farr illustrates, a Wak dynasty king who ultimately failed after presiding over a golden age was nevertheless revered and celebrated by ordinary people in a postroyal temple. So Inomata (this volume) is right that we require a nuanced and subtle approach to the matter of divinity in human form. That subtlety must, in my view, primarily derive from the synthesis of information about the Maya case based on all of our sources of evidence, as evinced in the substantial analysis presented in this volume. The comparative framework is ultimately and scientifically necessary. But as Geertz (1973) put it, we must also continue to be informed by local knowledge that has been elucidated as much as possible. I will come back to the nature of divine kingship after looking more at the archaeology now associated with it, as represented in this volume.

Detecting Dialogue in the Dirt

Archaeologists have embraced the hypothesis that there were divine kings for more than a generation, and the epistemology of how to detect the presence of divine kings in the context of sites lacking carved monuments with texts and images of divine rulers has been a problem that has been explicitly addressed for some time (e.g., Freidel and Schele 1988a; Freidel and Suhler 1998). The magisterial edited volume on the Terminal Classic (Demarest et al. 2004) referenced this problem in many ways. The chapters in this book evince a very welcome refinement and nuancing of contextual analysis in pursuit of that elusive quarry, the covenantal relationship of kings to followers. There are many other relations—to noble rivals and enemies, for example (Fash 1983; Fash et al. 1992)—and those also figure importantly. But with the clear current focus on commoners in Maya archaeology (e.g., Lohse and Valdez 2004), understanding their bridge to divine kings is a priority in forging consensus about direction in the field.

A salient issue the contributors in this volume pursue is their recognition that a great deal of the archaeological record, especially what Mayanists term above-floor deposits, is usefully analyzed as the product of intentional cultural behavior (Freidel 1998; Mock 1998a). When my colleagues at Cerros, especially James Garber (Figure 12.1), started recognizing the intentionality that lay behind the shattering of hard stuff such as jade preciosities and metates and pottery vessels and depositing them on plazas and next to buildings (Garber 1983; Robertson 1983; Robertson and Freidel 1986), we had not yet fully researched the history of "problematic deposits" in Maya archaeology (Coe 1959). Still, we knew that we were on the track of intentional behavior and that it was important to pursue the matter.

By the time I had initiated research at Yaxuna in the Yucatan (Stanton et al. 2010), I was explicitly looking for war-related deposits, and we found them in several places, particularly in the north acropolis, at Structure 6F-68. James Ambrosino (2003, 2007) systematically documented the intentional destruction of that building and the placement of deposits of ceramics and other artifacts in and around the destroyed building (figure 12.2).

When we encountered massive above-floor deposits at El Perú-Waka' adjacent to Structure M13-1, I knew that the documentation and elucidation of the behaviors that produced them would require an intense investigation of the ritual life of the community, and I assigned the task to Olivia Navarro-Farr. She succeeded in moving my understanding of such deposits away from the simple dichotomy of desecratory and reverential, and her ongoing efforts to do so are detailed in her chapter.

In her edited volume *The Sowing and the Dawning* (1988), Shirley Mock usefully brought together many substantial contributions to the question of interpreting above-floor deposits. These included Debra Walker's (1998) further analyses of the Cerros materials. One of the most intriguing insights Walker reported was the prospect that ceramic sherds from the termination ritual in the Structure 4B-1st Chamber 1 deposits were incorporated into the white marl foundations of some of the last homes built in the diminished community, long after its heyday as a royal seat but evidently when the memories of that time were still alive among the inhabitants. Lisa Lucero (2003) has proposed that divine rulers appropriated and amplified the dedication and termination ritual practices of commoner Maya followers as a strategy of legitimization during the evolution of Maya civilization from Preclassic to Classic. It would seem that royal practice, or at least the memory of it, flowed in the other direction as well, for Chamber 1 appears to have been a subsurface performance place for the resurrection ceremonies that accompanied the royal accession of divine rulers (Freidel and Suhler 1998).

Several contributors to this volume explore links between the material worlds of commoners and kings. For example, Takeshi Inomata makes the case that middens from households might have been deposited on some buildings in the Aguateca epicenter in the course of termination rituals

Above: Figure 12.1. James Garber excavating an above-floor deposit on Structure 4, OP 22, Cerros.

Left: Figure 12.2. Excavating sherds from termination rituals at Structure 6F-68 Yaxuna.

there. He suggests that the inclusion of such telltale signs as faunal remains, fragments of grinding stones, sherds from food preparation vessels, and numerous chipped-stone tools are evidence that the palace group buildings were strewn with midden trash. The context looks desecratory, so one might be tempted to see this as an act of profanation.

But the layering of materials from ordinary households on central edifice surfaces was in some instances evidently reverential. Olivia Navarro-Farr (Navarro-Farr et al. 2008; Navarro-Farr this volume) has come to the conclusion that the elaborate palimpsest of Terminal Classic materials she has documented on the main temple of the city center at El Perú-Waka' registers reverential intentions. Those materials are also quite diverse and include artifact categories that overlap with those Inomata listed in Aguateca contexts. Still, Inomata is very careful to contextually distinguish the different above-floor deposits he meticulously documented at Aguateca, and he chooses his identifications of intention with equal care.

Brett Houk, following advice from Navarro-Farr, cautions us to be wary of categorizing above-floor deposits by intention in his discussion of Dos Hombres, Chan Chich, and La Milpa. However, he does suggest that one of the Dos Hombres deposits look desecratory while another looks reverential. Those at Chan Chich look more likely to have been reverential. The La Milpa deposit looks like a midden to him, echoing the earlier focus on above-floor deposits as the product of squatters amid the ruins that was favored by archaeologists working the Central Acropolis at Tikal (Harrison 1999) More to the point, Houk thinks that all of these deposits were, in the last analysis, laid down by ordinary people responding to the failure of kingship.

Thomas Guderjan and Colleen Hanratty review the fine-grained evidence of late above-floor deposits at Blue Creek to make the case that these are indeed termination deposits that were followed by abandonment and not middens or the remains of feasting. They point to an absence of faunal and macrobotanical remains, to the significant number of partially restorable vessels, and the largely domestic nature of the other artifact categories. That last point bears on the theme of the relationships between royalty and followers. While Guderjan and Hanratty do not explicitly address the status of the people creating the termination deposits, they do suggest that these were people who were responding to the failure of the king and court and deliberately closing down the places associated with them. They speculate that the royalty were killed or driven off by these people before they performed the termination rituals. Clearly the epistemology of above-floor deposits remains an exciting and contested work in progress for Maya archaeologists, and I will have reason to touch on the theme again. But the Blue Creek case also raises another epistemological question here: How do we know that people had divine kings when we lack explicit texts and images declaring their presence in our places of research?

As one pioneer in the effort to establish that there were in fact divine kings in the Preclassic and that their presence was archaeologically detectable, I have been thinking about this problem for a long time (Freidel 2008). It was a controversial matter, but it was an argument based on data. When I excavated Cache I at Cerros (Freidel 1979), it was immediately clear to me that these materials had been deliberately arranged. They clearly represented a royal cosmogram, as a comparison to the Classic insignia demonstrated (Schele and Freidel 1990; Freidel et al. 1993). The royal insignia jewels were a concrete expression of kingship (Freidel 1991, 1992, 1993; Freidel and Suhler 1995) with significant distribution in sites lacking texts declaring kings.

But those efforts are part of a long history of investigation. William Coe (1965) implied the possibility that Preclassic rulership was continuous with the ensuing Classic practices based on the discoveries at Tikal, particularly in the North Acropolis excavations. I began my inquiry into the issue of divine kingship based on Cerros Cache 1 (Freidel 1979, 1981) and was fully committed to the idea by 1982 (Freidel and Schele 1988a). William Saturno (2009; Taube et al. 2010) decisively confirmed the Preclassic mythological rationale of royal accession with the discovery and interpretation of the Pinturas building at San Bartolo. In these cases, there are elusively brief glyphic references, but it is the explicit correspondence between the Preclassic material symbol systems and iconographic programs and Classic period ones that close the argument (Fields 1989).

Inomata rightfully cautions that we need to bear in mind that the Maya divine kingship varied and no doubt evolved through time. Indeed, I am of the view that it varied decisively through space, a point I return to shortly. Nevertheless, it is possible to identify Maya divine kingship in the absence of attestation by glyphic texts (*pace* our colleagues in epigraphy), not only in the largely preliterate Preclassic era but also in parts of the Classic period Maya lowlands where public inscriptions are rare or nonexistent. In this assertion I am in company with the contributors to this volume, many of whom marshal detailed empirical patterns of architectural and artifactual evidence to trace the paths of divine kingship.

One of the reasons I designed research at Yaxuna in Yucatan was to

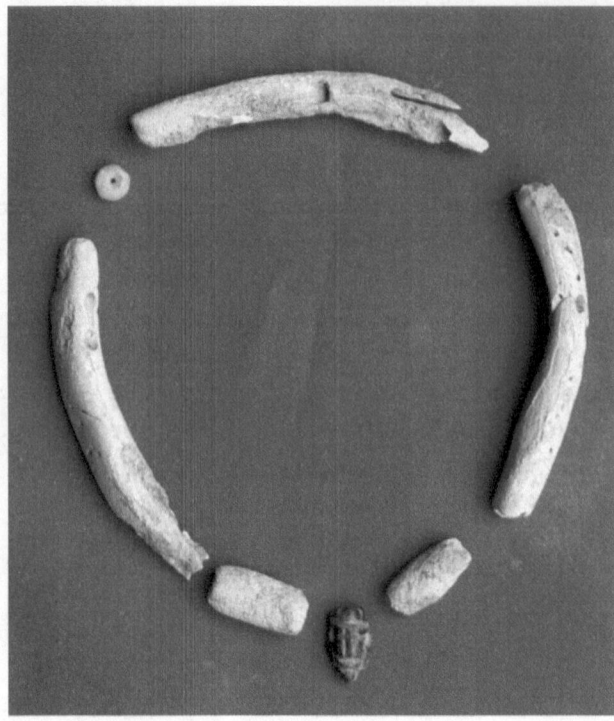

Figure 12.3. The royal crown worn by a sacrificed young woman, Burial 24, Yaxuna.

pursue the hypothesis that divine kingship existed in the northern lowlands despite the paucity of inscribed stelae celebrating it in this part of the Maya world (Proskouriakoff 1950). The Selz Foundation Yaxuna Project discovered two Early Classic royal tombs with clear material symbols of divine kingship, specifically *huunal* jewels (Ardren 2002; Freidel and Suhler 1998; Stanton et al. 2010; Suhler and Freidel 1998). As discussed at the outset of this chapter, to my knowledge the perishable headband with polished white shell sewn on and jade *huunal* jewel found in place on the skull of a young woman in Yaxuna Burial 24 is the only archaeological example of this major expression of the Maya *sak huunal* (white royal crown) that is depicted pervasively in the art corpus (figure 12.3).

The Nature of Divine Rulership and Material Expectations

As I mentioned, Eleanor Harrison-Buck (2012, this volume) is marshaling the arguments for Maya divine kingship and how to interpret the archaeological record in light of its existence, and I applaud her efforts. Gyles

Iannone (this volume) is contextualizing Maya divine kingship within the broader literature on divine kingship, with a particular eye to the king as the source of prosperity. Both of these are advances, and they show commitment to the legitimacy and scholarly importance of this undertaking. I take this opportunity to reflect on the matter, as a celebration of what is now a new generation's challenging task.

Regarding the premises behind the epistemology informing our views of the archaeological record, Linda Schele and I tried to make the case in *Maya Cosmos* (1993) that archaeologists should perceive the reality of the pre-Columbian Maya as mystical. By this I do not mean to imply that the Maya were unaware of the workings of the natural or social worlds but rather that their approach to explaining and interpreting those worlds was predicated on the firm belief that human mindfulness extended well beyond the physical body to include a variety of beings in the world, living, dead, immortal, and inorganic. Evon Z. Vogt taught that this predicate of reality obtained in modern times in his observations of the Zinacanteco Maya of highland Chiapas, Mexico. He regarded this as deeply ancient (Vogt 1969). Other ethnographers of the twentieth-century Mayan-language speakers also found this to be the case (e.g., Carlsen 1997; Christenson 2003; Hanks 1990; Tedlock 1982). This viewpoint is popular today and is well represented in the chapters of this book. It fits with the fashionable notion of things as agentive (Hendon 2012).

So it is worthwhile to accept and embrace the notion of divine kingship as part of a mystical cultural construction of reality (Harrison-Buck 2012b). The reason is explicit in the royal epithet *K'uhul Ajaw*, Holy Lord. The best gloss of this is still Lord of the Life Force. But as the contributors to this volume broadly acknowledge, the mystical reality of the Maya informs their behavior but does not relieve their rulers of the pragmatic responsibility to effectively rule over material conditions. This is at the crux of Iannone's (this volume) analysis of how and why divine kings fail.

On the practical side, from Middle Preclassic times (Freidel and Reilly 2010; Reilly 1987), this role as divine king elevated the selected official to a role as interlocutor in a complex and dynamic web of economic and political alliances in which the basic bottom line was the need to maintain access to food through exchange and marketing (Freidel 1986; Freidel and Shaw 2000; Masson and Freidel 2012; Schele and Freidel 1990, 93). Food was stored not in bins but in the exchange system and administered markets (Masson and Freidel 2012), and the divine rulers were exemplary of that system as not only Lords of the Life Force but also as Maize incarnate. In this we follow the inspiration of William Rathje (1972), but with some different trade items. The divine kings of the southern lowlands clearly failed if they had such central roles and stood by as the core-area routes collapsed (Demarest this volume). I think that they actually precipitated such collapse of trade routes through disastrous embargoes of the flow of commodities to adversaries and enemies. This may sound very modern, but in my opinion, the administrative motivations and functions of rulers in complex society have changed relatively little over the millennia, compared to the metaphors and tropes these rulers deployed and that guided their intentions.

But those tropes and metaphors do matter. The cosmological centrality of divine rulers is now firmly fixed in our epistemology and informs this volume's contributors. It is also a basis for contemplating the ruler as cultic object (Freidel 1992). Inomata (this volume), for example, suggests that the subjects of Maya rulers were loyal to them personally, more than they were to some abstract notion of polity. However, we do have some evidence that people also identified with places, as in the attribution *Mutal Winik*, man of Tikal, referencing King Nuun Ujol Chaak of Tikal on HS 2 at Dos Pilas (Fahsen 2002; Guenter n.d.). While there the phrase was meant as a slight, because the king was *K'uhul Mutal Ajaw*—dynastic successor and rival to the Dos Pilas King (who also claimed this title)—and not just a *Mutal Winik*, it still reveals the existence of the realm of Mutal as a place with which people identified.

But even if there is evidence that people identified with their polities, the cases that Charles Golden and his colleagues (this volume) make for the moral responsibility of the divine king for the health of his realm and that Gyles Iannone (this volume) makes for the king as ultimate arbiter of prosperity are worth serious consideration in the context of the dark times of the late eighth through ninth centuries in the southern lowlands. It is not just the disturbing and compelling evidence that Arthur Demarest and his research team (this volume) marshal for the sacrifice of the royal court at Cancuen by ordinary people and perhaps also by traditional allies from the south. Iannone (this volume) is likely right in his appeal to ethnological analogy to think that divine status in the Maya case gave potentially lethal responsibility as well as moral authority to rulers (Freidel and Shaw 2000). We all know the end of that story (Schele and Freidel 1990), so the death of kings, queens, royal families, and nobility surely accompanied the demise of divine kingship.

One of the intriguing themes in this book is the role of social memory in the dialogue between divine rulers and their followers. Golden and his colleagues (this volume) explore this as a way of understanding the decisions the royal courtiers of Piedras Negras made regarding the termination and rebuilding of court buildings. The same logic applies to the use of former royal facilities and sacred public ones, such as sweat baths, by nonroyal peoples. Likewise, Schwake and Iannone (this volume) review the remarkable evidence of memory at work in the location and relocation of cached offerings sealed into construction, and the very deliberate interment of royal architecture underneath more modest postroyal architecture at Minanha. Inomata (this volume) suggests that the termination of buildings at Aguateca was very deliberate and was guided by knowledge and memory of the particular works of the last king there. There are other examples, but the most dramatic seems to be the new evidence reported by Navarro-Farr (this volume) for the reuse of monument fragments in the final construction phase of the terrace of the city temple at El Perú-Waka', Structure M13-1.

I think that part of the fund of moral authority that Golden and his colleagues (this volume) allude to (see Houston and Inomata 2009) must have been cached in collective memories of the deeds of famous prior rulers. We can be quite certain that in the laconic texts that have survived for epigraphers to study there are examples of retrospective history and indeed attempts to anchor the descent of divine human rulers into deities as founding progenitors (Schele and Freidel 1990). Joyce Marcus (1992) has suggested that such efforts proved the mythological nature of Maya historical texts because the Palenque progenitor deity lived eons, like the patriarchs of Genesis. But we now know with some confidence that Maya scribes knew which parts of their story were myth and which were chronicle, at least as well as we moderns claim to know. But, like us, they were likely prone to view history as a force of destiny and its patterns as bearing some predictive value.

For example, in the case of the history of El Perú-Waka', I do not think it was coincidental that the name of the king of the realm and vassal to the Snake King Yuknoom Ch'een was K'inich Bahlam. This was the name of the Wak king that Sihyaj K'ahk' made a vassal in the fourth century. Sihyaj K'ahk' conquered Tikal a week after establishing order at Waka', according to the text on El Peru Stela 15 (Guenter 2005; Stuart 2000). Yuknoom Ch'een conquered Tikal soon after establishing his relationship with K'inich Bahlam II. Perhaps there were other K'inich Bahlams in the royal line at

Waka', but so far we have not discovered them. I stand by the proposition that Yuknoom Ch'een was manipulating memory and attempting to repeat history.

So divine rulers, as objects of memory work on the part of ordinary people, bore the force of millennia during which they were partnered agents in such work, as this volume documents. In the regions of the lowland Maya world where kings and other royalty did not write public texts as a regular practice, we can still identify their presence in the record and trace out this partnership with their people, as the contributions to this volume demonstrate. And everywhere we can see the final chapters of Classic period history archived in the material traces of the efforts of ordinary people to perpetuate their cultural realities in the face of social catastrophe. The essential fact is that history is lived before it is written. And if it is not written, archaeologists can still apprehend it forensically. The lowland Maya survived the demise of divine kingship and carried forward their cosmos. The ultimate viability of the gods and the world was not contingent on the presence of divine kings but on ordinary people, even as parts of that world were abandoned by those people and returned to the gods. This history is written not on stones, but with them.

References

Abercrombie, Nicholas, and Bryan S. Turner
1978   The Dominant Ideology Thesis. *British Journal of Sociology* 29(2):149–170.
Acuña, Mary Jane
2014   Royal Alliances, Ritual Behavior, and the Abandonment of the Royal Couple Building at El Peru-Waka'. In *Archaeology at El Peru-Waka': Ancient Maya Performances of Ritual, Memory, and Power*, edited by Olivia C. Navarro-Farr and Michelle Rich, pp. 53–65. University of Arizona Press, Tucson.
Adamek, Wendi L.
2005   The Impossibility of the Given: Representations of Merit and Emptiness in Medieval Chinese Buddhism. *History of Religion* 45(2):135–180.
Adams, Richard E. W.
1973a   Maya Collapse: Transformation and Termination in the Ceramic Sequence at Altar de Sacrificios. In *The Classic Maya Collapse*, edited by T. Patrick Culbert, pp. 133–163. School of American Research, University of New Mexico Press, Albuquerque.
1973b   The Collapse of Maya Civilization: A Review of Previous Theories. In *The Classic Maya Collapse*, edited by T. Patrick Culbert, pp. 21–34. School of American Research, University of New Mexico Press, Albuquerque.
Adams, R. E. W., Hubert R. Robichaux, Fred Valdez, Jr., Brett A. Houk, and Ruth Mathews
2004   Transformations, Periodicity, and Urban Development in the Three Rivers Region. In *The Terminal Classic in the Maya Lowlands: Collapse, Transition, and Transformation*, edited by Arthur A. Demarest, Prudence M. Rice, and Don S. Rice, pp. 324–341. University Press of Colorado, Boulder.
Aimers, James
2007   What Maya Collapse? Terminal Classic Variation in the Maya Lowlands. *Journal of Archaeological Research* 15:329–377.
2012   Environment and Agency in the Ancient Maya Collapse. In *Climates, Landscapes, and Civilizations*, edited by Liviu Giosan, Dorian Q. Fuller, Kathleen Nicoll, Rowan K. Flad, and Peter D. Clift, pp. 27–33. Geophysical Monograph Series 198. American Geophysical Union, Washington, D.C.
Akkeren, Ruud van
2000   *Place of the Lord's Daughter: Rab'inal, Its History, Its Dance-Drama*. Research School CNWS, Leiden.

2012 *Xib'balba y el nacimiento del Nuevo sol: una visión postclásica del colapso Maya.* Editorial Piedra Santa, Guatemala City.

Alschuler, Milton
1958 On the Environmental Limitations of Maya Cultural Development. *Southwest Journal of Anthropology* 14(2):189–198.

Alvarado, Carlos, Carrie Anne Berryman, Ana Novotny, and Kristen Demarest
2006 Investigaciones en el Puerto Principal de Cancuén. In *Proyecto Arqueológico Cancuén Informe de Temporada 2004–2005*, edited by Tomas Barrientos, Arthur Demarest, Claudia Quintanilla, and Luis F. Luin, pp. 435–453. Vanderbilt University and Universidad del Valle, Dirección General de Patrimonio Cultural y Natural, Guatemala City.

Alvarado, Silvia
2011 Análisis Funcional de las Reservas de Agua en Cancuen. Licenciatura Thesis. Universidad de San Carlos, Guatemala City.

Ambrosino, James N.
1998 The Archaeological Deposit Associated with a Palace at Yaxuna, Yucatan: A Cautionary Tale. Paper presented at the 63rd annual meeting of the Society for American Archaeology, Seattle.
2003 The Function of a Maya Palace at Yaxunah. In *Maya Palaces and Elite Residences: An Interdisciplinary Approach*, edited by Jessica Joyce Christie, pp. 253–273. University of Texas Press, Austin.
2007 Warfare and Destruction in the Maya Lowlands: Pattern and Process in the Archaeological Record of Yaxuna, Yucatan, Mexico. Unpublished PhD dissertation, Southern Methodist University, Dallas, Texas.

Anaya Hernández, Armando
2001 *Site Interaction and Political Geography in the Upper Usumacinta Region during the Late Classic: A GIS Approach.* BAR International Series 994. British Archaeological Reports, Oxford.
2005 Strategic Location and Territorial Integrity: The Role of Subsidiary Sites in the Classic Maya Kingdoms of the Upper Usumacinta Region. *Internet Archaeology* 19.

Anaya Hernández, Armando, Stanley P. Guenter, and Marc U. Zender
2003 Sak Tz'i', a Classic Maya Center: A Locational Model Based on GIS and Epigraphy. *Latin American Antiquity* 14:179–191.

Anderson, A. H.
1959 More Discoveries at Caracol, British Honduras. *Congreso Internacional de Americanistas* 33:211–218.

Andres, Christopher
2009 Architecture and Sociopolitical Transformation at Chau Hiix, Belize. *Journal of Field Archaeology* 34(1):1–34.

Andrews, Anthony P.
1983 *Maya Salt Production and Trade.* University of Arizona Press, Tucson.
1990 The Role of Trading Ports in Maya Civilization. In *Vision and Revision in Maya Studies*, edited by Flora S. Clancy and Peter D. Harrison, pp. 159–168. University of New Mexico Press, Albuquerque.

Andrews, Anthony P., and Shirley B. Mock
2002   New Perspectives on the Prehistoric Salt Trade. In *Ancient Maya Political Economies*, edited by Marilyn A. Masson and David A. Freidel, pp. 317–335. Altamira Press, Walnut Creek, California.

Andrews, E. Wyllys, and Barbara W. Fash
1992   Continuity and Change in a Royal Maya Residential Complex at Copan. *Ancient Mesoamerica* 3:63–88.

Andrieu, Chloe, and Douglas Quiñonez
2010   Análisis Lítico. In *Proyecto Arqueológico Cancuen Informe Final No. 10, Temporada 2010*, edited by Arthur Demarest and Horacio Martínez, pp. 164–184. Ministerio de Cultura y Deportes de Guatemala, Guatemala City.

Andrieu, Chloé, Douglas Quiñonez, and Edna Rodas
2011a   La lítica de Cancuen, In *Proyecto Cancuen, Informe Final No. 11, Temporada 2011*, edited by Arthur A. Demarest, Horacio Martínez, Claudia Quintanilla, and Paola Torres, pp. 262–273. Ministerio de Cultura y Deportes de Guatemala, Guatemala City.

2011b   La interpretación económica de los depósitos de lascas. In *XXIV Simposio Internacional de Arqueología*, edited by B. Arroyo, A. Linares Palma, and L. Paiz Aragón, pp. 321–344, Museo Nacional de Arqueología y Etnología, Guatemala City.

Ardren, Traci
1999   Palace Termination Rituals at Xkanha and Yaxuna, Yucatan, Mexico. In *Land of the Pheasant and the Deer*, edited by Ruth Gubler, pp. 25–36. Labyrinthos Press, Lancaster, California.

2002   Death Became Her: Images of Female Power from Yaxuna Burials. In *Ancient Maya Women*, edited by Traci Ardren, pp. 68–88. Altamira Press, Walnut Creek, California.

Aung-Thwin, Michael
1985   *Pagan: The Origins of Modern Burma*. University of Hawaii Press, Honolulu.

Aung-Thwin, Michael A., and Maitrii Aung-Thwin
2012   *A History of Myanmar since Ancient Times*. Reaktion, London.

Ayala, Maricela
1994   The History of Toniná through Its Inscriptions. Unpublished PhD dissertation. The University of Texas at Austin.

Bachand, Bruce R.
2010   Onset of the Early Classic Period in the Southern Maya Lowlands: New Evidence from Punta de Chimino, Guatemala. *Ancient Mesoamerica* 21:21–44.

Baines, John, and Norman Yoffee
2000   Order, Legitimacy, and Wealth: Setting the Terms. In *Order, Legitimacy, and Wealth in Ancient States*, edited by Janet Richards and Mary Van Buren, pp. 13–17. Cambridge University Press, Cambridge.

Baker, Jeffrey
2003   Maya Wetlands: Ecology and Prehispanic Utilization of Wetlands in Northwestern Belize. Unpublished PhD dissertation, Anthropology Department, University of Arizona, Tucson.

Ball, Joseph W., and Jennifer T. Taschek
1989   Teotihuacan's Fall and the Rise of the Itza: Realignments and Role Changes in the Terminal Classic Maya Lowlands. In *Mesoamerica after the Decline of Teotihuacan AD 700–900*, edited by Richard A. Diehl and Janet C. Berlo, pp. 187–200. Dumbarton Oaks, Washington, D.C.

Barrett, Jason W., and Thomas H. Guderjan
2006   A River Docking Feature at Blue Creek, Belize. *Latin American Antiquity* 17:227–239.

Barrett, Jason W., and Andrew K. Scherer
2005   Stones, Bones, and Crowded Plazas: Evidence for Terminal Classic Maya Warfare at Colha, Belize. *Ancient Mesoamerica* 16:101–118.

Barrientos, Tomas
2014   The Royal Palace of Cancuen: The Structure of Lowland Maya Architecture and Politics at the End of the Late Classic Period. Unpublished PhD dissertation, Department of Anthropology, Vanderbilt University, Nashville, Tennessee.

Barrientos, Tomas, Moises Arriaza, Blanca Mijangos, Adriana Linares, Claudia Quintanilla, and Silvia Alvarado
2006   Excavaciones en la Estructura L7-27 de Cancuen. In *Proyecto Arqueológico Cancuen, Informe de Temporadas 2004–2005*, edited by Tomas Barrientos, Arthur Demarest, Luis Luin, Claudia Quintanilla, and Elisa Mencos, pp. 259–314. Ministerio de Cultura y Deportes de Guatemala, Guatemala City.

Barrientos, Tomas, and Arthur Demarest
2007   Cancuen: Puerta al mundo maya. In *XX Simposio de Investigaciones Arqueológicas en Guatemala, 2006*, edited by Juan Pedro Laporte, Bárbara Arroyo, and Hector Mejía, pp. 611–628. Museo Nacional de Arqueología y Etnología, Guatemala City.

Barrientos, Tomás, Arthur Demarest, Silvia Alvarado, Horacio Martínez, Marc Wolf, and Luis Fernando Luin
2006   Hidráulica, ecología, ideología y poder: Nueva evidencia y teorías en el Sur de Petén. In *XIX Simposio de Investigaciones Arqueológicas en Guatemala, 2005*, edited by J. P. Laporte, B. Arroyo, and H. Mejía, pp. 291–302. Museo Nacional de Arqueología y Etnología, Guatemala City.

Beach, Timothy, Sheryl Luzzadder-Beach, Steve Bozarth, Nicholas Dunning, Thomas Guderjan, John Jones, Jon Lohse, Sarah Millspaugh, and Tripti Bhattacharya
2009   Maya Marshes: Human and Natural Changes in Wetlands of the Maya Lowlands. *Quaternary Science Reviews* 28:1–15.

Beach, Timothy, Sheryl Luzzadder-Beach, Nicholas Dunning, Jon Hageman, and Jon Lohse
2002   Upland Agriculture in the Maya Lowlands: Ancient Maya Soil Conservation in Northwestern Belize. *Geographic Review* 92:372–397.

Becker, Marshall J.
1971   Identification of a Second Plaza Plan at Tikal, Guatemala, and Its Implications for Ancient Maya Social Complexity. Unpublished PhD dissertation, University of Pennsylvania, Philadelphia.

Bedford, Peter R.
2009   The Neo-Assyrian Empire. In *The Dynamics of Ancient Empires*, edited by Ian Morris and Walter Scheidel, pp. 30–65. Oxford University Press, New York.
Beetham, David
1991   Max Weber and the Legitimacy of the Modern State. *Analyse & Kritik* 13:34–45.
Bell, Eleanor E., Marcelo Canuto, and Robert Sharer
2004   *Understanding Early Classic Copan*. University of Pennsylvania Museum, Philadelphia.
Berdan, Francis, and Patricia R. Anawalt
1992   *The Codex Mendoza*. University of California Press, Berkeley.
Berlin, Heinrich
1958   El glifo "emblema" en las inscripciones mayas. *Journal de la Société des Américanistes* 47:111–119.
1968   Estudios Epigraphicos II. *Antropología e Historia de Guatemala* 20(1):13–24. Instituto de Antropología e Historia de Guatemala.
Bernbeck, Reinhard
2008   Royal Deification: An Ambiguation Mechanism for the Creation of Courtier Subjectivities. In *Religion and Power: Divine Kingship in the Ancient World and Beyond*, edited by Nicole Brisch, pp. 157–170. University of Chicago, Chicago.
Berryman, Carrie Anne, and Ana Novotny
2004   Excavaciones y Análisis Bioarqueologico de Cancuen: 2003. In *Proyecto Arqueológico Cancuen, Informe No. 5, Temporada 2003*, edited by Arthur A. Demarest, Tomas Barrientos Q., Brigitte Kovacevich, Michael Callaghan, Brent Woodfill, and Luis F. Luin, pp. 515–528. Instituto de Antropología e Historia de Guatemala, Guatemala City.
Binford, Michael, Mark Brenner, Thomas J. Whitmore, Antonia Higuera-Gundy, E. S. Deevey, and Barbara Leyden
1983   Ecosystems, Paleoecology and Human Disturbance in Subtropical and Tropical America. *Quaternary Science Reviews* 6(2):115–128.
Birbhushan, Chakrabarti, Tim Yates, and Andrew Lewry
1996   Effect of Fire Damage on Natural Stonework in Buildings. *Construction and Building Materials* 10:539–544.
Bishop, Ronald L.
1994   Pre-Columbian Pottery: Research in the Maya Region. In *Archaeometry of Pre-Columbian Sites and Artifacts*, edited by David A. Scott and Pieter Meyers, pp. 15–66. J. Paul Getty Trust, Los Angeles, California.
Bishop, Ronald, L., Erin L. Sears, and M. James Blackman
2005   A Través del Río del Cambio. *Estudios de Cultura Maya* 26:17–40.
Blanton, Richard, and Gary Feinman
1984   The Mesoamerican World System. *American Anthropologist* 86:673–82.
Blau, Peter M.
1963   Critical Remarks on Weber's Theory of Authority. *American Political Science Review* 57:305–316.
Bloch, Maurice, and Jonathan Parry (editors)
1982   *Death and the Regeneration of Life*. Cambridge University Press, Cambridge.

Bourdieu, Pierre
1977   *Outline of a Theory of Practice.* Cambridge University Press.
1990   *The Logic of Practice.* Polity Press, Cambridge.
Bozarth, Steven, and Thomas Guderjan
2004   Results of Biosilicate Analysis of Residue in Maya Dedicatory Cache Vessels. *Journal of Archaeological Science* 31:2:205–215.
Brainerd, George W.
1958   *The Archaeological Ceramics of Yucatan.* University of California Press, Berkeley.
Braswell, Geoffrey E.
2001   Post-Classic Maya Courts of the Guatemalan Highlands: Archaeological and Ethnohistorical Approaches. In *Royal Courts of the Ancient Maya,* vol. 2, *Data and Case Studies,* edited by Takeshi Inomata and Stephen D. Houston, pp. 308–344. Westview Press, Boulder, Colorado.
2004   A Forest of Trees: Postclassic K'iche'an Identity and the Anthropological Problem of Ethnicity. In *Maya Ethnicity: The Construction of Ethnic Identity from the Preclassic to Modern Times,* edited by Frauke Sachse, pp. 125–140. Acta Mesoamericana 19. Saurwein, Markt Schwaben.
Brenner, Neil
1994   Foucault's New Functionalism. *Theory and Society* 23:679–709.
Brenner, Mark, Michael F. Rosenmeier, David A. Hodell, and Jason H. Curtis
2002   Paleolimnology of the Maya Lowlands: Long-term Perspectives on Interactions among Climate, Environment, and Humans. *Ancient Mesoamerica* 13:141–157.
Brisch, Nicole
2008   Introduction. In *Religion and Power: Divine Kingship in the Ancient World and Beyond,* edited by Nicole Brisch, pp. 1–11. University of Chicago, Chicago.
Brown, Bill
2001   Thing Theory. *Critical Inquiry* 28(1):1–22.
Brown, Linda A.
2004   Dangerous Places and Wild Spaces: Creating Meaning with Materials and Space at Contemporary Maya Shrines on El Duende Mountain. *Journal of Archaeological Method and Theory* 11(1):31–58.
Brown, Linda A., and Kitty F. Emery
2008   Negotiations with the Animate Forest: Hunting Shrines in the Guatemalan Highlands. *Journal of Archaeological Method and Theory* 15:300–337.
Brown, M. Kathryn, and Travis Stanton (editors)
2003   *Ancient Mesoamerican Warfare.* Altamira Press, Walnut Creek, California.
Brumfiel, Elizabeth M.
1992   Distinguished Lecture in Archeology: Breaking and Entering the Ecosystem—Gender, Class, and Faction Steal the Show. *American Anthropologist* 94(3):551–567.
2000   The Politics of High Culture: Issues of Worth and Rank. In *Order, Legitimacy, and Wealth in Ancient States,* edited by Janet Richards and Mary Van Buren, pp. 131–139. Cambridge University Press, New York.
Butler, Mary
2005 [1935]   Piedras Negras Pottery. In *Piedras Negras Archaeology, 1931–1939,* edited by

John M. Weeks, Jane A. Hill, and Charles W. Golden, pp. 90–120. University of Pennsylvania Museum Press, Philadelphia.

Buttles, Palma J.
2002   Material and Meaning: A Contextual Examination of Select Portable Material Culture from Colha, Belize. Unpublished PhD dissertation, The University of Texas at Austin.

Buttles, Palma J., and Fred Valdez Jr.
2007   Terminal Classic Events: Colha and the Central Maya Lowlands. *Research Reports in Belizean Archaeology* 4:147–153.
2011   Socio-Political Events of the Terminal Classic at Colha, Northern Belize. Paper presented at the 76th Annual Meeting of the Society for American Archaeology, Sacramento, California.

Butzer, Karl W.
2012   Collapse, Environment, and Society. *Proceedings of the National Academy of Sciences* 109(10):3632–3639.

Butzer, Karl W., and Georgina H. Endfield
2012   Critical Perspectives on Historical Collapse. *Proceedings of the National Academy of Sciences* 109(10):3628–3631.

Cancian, Frank
1996   The Hamlet as Mediator. *Ethnology* 35:215–228.

Canuto, Marcello A., and Tomás Barrientos Q.
2013   The Importance of La Corona. *La Corona Notes* 1(1):1–5.

Canuto, Marcello A., and William L. Fash
2004   *The Blind Spot: Where the Elite and Non-Elite Meet*, edited by Charles W. Golden and Greg Borgstede, pp. 51–76. Routledge, New York.

Carlsen, Robert S.
1997   *War for the Heart and Soul of a Highland Maya Town*. University of Texas Press, Austin.

Carmack, Robert M.
1981   *The Quiché Mayas of Utatlan*. University of Oklahoma Press, Norman.

Caso Barrera, Laura, and Marie Aliphat Fernández
2006   Cacao, Vanilla, and Annatte: Three Production and Exchange Systems in the Southern Maya Lowlands, XVI–XVII Centuries. *Journal of Latin American Geography* 5(2):29.
2012   Mejores son huertos de cacao y achiote que minas de oro y plata: Huertos especializados de los choles del Manche y de los k'eckhi'es. *Latin American Antiquity* 23:292–299.

Chase, Arlen F.
1985   Troubled Times: The Archaeology and Iconography of the Terminal Classic Southern Lowland Maya. In *Fifth Palenque Round Table, 1983*, edited by Merle G. Robertson and Virginia M. Fields, pp. 103–114. Pre-Columbian Art Research Institute, San Francisco.

Chase, Arlen F., and Diane Z. Chase
1987   *Investigations at the Classic Maya City of Caracol, Belize: 1985–87*. Monograph 3. Pre-Columbian Art Research Institute, San Francisco.

Chase, Diane Z., and Arlen F. Chase
1982   Yucatec Influence in Terminal Classic Northern Belize. *American Antiquity* 47:596–614.

Chase, Diane Z., and Arlen F. Chase (editors)
1992   *Mesoamerican Elites: An Archaeological Assessment*. University of Oklahoma Press, Norman.

Chase, Arlen F., Nikolai Grube, and Diane Z. Chase
1991   *Three Terminal Classic Monuments from Caracol, Belize*. Research Reports on Ancient Maya Writing 36. Center for Maya Research, Washington, D.C.

Child, Mark B.
2006   The Archaeology of Religious Movements: The Maya Sweatbath Cult of Piedras Negras. Unpublished PhD dissertation, Department of Anthropology, Yale University.

Child, Mark B., and Charles Golden
2008   The Transformation of Abandoned Architecture at Piedras Negras. In *Ruins of the Past: The Use and Perception of Abandoned Structures in the Maya Lowlands*, edited by Travis W. Stanton and Aline Magnoni, pp. 65–89. University Press of Colorado, Boulder.

Childe, V. Gordon
1950   The Urban Revolution. *Town Planning Review* 21:3–17.

Christenson, Allen
2003   Manipulating the Cosmos: Shamanic Tables among the Highland Maya. In *Mesas and Cosmologies in Mesoamerica*, edited by Douglas Sharon, p. 93–104. Papers 42. San Diego Museum of Man, California.
2007   *Popol Vuh: The Sacred Book of the Maya. The Great Classic of Central American Spirituality, Translated from the Original Maya Text*. University of Oklahoma Press, Norman.

Claessen, Henri J. M.
2005   Chiefs and Kingship in Polynesia. In *The Character of Kingship*, edited by Declan Quigley, pp. 233–250. Berg, New York.

Claessen, Henri J. M., and Pieter van de Velde
1991   Introduction. In *Early State Economics*, edited by Henri Claessen and Pieter van de Velde, pp. 1–29. Transaction, London.

Clayton, Sarah C., David W. Driver, and Laura J. Kosakowsky
2005   Rubbish or Ritual? Contextualizing a Terminal Classic Problematical Deposit at Blue Creek, Belize: A Response to "Public Architecture, Ritual, and Temporal Dynamics at the Maya Center of Blue Creek, Belize" by Thomas H. Guderjan. *Ancient Mesoamerica* 16:119–130.

Coe, Michael D.
2003   *Angkor and the Khmer Civilization*. Thames and Hudson, New York.

Coe, Michael D., and Richard A. Diehl
1980   *In the Land of the Olmec: The Archaeology of San Lorenzo Tenochtitlan*. University of Texas Press, Austin.

Coe, William R.
1959   *Piedras Negras Archaeology: Artifacts, Caches, and Burials*. University Museum

Monographs no. 18. University Museum, University of Pennsylvania, Philadelphia.
1965 A Model of Ancient Community Structure in the Maya Lowlands. *Southwestern Journal of Anthropology* 21:97–114.
1988 *Tikal: A Handbook of the Ancient Maya Ruins*. University Museum, University of Pennsylvania, Philadelphia.
1990 *Excavations in the Great Plaza, North Terrace, and North Acropolis of Tikal*. Tikal Report 14. The University Museum, University of Pennsylvania, Philadelphia.

Cohodas, Marvin
1989 The Epiclassic Problem: A Review and Alternative Model. In *Mesoamerica after the Decline of Teotihuacan AD 700–900*, edited by Richard A. Diehl and Janet C. Berlo, pp. 219–251. Dumbarton Oaks, Washington, D.C.

Cowgill, George L.
1964 The End of Classic Maya Culture: A Review of Recent Evidence. *Southwestern Journal of Anthropology* 20:145–159.
1988 Onward and Upward with Collapse. In *The Collapse of Ancient States and Civilizations*, edited by Norman Yoffee and George L. Cowgill, pp. 244–276. University of Arizona Press, Tucson.

Cresson, Frank M.
2005a [1939] Appendix 4: Carved Orange and Carved Gray Wares at Piedras Negras. In *Piedras Negras Archaeology, 1931–1939*, edited by John M. Weeks, Jane A. Hill, and Charles W. Golden, pp. 395–397. University of Pennsylvania Museum of Archaeology and Anthropology, Philadelphia.
2005b [1939] Appendix 5: Pottery Types of Yucatan in the Usumacinta Area. In *Piedras Negras Archaeology, 1931–1939*, edited by John M. Weeks, Jane A. Hill, and Charles W. Golden, pp. 398–400. University of Pennsylvania Museum of Archaeology and Anthropology, Philadelphia.

Culbert, T. Patrick
1974 *The Lost Civilization: The Story of the Classic Maya*. Harper and Row, New York.
1988 The Collapse of Classic Maya Civilization. In *The Collapse of Ancient States and Civilizations*, edited by Norman Yofee and George L. Cowgill, pp. 69–101. University of Arizona Press, Tucson.

Culbert, T. Patrick (editor)
1973 *The Classic Maya Collapse*. School of American Research, University of New Mexico Press, Albuquerque.

Culbert T. Patrick, and Don S. Rice (editors)
1990 *Precolumbian Population History in the Maya Lowlands*. University of New Mexico Press, Albuquerque.

Curtis, J. H., D. A. Hodell, and M. Brenner
1996 Climate Variability on the Yucatan Peninsula (Mexico) during the Past 3500 Years, and Implications for Maya Cultural Evolution. *Quaternary Research* 46(1):37–47.

Cusick, James G. (editor)
1998 *Studies in Culture Contact: Interaction, Culture Change and Archaeology*. Occasional Paper No. 25. Center for Archaeological Investigations, Southern Illinois University, Carbondale.

De Casparis, J. G., and Ian W. Mabbett
1992   Religion and Popular Beliefs of Southeast Asia before c. 1500. In *The Cambridge History of Southeast Asia*, vol. 1, *From Early Times to c. 1500*, edited by Nicholas Tarding, pp. 276–339. Cambridge University Press, New York.

Deetz, James
1996   *In Small Things Forgotten: An Archaeology of Early American Life*. Exp. and rev. ed. Anchor-Doubleday, New York.

Demarest, Arthur
1992   Ideology in Ancient Maya Cultural Evolution. In *Ideology and the Evolution of Precolumbian Civilization*, edited by Arthur Demarest and Geoffery Conrad, pp. 135–157. University of New Mexico Press, Albuquerque.
1997   The Vanderbilt Petexbatun Regional Archaeological Project 1989–1994: Overview, History, and Major Results of a Multidisciplinary Study of the Classic Maya Collapse. *Ancient Mesoamerica* 8(2):209–227.
2004a *Ancient Maya: The Rise and Fall of a Rainforest Civilization*. Cambridge University Press, Cambridge.
2004b After the Maelstrom: The Classic Maya Collapse and the Terminal Classic in the Western Peten. In *The Terminal Classic in Maya Lowlands: Collapse, Transition, and Transformation*, edited by Arthur A. Demarest, Prudence M. Rice, and Don S. Rice, pp. 102–124. University Press of Colorado, Boulder.
2006   *The Petexbatun Regional Archaeological Project: A Multidisciplinary Study of the Maya Collapse*. Vanderbilt Institute of Mesoamerican Archaeology Monograph Series, vol. 1. Vanderbilt University Press, Nashville, Tennessee.
2013   Ideological Pathways to Economic Exchange: Religion, Economy, and Legitimation at the Classic Maya Royal Capital of Cancuén. *Latin American Antiquity* 24(4):371–402.

Demarest, Arthur A., Chloé Andrieu, Paola Torres, Melanié Forné, Tomas Barrientos, and Marc Wolf
2014   Economy, Exchanges, and Power: New Evidence from the Late Classic Maya Port City of Cancuen. *Ancient Mesoamerica* 25(1):187–219.

Demarest, Arthur A., Tomás Barrientos, Melanié Forné, Marc Wolf, and Ronald Bishop
2008   La nueva historia de la puerta a las Tierras Bajas: descubrimientos recientes sobre la interacción, arqueología y epigrafía de Cancuén. In *XXI Simposio de Investigaciones Arqueológicas en Guatemala, 2007*, edited by Juan Pedro Laporte, Bárbara Arroyo, and Héctor Mejía, pp. 515–531. Museo Nacional de Arqueología y Etnología, Guatemala City.

Demarest, Arthur A., and Horacio Martínez
2010   El Intento Infructuoso a una Transición Clásico/Postclásico en Cancuen. In *XXIII Simposio de Investigaciones de Arqueología en Guatemala, 2009*, edited by Bárbara Arroyo, Adriana Linares Palma, and Lorena Paiz Aragón, pp. 609–620. Museo Nacional de Arqueología y Etnología, Guatemala City.

Demarest, Arthur, Horacio Martínez, Marc Wolf, Paola Torres, Waleska Belches, Chloé Andrieu, Luis Fernando Luin, Matt O'Mansky, and Claudia Quintanilla
2009   Economía interna relaciones internacionales de Cancuen y de sitios de su reinado. In *XXII Simposio de Investigaciones de Arqueología en Guatemala, 2008*,

edited by Juan Pedro Laporte, Bárbara Arroyo, and Héctor E. Mejía, pp. 655–674. Museo Nacional de Arqueología y Etnología, Guatemala City.

Demarest, Arthur A., Kim Morgan, Claudia Wolley, and Héctor Escobedo
2003   The Political Acquisition of Sacred Geography: The Murciélagos Complex at Dos Pilas. In *Maya Palaces and Elite Residences*, edited by Jessica Christie, pp. 120–153. University of Texas, Austin.

Demarest, Arthur A., Matt O'Mansky, Q. Joshua Hinson, José S. Suasnavar, and Coral Rasmussen
1997   Classic Maya Defensive Systems and Warfare in the Petexbatun Region. *Ancient Mesoamerica* 8:229–253.

Demarest, Arthur A., Prudence M. Rice, and Don S. Rice (editors)
2004   *The Terminal Classic in the Maya Lowlands: Collapse, Transition, and Transformation*. University Press of Colorado, Boulder.

Demarest, Arthur, Brent Woodfill, Tomás Barrientos, Federico Fahsen, and Mirza Monterroso
2007   La ruta altiplano-tierras bajas del occidente, y el surgimiento y caída de la civilización Clásica Maya. In *XX Simposio de Investigaciones Arqueológicas en Guatemala, 2006*, edited by Juan Pedro Laporte, Bárbara Arroyo, and Héctor Mejía, pp. 27–44. Museo Nacional de Arqueología y Etnología, Guatemala City.

Diamond, Jared
2005   *Collapse: How Societies Choose to Fail or Succeed*. W. W. Norton, New York.

Dietler, Michael
2001   Theorizing the Feast: Rituals of Consumption, Commensal Politics, and Power in African Contexts. In *Feasts: Archaeological and Ethnographic Perspectives on Food, Politics, and Power*, edited by Michael Dietler and Brian Hayden, pp. 65–14. Smithsonian Institution Press, Washington.

Dirks, Nicholas B.
1987   *The Hollow Crown: Ethnohistory of an Indian Kingdom*. Cambridge University Press, Cambridge.

Dornan, Jennifer
2002   Agency and Archaeology: Past, Present, and Future Directions. *Journal of Archaeological Method and Theory* 9(4):303–329.

Driver, David
2002   An Early Classic Columned Temple at Blue Creek, Belize. *Latin American Antiquity* 13:63–85.
2008   The Construction of Intrapolity Sociopolitical Identity through Architecture at the Ancient Maya Site of Blue Creek. Unpublished PhD dissertation, Department of Anthropology, Southern Illinois University at Carbondale.

Driver, W. David, and Phil Wanyerka
2002   Creation Symbolism in the Architecture and Ritual at Structure 3, Blue Creek, Belize. *Mexicon* 24:1:6–8.

Drucker-Brown, Susan
2005   King House: The Mobile Polity in Northern Ghana. In *The Character of Kingship*, edited by Declan Quigley, pp. 171–186. Berg, New York.

Dumarcay, Jacques
1978   *Borobudur*. Oxford University Press, Oxford.
Duncan, William N.
2005   Understanding Veneration and Violation in the Archaeological Record. In *Interacting with the Dead: Perspectives on Mortuary Archaeology for the New Millennium*, edited by Gordon F. M. Rakita, Jane E. Buikstra, Lane A. Beck, and Sloan R. Williams, pp. 207–227. University Press of Florida, Gainesville.
Duncan, William N., and Charles Andrew Hofling
2011   Why the Head? Cranial Modification as Protection and Ensoulment among the Maya. *Ancient Mesoamerica* 22:199–210.
Dunning, Nicholas P., Timothy Beach, Pat Farrell, and Sheryl Luzzadder-Beach
1998   Prehispanic Agrosystems and Adaptive Regions in the Maya Lowlands. *Culture & Agriculture* 20:87–101.
Dunning, Nicholas P., Timothy P. Beach, and Sheryl S. Luzzadder-Beach
2009   Creating a Stable Landscape: Soil Conservation among the Ancient Maya. In *The Socio-Natural Connection: Integrating Archaeology and Environmental Studies for 21st Century Conservation*, edited by Chris Fisher, James Brett Hill, and Gary Feinman, pp. 85–105. University of Arizona Press, Tucson.
2012   Kax and Kol: Collapse and Resilience in Lowland Maya Civilization. *Proceedings of the National Academy of Sciences* 109(10):3652–3657.
Eaton, Jack D.
1980   Operation 2011: Investigations within the Main Plaza of the Monumental Center at Colha. In *The Colha Project, Second Season, 1980 Interim Report*, edited by Thomas R. Hester, Jack D. Eaton, and Harry J. Shafer, pp. 145–162. Center for Archaeological Research, The University of Texas at San Antonio, San Antonio, and Centro Studi e Ricerche Ligabue, Venice.
Eberl, Marcus
2007   Community Heterogeneity and Integration: The Maya Sites of Nacimiento, Dos Ceibas, and Cerro de Cheyo (El Peten, Guatemala). Unpublished PhD dissertation, Department of Anthropology, Tulane University, New Orleans.
2013   Nourishing Gods: Birth and Personhood in Highland Mexican Codices. *Cambridge Archaeological Journal* 3:1–23.
2014   *Community and Difference. Change in Late Classic Maya Villages of the Petexbatun Region*. Vanderbilt Institute of Mesoamerican Archaeology Series. Vanderbilt University Press, Nashville.
Eberl, Markus, and Marco Antonio Monroy
2007   Refinando la Secuencia cerámica del Clásico Tardío en la región Petexbatun. In *XX Simposio de Investigaciones Arqueológicas en Guatemala, 2006*, edited by Juan P. Laporte, Bárbara Arroyo, and Héctor Mejía, pp. 464–477. Museo Nacional de Arqueología y Etnología, Guatemala City.
Edmonson, Munro
1986   *Heaven Born Merida and Its Destiny: The Book of Chilam Balam of Chumayel*. University of Texas Press, Austin.

Elson, Christina M., and R. Alan Covey
2006   *Intermediate Elites in Pre-Columbian States and Empires*. University of Arizona Press. Tucson.
Emery, Kitty
2008   A Zooarchaeological Test for Dietary Resource Depression at the End of the Classic Period in the Petexbatun, Guatemala. *Human Ecology* 36:617–634.
Eppich, E. Keith
2010   Tracking the Late to Terminal Classic Transition at El Perú-Waka': A Ceramic Perspective. Paper Presented at the 75th Annual Meeting of the Society for American Archaeology, St. Louis, Missouri.
2011   Lineage and State at El Peru-Waka': Ceramic and Architectural Perspectives on the Classic Maya Social Dynamic. Unpublished PhD dissertation, Southern Methodist University, Dallas.
Eppich, Evan Keith, Griselda Pérez Robles, Ana Lucía Arroyave, Fabiola Quiroa, Juan Carlos Meléndez, and Edwin Romàn
2005   La Secuencia de la Tradición Cerámica de El Perú: Un Estudio Cerámico. In *Proyecto Arqueológico El Perú-Waka': Informe No. 2, Temporada 2004*, edited by Hector L. Escobedo and David A. Freidel, pp. 313–350. Report presented to the Instituto de Antropología e Historia, Guatemala.
Errington, Shelly
1989   *Meaning and Power in a Southeast Asian Realm*. Princeton University Press, Princeton, New Jersey.
Escobedo, Héctor L.
2004   Tales from the Crypt: The Burial Place of Ruler 4, Piedras Negras. In *Courtly Art of the Ancient Maya*, edited by Mary E. Miller and Simon Martin, pp. 277–280. Thames and Hudson, New York.
Escobedo, Héctor L., and Mary Jane Acuña
2004   WK-02: Excavaciones en la Estructura M12-35. In *Proyecto Arqueológico El Perú-Waka'Informe No. 1, Temporada 2003*, edited by Héctor L. Escobedo and David Freidel, pp. 43–80. Instituto de Antropología e Historia, Guatemala.
Evans-Pritchard, E. E., and Meyer Fortes (editors)
1940   *African Political Systems*. Oxford University Press, Oxford.
Fagan, Brian
1999   *Floods, Famines, and Emperors: El Niño and the Fate of Civilizations*. Basic Books, New York.
Fahsen, Federico
2002   Rescuing the Origins of Dos Pilas Dynasty: A Salvage of Hieroglyphic Stairway 2, Structure L5-49. Electronic document, http://www.famsi.org/reports/01098/01098Fahsen01.pdf, accessed May 12, 2013.
Fahsen, Federico, and Tomas Barrientos
2006   Los Monumentos de Taj Chan Ahk and Kan Maax. In *Proyecto Arqueológico Cancuen, Informe de Temporada 2004–2005*, edited by Tomas Barrientos, Arthur Demarest, Luis Luin, Claudia Quintanilla, and Elisa Mencos, pp. 35–56. Ministerio de Cultura y Deportes de Guatemala, Guatemala City.

Fash, Barbara, William Fash, S. Lane, Rudy Larios, Linda Schele, J. Stomper, and David Stuart
1992   Investigation of a Classic Maya Council House at Copan, Honduras. *Journal of Field Archaeology* 19:419–442.

Fash, William L.
1983   Classic Maya State Formation: A Case Study and Its Implications. Unpublished PhD dissertation, Department of Anthropology, Harvard University.
1991   *Scribes, Warriors and Kings: the City of Copan and the Ancient Maya.* Thames and Hudson, New York and London.

Fash, William L., E. Wylls Andrews, and T. Kam Manahan
2004   Political Decentralization, Dynastic Collapse, and the Early Postclasic in the Urban Center of Copán, Honduras. In *The Terminal Classic in the Maya Lowlands: Collapse, Transition, and Transformation*, edited by Arthur A. Demarest, Prudence M. Rice, and Don S. Rice, pp. 260–287. University Press of Colorado, Boulder.

Fash, William, and David Stuart
1991   Dynastic History and Cultural Evolution at Copan, Honduras. In *Classic Maya Political History: Hieroglyphic and Archaeological Evidence*, edited by T. Patrick Culbert, pp. 147–180. Cambridge University Press, New York.

Fash, William L., Alexandre Tokovinine, and Barbara W. Fash
2009   The House of New Fire at Teotihuacan and Its Legacy in Mesoamerica. In *Art of Urbanism: How Mesoamerican Kingdoms Represented Themselves in Architecture and Imagery*, edited by William L. Fash and Leonardo López Luján, pp. 201–229. Dumbarton Oaks, Washington, D.C.

Feeley-Harnik, Gillian
1985   Issues in Divine Kingship. *Annual Review of Anthropology* 14:273–313.

Fernández Aguilar, Carlos Enrique
2010   *Símbolos de Poder. Análisis Simbólico-cognitivo de los Estucos de la Estructura M7-1 de Cancuen.* Tesis de Licenciatura en Ciencias Sociales, Universidad del Valle, Guatemala City.

Fialko, Vilma
2009   Archaeological Research and Rescue Project at Naranjo: Emerging Documentation in Naranjo's, Palacio de la Realeza, Petén, Guatemala. Electronic document, http://www.famsi.org/reports/05005/index.html, accessed September 28, 2012.

Fields, Virginia M.
1989   The Origins of Divine Kingship among the Lowland Classic Maya. Unpublished PhD dissertation, The University of Texas, Austin.

Fields, Virginia M., and Dorie Reents-Budet
2005   *Lords of Creation: The Origins of Sacred Maya Kingship.* Scala Publishers, New York.

Finamore, Daniel, and Stephen D. Houston
2010   *Fiery Pool: The Maya and the Mythic Sea.* Yale University Press, New Haven, Connecticut.

Fitzsimmons, James L.
1998   Classic Maya Mortuary Anniversaries at Piedras Negras, Guatemala. *Ancient Mesoamerica* 9:271–278.
1999   PN 51: Excavaciones en la Estructura O-17. In *Proyecto Arqueológico Piedras Negras: Informe Preliminar No. 3, Tercera Temporada 1999*, edited by Héctor L. Escobedo and Stephen D. Houston, pp. 285–294. Proyecto Arqueológico Piedras Negras, Guatemala City.

Flannery, Kent V.
1972   The Cultural Evolution of Civilizations. *Annual Review of Ecology and Semantics* 3:399–426.

Flannery, Kent, and Joyce Marcus
2012   *The Creation of Inequality*. Harvard University Press, Cambridge.

Foias, Antonia E.
1996   Changing Ceramic Production and Exchange Systems and the Classic Maya Collapse in in the Petexbatun Region. Unpublished PhD dissertation, Department of Anthropology, Vanderbilt University, Nashville, Tennessee.

Foias, Antonia E., and Ronald L. Bishop
1997   Changing Ceramic Production and Exchange in the Petexbatun Region, Guatemala: Reconsidering the Classic Maya Collapse. *Ancient Mesoamerica* 8:275–291.

Forné, Mélanie
2006   *La Cronología Cerámica de La Joyanca, Noroeste del Petén, Guatemala*. BAR International Series 1572. British Archaeological Reports, Oxford.

Forné, Mélanie, Ronald L. Bishop, Arthur A. Demarest, M. James Blackman, and Erin L. Sears
2010   Gris Fino, Naranja Fino: Presencia temprana y fuentes de producción, el caso de Cancuen. In *XXIII Simposio de Investigaciones Arqueológicas en Guatemala, 2009*, edited by Barbara Arroyo, Lorena Paiz Aragón, Adriana Linares Palma, and Ana Lucia Arroyave, pp. 1163–1182. Museo Nacional de Arqueología y Etnología, Guatemala City.

Forné, Mélanie, Arthur A. Demarest, Horacio Martínez, Paola Torres, Silvia Alvarado, and Claudia Arriaza
2009   Intercambio y afiliación cultural en Cancuén: la complejidad cultural en las vísperas del colapso." In *XXII Simposio de Investigaciones Arqueológicas en Guatemala, 2008*, edited by J. P. Laporte, B. Arroyo and H. E. Mejía, pp. 1017–1036. Museo Nacional de Arqueología y Etnología, Guatemala City.

Fowles, Severin
2010   People without Things. In *An Anthropology of Absence: Materializations of Transcendence and Loss*, edited by Mikkel Bille, Frida Hastrup, and Tim Flohr Soerensen, pp. 23–41. Springer Science + Business Media, New York.

Fox, John W.
1996   Playing with Power: Ballcourts and Political Ritual in Southern Mesoamerica. *Current Anthropology* 37:483–509.

Fox, Richard
1977   *Urban Anthropology*. Prentice Hall, Englewood Cliffs, New Jersey.

Frazer, James G.
1993 [1922]   *The Golden Bough*. Wordworth Reference, Ware, Hertfordshire.

Freidel, David A.
1979   Culture Areas and Interaction Spheres: Contrasting Approaches to the Emergence of Civilization in the Maya Lowlands. *American Antiquity* 44:36–54.
1981   Civilization as a State of Mind: The Cultural Evolution of the Lowland Maya. In *The Transition to Statehood in the New World*, edited by G. D. Jones and R. R. Kautz, pp. 188–227. Cambridge University Press, Cambridge.
1985   Polychrome Facades of the Lowland Maya Preclassic. In *Painted Architecture and Polychrome Monumental Sculpture in Mesoamerica*, edited by Elizabeth Boone, pp. 5–30. Dumbarton Oaks, Washington, D.C.
1986   The Monumental Architecture. In *Archaeology at Cerros, Belize, Central America*, edited by David A. Freidel and Robin Robertson-Freidel, pp. 1–21. Southern Methodist University Press, Dallas.
1988   The Late Preclassic Antecedents of Classic Maya Discourse. *Journal of Mayan Linguistics* 6:23–46.
1991   The Jester God: The Beginning and End of a Maya Royal Symbol. In *Vision and Revision in Maya Studies*, edited by Flora Clancy and Peter D. Harrison, pp. 67–78. University of New Mexico Press, Albuquerque.
1992   Ahau as Idea and Artifact. In *Ideology and Pre-Columbian Civilization*, edited by Arthur A. Demarest and Geoffrey W. Conrad, pp.115–133. School of American Research Press, Santa Fe, New Mexico.
1998   Sacred Work: Dedication and Termination in Mesoamerica. In *The Sowing and the Dawning: Termination, Dedication, and Transformation in the Archaeological and Ethnographic Record of Mesoamerica*, edited by Shirley Boteler Mock, pp. 189–194. University of New Mexico Press.
2008   Maya Divine Kingship. In *Religion and Power: Divine Kingship in the Ancient World and Beyond*, edited by Nicole Brisch, pp. 191–206. University of Chicago, Chicago.

Freidel, David A., Héctor L. Escobedo, and Stanley P. Guenter
2007   A Crossroads of Conquerors: 'Waka' and Gordon Willey's 'Rehearsal for the Collapse' Hypothesis. In *Gordon R. Willey and American Archaeology: Contemporary Perspectives*, edited by Jeremy A. Sabloff and William Fash, pp. 187–208. University of Oklahoma Press, Norman.

Freidel, David A., Héctor L. Escobedo, and Juan Carlos Meléndez
2013   Mountain of Memories: Structure M12-32 at El Perú. In *Millenary Maya Societies: Past Crises and Resilience*, edited by M. Charlotte Arnauld and Alain Breton, pp. 235–248. Electronic document, published online at Mesoweb: www.mesoweb.com/publications/MMS/15_Freidel_etal.pdf.

Freidel, David, and F. Kent Reilly
2010   The Flesh of God: Cosmology, Food, and the Origins of Political Power in Ancient Southeastern Mesoamerica. In *Pre-Columbian Foodways: Interdisciplinary Approaches to Food, Culture, and Markets in Ancient Mesoamerica*, edited by John Edward Staller and Michael Carrasco, pp. 635–680. Springer, New York and Hidelberg.

Freidel, David A., and Linda Schele
1988a   Kingship in the Late Preclassic Maya Lowlands: The Instruments and Places of Ritual Power. *American Anthropologist* 90:547–567.
1988b   Symbol and Power: A History of the Lowland Maya Cosmogram. In *Maya Iconography*, edited by Elizabeth Benson and Gillett Griffin, pp. 44–93. Princeton University Press, Princeton, New Jersey.
1989   Dead Kings and Living Temples: Dedication and Termination Rituals among the Ancient Maya. In *Word and Image in Maya Culture*, edited by W. F. Hanks and Don S. Rice, pp. 233–243. University of Utah Press, Salt Lake City.

Freidel, David A., Linda Schele, and Joy Parker
1993   *Maya Cosmos: Three Thousand Years on the Shaman's Path*. William Morrow and Co., New York.

Freidel, David A., and Justine Shaw
2000   The Lowland Maya Civilization: Historical Consciousness and Environment. In *The Way the Wind Blows: Climate, History, and Human Action* edited by Roderick J. McIntosh, Joseph A. Tainter, and Susan Keech McIntosh, pp. 271–300. Columbia University Press, New York.

Freidel, David A., and Charles K. Suhler
1995   Crown of Creation: The Development of the Maya Royal Diadems in the Late Preclassic and Early Classic Periods. In *The Emergence of Lowland Maya Civilization, The Transition from the Preclassic to the Early Classic*, edited by Nikolai Grube, pp. 137–150. Verlag Von Flemming, Mockmuhl.
1998   Visiones serpentinas y laberintos mayas. *Arqueología Mexicana* 6(34):28–37.

Freidel, David A., Charles K. Suhler, and Rafael Cobos Palma
1998   Termination Ritual Deposits at Yaxuna: Detecting the Historical in Archaeological Contexts. In *The Sowing and the Dawning: Termination, Dedication, and Transformation in the Archaeological and Ethnographic Record of Mesoamerica*, edited by Shirley Boteler Mock, pp. 135–146. University of New Mexico Press, Albuquerque.

Friedrich, Carl J.
1963   *Man and His Government*. McGraw-Hill, New York.

Gann, Thomas
1918   *The Maya Indians of Southern Yucatan and Northern British Honduras*. Bulletin No. 64. Bureau of American Ethnology, Washington, D.C.

Garber, James F.
1983   Patterns of Jade Consumption and Disposal at Cerros, Northern Belize. *American Antiquity* 48:800–807.
1986   The Artifacts. In *Archaeology at Cerros Belize, Central America*, vol. 1, *An Interim Report*, edited by Robin A. Robertson and David A. Freidel, pp. 117–126. Southern Methodist University Press, Dallas.

Garber, James F., W. David Driver, Lauren A. Sullivan, and David M. Glassman
1998   Bloody Bowls and Broken Pots: The Life, Death, and Rebirth of a Maya House. In *The Sowing and the Dawning: Termination, Dedication, and Transformation in the Archaeological and Ethnographic Record of Mesoamerica*, edited by Shirley Boteler Mock, pp. 125–133. University of New Mexico Press, Albuquerque.

García Moll, Roberto
2003 *La Arquitectura De Yaxchilan*. Instituto de Antropología e Historia, Mexico City.
2005 *Pomona: Un Sitio Del Clásico Maya En Las Colinas Tabasqueñas*. Instituto de Antropología e Historia, Mexico City.

Garrison, Thomas G., and Nicholas P. Dunning
2009 Settlement, Environment, and Politics in the San Bartolo-Xultun Territory, El Peten, Guatemala. *Latin American Antiquity* 20:525–552.

Gečienė, Ingrida
2002 The Notion of Power in the Theories of Bourdieu, Foucault and Baudrillard. *Sociologija* 2:116–124.

Geertz, Clifford
1973 *The Interpretation of Cultures*. Basic Books, New York.
1980 *Negara: The Theatre State in Nineteenth-Century Bali*. Princeton University Press, Princeton, New Jersey.

Geller, Pamela
2012 Parting (with) the Dead: Body Partibility as Evidence of Commoner Ancestor Veneration. *Ancient Mesoamerica* 23:115–130.

Gilbert, Michelle
2008 The Sacralized Body of the Akwapim King. In *Religion and Power: Divine Kingship in the Ancient World and Beyond*, edited by Nicole Brisch, pp. 171–190. University of Chicago, Chicago.

Gill, Richardson B.
2000 *The Great Maya Droughts: Water, Life, and Death*. University of New Mexico Press, Albuquerque, New Mexico.

Gillespie, Susan D.
2000 Rethinking Ancient Maya Social Organization: Replacing "Lineage" with "House." *American Anthropologist* 102:467–484.
2001 Personhood, Agency, and Mortuary Ritual: A Case Study from the Ancient Maya. *Journal of Anthropological Archaeology* 20:73–112.
2008 Embodied Persons and Heroic Kings in Late Classic Maya Sculpture. In *Past Bodies: Body-Centered Research in Archaeology*, edited by Dušan Borić and John E. Robb, pp. 125–134. Oxbow Press, Oxford.

Golden, Charles W.
2002 Disentangling Culture Change from Chronology: The Early Classic/Late Classic Divide at Piedras Negras, Guatemala. Unpublished PhD dissertation, Department of Anthropology, University of Pennsylvania.
2003 The Politics of Warfare in the Usumacinta Basin: La Pasadita and the Realm of Bird Jaguar. In *Ancient Mesoamerican Warfare*, edited by M. Kathryn Brown and Travis W. Stanton, pp. 31–48. Alta Mira, Walnut Creek, California.

Golden, Charles W., and Andrew K. Scherer
2006 Border Problems: Recent Archaeological Research along the Usumacinta River. *PARI Journal* 7(2):1–16.
2012 Un Mundo Mojado: Paisaje y Poder en los Reinos Mayas del Oeste. *Los Investigadores de la Cultura Maya* 21:65–84.

2013a Territory, Trust, Growth and Collapse in Classic Period Maya Kingdoms. *Current Anthropology* 54.
2013b All of a Piece: The Politics of Growth and Collapse in Classic Maya Kingdoms. *Contributions in New World Archaeology* 4:157–171.

Golden, Charles, Andrew K. Scherer, A. René Muñoz, and Zachary X. Hruby
2012 Polities, Boundaries, and Trade in the Classic Period Usumacinta River Basin. *Mexicon* 34(1):11–19.

Golden, Charles W., Andrew K. Scherer, A. René Muñoz, and Rosaura Vasquez
2008 Piedras Negras and Yaxchilan: Divergent Political Trajectories in Adjacent Maya Polities. *Latin American Antiquity* 19:249–274.

González Cruz, Arnoldo
2003 *The Throne of Ahkal Mo' Nahb' III: A Unique Finding at Palenque*. INAH/Nestlé. INAH, Mexico, D.F.

Gossen, Gary
1994 From Olmecs to Zapatistas: A Once and Future History of Souls. *American Anthropologist* 96:553–570.
1996 Maya Zapatistas Move to the Ancient Future. *American Anthropologist* 96:528–538.

Graffam, Gray
1992 Beyond State Collapse: Rural History, Raised Fields, and Pastoralism in the South Andes. *American Anthropologist* 94:882–904.

Grafstein, Robert
1981 The Failure of Weber's Conception of Legitimacy: Its Causes and Implications. *Journal of Politics* 43(2):456–472.

Graham, Elizabeth A.
2004 Lamanai Reloaded: Alive and Well in the Early Postclassic. *Research Reports in Belizean Archaeology* 1:223–241.

Graham, Ian
1967 *Archaeological Explorations in El Peten, Guatemala*. Publication 33. Middle American Research Institute, Tulane University, New Orleans.

Graham, John
1973 Aspects of Non-Classic Presences in the Inscriptions and Sculptural Art of Seibal. In *The Classic Maya Collapse*, edited by T. Patrick Culbert, pp. 207–219. School of American Research, University of New Mexico Press, Albuquerque.

Griffin, Robert, Robert Oglesby, Thomas Sever, and Udaysankar Nair
2014 An Archaeological Consideration of Long-Term Socio-Ecological Dynamics on the Vaca Plateau, Belize. In *The Great Maya Droughts in Cultural Context: Case Studies in Resilience and Vulnerability*, edited by Gyles Iannone, pp. 71–85. University Press of Colorado, Boulder.

Grove, David C.
1981 Olmec Monuments: Mutilation as a Clue to Meaning. In *The Olmec and Their Neighbors: Essays in Memory of Matthew W. Stirling*, edited by Elizabeth P. Benson, pp. 49–68. Dumbarton Oaks, Washington, D.C.

Grube, Nikolai
1994 Epigraphic Research at Caracol, Belize. In *Studies in the Archaeology of Caracol,*

Belize, edited by Diane Z. Chase and Arlen F. Chase, pp. 83–122. Monograph 7. Pre-Columbian Art Research Institute, San Francisco.

Grube, Nikolai, Thomas Guderjan, and Helen R. Haines
1995 Late Classic Architecture and Iconography at the Blue Creek Ruin, Belize. *Mexicon* 17(3):51–57.

Guderjan, Thomas H.
1995 Maya Settlement and Trade on Ambergris Caye, Belize. *Ancient Mesoamerica* 6:147–159.
1998 The Blue Creek Jade Cache: Early Classic Ritual in Northwest Belize. *The Sowing and the Dawning: Termination, Dedication and transformation in the Archaeological and Ethnographic Record of Mesoamerica*, edited by Shirley Boetler Mock, pp. 101–111. University of New Mexico Press, Albuquerque.
2000 The Discovery of Tomb 5 at Blue Creek, Belize. *Pre-Columbian Art Research Institute Journal* 1:1–3.
2004 Architecture, Ritual and Temporal Dynamics at the Maya Center of Blue Creek, Belize. *Ancient Mesoamerica* 15:235–250.
2005 The Early Classic Period at the Maya Site of Blue Creek. *Research Reports in Belizean Archaeology* 2:131–142.
2006 E-Groups, Pseudo E-Groups, and the Development of the Classic Maya Identity in the Eastern Petén. *Ancient Mesoamerica* 17:97–104.
2007 *The Nature of a Maya City: Resources, Interaction and Power at Blue Creek, Belize.* University of Alabama Press, Tuscaloosa.

Guderjan, Thomas, Jeffery Baker, and Robert J. Lichtenstein
2003 Environmental and Cultural Diversity at Blue Creek. *Heterarchy, Political Economy, and the Ancient Maya*, edited by Vernon Scarborough, Fred Valdez Jr. and Nicholas Dunning, pp. 77–91. University of New Mexico Press, Albuquerque.

Guderjan, Thomas H., Timothy Beach, Sheryl Luzzadder-Beach, and Steve Bozarth
2009 Understanding the Causes of Abandonment in the Maya Lowlands. *Archaeological Review of Cambridge* 24(2):99–122.

Guderjan, Thomas H., Timothy Beach, Steve Bozarth, Colleen Hanratty, Sheryl Luzzadder-Beach, and Timothy Preston
2010 New Information about the Demise of a Maya City: Fieldwork at Blue Creek, Belize, 2006 and 2007. *Mexicon* 3(2):15–22.

Guderjan, Thomas H., and James F. Garber
1995 *Maya Maritime Trade, Settlement and Populations on Ambergris Cay, Belize.* Labyrinthos, Culver City, California.

Guderjan, Thomas H., Helen R. Haines, Michael Lindeman, Shirley Mock, Ellen Ruble, Froyla Salam, and Lea Worchester
1993 *Excavations at the Blue Creek Ruin, Northwestern Belize: 1992 Interim Report.* Maya Research Program, St. Mary's University, San Antonio, Texas.

Guderjan, Thomas H., and C. Colleen Hanratty
2006 A Thriving Non-Royal Lineage at Blue Creek; Evidence from a Sequence of Burials Caches and Architecture. *Acta Mesoamerica* 19.
2007 Factors of Stress and Processes Leading to the End of the Classic Period at Blue Creek. *Research Reports in Belizean Archaeology* 5:155–165.

2012   BC21: *The 20th Annual Report of the Blue Creek Archaeological Project.* Maya Research Program, The University of Texas at Tyler.
Guderjan, Thomas H., and Samantha Krause
2011   Identifying the Extent of Ancient Maya Ditched Field Systems in the Río Hondo Valley of Belize and Mexico. *Research Reports in Belizean Archaeology* 8:126–137.
Guderjan, Thomas H., Robert J. Lichtenstein, and C. Colleen Hanratty
2003   Elite Residences at Blue Creek, Belize. In *Maya Palaces and Elite Residences: An Interdisciplinary Approach*, edited by Jessica J. Christie, pp. 13–45. University of Texas Press, Austin.
Guenter, Stanley Paul
2005   Informe Preliminar de la Epigrafía de El Perú. In *Proyecto Arqueológico El Perú-Waka': Informe No. 2, Temporada 2004*, edited by Héctor L. Escobedo and David Freidel, pp. 359–400. Southern Methodist University. Dallas, Texas.
2014   The Epigraphy of El Peru-Waka'ak. In *Archaeology at El Peru-Waka': Ancient Maya Performances of Ritual, Memory, and Power*, edited by Olivia C. Navarro-Farr and Michelle Rich, pp. 147–166. University of Arizona Press, Tucson.
n.d.   The Inscriptions of Dos Pilas Associated with B'AJLAJ CHAN K'AWIIL. Electronic document, www.mesoweb.com/features/guenter/DosPilas.pdf, accessed May 10, 2013.
Gunn, Joel D., and Richard E. W. Adams
1982   Climatic Change, Culture, and Civilization in North America. *World Archaeology* 13(1):87–100.
Gunn, Joel D., Richard T. Matheny, and William J. Folan
2002   Climate-Change Studies in the Maya Area: A Diachronic Analysis. *Ancient Mesoamerica* 13:79–84.
Habermas, Jürgen
1975   *Legitimation Crisis.* Beacon Press, London.
Hall, Kenneth R.
2011   *A History of Early Southeast Asia: Maritime Trade and Societal Development, 100–1500.* Rowan and Littlefield, Toronto.
Hamblin, Robert L., and Brian L. Pitcher
1980   The Classic Maya Collapse: Testing Class Conflict Hypotheses. *American Antiquity* 45:246–267.
Hammond, Norman
1972   Obsidian Trade Routes in the Maya Area. *Science* 178:1092–1093.
1999a "Pillar of State . . . Majestic, Though in Ruin": The Royal Acropolis of La Milpa. *Context* 14(1):11–15.
1999b A Maya Throne Room at La Milpa. *Pre-Columbian Art Research Institute Newsletter* 28:12–13.
Hammond, Norman, and Matthew R. Bobo
1994   Pilgrimage's Last Mile: Late Maya Monument Veneration at La Milpa, Belize. *World Archaeology* 26:19–34.
Hammond, Norman, and Ben Thomas
1999   Another Maya Throne Room at La Milpa. *Context* 14:15–16.

Hammond, Norman, and Gair Tourtellot
2004   Out with a Whimper: La Milpa in the Terminal Classic. In *The Terminal Classic in the Maya Lowlands: Collapse, Transition, and Transformation*, edited by Arthur A. Demarest, Prudence M. Rice, and Don S. Rice, pp. 288–301. University Press of Colorado, Boulder.

Hammond, Norman, Gair Tourtellot III, Gloria Everson, Kerry L. Sagebiel, Ben Thomas, and Marc Wolf
2000   Survey and Excavation at La Milpa, Belize, 1998. *Mexicon* 22(2):38–45.

Hanks, William F.
1990   *Referential Practice, Language and Lived Space among the Maya*. University of Chicago Press, Chicago.
2010   *Converting Words: Maya in the Age of the Cross*. University of California Press, Berkley.

Hanratty, C. Colleen
2002   Excavations in the Structure 37 Plazuela. In *The Blue Creek Project: Working Papers from the 1998 and 1999 Seasons*, edited by Thomas H. Guderjan and Robert J. Lichtenstein, pp. 73–80. Maya Research Program, Texas Christian University, Fort Worth.

Hanratty, C. Colleen, and Thomas H. Guderjan
2007   Factors of Stress and Processes Leading to the End of the Classic Period at Blue Creek. *Research Reports in Belizean Archaeology* 5:155–165.

Hansen, Thomas Blom, and Finn Stepputat
2006   Sovereignty Revisited. *Annual Review of Anthropology* 35:295–315.

Harris, Peter
2007   *Zhou Daguan: A Record of Cambodia: The Land and Its People*. Silk Worm Books, Chiang Mai.

Harrison, Ellie
2000   Structure C-6: Excavation of an Elite Compound. In *The 1998 and 1999 Seasons of the Chan Chich Archaeological Project*, edited by Brett A. Houk, pp. 71–94. Papers of the Chan Chich Archaeological Project no. 4. Mesoamerican Archaeological Research Laboratory, University of Texas, Austin.

Harrison, Peter D.
1979   The Lobil Postclassic Phase in the Southern Interior of the Yucatan Peninsula. In *Mesoamerican Archaeology and Ethnohistory*, edited by Norman Hammond and Gordon Willey, pp. 189–207. University of Texas Press, Austin.
1981   Some Aspects of Precolumbian Settlement in Southern Quintana Roo, Mexico. In *Lowland Maya Settlement Patterns*, edited by Wendy Ashmore, pp. 259–286. University of New Mexico Press, Albuquerque.
1999   *The Lords of Tikal: Rulers of an Ancient Maya City*. Thames and Hudson, London.

Harrison-Buck, Eleanor
2007   Materializing Identity among the Terminal Classic Maya: Architecture and Ceramics in the Sibun Valley, Belize. Unpublished PhD dissertation, Boston University, Boston.
2012a   Rituals of Death and Disempowerment among the Maya. In *Power and Identity in Archaeological Theory and Practice: Case Studies from Ancient Mesoamerica*,

edited by Eleanor Harrison-Buck, pp. 103–115. Foundations of Archaeological Inquiry. University of Utah Press, Salt Lake City.
2012b   Architecture as Animate Landscape: Circular Shrines in the Ancient Maya Lowlands. *American Anthropologist* 114:64–80.
2014   Reevaluating Chronology and Historical Content in the Maya Books of Chilam Balam. *Ethnohistory* 61(4):681–713.

Harrison-Buck, Eleanor, and Julia A. Hendon
2013   Epistemologies and Ontologies of Agency and Personhood: An Introduction. Paper presented at the 78th Annual Meeting of the Society for American Archaeology, Honolulu, Hawaii.

Harrison-Buck, Eleanor, and Patricia A. McAnany
2006   Terminal Classic Circular Shrines and Ceramic Material in the Sibun Valley, Belize: Evidence of Northern Yucatec Influence in the Eastern Maya Lowlands. *Research Reports in Belizean Archaeology* 3:287–299.
2013   Terminal Classic Circular Architecture in the Sibun Valley, Belize. *Ancient Mesoamerica* 24(2):295–306.

Harrison-Buck, Eleanor, Patricia A. McAnany, and Rebecca Storey
2007   Empowered and Disempowered During the Late to Terminal Classic Transition: Maya Burial and Termination Rituals in the Sibun Valley, Belize. In *New Perspectives on Human Sacrifice and Ritual Body Treatments in Ancient Maya Society*, edited by Vera Tiesler and Andrea Cucina, pp. 74–101. Springer Science + Business Media, New York.

Harrison-Buck, Eleanor, Ellen Spensley Moriarty, and Patricia A. McAnany
2013   Classic Maya Ceramic Hybridity in the Sibun Valley of Belize. In *The Archaeology of Hybrid Material Culture*, edited by Jeb Card, pp. 185–206. Center for Archaeological Investigation, Occasional Paper No. 39. Southern Illinois University, Carbondale.

Hauser-Schäublin, Brigitta
2003   The Precolonial Balanese State Reconsidered. *Current Anthropology* 44(3):153–181.
2005   Temple and King: Resource Management, Rituals and Redistribution in Early Bali. *Journal of the Royal Anthropological Institute* 11:747–771.

Haviland, William
1969   A New Population Estimate for Tikal, Guatemala. *American Antiquity* 34:429–433.

Heath, Joseph
2010   "Legitimation Crisis" in the Later Work of Jürgen Habermas. *The Journal of Shanghai Administrative Institute* 11(5):103–109.

Heitzman, James
1997   *Gifts of Power: Lordship in an Early Indian State*. Oxford University Press, Oxford.

Helms, Mary W.
1993   *Craft and the Kingly Ideal: Art, Trade, and Power*. University of Texas Press, Austin.
1999   Observations on Political Ideology in Complex Societies in the Tropics—and Elsewhere. In *Complex Polities in the Ancient Tropical World*, edited by Elisabeth

A. Bacus and Lisa J. Lucero, pp. 195–200. American Anthropological Association, Arlington, Virginia.

Hendon, Julia A.
2010   *Houses in a Landscape: Memory and Everyday Life in Mesoamerica.* Duke University Press, Durham, North Carolina.
2012   Objects as Persons: Integrating Maya Beliefs and Anthropological Theory. In *Power and Identity in Archaeological Theory and Practice: Case Studies from Ancient Mesoamerica*, edited by Eleanor Harrison-Buck, pp. 82–89. Foundations of Archaeological Inquiry. University of Utah Press, Salt Lake City.

Hester, Thomas R.
1982   The Maya Lithic Sequence in Northern Belize. In *Archaeology at Colha, Belize: The 1981 Interim Report*, edited by Thomas R. Hester, Harry J. Shafer, and Jack D. Eaton, pp. 39–59. Center for Archaeological Research, The University of Texas at San Antonio.

Hester, Thomas R. (editor)
1985   Late Classic–Early Postclassic Transitions: Archaeological Investigations at Colha, Belize. Final Performance Report submitted to the National Endowment for the Humanities, Grants RO 20534-83 and RO-20755. Center for Archaeological Research, The University of Texas at San Antonio.

Heusch, Luc de
1997   The Symbolic Mechanism of Sacred Kingship: Rediscovering Frazer. *Journal of the Royal Anthropological Institute* 3:213–232.
2005   Forms of Sacralized Power in Africa. In *The Character of Kingship*, edited by Declan Quigley, pp. 25–37. Berg, New York.

Higham, Charles
1989   *The Archaeology of Mainland Southeast Asia: From 10,000 B.C. to the Fall of Angkor.* Cambridge University Press, Cambridge.
2001   *The Civilization of Angkor.* University of California Press, Los Angeles.

Hill, Robert M., II
1996   Eastern Chajoma (Cakchiquel) Political Geography. Ethnohistorical and Archaeological Contributions to the Study of a Late Postclassic Highland Maya Polity. *Ancient Mesoamerica* 7:63–87.

Hill, Robert M., II, and John Monaghan
1987   *Continuities in Highland Maya Social Organization: Ethnohistory in Sacapulas, Guatemala.* University of Pennsylvania Press, Philadelphia.

Hocart, A. M.
1936   *Kings and Councilors.* University of Chicago Press, Chicago.

Hodder, Ian
2011   Human-Thing Entanglement: Towards an Integrated Archaeological Perspective. *Journal of the Royal Anthropological Institute* 17:154–177.

Hoffman, Michael A.
1979   *Egypt Before the Pharaohs.* Marboro, London.

Holley, George
1983   Ceramic Changes at Piedras Negras, Guatemala. Unpublished PhD Thesis, Department of Anthropology, Southern Illinois University, Carbondale.

Houk, Brett A.
1996   The Archaeology of Site Planning: An Example from the Maya Site of Dos Hombres, Belize. Unpublished PhD dissertation, Department of Anthropology, University of Texas at Austin.
2000   Life, the Universe, and Everything: Re-evaluating Problematic Deposit 2 from Dos Hombres, Belize. In *The 1998 and 1999 Seasons of the Chan Chich Archaeological Project*, edited by Brett A. Houk, pp. 141–150. Papers of the Chan Chich Archaeological Project no. 4. Mesoamerican Archaeological Research Laboratory, University of Texas, Austin.
2011   The Deadly Years: Terminal Classic Problematic Deposits and the Fates of Dos Hombres and Chan Chich, Belize. Paper presented at the 76th annual meeting of the Society for American Archaeology, Sacramento, California.
2015   *Ancient Maya Cities of the Eastern Lowlands*. University Press of Florida, Gainesville.
Houk, Brett A., Lauren A. Sullivan, and Fred Valdez Jr.
2008   Rethinking the Postclassic in Northwest Belize. *Research Reports in Belizean Archaeology* 5:93–102.
Houston, Stephen D.
1993   *Hieroglyphs and History at Dos Pilas: Dynastic Politics of the Classic Maya*. University of Texas Press, Austin.
2008   The Epigraphy of El Zotz. Electronic document, http://www.mesoweb.com/zotz/articles/ZotzEpigraphy.pdf, accessed April, 15 2013.
2014   A Game with a Throne. Maya Decipherment: Ideas on Ancient Maya Writing and Iconography. http://decipherment.wordpress.com/2014/01/24/a-game-with-a-throne/. Accessed April 1, 2014.
Houston, Stephen D., and Ernesto Arredondo Leiva
1999a   PN 34: Excavaciones en el Patio 1 de la Acropolis. In *Proyecto Arqueologico Piedras Negras: Informe Preliminar No. 3, Tercera Temporada 1999*, edited by Héctor L. Escobedo and Stephen D. Houston, pp. 105–118. Proyecto Arqueologico Piedras Negras, Guatemala City.
1999b   PN 48: Excavaciones en la Plataforma J-1. In *Proyecto Arqueológico Piedras Negras: Informe Preliminar No. 3, Tercera Temporada 1999*, edited by edited by Héctor L. Escobedo and Stephen D. Houston, pp. 249–268. Proyecto Arqueológico Piedras Negras, Guatemala City.
2000   PN 32: Excavaciones en el Patio 2 y 3 de la Acrópolis. In *Proyecto Arqueologico Piedras Negras: Informe Preliminar No. 4, Cuarta Temporada 2000*, edited by edited by Héctor L. Escobedo and Stephen D. Houston, pp. 37–61. Proyecto Arqueológico Piedras Negras, Guatemala City.
Houston, Stephen D, Héctor L. Escobedo, Mark Child, Charles Golden, and A. Rene Muñoz
2001   Crónica de una Muerte Anunciada: Los Años Finales de Piedras Negras. In *Reconstruyendo La Ciudad Maya: El Urbanismo en Las Sociedades Antiguas*, edited by Andrés Ciudad Ruiz, Mario Humberto Ruz Sosa, and M. Josefa Iglesias Ponce de León, pp. 65–93. Sociedad Española de Estudios Mayas, Madrid.

Houston, Stephen D., Héctor L. Escobedo, Mark Child, Charles Golden, René Muñoz, and Monica Urquizú
1998   Monumental Architecture at Piedras Negras, Guatemala: Time, History, and Meaning. *Mayab* 11:40–56.
Houston, Stephen D., Héctor L. Escobedo, Mark Child, Charles Golden, Richard Terry, and David Webster
2000   In the Land of the Turtle Lords: Archaeological Investigations at Piedras Negras, Guatemala, 2000. *Mexicon* 22:97–110.
2003   The Moral Community: Maya Settlement Transformation at Piedras Negras, Guatemala. In *The Social Construction of Ancient Cities*, edited by Monica L. Smith, pp. 212–253. Smithsonian Institution Press, Washington, D.C.
Houston, Stephen D., Héctor L. Escobedo, Perry Hardin, Richard Terry, David L. Webster, Mark Child, Charles Golden, Kitty Emery, and David Stuart
1999   Between Mountains and Sea: Investigations at Piedras Negras, Guatemala, 1998. *Mexicon* 21:10–17.
Houston, Stephen, Héctor L. Escobedo, Andrew Scherer, Mark Child, and James Fitzsimmons
2003   Classic Maya Death at Piedras Negras, Guatemala. In *Antropología de la Eternidad: La Muerte en la Cultura Maya*, edited by Andrés Ciudad Ruiz, Mario Humberto Ruz Sosa, and M. Josefa Iglesias Ponce de León, pp. 113–143. Sociedad Española de Estudios Mayas, Madrid.
Houston, Stephen D., Héctor L. Escobedo, Richard Terry, David L. Webster, George Veni, and Kitty F. Emery
2000   Among the River Kings: Archaeological Research at Piedras Negras, Guatemala, 1999. *Mexicon* 22:8–17.
Houston, Stephen D., and Takeshi Inomata
2009   *The Classic Maya*. Cambridge University Press, New York.
Houston, Stephen, and David Stuart
1989   *The Way Glyph: Evidence for "Co-essences" among the Classic Maya*. Research Reports on Ancient Maya Writing no. 30. Center for Maya Research, Barnardsville, North Carolina.
1996   Of Gods, Glyphs, and Kings: Divinity and Rulership among the Classic Maya. *Antiquity* 70:289–312.
1998   The Ancient Maya Self: Personhood and Portraiture in the Classic Period. *Res: Anthropology and Aesthetics* 33:73–101.
Houston, Stephen D., David Stuart, and Karl A. Taube
2006   *The Memory of Bones: Body, Being, and Experience among the Classic Maya*. University of Texas Press, Austin.
Houston, Stephen D., and Monica Urquizú
1998   PN 34: Excavaciones en el Patio 1 de La Acrópolis. In *Proyecto Arqueologico Piedras Negras: Informe Preliminar No. 2, Segunda Temporada 1998*, edited by Héctor L. Escobedo and Stephen D. Houston, pp. 243–256. Proyecto Arqueológico Piedras Negras, Guatemala City.

Hruby, Zachary X.
2006   The Organization of Chipped-Stone Economies at Piedras Negras, Guatemala. Unpublished PhD dissertation, Department of Anthropology, University of California, Riverside.

Hughes, Donald L.
2001   *An Environmental History of the World*. Routledge, New York.

Hüsken, Ute
2007   Ritual Dynamics and Ritual Failure. In *When Rituals Go Wrong: Mistakes, Failure, and the Dynamics of Ritual*, edited by Ute Hüsken, pp. 337–366. Brill Academic Publishers, Boston.

Iannone, Gyles
2005   The Rise and Fall of an Ancient Maya Petty Royal Court. *Latin American Antiquity* 16:26–44.
2006   Investigations in the Buried Royal Residential Courtyard at Minanha, Belize. *Research Reports in Belizean Archaeology* 3:149–160.
2007   On Drought and the "Collapse" of the Ancient Maya. *Research Reports in Belizean Archaeology* 4:55–65.
2009   The Jungle Kings of Minanha: Constellations of Authority and the Ancient Maya Socio-Political Landscape. *Research Reports in Belizean Archaeology* 6:33–41.
2010a   Collective Memory in the Frontiers: A Case Study from the Ancient Maya Center of Minanha, Belize. *Ancient Mesoamerica* 21:353–371.
2010b   The Ritual "Termination" of Royal Residential Courtyards During the Terminal Classic Period: Implications for Understanding Ancient Maya Societal Structure, and the Terminal Classic "Collapse." *Research Reports in Belizean Archaeology* 7:267–280.
2014   Introduction: Resilience, Vulnerability, and the Study of Socio-Ecological Dynamics. In *The Great Maya Droughts in Cultural Context: Case Studies in Resilience and Vulnerability*, edited by Gyles Iannone, pp. 1–19. University Press of Colorado, Boulder.

Iannone, Gyles, Arlen F. Chase, Diane Z. Chase, Jaime Awe, Holley Moyes, George Brook, Jason Polk, James Webster, and James Conolly
2014   An Archaeological Consideration of Long-Term Socio-Ecological Dynamics on the Vaca Plateau, Belize. In *The Great Maya Droughts in Cultural Context: Case Studies in Resilience and Vulnerability*, edited by Gyles Iannone, pp. 271–300. University Press of Colorado, Boulder.

Iannone, Gyles, and Matthew Longstaffe
2010   The 2010 Excavations in the Stairway Leading to Minanha's Royal Residential Compound (Group J). In *Archaeological Investigations in the North Vaca Plateau, Belize: Progress Report of the Twelfth (2010) Field Season*, edited by Gyles Iannone, Jaime J. Awe, Maxime Lamoureux St-Hilaire, and Matthew Longstaffe, pp. 63–73. Trent University, Peterborough, Ontario.

Iannone, Gyles, Jason Yaeger, and David Hodell
2014   The Great Maya Droughts: A Critical Introduction. In *The Great Maya Droughts in Cultural Context: Case Studies in Resilience and Vulnerability*, edited by Gyles Iannone, pp. 51–70. University Press of Colorado, Boulder.

Inomata, Takeshi
1997   The Last Day of a Fortified Classic Maya Center: Archaeological Investigations at Aguateca, Guatemala. *Ancient Mesoamerica* 8:337–351.
2001   King's People: Classic Maya Royal Courtiers in a Comparative Perspective. In *Royal Courts of the Ancient Maya*, vol. 1, *Theory, Comparison, and Synthesis*, edited by Takeshi Inomata and Stephen Houston, pp.27–53. Westview Press, Boulder.
2003   War, Destruction, and Abandonment: The Fall of the Classic Maya Center of Aguateca, Guatemala. In *The Archaeology of Settlement Abandonment in Middle America*, edited by Takeshi Inomata and Ronald W. Webb, pp. 43–60. University of Utah Press, Salt Lake City.
2006a   Politics and Theatricality in Mayan Society. In *Archaeology as Performance: Theaters of Power, Community, and Politics*, edited by Takeshi Inomata and Lawrence S. Coben, pp. 187–221. Alta Mira Press, Lanham, Maryland.
2006b   Plazas, Performers, and Spectators: Political Theaters of the Classic Maya. *Current Anthropology* 47:805–842.
2008a   *Settlements and Fortifications of Aguateca: Archaeological Maps of a Petexbatun Center*. Vanderbilt University Press, Nashville.
2008b   Women in Classic Maya Royal Courts. In *Servants of the Dynasty: Palace Women in World History*, edited by Anne Walthall, pp. 45–64. University of California Press, Berkeley.
2008c   *Warfare and the Fall of a Fortified Center: Archaeological Investigations at Aguateca*. Vanderbilt Institute of Mesoamerican Series, vol. 3. Vanderbilt University Press, Nashville.
2010   Test Pits in Other Locations. In *Burned Palaces and Elite Residences of Aguateca: Excavations and Ceramics*, edited by Takeshi Inomata and Daniela Triadan, pp. 149–155. Monographs of the Aguateca Archaeological Project First Phase, vol. 1. University of Utah Press, Provo.
2014   Fire Intensity Assessment through the Analysis of Artifacts and Building Materials: Burning and Abandonment at the Classic Maya Sites of Aguateca and Ceibal, Guatemala. *Advances in Archaeological Practice* 2:50–63.
Inomata, Takeshi, and Markus Eberl
2010   The Barranca Escondida. In *Burned Palaces and Elite Residences of Aguateca: Excavations and Ceramics*, edited by Takeshi Inomata and Daniela Triadan, pp. 138–148. Monographs of the Aguateca Archaeological Project First Phase, vol. 1. University of Utah Press, Provo.
Inomata, Takeshi, and Stephen D. Houston
2001   Opening the Royal Maya Court. In *Royal Courts of the Ancient Maya*, vol. 1, *Theory, Comparison, and Synthesis*, edited by Takeshi Inomata and Stephen D. Houston, pp. 3–23. Westview Press, Boulder, Colorado.
Inomata, Takeshi, Erick Ponciano, Oswaldo Chinchilla, Otto Román, Véronique Breuil-Martínez, and Oscar Santos
2004   An Unfinished Temple at the Classic Maya Center of Aguateca, Guatemala. *Antiquity* 78(302):798–811.
Inomata, Takeshi, and Daniela Triadan
2003   Where Did Elites Live? Identifying Elite Residences at Aguateca, Guatemala. In

Maya Palaces and Elite Residences: An Interdisciplinary Approach, edited by Jessica J. Christie, pp. 154–183. University of Texas Press, Austin.

Inomata, Takeshi, and Daniela Triadan (editors)
2010   *Burned Palaces and Elite Residences of Aguateca: Excavations and Ceramics.* Aguateca Archaeological Project First Phase Monograph Series, vol. 1. University of Utah Press, Salt Lake City.
2014   *Life and Politics at the Royal Court of Aguateca: Artifacts, Analytical Data, and Synthesis.* Aguateca Archaeological Project First Phase Monograph Series, vol. 3. University of Utah Press, Salt Lake City.

Inomata, Takeshi, Daniela Triadan, Erick Ponciano, and Kazuo Aoyama (editors)
2009   *La Política De Lugares y Comunidades En La Antigua Sociedad Maya De Petexbatun: Las Investigaciones Del Proyecto Arqueológico Aguateca Segunda Fase.* Ministerio de Cultura y Deportes, Dirección General del Patrimonio Cultural y Natural, and Instituto de Antropología e Historia, Guatemala.

Inomata, Takeshi, Daniela Triadan, Erick Ponciano, Estela Pinto, Richard E. Terry, and Markus Eberl
2002   Domestic and Political Lives of Classic Maya Elites: The Excavation of Rapidly Abandoned Structures at Aguateca, Guatemala. *Latin American Antiquity* 13:305–330.

Inomata, Takeshi, Daniela Triadan, Erick Ponciano, Richard Terry, and Harriet F. Beaubien
2001   In the Palace of the Fallen King: The Royal Residential Complex at Aguateca, Guatemala. *Journal of Field Archaeology* 28:287–306.

Inomata, Takeshi, and Ronald W. Webb (editors)
2003   *The Archaeology of Settlement Abandonment in Middle America.* Foundations of Archaeological Inquiry. University of Utah Press, Salt Lake City.

Jackson, Sarah
2005   Deciphering Classic Maya Political Hierarchy: Epigraphic, Archaeological, and Ethno-Historic Perspectives on the Courtly Elite. Unpublished PhD dissertation, Department of Anthropology, Harvard University.

Jacobsen, Trudy
2003   Autonomous Queenship in Cambodia, 1st–9th Centuries AD. *Journal of the Royal Asiatic Society,* 3rd Series 13(3):357–375.

Jameson, Fredric
1981   *The Political Unconscious.* Cornell University Press, Ithaca, New York.

Johnston, Kevin, Takeshi Inomata, and Joel Palka
1989   Excavaciones de Rescate del Campamento y Análisis de los Artefactos Recuperados. In *El Proyecto Arqueologico Regional Petexbatun,* edited by Arthur Demarest and Stephen Houston, pp. 29–52. Instituto de Antropologia e Historia, Guatemala City.

Jones, Christopher
1996   *Excavations in the East Plaza of Tikal.* Tikal Report no. 16. University Museum Monograph 92. University Museum, University of Pennsylvania, Philadelphia.

Joyce, Arthur
2000   The Founding of Monte Alban: Sacred Propositions and Social Practices. In

Agency in Archaeology, edited by Marcia-Anne Dobres and John Robb, pp. 72–91. Routledge, New York.

Joyce, Arthur A., and Erin T. Weller
2007   Commoner Rituals, Resistance, and the Classic-to-Postclassic Transition in Ancient Mesoamerica. In *Commoner Ritual and Ideology in Ancient Mesoamerica*, edited by Nancy Gonlin and Jon C. Lohse, pp. 143–184. University Press of Colorado, Boulder.

Kennett, Douglas J., Sebastian F. M. Breitenbach, Valorie V. Aquino, Yemane Asmerom, Jaime Awe, James U. L. Baldini, Patrick Bartlein, Brendan J. Culleton, Claire Ebert, Christopher Jazwa, Martha J. Macri, Norbert Marwan, Victor Polyak, Keith M. Prufer, Harriet E. Ridley, Harald Sodemann, Bruce Winterhalder, and Gerald H. Haug
2012   Development and Disintegration of Maya Political Systems in Response to Climate Change. *Science* 338:788–791.

Kepecs, Susan
2007   Chichén Itzá, Tula and the Epiclassic Early Postclassic Mesoamerican World System. In *Twin Tollans: Chichén Itzá, Tula, and the Epiclassic to Early Postclassic Mesoamerican World*, edited by Jeff K. Kowalski, and Cynthia Kristan-Graham. Dumbarton Oaks, Washington, D.C.

Kingsley, Melanie J., David del Cid, and Alejandro Gillot
2010   Excavaciones en la Estructura H10-1, Sector Norte de El Kinel. In *Proyecto Regional Arqueológico Sierra del Lacandón, 2010: Informe Preliminar, No. 8*, edited by Melanie J. Kingsley, Charles Golden, Andrew K. Scherer, and Luz Midilia Marroquín Franco, pp. 116–134. Informe Presentado a la Dirección General del Patrimonio Cultural y Natural de Guatemala.

Kingsley, Melanie J., Charles Golden, Andrew Scherer, and Luz Midilia Marroquín Franco
2012   Parallelism in Occupation: Tracking the Pre- and Post-Dynastic Occupation of Piedras Negras, Guatemala Through Its Secondary Site, El Porvenir. *Mexicon* 34(5):109–117.

Knapp, A. Bernard
2008   *Prehistoric and Protohistoric Cyprus: Identity, Insularity and Connectivity*. Oxford University Press, Oxford.

Knappett, Carl, and Lambros Malafouris (editors)
2008   *Material Agency: Towards a Non-Anthropocentric Approach*. Springer Science + Business Media, New York.

Kowalski, Jeff K.
1989   Who Am I among the Itza?: Links between Northern Yucatan and the Western Maya Lowlands and Highlands. In *Mesoamerica after the Decline of Teotihuacan AD 700–900*, edited by Richard A. Diehl and Janet C. Berlo, pp. 173–186. Dumbarton Oaks, Washington, D.C.

Kowalski, Jeff K., Alfredo Barrera Rubio, Heber Ojeda Más, and Jose Huchim Herrera
1994   Archaeological Excavations of a Round Temple at Uxmal: Summary Discussion and Implications for Northern Maya Culture History. In *Eighth Palenque Round Table, 1993*, edited Martha J. Macri and Jan McHargue, pp. 281–296. Pre-Columbian Art Research Institute, San Francisco.

Kristan-Graham, Cynthia, and Jeff K. Kowalski
2007 Chichén Itzá, Tula, and Tollan: Changing Perspectives on a Recurring Problem in Mesoamerican Archaeology and Art History. In *Twin Tollans: Chichén Itzá, Tula, and the Epiclassic to Early Postclassic Mesoamerican World*, edited by Jeff K. Kowalski, and Cynthia Kristan-Graham, pp. 13–83, Dumbarton Oaks, Washington, D.C.
Kunen, Julie L., Mary Jo Galindo, and Erin Chase
2002 Pits and Bones, Identifying Maya Ritual Behavior in the Archaeological Record. *Ancient Mesoamerica* 13:197–211.
Landa, Diego de
1978 *Yucatan Before and After the Conquest*. Dover Press, New York.
LaPorte, Juan Pedro, and Vilma Fialko C.
1990 New Perspectives on Old Problems: Dynastic References for the Early Classic at Tikal. In *Vision and Revision in Maya Studies*, edited by Flora S. Clancy and Peter D. Harrison, pp. 33–66. University of New Mexico Press, Albuquerque.
1995 Un reencuentro con Mundo Perdido, Tikal, Guatemala. *Ancient Mesoamerica* 6:41–94.
Laporte, Juan Pedro, and Hector E. Mejía
2000 *Registro de Sitios Arqueologicos del Sureste de Petén*. Report No. 14. Atlas Arqueológico de Guatemala, IDAEH, Guatemala City.
Latour, Bruno
1993 *We Have Never Been Modern*. Harvard University Press, Cambridge, Massachusetts.
LeCount, Lisa J.
1999 Polychrome Pottery and Political Strategies in Late and Terminal Classic Lowland Maya Society. *Latin American Antiquity* 10:239–258.
2001 Like Water for Chocolate: Feasting and Political Ritual among the Late Classic Maya at Xunantunich, Belize. *American Anthropologist* 103:935–953.
LeCount, Lisa J., and Jason Yaeger (editors)
2010 *Classic Maya Provincial Politics: Xunantunich and Its Hinterlands*. University of Arizona Press, Tucson.
LeCount, Lisa J., Jason Yaeger, Richard M. Leventhal, and Wendy Ashmore
2002 Dating the Rise and Fall of Xunantunich, Belize. *Ancient Mesoamerica* 13:41–63.
Lichtenstein, Robert
2000 *Settlement Zone Communities of the Greater Blue Creek Area*. Occasional Paper 2. Maya Research Program, Texas Christian University, Fort Worth.
Lieberman, Victor
2003 *Strange Parallels—Southeast Asia in Global Context, c. 800–1300*, vol. 1: *Integration on the Mainland*. Cambridge University Press, New York.
2009 *Strange Parallels—Southeast Asia in Global Context, c. 800–1300*, vol. 2: *Mainland Mirrors: Europe, Japan, China, South Asia, and the Island*. Cambridge University Press, New York.
Liendo Stuardo, Rodrigo
2007 The Problem of Political Integration in the Kingdom of Baak: A Regional Perspective for Settlement Patterns in the Palenque Region. In *Palenque: Recent In-*

vestigations at the Classic Maya Center, edited by Damien B. Marken, pp. 85–106. Altamira Press, Lanham, Maryland.

Liston, Maria A.
2007   Secondary Cremation Burials at Kavousi Vronda, Crete: Symbolic Representation in Mortuary Practice. *Hesperia* 76:51–71.

Lohse, Jon C., and Fred Valdez Jr. (editors)
2004   *Ancient Maya Commoners*. University of Texas Press, Austin.

Longstaffe, Matthew, and Gyles Iannone
2011   Households and Social Trajectories: The Site Core Community at Minanha, Belize. *Research Reports in Belizean Archaeology* 8:45–59.

López Varela, Sandra L.
1989   *Análisis y Clasificación de la Cerámica de un Sitio Maya del Clásico: Yaxchilan, Mexico*. BAR International Series 535. British Archaeological Reports, Oxford.
2005   Dynamics of Engagement in the Usumacinta River Valley and the Coastal Plains of Tabasco: Traversing Terminal Classic Hypotheses. In *Geographies of Power: Understanding the Nature of Terminal Classic Pottery in the Maya Lowlands*, edited by Sandra L. López Varela and Antonia E. Foias, pp. 41–61. BAR International Series 1447. British Archaeological Reports, Oxford.

Lucero, Lisa J.
1999   Water Control and Maya Politics in the Southern Maya Lowlands. In *Complex Polities in the Ancient Tropical World*, edited by E. A. Bacus and L. J. Lucero, pp. 35–49. Archaeological Papers of the American Anthropological Association no. 9. American Anthropological Association, Arlington.
2002   The Collapse of the Classic Maya: A Case for the Role of Water Control. *American Anthropologist* 104:814–826.
2003   The Politics of Ritual: The Emergence of Classic Maya Rulers. *Current Anthropology* 44:523–558.
2006   *Water and Ritual: The Rise and Fall of Classic Maya Rulers*. University of Texas Press, Austin.

Luzzadder-Beach, Sheryl, and Timothy Beach
2009   Arising from the Wetlands: Mechanisms and Chronology of Landscape Aggradation in the Northern Coastal Plain of Belize. *Annals of the Association of American Geographers* 99:1–26.

Mabbett, Ian W.
1978   Kingship at Angkor. *Journal of the Siam Society* 66(2):1–58.

Mackie, Euan W.
1985   *Excavations at Xunantunich and Pomona, Belize, in 1959–60*. BAR International Series 251. British Archaeological Reports, Oxford.

Macrae, Scott, and Gyles Iannone
2011   Investigations of the Agricultural Terracing Surrounding the Ancient Maya Centre of Minanha, Belize. *Research Reports in Belizean Archaeology* 8:183–197.

Magaña, Victor, Jorge A. Amador, and Socorro Medina
1999   The Midsummer Drought over Mexico and Central America. *Journal of Climate* 12:1577–1588.

Magaña, Victor O., Jorge L. Vásquez, José L. Pérez, and Joel B. Pérez
2003   Impact of El Niño on Precipitation in Mexico. *Geofísica Internacional* 42:313–330.
Maler, Teobert
1908   *Explorations in the Department of Peten, Guatemala and Adjacent Region: Topoxté; Yaxhá, Benque Viejo, and Naranjo*. Memoirs of the Peabody Museum of American Archaeology and Ethnology, vol. 4, no. 2. Harvard University, Cambridge, Massachusetts.
Malešević, Siniša
2002   *Ideology, Legitimacy and the New State: Yugoslavia, Serbia and Croatia*. Routledge, Oxford.
Manahan, T. Kam
2004   The Way Things Fall Apart: Social Organization and the Classic Maya Collapse of Copan. *Ancient Mesoamerica* 15:107–125.
Manahan, T. Kam, and Marcello Canuto
2009   Bracketing the Copan Dynasty: Late Preclassic and Early Postclassic Settlements at Copan, Honduras. *Latin American Antiquity* 20:553–580.
Marcus, Joyce
1992   Political Fluctuations in Mesoamerica. *National Geographic Research and Exploration* 8:392–411.
2003   Recent Advances in Maya Archaeology. *Journal of Archaeological Research* 11(2):71–148.
Marken, Damien B.
2007   The Construction Chronology of Palenque: Seriation Within an Architectural Form. In *Palenque: Recent Investigations at the Classic Maya Center*, edited by Damien B. Marken, pp. 57–84. AltaMira Press, Walnut Creek, California.
Marken, Damien B., and Arnoldo González Cruz
2007   Elite Residential Compounds at Late Classic Palenque. In *Palenque: Recent Investigations at the Classic Maya Center*, edited by Damien B. Marken, pp. 135–160. AltaMira Press, Walnut Creek, California.
Marken, Damien B., and Kirk D. Straight
2007   Conclusion: Reconceptualizing the Palenque Polity. In *Palenque: Recent Investigations at the Classic Maya Center*, edited by Damien B. Marken, pp. 279–324. AltaMira Press, Walnut Creek, California.
Martin, Simon, and Nikolai Grube
2008   *Chronicle of the Maya Kings and Queens*. 2nd ed. Thames and Hudson, New York.
Mason, J. Alden
1935   Preserving America's Finest Sculptures. *National Geographic Magazine* 68:537–570.
Massey, Virginia
1989   *The Human Skeletal Remains from a Terminal Classic Skull Pit at Colha Belize*. Papers of the Colha Project, vol. 3. Texas Archeological Research Laboratory, The University of Texas at Austin, and Department of Anthropology, Texas A&M University, College Station.
Masson, Marilyn A.
1989   Lithic Production Changes in Late Classic Maya Workshops at Colha, Belize: A

Study of Debitage Variation. Unpublished Master's thesis, Department of Anthropology, Florida State University.

Masson, Marilyn A., and David Freidel
2012   An Argument for Classic Era Maya Market Exchange. *Journal of Anthropological Archaeology* 31:455–484.

Mathews, Peter
1985   Maya Early Classic Monuments and Inscriptions. In *A Consideration of the Early Classic Period in the Maya Lowlands*, edited by Gordon R. Willey and Peter Mathews, pp. 5–54. Institute for Mesoamerican Studies, State University of New York at Albany.

Mathews, Peter, and Mario M. Aliphat Fernandez
1997   Informe de la Temporada de Campo 1993, Proyecto El Cayo. Informe Presentado ante el Consejo de Arqueologia del Instituto Nacional de Antropologia e Historia, Mexico, DF.

Mauss, Marcel
1954   *The Gift: Forms and Functions of Exchange in Archaic Societies*. Cohen and West, London.

McAnany, Patricia A.
1995   *Living with the Ancestors: Kinship and Kingship in Ancient Maya Society*. University of Texas Press, Austin.
1998   Ancestors and the Classic Maya Built Environment. In *Function and Meaning in Classic Maya Architecture*, edited by Stephen D. Houston, pp. 271–298. Dumbarton Oaks, Washington, D.C.
2010   *Ancestral Maya Economies in Archaeological Perspective*. Cambridge University Press, New York.
2013   Artisans, Ikatz, and Starcraft: Provisioning Classic Maya Royal Courts. In *Merchants, Markets, and Exchange in the PreColumbian World*, edited by Kenneth Hirth and Joanne Pillsbury. Dumbarton Oaks, Washington, D.C.

McAnany, Patricia A., and Tomas Gallareta Negrón
2010   Bellicose Rulers and Climatological Peril?: Retrofitting 21st Century Woes on 8th Century Maya Society. In *Questioning Collapse Human Resilience, Ecological Vulnerability, and the Aftermath of Empire*, edited by Patricia A. McAnany and Norman Yoffee, pp. 142–175. Cambridge University Press, New York.

McAnany, Patrica, and Norman Yoffee (editors)
2010   *Questioning Collapse: Human Resilience, Ecological Vulnerability, and the Aftermath of Empire*. Cambridge University Press, New York.

McCane, Carmen A., Scott A. Macrae, and Gyles Iannone
2009   A Consideration of the Spatial Arrangement of Settlement Groups and Terraces in Contreras, Minanha, Belize. *Research Reports in Belizean Archaeology* 6:141–152.

McGee, R. Jon
1998   The Lacandon Incense Burner Renewal Ceremony: Termination and Dedication Ritual among the Contemporary Maya. In *The Sowing and the Dawning: Termination, Dedication, and Transformation in the Archaeological and Ethnographic*

Record of Guatemala, edited by Shirely Boteler Mock, pp. 41–46. University of New Mexico Press, Albuquerque.

McGuire, Randall H.
2002   *A Marxist Archaeology*. Percheron Press, Clinton Corners, New York.
2008   *Archaeology as Political Action*. University of California Press, Los Angeles.

McKillop, Heather I.
1996   Ancient Maya Trading Ports and the Integration of Long-Distance and Regional Economies: Wild Cane Cay in South Coastal Belize. *Ancient Mesoamerica* 7:49–62.
2002   *Salt: White Gold of the Ancient Maya*. University Press of Florida, Gainesville.

McKillop, Heather I., and Paul Healy
1989   *Coastal Maya Trade*. Occasional Papers in Anthropology 8. Department of Anthropology, Trent University, Peterborough, Canada.

McNeeley, Jeffrey A.
1994   Lessons from the Past: Forests and Biodiversity. *Biodiversity and Conservation* 3:3–20.

McNeil, Cameron L., David A. Burney, and Lida Pigott Burney
2010   Evidence Disputing Deforestation as the Cause for the Collapse of the Ancient Maya Polity of Copan, Honduras. *Proceedings of the National Academy of Sciences* 107(3):1017–1022.

Meadows, Richard
1998   Test Pit Program in Group C. In *The 1997 Season of the Chan Chich Archaeological Project*, edited by Brett A. Houk, pp. 59–66. Papers of the Chan Chich Archaeological Project no. 3. Center for Maya Studies, San Antonio, Texas.

Me-Bar, Yoav, and Fred Valdez Jr.
2003   Droughts as Random Events in the Maya Lowlands. *Journal of Archaeological Science* 30:1599–1606.
2004   Recovery Time after a Disaster and the Ancient Maya. *Journal of Archaeological Science* 31:1311–1324.

Medina Martín, Cecilia, and Mirna Sánchez Vargas
2007   Posthumous Body Treatments and Ritual Meaning in the Classic Period Northern Petén. A Taphonomic Approach. In *New Perspectives on Human Sacrifice and Ritual Body Treatments in Ancient Maya Society*, edited by Vera Tiesler and Andrea Cucina, pp. 102–119. Springer, New York.

Middleton, Guy D.
2012   Nothing Lasts Forever: Environmental Discourses on the Collapse of Past Societies. *Journal of Archaeological Research* 20(3):257–307.

Miles, S. W.
1957   The Sixteenth-Century Pokom-Maya: A Documentary Analysis of Social Structure and Archaeological Setting. *Transactions of the American Philosophical Society* 47:733–781.

Miller, Julia C.
2000   *The 2000 Season of the Cross Group Project and a Brief Review of Previous Work*. Electronic document, http://www.mesoweb.com/palenque/dig/report/report_00_text.html, accessed December 21, 2012.

Mills, Barbara, and William Walker (editors)
2008   *Memory Work: Archaeologies of Material Practice*. School for Advanced Research, Santa Fe, New Mexico.

Moats, Lindsey R., Walter Beckwith, and Gregory Zaro
2012   The 2011 Excavations at Courtyard 100. In *The 2011 Season of the La Milpa Core Project*, edited by Brett A. Houk, pp. 39–76. Occasional Papers no. 13. Mesoamerican Archaeological Research Laboratory, The University of Texas at Austin.

Mock, Shirley Boteler
1998a   Prelude. In *The Sowing and the Dawning: Termination, Dedication, and Transformation in the Archaeological and Ethnographic Record of Mesoamerica*, edited by Shirley Boteler Mock, pp. 3–18. University of New Mexico Press, Albuquerque.
1998b   The Defaced and the Forgotten: Decapitation and Flaying/Mutilation as a Termination Event at Colha, Belize. In *The Sowing and the Dawning: Termination, Dedication, and Transformation in the Archaeological and Ethnographic Record of Mesoamerica*, edited by Shirley Boteler Mock, pp. 113–123. University of New Mexico Press, Albuquerque.

Mock, Shirley Boteler (editor)
1998   *The Sowing and the Dawning: Termination, Dedication, and Transformation in the Archaeological and Ethnographic Record of Mesoamerica*. University of New Mexico Press, Albuquerque.

Monaghan, John D.
2000   Theology and History in the Study of Mesoamerican Religions. In *Supplement to the Handbook of Middle American Indians*, vol. 6, *Ethnology*, edited by John D. Monaghan, pp. 24–49. University of Texas Press, Austin.

Monterroso, Jorge Mario, Mauro Montejo, and Leonel Ziesse
2009   Prospección Arqueológica en El Porvenir, Periferia Norte de Piedras Negras. In *Proyecto Regional Arqueológico Sierra Lacandon: Informe Preliminar No. 7*, edited by C. Golden, Andrew K. Scherer and Rosaura Vásquez, pp. 155–168. Report presented to the Instituto de Antropología e Historia de Guatemala, Guatemala.

Montmollin, Olivier de
1997   A Regional Study of Classic Maya Ballcourts from the Upper Grijalva Basin, Chiapas, Mexico. *Ancient Mesoamerica* 8:23–42.

Morley, Sylvanius
1946   *The Ancient Maya*. Stanford University Press, Stanford, California.

Moyes, Holley, Jaime J. Awe, George A. Brook, and James Webster
2009   The Ancient Maya Drought Cult: Late Classic Cave Use in Belize. *Latin American Antiquity* 20:175–206.

Mulhare, Eileen M.
1996   Barrio Matters: Toward an Ethnology of Mesoamerican Customary Social Units. *Ethnology* 35:93–106.

Muñoz, A. René
2006   Power, Practice, and Production: Technological Change in the Late Classic Ceramics of Piedras Negras, Guatemala. Unpublished PhD dissertation, Department of Anthropology, University of Arizona.

Munson, Jessica L., and Martha J. Macri
2009   Sociopolitical Network Interactions: A Case Study of the Classic Maya. *Journal of Anthropological Archaeology* 28:424–438.
Nalda, Enrique
2005   Kohunlich and Dzibanche: Parallel Histories. In *Quintana Roo Archaeology*, edited by Justine M. Shaw and Jennifer P. Matthews, pp. 228–244. University of Arizona Press, Tucson.
Navarro-Farr, Olivia C.
2005   WK-01: Excavaciones en la Estructura M13-1, Segunda Temporada. In *Proyecto Arqueológico El Perú-Waka': Informe No. 2, Temporada 2004*, edited by Héctor L. Escobedo and David A. Freidel, pp. 5–36. Report submitted to the Instituto de Antropología e Historia, Guatemala.
2009   Ritual, Process, and Continuity in the Late to Terminal Classic Transition: Investigations at Structure M13-1 in the Ancient Maya Site of El Perú-Waka', Petén, Guatemala. Unpublished PhD dissertation, Southern Methodist University, Dallas, Texas.
Navarro-Farr, Olivia C., and Ana Lucía Arroyave Prera
2014   A Palimpsest Effect: The Multi-Layered Meanings of Late-to-Terminal Classic Era, Above-Floor Deposits at Structure M13-1. In *Archaeology at El Peru-Waka'akaaeology at El Peru-Waka': Ritual, Memory, and Power*, edited by Olivia C. Navarro-Farr and Michelle Rich, pp. 34–52. University of Arizona Press, Tucson.
Navarro-Farr, Olivia C., David A. Freidel, and Ana Lucía Arroyave Prera
2008   Manipulating Memory in the Wake of Dynastic Decline at El Peru-Waka: Termination Deposits at Abandoned Structure M13-1. In *Ruins of the Past: The Use and Perception of Abandoned Structures in the Maya Lowlands*, edited by Travis W. Stanton and Aline Magnoni, pp. 113–146. University Press of Colorado, Boulder.
Navarro-Farr, Olivia C., Griselda Pérez Robles, and Damaris Menéndez Bolaños
2013   WK-01: Excavaciones en la Estructura M13-1. In *Proyecto Arqueológico El Perú-Waka': Informe No. 10, Temporada 2012*, edited by Juan Carlos Pérez Calderón, pp. 12–100. Instituto de Antropología e Historia, Guatemala.
Neff, Hector, and Ronald L. Bishop
1988   Plumbate Origins and Development. *American Antiquity* 53:505–522.
Neff, Hector, and Fredrick J. Bove
1999   Mapping Ceramic Compositional Variation and Prehistoric Interaction in Pacific Coastal Guatemala. *Journal of Archaeological Science* 26:1037–1051.
Neff, Hector, Fredrick J. Bove, B. Lou, and M. F. Piechowski
1992   Ceramic Raw Materials Survey in Pacific Coastal Guatemala. In *Chemical Characterization of Ceramic Pastes in Archaeology*, edited by Hector Neff, pp. 59–84. Prehistory Press, Madison.
Nelson, Sarah M.
2008   *Shamanism and the Origin of States: Spirit, Power, and Gender in East Asia*. Left Coast Press, Walnut Creek, California.

Nelson, Zachary N.
2005   Settlement and Population at Piedras Negras, Guatemala. Unpublished PhD dissertation, Department of Anthropology, Pennsylvania State University.

O'Connor, David
1983   *A Theory of Indigenous Southeast Asian Urbanism.* ISEAS, Singapore.
2000   Society and Individual in Early Egypt. In *Order, Legitimacy, and Wealth in Ancient States*, edited by Janet Richards and Mary Van Buren, pp. 21–35. Cambridge University Press, New York.

Olsen, Bjørnar
2007   Keeping Things at Arm's Length: A Genealogy of Asymmetry. *World Archaeology* 39(4): 579–588.

O'Mansky, Matt, and Nicholas P. Dunning
2004   Settlement and Late Classic Political Disintegration in the Petexbatun Region, Guatemala. In *The Terminal Classic in the Maya Lowlands: Collapse, Transition, and Transformation*, edited by Arthur A. Demarest, Prudence M. Rice, and Don S. Rice, pp. 83–101. University Press of Colorado, Boulder.

Orenstein, Henry
1980   Asymmetrical Reciprocity: A Contribution to the Theory of Political Legitimacy. *Current Anthropology* 21(1):69–91.

Padilla, Antonio
2007   Akab Muclil: A Classic to Postclassic Hinterland Settlement in Northwestern Belize. Unpublished Master's thesis, Department of Anthropology, Texas Tech University, Lubbock.

Pagliaro, Jonathan, James F. Garber, and Travis W. Stanton
2003   Evaluating the Archaeological Signatures of Maya Ritual and Conflict. In *Ancient Mesoamerican Warfare*, edited by M. Kathryn Brown and Travis W. Stanton, pp. 75–89. Alta Mira Press, Walnut Creek, California.

Palka, Joel W.
1995   Classic Maya Social Inequality and the Collapse at Dos Pilas, Peten, Guatemala. Unpublished PhD dissertation, Department of Anthropology, Vanderbilt University, Nashville.
1997   Reconstructing Classic Maya Socioeconomic Differentiation and the Collapse at Dos Pilas, Peten, Guatemala. *Ancient Mesoamerica* 8:293–306.

Pendergast, David
1981   Lamanai, Belize: Summary of Excavation Results: 1974–1980. *Journal of Field Archaeology* 8:29–53.
1986   Stability through Change: Lamanai, Belize from the Ninth to the Seventeenth Century. In *Late Lowland Maya Civilization*, edited by Jeremy A. Sabloff and E. Wyllys Andrews V., pp. 223–249. University of New Mexico Press, Albuquerque.
1990   Up from the Dust: The Central Lowlands Postclassic as seen from Lamanai and Marco Gonzalez, Belize. In *Vision and Revision in Maya Studies*, edited by Flora S. Clancy and Peter D. Harrison, pp. 169–177. University of New Mexico Press, Albuquerque.

Penn, Malcolm G., David A. Sutton, and Alex Munro
2004   Vegetation of the Greater Maya Mountains, Belize. *Systematics and Biodiversity* 2(1):21–44.

Peregrine, Peter
1999   Legitimation Crisis in Prehistoric Worlds. In *World Systems Theory in Practice: Leadership, Production, and Exchange*, edited by P. Nick Kardulias, pp. 37–52. Rowman and Littlefield, Lanham, Maryland.
2012   Power and Legitimation: Political Strategies, Typology, and Cultural Evolution. In *The Comparative Archaeology of Complex Societies*, edited by Michael E. Smith, pp. 165–191. Cambridge University Press, New York.

Pérez Robles, Griselda
2004   ES: Excavaciones de Sondeo en las Plazas 1, 2, 3 y 4. In *Proyecto Arqueológico El Perú-Waka' Informe No. 1, Temporada 2003*, edited by Héctor L. Escobedo and David A. Freidel, pp. 257–282. Instituto de Antropología e Historia, Guatemala.

Pérez Robles, Griselda, Ana Lucia Arroyave Prera, Armando Rodríguez, Joel López, Fabiola Quiroa, and Varinia Matute
2008   Tipología Cerámica Preliminar de El Perú. In *Proyecto Arqueológico El Perú-Waka': Informe No.5, Temporada 2007*, edited by Héctor L. Escobedo, Juan Carlos Meléndez, and David A. Freidel, pp. 207–260. Instituto de Antropología e Historia, Guatemala.

Piehl, Jennifer C.
2005   Performing Identity in an Ancient Maya City: The Archaeology of Houses, Health, and Social Differentiation at the Site of Baking Pot, Belize. Unpublished PhD Dissertation Tulane University, New Orleans, Louisiana.
2008   Análisis Preliminar de los Restos Humanos de Contextos Mortuarios y Rituales en Waka' y Chakah. In *Proyecto Arqueológico El Perú-Waka': Informe No.7, Temporada 2009*, edited by Héctor L. Escobedo, Juan Carlos Meléndez, and David A. Freidel, pp. 173–206. Instituto de Antropología e Historia, Guatemala.
2010   Análisis de Laboratorio de los Restos Humanos de las Operaciones 1, 3, 11, y ES. In *Proyecto Arqueológico El Perú-Waka': Informe No.7, Temporada 2009*, edited by Mary Jane Acuña and Jennifer Piehl, pp. 188–225. Instituto de Antropología e Historia, Guatemala.

Pitkin, Hanna
1972   *Wittgenstein and Justice*. University of California Press, Berkeley.

Plank, Shannon
2004   *Maya Dwellings in Hieroglyphs and Archaeology: An Integrative Approach to Ancient Architecture and Spatial Cognition*. BAR International Series 1324. British Archaeological Reports, Oxford.

Plant, Raymond
1980   Jürgen Habermas and the Idea of Legitimation Crisis. *European Journal of Political Research* 10:341–352.

Polk, Jason S., Philip E. van Beynen, and Philip P. Reeder
2007   Late Holocene Environmental Reconstruction Using Cave Sediments from Belize. *Quaternary Research* 68:53–63.

Pollock, H. E. D.
1936   *Round Structures of Aboriginal Middle America*. Publication No. 471. Carnegie Institution of Washington, Washington, D.C.

Ponciano, Erick
2009   Estructura M7-22 Del Grupo Palacio y La Zona Norte De Aguateca (Operaciones AG22C y AG28A). In *La Política De Lugares y Comunidades En La Antigua Sociedad Maya De Petexbatun: Las Investigaciones Del Proyecto Arqueológico Aguateca Segunda Fase*, edited by Takeshi Inomata, Daniela Triadan, Erick Ponciano, and Kazuo Aoyama, pp. 14–19. Instituto de Antropologia e Histora, Guatemala.

Ponciano, Erick, Takeshi Inomata, Estela Pinto, and Marco Antonio Monroy
2009   Excavaciones En La Plaza Principal: Estructuras L8-6 (Operación AG32A) y L8-7 (Operación AG33A). In *La Política De Lugares y Comunidades En La Antigua Sociedad Maya De Petexbatun: Las Investigaciones Del Proyecto Arqueológico Aguateca Segunda Fase*, edited by Takeshi Inomata, Daniela Triadan, Erick Ponciano, and Kazuo Aoyama, pp. 19–27. Instituto de Antropologia e Histora, Guatemala.

Ponting, Clive
2007   *A New Green History of the World: The Environment and the Collapse of Great Civilizations*. Penguin, Toronto.

Popson, Colleen
2000   Political Economy of the community of Chan Cahal at the Maya Center of Blue Creek, Belize. Unpublished Master's thesis, Department of Anthropology, State University of New York, Albany.

Potter, Daniel R.
1980   Archaeological Investigations at Operation 2012. In *The Colha Project Second Season, 1980 Interim Report*, edited by Thomas R. Hester, Jack D. Eaton, and Harry J. Shafer, pp. 173–184. Center for Archaeological Research, The University of Texas at San Antonio, and Centro Studi e Ricerche Ligabue, Venezia.

Preston, Tim
2007   Examining Power Heterarchies within an Ancient Maya Community. Unpublished Master's thesis, Department of Anthropology, San Francisco State University, San Francisco.
2008   Excavations at the Rosita Group. In *Blue Creek Archaeological Project: Report of 2007 Fieldwork*, edited by Thomas H. Guderjan, Timothy Beach, Sheryl Luzzadder-Beach, C. Colleen Hanratty, Tim Preston, and Steve Shaw, pp. 9–30. Submitted to the Institute of Archaeology, Belmopan.

Preston, Tim, and Thomas H. Guderjan
2012   Excavations at the Rempel Group, Blue Creek. In *BC-2011: The 20th Annual Report of the Blue Creek Archaeological Project*, edited by Thomas H. Guderjan and C. Colleen Hanratty, pp. 17–28. Maya Research Program, Tyler.

Primrose, J. Ryan
2003   The Ancient Maya Water Management System at Minanha, West Central, Belize. Unpublished Master's thesis, Department of Anthropology, Trent University, Peterborough.

Prince, Peter V.
1999   Preliminary Investigations at Structure 7A, Minanha, Belize. In *Archaeological Investigations in the North Vaca Plateau, Belize: Progress Report of the First (1999)*

Field Season, edited by Gyles Iannone, Jeffrey Seibert, and Nadine Gray, pp. 72–84. Trent University, Peterborough.

Pring, Duncan, and Norman Hammond
1975   Investigation of a Possible Port Installation at Nohmul. In *Archaeology in Northern Belize: British Museum-Cambridge University Corozal Project: 1974–75 Interim Report*, edited by Norman Hammond, pp. 117–131. Centre for Latin American Studies, Cambridge University, Cambridge.

Proskouriakoff, Tatiana
1950   *A Study of Classic Maya Sculpture*. Carnegie Institution of Washington, Publication 593. Washington, D.C.
1960   Historical Implications of a Pattern of Dates at Piedras Negras, Guatemala. *American Antiquity* 25:454–475.
1963   Historical Data in the Inscriptions of Yaxchilán, Part I. *Estudios de Cultura Maya* 3:149–167.
1964   Historical Data in the Inscriptions of Yaxchilán, Part II. *Estudios de Cultura Maya* 4:177–201.

Quigley, Declan
2000   The Killing of Kings and Ordinary People. *The Journal of the Royal Anthropological Institute* 6(2):237–254.
2005   Introduction: The Character of Kingship. In *The Character of Kingship*, edited by Declan Quigley, pp. 1–23. Berg, New York.

Quintanilla, Claudia
2013   Estudio y Análisis de los Enterramientos Humanos de Sitio Arqueológico Cancuen. Unpublished Licenciatura thesis. Universidad de San Carlos, Escuela de Historia, Guatemala.

Quintanilla, Claudia, and Arthur Demarest
2013   Variantes de la Destrucción de las Ciudades del Valle del Rio La Pasión: Implicaciones del Colapso en el Suroeste del Peten. In *XXVI Simposio de Investigaciones Arqueológicas en Guatemala, 2012*, edited by Bárbara Arroyo, and L. Méndez, pp. 977–922. Museo Nacional de Arqueología y Etnología, Guatemala. Rathje, William L.
1971   The Origin and Development of Classic Maya Civilization. *American Antiquity* 36:275–285.
1972   Praise the Gods and Pass the Metates: A Hypothesis of the Development of Lowland Rainforest Civilizations in Mesoamerica. In *Contemporary Archaeology: A Guide to Theory and Contributions*, edited by Michael P. Leone, pp. 365–392. Southern Illinois University Press, Carbondale.
1973   Classic Maya Development and Denouement: A Research Design. In *The Classic Maya Collapse*, edited by T. Patrick Culbert, pp. 405–456. University of New Mexico Press, Albuquerque.

Redman, Charles L.
1999   *Human Impact on Ancient Environments*. University of Arizona Press, Tucson.

Reeder, Philip, Robert Brinkman, and Edward Alt
1996   Karstification on the Northern Vaca Plateau, Belize. *Journal of Cave and Karst Studies* 58(2):121–130.

Reents-Budet, Dorie
1994   *Painting the Maya Universe: Royal Ceramics of the Classic Period*. Duke University Museum of Art, Durham.

Reese-Taylor, Kathryn
2003   *The Eastern Riverine Corridor during the Late Classic Period*. Submitted to the Foundation for the Advancement of Mesoamerican Studies, Crystal River.

Reese-Taylor, Peter Mathews, Julia Guernsey, and Marlene Fritzler
2009   Warrior Queens among the Classic Maya. In *Blood and Beauty: Organized Violence in the Art and Archaeology of Mesoamerica and Central America*, edited by Heather Orr and Rex Koontz, pp. 39–72. Cotsen Institute of Archaeology, University of California-Los Angeles.

Reilly, F. Kent
1987   The Ecological Origins of Olmec Symbols of Rulership. Unpublished Master's thesis, The University of Texas at Austin.

Reina, Ruben E., and John Monaghan
1981   The Ways of the Maya: Salt Production in Sacapulas, Guatemala. *Expedition* 23(3)13–33.

Restall, Matthew
1997   *The Maya World: Yucatec Culture and Society, 1550–1850*. Stanford University Press, Stanford, California.
1998   *Maya Conquistador*. Beacon Press, Boston.

Rice, Prudence M.
2004   *Maya Political Science: Time, Astronomy, and the Cosmos*. University of Texas Press, Austin.
2007   The Classic Maya "Collapse" and Its Causes: The Role of Warfare? In *Gordon R. Willey and American Archaeology: Contemporary Perspectives*, edited by Jeremy A. Sabloff and William L. Fash, pp. 141–186. University of Oklahoma Press, Norman.

Richards, Janet
2000   Modified Order, Responsive Legitimacy, Redistributed Wealth: Egypt, 2260–1650 BC. In *Order, Legitimacy, and Wealth in Ancient States*, edited by Janet Richards and Mary Van Buren, pp. 36–45. Cambridge University Press, New York.

Ringle, William M., Tomás Gallareta Negrón, and George J. Bey III
1998   The Return of Quetzalcoatl: Evidence for the Spread of a World Religion During the Epiclassic Period. *Ancient Mesoamerica* 9:183–232.

Robertson, Robin A.
1983   Functional Analysis and Social Process in Ceramics: The Pottery from Cerrros, Belize. In *Civilization in the Ancient Americas: Essays in Honor of Gordon R. Willey*, edited by Richard M. Leventhal and Alan L. Kolata, pp. 105–142. University of New Mexico Press, Albuquerque.

Robertson, Robin A., and David A. Freidel
1986   *Archaeology at Cerros, Belize, Central America*, vol. 1: *An Interim Report*. Southern Methodist University Press, Dallas.

Rosen, Arlene Miller
2007   *Civilizing Climate: Social Responses to Climate Change in the Near East*. Altamira Press, Lanham.

Rotberg, Robert I.
2003   Failed States, Collapsed States, Weak States: Causes and Indicators. In *State Failure and State Weakness in a Time of Terror*, edited by Robert I. Rotberg, pp. 1–25. The World Peace Foundation and Brookings Institution Press, Cambridge, Massachusetts and Washington, D.C.
2004   The Failure and Collapse of Nation-States: Breakdown, Prevention, and Repair. In *When States Collapse: Causes and Consequences*, edited by Robert I. Rotberg, pp. 1–49. Princeton University Press, Princeton.

Rovner, Irwin
1975   *Implications of the Lithic Analysis at Becan*. Publication 31. Middle American Research Institute, Tulane University, New Orleans.

Roys, Ralph L.
1957   *The Political Geography of the Yucatan Maya*. Carnegie Institution of Washington Publication 613. Washington, D.C.
1967   *The Book of Chilam Balam of Chumayel*. University of Oklahoma Press, Norman.

Rudolph, Susanne H.
2006   Weber and Foucault: Convergences and Divergences. Paper presented at the International Political Science Association meetings, Fukuoka, Japan.

Ruppert, Karl
1935   *The Caracol at Chichén Itzá, Yucatan, Mexico*. Publication no. 454. Carnegie Institution of Washington, Washington, D.C.
1952   *Chichén Itzá: Architectural Notes and Plans*. Publication no. 593. Carnegie Institution of Washington, Washington, D.C.

Ruz Lhuillier, Alberto
1991   *Costumbres Funerarias de Los Antiguos Mayas*. Universidad Nacional Autónoma de México, Mexico City.

Sabloff, Jeremy A.
1973   Continuity and Disruption during Terminal Late Classic Times at Seibal: Ceramic and Other Evidence. In *The Classic Maya Collapse*, edited by T. Patrick Culbert, pp. 107–132. School of American Research, University of New Mexico Press, Albuquerque.
1975   *Excavations at Seibal: Ceramics*. Memoirs of the Peabody Museum of Archaeology and Ethnology, vol. 13, no. 2. Harvard University, Cambridge.
1977   Old Myths, New Myths: The Role of Sea Trades in the Development of Maya Civilization. In *The Sea and the Pre-Columbian World*, edited by Elizabeth P. Bensen, pp. 67–95. Dumbarton Oaks, Washington, D.C.

Sabloff, Jeremy A., and William Rathje
1975   The Rise of a Maya Merchant Class. *Scientific American* 233:73–82.

Sabloff, Jeremy A., and Gordon R. Willey
1967   The Collapse of Maya Civilization in the Southern Lowlands: A Consideration of History and Process. *Southwestern Journal of Anthropology* 23(4):311–336.

Sagebiel, Kerry
2005   Shifting Allegiances at La Milpa, Belize: A Typological, Chronological and Formal Analysis of the Ceramics. Unpublished PhD dissertation, Department of Anthropology, University of Arizona, Tucson.

Sanders, William T., and David Webster
1988 The Mesoamerican Urban Tradition. *American Anthropologist* 90:521–546.
Satterthwaite, Linton, Jr.
1935 The Black Rocks. *University Museum Bulletin* 8:7–15.
1937 Thrones at Piedras Negras. *University Museum Bulletin* 7:18–23.
1958 *The Problem of Abnormal Stela Placement at Tikal and Elsewhere.* Tikal Report no. 3. University Museum, Philadelphia.
2005 [1933] The South Group Ball Court (Structures R-11-A and R-11-B); with a Preliminary Note on the West Group Ball Court (Structures K-6-A and K-6-B). In *Piedras Negras Archaeology, 1931–1939*, edited by John M. Weeks, Jane A. Hill, and Charles W. Golden, pp. 30–49. University of Pennsylvania Museum Press, Philadelphia.
2005 [1935] Palace Structures J-2 and J-6, with Notes on Structure J-6-2nd and Other Buried Structures in Court 1. In *Piedras Negras Archaeology, 1931–1939*, edited by John M. Weeks, Jane A. Hill, and Charles W. Golden, pp. 50–89. University of Pennsylvania Museum Press, Philadelphia.
2005 [1958] Unclassified Buildings and Substructures. In *Piedras Negras Archaeology, 1931–1939*, edited by John M. Weeks, Jane A. Hill, and Charles W. Golden, pp. 318–383. University of Pennsylvania Museum Press, Philadelphia.
Saturno, William
2009 Centering the Kingdom, Centering the King: Maya Creation and Legitimization at San Bartolo. In *Art of Urbanism: How Mesoamerican Kingdoms Represented Themselves in Architecture and Imagery*, edited by William L. Fash and Leonardo López Luján, pp. 111–134. Dumbarton Oaks, Washington, D.C.
Saul, Frank
1973 Disease in the Maya Area: The Pre-Columbian Evidence. In *The Classic Maya Collapse*, edited by T. Patrick Culbert, pp. 301–324. School of American Research, University of New Mexico Press, Albuquerque.
Scarborough, Vernon L.
1998 Ecology and Ritual: Water Management and the Maya. *Latin American Antiquity* 8:135–159.
Scarborough, Vernon L., and William R. Burnside
2010 Complexity and Sustainability: Perspectives from the Ancient Maya and the Modern Balinese. *American Antiquity* 75:327–363.
Schaar, John
1970 Legitimacy in the Modern State. In *Power and Community*, edited by Philip Green and Sanford Levinson, pp. 276–327. Pantheon, New York.
Scheffer, Marten
2009 *Critical Transitions in Nature and Society.* Princeton University Press, Princeton, New Jersey.
Schele, Linda
1991 *Another Look at Stela 11.* Copan Mosaic's Project Note 103. Copan Acropolis Archaeological Project and the Instituto Hondureno de Antropologia e Historia, Austin.

Schele, Linda, and David Freidel
1990   *A Forest of Kings: The Untold Story of the Ancient Maya*. William Morrow, New York.

Schele, Linda, and Nikolai Grube
1994   Notes on the Chronology of Piedras Negras Stela 12. *Texas Notes on Precolumbian Art, Writing, and Culture* 70:1–4.
1995   *Notebook for the XIX Maya Hieroglyphic Workshop at Texas: Late Classic and Terminal Classic Warfare*. Department of Art, University of Texas, Austin.

Schele, Linda, and Peter Mathews
1998   *The Code of Kings: The Language of Seven Sacred Maya Temples and Tombs*. Scribner, New York.

Schele, Linda, and Mary Ellen Miller
1986   *The Blood of Kings: Dynasty and Ritual in Maya Art*. Kimball Art Museum, Fort Worth.

Scherer, Andrew K., and Charles Golden
2009   Tecolote, Guatemala: Archaeological Evidence for a Fortified Late Classic Maya Political Border. *Journal of Field Archaeology* 34:285–304.
2012   *Revisiting Maler's Usumacinta: Recent Archaeological Investigation in Chiapas, Mexico*. Monograph 1. The Pre-Columbian Art Research Institute, San Francisco.
2013   Water in the West: Chronology and Collapse of the Classic Maya River Kingdoms. In *The Great Maya Droughts in Cultural Context*, edited by Gyles Iannone, pp. 224–248. University of Colorado Press, Boulder.

Scherer, Andrew K., Lori E. Wright, and Cassady J. Yoder
2007   Bioarchaeological Evidence for Social and Temporal Differences in Subsistence at Piedras Negras, Guatemala. *Latin American Antiquity* 18:85–104.

Schieffelin, Edward L.
2007   Introduction. In *When Rituals Go Wrong: Mistakes, Failure, and the Dynamics of Ritual*, edited by Ute Hüsken, pp. 1–20. Brill Academic Publishers, Boston.

Schnepel, Burkhard
2002   *The Jungle Kings: Ethnohistorical Aspects of Politics and Ritual in Orissa*. Manohar, New Delhi.
2005   Kings and Tribes in East India: The Internal Political Dimension. In *The Character of Kingship*, edited by Declan Quigley, pp. 1–23. Berg, New York.

Scholes, France V., and Ralph L. Roys
1968   *The Maya Chontal Indians of Acalan-Tixchel: A Contribution to the History and Ethnography of the Yucatan Peninsula*. University of Oklahoma Press, Norman.

Schortman, Edward, and Patricia Urban
2011   Power, Memory, and Prehistory: Constructing and Erasing Political Landscapes in the Naco Valley, Northwestern Honduras. *American Anthropologist* 113(1):5–21.

Schwake, Sonja A.
1999   Public Architecture, Elite Power: Preliminary Investigations of an E-Group at Minanha, Belize. In *Archaeological Investigations in the North Vaca Plateau, Belize: Progress Report of the First (1999) Field Season*, edited by Gyles Iannone, Jeffrey Seibert, and Nadine Gray, pp. 41–56. Trent University, Peterborough.
2001   Investigations within Structure 3A and 4A at Minanha, Belize: The 2001 Research.

In *Archaeological Investigations in the North Vaca Plateau, Belize: Progress Report of the Third (2001) Field Season*, edited by Gyles Iannone, Ryan Primrose, Adam Menzies, and Lisa McParland, pp. 15–28. Trent University, Peterborough.
2008 The Social Implications of Ritual Behavior in the Maya Lowlands: A Perspective from Minanha, Belize. Unpublished PhD dissertation, University of California, San Diego.

Schwake, Sonja A., and Gyles Iannone
2010 Ritual Remains and Collective Memory: Maya Examples from West Central Belize. *Ancient Mesoamerica* 21(2):331–339.

Scott, James C.
1972 Patron-Client Politics and Political Change in Southeast Asia. *The American Political Science Review* 66(1):91–113.
1990 *Domination and the Arts of Resistance: Hidden Transcripts*. Yale University Press, New Haven, Connecticut.

Seager, Richard, Mingfang Ting, M. Davis, Mark Cane, Naomi Naik, Jennie Nakamura, Cuihua Li, Ed Cook, and David W. Stahle
2009 Mexican Drought: An Observational Modeling and Tree Ring Study of Variability and Climate Change. *Atmósfera* 22:1–31.

Seibert, Jeffrey
2001 Residential Architecture as an Indicator of Social Status among the Ancient Maya of the Belize Valley. Unpublished Master's thesis, Department of Anthropology, Trent University.

Sharer, Robert
1982 Did the Maya Collapse? A New World Perspective on the Demise of the Harappan Civilization. In *Harappan Civilization: A Contemporary Perspective*, edited by Gregory Possehl, pp. 367–383. Oxford and IBH, New Delhi.

Sharer, Robert, and Loa Traxler
2006 *The Ancient Maya*. 6th ed. Stanford University Press, Stanford, California.

Shaw, Justine M.
2003 Climate Change and Deforestation: Implications for the Maya Collapse. *Ancient Mesomerica* 14:157–167.
2005 The Late to Terminal Classic Settlement Shifts at Yo'okop. In *Quintana Roo Archaeology*, edited by Justine M. Shaw and Jennifer P. Matthews, pp. 144–157. University of Arizona Press, Tucson.

Shepard, Anna O.
1948 *Plumbate: A Mesoamerican Tradeware*. Publication no. 573. Carnegie Institution of Washington, Washington, D.C.

Simonse, Simon
2005 Tragedy, Ritual and Power in Nilotic Regicide: The Regicidal Dramas of the Eastern Nilotes of Sudan in Comparative Perspective. In *The Character of Kingship*, edited by Declan Quigley, pp. 67–100. Berg, New York.

Smith, Michael E.
2008 *Aztec City-State Capitals*. University Press of Florida, Gainesville.
2009 V. Gordon Childe and the Urban Revolution: An Historical Perspective on a Revolution in Urban Studies. *Town Planning Review* 80(1):3–29.

Smith, Robert Eliot
1971   *The Pottery of Mayapan: Including Studies of Ceramic Material from Uxmal, Kabah, and Chichen Itza*. Papers of the Peabody Museum of Archaeology and Ethnology vol. 66. Peabody Museum of Archaeology and Ethnology, Cambridge.
Snetsinger, Andrew
2012   Burials and Mortuary Behaviour of the Ancient Maya at Minanha, Belize. Unpublished Master's thesis, Department of Anthropology, Trent University, Peterborough.
Stahle, David W., Edward R. Cook, Jose Villanueva Díaz, Falko K. Fye, Dorian J. Burnette, R. Daniel Griffin, Rodolfo Acuña Soto, Richard Seager, and Richard R. Heim Jr.
2009   Early 21st-Century Drought in Mexico. *Eos* 90:89–100.
Stanton, Travis W., and M. Kathryn Brown
2003   Studying Warfare in Ancient Mesoamerica. In *Ancient Mesoamerican Warfare*, edited by M. Kathryn Brown and Travis W. Stanton, pp. 1–16. AltaMira Press, Walnut Creek, California.
Stanton, Travis W., M. Kathryn Brown, and Jonathan B. Pagliaro
2008   Garbage of the Gods? Squatters, Refuse Disposal, and Termination Rituals among the Ancient Maya. *Latin American Antiquity* 19(3):227–247.
Stanton, Travis W., David A. Freidel, Charles K. Suhler, Traci Ardren, James N. Ambrosino, Justine M. Shaw, and Sharon Bennett
2010   *Archaeological Investigations at Yaxuná, 1986–1996*. BAR International Series S2056. Archaeopress, Oxford.
Stirling, Mathew
1941   Expedition Unearths Buried Masterpieces of Carved Jade. *National Geographic Magazine* 80:277–302.
Stone, Andrea
1989   Disconnection, Foreign Insignia, and Political Expansion: Teotihuacan and the Warrior Stelae of Piedras Negras. In *Mesoamerica after the Decline of Teotihuacan, A.D. 700–900*, edited by Richard Diehl and Janet C. Berlo, pp. 153–172. Dumbarton Oaks, Washington, D.C.
Straight, Kirk D.
2007   A House of Cards: Construction, Proportion and Form at Temple XIX, Palenque, Chiapas, Mexico. In *Palenque: Recent Investigations at the Classic Maya Center*, edited by Damien B. Marken, pp. 175–206. AltaMira Press, Walnut Creek, California.
Straight, Kirk D., and Damien B. Marken
2007   Conclusion: Reconceptualizing the Palenque Polity. In *Palenque: Recent Investigations at the Classic Maya Center*, edited by Damien B. Marken, pp. 279–324. AltaMira Press, Walnut Creek, California.
Straight, Kirk D., and Damien B. Marken (editors)
2007   *Palenque: Recent Investigations at the Classic Maya Center*. AltaMira Press, Walnut Creek, California.
Stross, Brian
1998   Seven Ingredients in Mesoamerican Ensoulment: Dedication and Termination in Tenejapa. In *The Sowing and the Dawning: Termination, Dedication, and Transfor-

Stuart, David
1984   Royal Auto-Sacrifice among the Maya: A Study in Image and Meaning. *Res: Anthropology and Aesthetics* 7–8:6–20.
1988   Blood Symbolism in Maya Iconography. In *Maya Iconography*, edited by Elizabeth Benson and Gillett Griffin, pp. 175–221. Princeton University Press, Princeton, New Jersey.
1996   Kings of Stone: A Consideration of Stelae in Ancient Maya Ritual and Representation. *Res: Anthropology and Aesthetics* 29–30:148–171.
1998a   Una Guerra Entre Yaxchilan y Piedras Negras. In *Proyecto Arqueológico Piedras Negras: Informe Preliminar No. 2, Segunda Temporada 1998*, edited by Héctor L. Escobedo and Stephen D. Houston, pp. 389–392. Proyecto Arqueológico Piedras Negras, Guatemala City.
1998b   "The Fire Enters His House": Architecture and Ritual in Classic Maya Texts. In *Function and Meaning in Classic Maya Architecture*, edited by Stephen D. Houston, pp. 373–426. Dumbarton Oaks, Washington, D.C.
2000   "The Arrival of Strangers": Teotihuacan and Tollan in Classic Maya History. In *Mesoamerica's Classic Heritage: Teotihuacán to the Aztecs*, edited by Davíd Carrasco, Lindsay Jones, and Scott Sessions, pp. 465–513. University Press of Colorado, Niwot.
2004   The Paw Stone: The Place Name of Piedras Negras, Guatemala. *The PARI Journal* 4(3):1–6.
2007   Gods and Histories: Mythology and Dynastic Succession at Temples XIX and XXI at Palenque. In *Palenque: Recent Investigations at the Classic Maya Center*, edited by Damien B. Marken, pp. 207–232. AltaMira Press, Walnut Creek, California.
Suasnavar, José, Alan Robinson, Heidy Quezada, Oscar Ixpatá, Guillermo Vásquez, and Patricia Ixcot
2007   *Investigación Antropológico Forense de La Aguada Sur del Sitio Arqueológico Cancuen, Operación 42*. Report on the Proyecto Arqueológico Cancuen, Guatemala. Fundación de Antropología Forense de Guatemala, Guatemala City.
Suhler, Charles K.
1996   *Excavations at the North Acropolis Yaxuná, Yucatan, Mexico*. 2 vols. Southern Methodist University, Dallas.
Suhler, Charles, and David A. Freidel
1998   Life and Death in the Maya War Zone. *Archaeology* 51(3):28–34.
2003   The Tale End of Two Cities: Tikal, Yaxuna, and Abandonment Contexts in the Lowland Maya Archaeological Record. In *Archaeology of Settlement Abandonment in Middle America*, edited by Takeshi Inomata and Ronald Webb, pp. 135–147. University of Utah Press, Salt Lake City.
Sullivan, Lauren A.
2012   Report on Ceramic Analysis for La Milpa Terminal Classic Project. In *The 2011 Season of the La Milpa Core Project*, edited by Brett A. Houk, pp. 77–106. Occasional Papers no. 13. Mesoamerican Archaeological Research Laboratory, The University of Texas at Austin.

Symes, Steven A., Christopher W. Rainwater, Erin N. Chapman, Desina Rachael Gipson, and Andrea L. Piper
2008   Patterned Thermal Destruction of Human Remains in a Forensic Setting. In *The Analysis of Burned Human Remains*, edited by Christopher W. Schmidt and Steven A. Symes, pp. 15–54. Academic Press, London.

Tainter, Joseph A.
1988   *The Collapse of Complex Societies*. Cambridge University Press, New York.
2000   Problem Solving: Complexity, History, Sustainability. *Population and Environment* 22(1):3–41.

Talbot, Cynthia
1991   Temples, Donors, and Gifts: Patterns of Patronage in Thirteenth-Century South India. *The Journal of Asian Studies* 50(2):308–340.

Taube, Karl
1985   The Classic Maya Maize God: A Reappraisal. In *Fifth Palenque Round Table, 1983*, vol. 7, edited by Virginia M. Fields, pp. 171–181. Pre-Columbian Art Research Institute, San Francisco.
2004   Structure 10-L16 and Its Early Classic Antecedents: Fire and the Evocation and Resurrection of K'inich Yax K'uk' Mo'. In *Understanding Early Classic Copan*, edited by Ellen E. Bell, Marcello A. Canuto, and Robert J. Sharer, pp. 265–295. University of Pennsylvania Museum of Archaeology and Anthropology, Philadelphia.

Taube, Karl A., William A. Saturno, David Stuart, and Heather Hurst
2010   *The Murals of San Bartolo, El Petén, Guatemala, Part 2: The West Wall*. Ancient Mesoamerica no. 10. Boundary End Archaeology Research Center, Barnardsville, North Carolina.

Taylor, Christopher
2010   Rwandan Genocide: Toward an Explanation in Which History and Culture Matter. In *Questioning Collapse: Human Resilience, Ecological Vulnerability, and the Aftermath of Empire*, edited by Patricia McAnany and Norman Yoffee, pp. 239–268. Cambridge University Press, Cambridge and New York.

Tedlock, Barbara
1982   *Time and the Highland Maya*. University of New Mexico Press, Albuquerque.

Thompson, J. Eric S.
1954   *The Rise and Fall of Maya Civilization*. Oklahoma University Press, Norman.
1970   *Maya History and Religion*. University of Oklahoma Press, Norman.

Tiesler, Vera, and Arturo Romano
2008   El modelado del cráneo en Mesoamérica. Emblemática costumbre milenaria. *Arqueología Mexicana* 94:18–25.

Tokovinine, Alexandre, and Vilma Fialko
2007   Stela 45 of Naranjo and the Early Classic Lords of Sa'aal. *The PARI Journal* 7(4):1–14.

Torres, Paola
2011   Los Juegos de Pelota Como Evidencia de un Sitio Fronterizo: El Caso de Cancuen. Licenciatura Thesis, Universidad de San Carlos de Guatemala, Guatemala City.

Tourtellot, Gair, and Jason J. Gonzalez
2004   The Last Hurrah: Continuity and Transformation at Seibal. In *The Terminal Classic in the Maya Lowlands: Collapse, Transition, and Transformation*, edited by Arthur A. Demarest, Prudence M. Rice, and Don S. Rice, pp. 60–82. University Press of Colorado, Boulder.

Trein, Debora
2011   Investigating Monumental Architecture at La Milpa: The 2010 Season. In *Research Reports from the Programme for Belize Archaeological Project*, vol. 5, edited by Brett A. Houk and Fred Valdez Jr., pp. 39–66. Occasional Papers no. 12. Mesoamerican Archaeological Research Laboratory, University of Texas at Austin.

Trigger, Bruce G.
2003   *Understanding Early Civilizations: A Comparative Study*. Cambridge University Press, New York.

Turner, Victor
1967   *The Forest of Symbols: Aspects of Ndemba Ritual*. Cornell University Press, Ithaca, New York.

Turner, B. L., II, and Jeremy A. Sabloff
2012   Classic Period Collapse of the Central Maya Lowlands: Insights about Human-Environment Relationships for Sustainability. *Proceedings of the National Academy of Sciences* 109(35):13908–13914.

Ubelaker, Douglas H., and Joseph L. Rife
2007   The Practice of Cremation in the Roman-Era Cemetery at Kenchreai, Greece: The Perspective from Archeology and Forensic Science. *Bioarchaeology of the Near East* 1:35–57.

Valdés, Juan Antonio, Mónica Urquizú, Carolina Díaz Samayoa, and Horacio Martínez Paíz
1999   *Informe Anual Del Proyecto De Restauración Aguateca*. Report submitted to the Institute de Antropología e Historia de Guatemala, Guatemala City.

Valdez, Fred, Jr.
1987   The Ceramics of Colha. Unpublished PhD dissertation, Department of Anthropology, Harvard University, Cambridge.

Valdez, Fred, Jr., and Shirley B. Mock
1991   Additional Considerations for Prehispanic Saltmaking in Belize. *American Antiquity* 56:520–525.

Valdez, Fred, Jr., and Vernon L. Scarborough
2014   The Prehistoric Maya of Northern Belize: Issues of Drought and Cultural Transformations. In *The Great Maya Droughts in Cultural Context: Case Studies in Resilience and Vulnerability*, edited by Gyles Iannone, pp. 255–270. University of Colorado Press, Boulder.

Van Buren, Mary
2000   Political Fragmentation and Ideological Continuity in the Andean Highlands. In *Order, Legitimacy, and Wealth in Ancient States*, edited by Janet Richards and Mary Van Buren, pp. 80–87.Cambridge University Press, Cambridge.

Van Buren, Mary, and Janet Richards
2000   Introduction: Ideology, Wealth, and the Comparative Study of 'Civilizations.' In *Order, Legitimacy, and Wealth in Ancient States*, edited by Janet Richards and Mary Van Buren, pp. 3–12. Cambridge University Press, Cambridge.

Van Dyke, Ruth M., and Susan E. Alcock (editors)
2003   *Archaeologies of Memory*. Blackwell Publishing, Oxford.

Vargas, Ernesto
2001   *Itzamkanac y Acalan: tiempos de crisis anticipando el futuro*. Universidad Nacional Autónoma de México, Instituto de Investigaciones Antropológicas, México, D.F.

Villamil, Laura, and Jason Sherman
2005   Investigating Urban Diversity in South-Central Quintana Roo. In *Quintana Roo Archaeology*, edited by Justine M. Shaw and Jennifer P. Matthews, pp. 197–213. University of Arizona Press, Tucson.

Vogt, Evon Z.
1965a   Zinacanteco "Souls." *Man* 65:33–35.
1965b   Structural and Conceptual Replication in Zinacantan Culture. *American Anthropologist* 67(2):342–353.
1969   *Zinacantan: A Maya Community in the Highlands of Chiapas*. Harvard University Press, Cambridge.
1976   *Tortillas for the Gods: A Symbolic Analysis of Zinacanteco Rituals*. University of Oklahoma Press, Norman.
1998   Zinacanteco Dedication and Termination Rituals. In *The Sowing and the Dawning: Termination, Dedication, and Transformation in the Archaeological Record of Mesoamerica*, edited by Shirley Boteler Mock, pp. 21–30. University of New Mexico Press, Albuquerque.

Walker, Debora S.
1995   Ceremonial Trash? In *Expanding Archaeology*, edited by William H. Walker, James M. Skibo, and Axel E. Nielson, pp. 67–79. University of Utah Press, Salt Lake City.
1998   Smashed Pots and Shattered Dreams: The Material Evidence for an Early Classic Maya Site Termination at Cerros, Belize. In *The Sowing and the Dawning: Termination, Dedication, and Transformation in the Archaeological and Ethnographic Record of Mesoamerica*, edited by Shirley Boteler Mock, pp. 81–99. University of New Mexico Press, Albuquerque.

Watanabe, John
1992   *Maya Saints and Souls in a Changing World*. University of Texas Press, Austin.

Watts, Christopher (editor)
2013   *Relational Archaeologies: Humans, Animals, Things*. Routledge, New York, New York.

Webster, David
2000   The Not So Peaceful Civilization: A Review of Maya War. *Journal of World Prehistory* 14:65–118.
2002a   *The Fall of the Ancient Maya*. Thames and Hudson, London.

2002b Groundhogs and Kings: Issues of Divine Rulership among the Classic Maya. In *Incidents of Archaeology in Central America and Yucatan*, edited by Michael Love, Marion Popenoe de Hatch, and Héctor L. Escobedo, pp. 433–458. University Press of America, New York.

Webster, David, AnnCorinne Freter, and Nancy Gonlin
2000 *Copán: The Rise and Fall of an Ancient Maya Kingdom*. Harcourt Brace, Fort Worth.

Webster, David, and Nancy Gonlin
1988 Household Remains of the Humblest Maya. *Journal of Field Archaeology* 15:169–190.

Webster, James W., George A. Brook, L. Bruce Railsback, Hai Cheng, R. Lawrence Edwards, Clark Alexander, and Philip P. Reeder
2007 Stalagmite Evidence from Belize Indicating Significant Droughts at the Time of the Preclassic Abandonment, the Maya Hiatus, and the Classic Maya Collapse. *Palaeogeography, Palaeoclimatology, Palaeoecology* 250:1–17.

Weeks, John M., Jane A. Hill, and Charles W. Golden
2005 *Piedras Negras Archaeology, 1931–1939*. University of Pennsylvania Museum of Archaeology and Anthropology, Philadelphia.

Weiss, Harvey, and Raymond S. Bradley
2001 What Drives Societal Collapse? *Science* 291(5504):609–610.

Westermark, Edward
1908 The Killing of the Divine King. *Man* 8:22–24.

Whittington, Stephen L., and David M. Reed (editors)
1997 *Bones of the Maya*. The University of Alabama Press, Tuscaloosa.

Wiesehöfer, Josef
2009 The Achaemenid Empire. In *The Dynamics of Ancient Empires*, edited by Ian Morris and Walter Scheidel, pp. 66–98. Oxford University Press, New York.

Wilk, Richard R.
1985 The Ancient Maya and the Political Present. *Journal of Anthropological Research* 41:307–326.

Williams, Raymond
1977 *Marxism and Literature*. Oxford University Press, Oxford.

Winburn, Amanda, Tiffiny Tung, Larisa DeSantis, and Claudia Quintanilla
2014 Resultados preliminares: análisis de isotopos estables de carbono y oxigeno de las muestra humano esquelética de la reserva de agua sur de Cancuen. *Apuntes Arqueológicos* (in press).*

Witmore, Christopher L.
2007 Symmetrical Archaeology: Excerpts of a Manifesto. *World Archaeology* 39:546–562.

Wolters, O. W.
1979 Khmer "Hinduism" in the Seventh Century. In *Early South East Asia: Essays in Archaeology, History and Historical Geography*, edited by R. B. Smith and W. Watson, pp. 427–442. Oxford University Press, New York.

Woodfill, Brent
2010 *Ritual and Trade in the Pasión-Verapaz Region, Guatemala*. Vanderbilt Institute

of Mesoamerican Archaeology Monographs, vol. 6. Vanderbilt University Press, Nashville, Tennessee.

Woodfill, Brent, and Chloe Andrieu
2012 Tikal's Early Classic Domination of the Great Western Trade Route: Ceramic, Lithic, and Iconographic Evidence. *Ancient Mesoamerica* 23:189–209.

Woodfill, Brent, Stanley Guenter, and Mirza Monterroso
2012 Changing Patterns of Ritual Activity in an Unlooted Cave in Central Guatemala. *Latin America Antiquity* 23(1):93–119.

Wright, Lori E.
1990 Resultados preliminaries del analisis osteologico de los restos humanos de las excavaciones de 1990. In *Proyecto Arqueologico Regional Petexbatun*, edited by Arthur Demarest and Stephen Houston, pp. 579–584. Instituto de Antropologia e Historia and Vanderbilt University, Guatemala City and Nashville, Tennessee.

Wright, Lori E., and Christine D. White
1996 Human Biology in the Classic Maya Collapse: Evidence from Paleopathology and Paleodiet. *Journal of World Prehistory* 10(2):147–198.

Yaeger, Jason
2010 Shifting Political Dynamics as Seen from the Xunatunich Palace. In *Classic Maya Provincial Politics: Xunantunich and Its Hinterlands*, edited by Lisa J. LeCount and Jason Yaeger, pp. 145–160. University of Arizona Press, Tucson.

Yaeger, Jason, and David A. Hodell
2009 The Collapse of Maya Civilization: Assessing the Interaction of Culture, Climate, and Environment. In *El Niño, Catastrophism, and Culture Change*, edited by Daniel H. Sandweiss and Jeffrey Quilter, pp. 187–242. Dumbarton Oaks, Washington, D.C.

Yoffee, Norman
1979 The Decline and Rise of Mesopotamian Civilization: An Ethnoarchaeological Perspective on the Evolution of Social Complexity. *American Antiquity* 44:5–35.
2000 Law Courts and the Mediation of Social Conflict in Ancient Mesopotamia. In *Order, Legitimacy, and Wealth in Ancient States*, edited by Janet Richards and Mary Van Buren, pp. 46–63. Cambridge University Press, New York.

Young, Marianne N., Rik Leemans, Roelof M. J. Boumans, Robert Costanza, Bert J. M. de Vries, John Finnigan, Uno Svedin, and Michael D. Young
2007 Group Report: Future Scenarios of Human Environment Systems. In *Sustainability or Collapse? An Integrated History and Future of People on Earth*, edited by Robert Costanza, Lisa J. Graumlich, and Will Steffan, pp. 447–470. MIT Press, Cambridge.

Zaro, Gregory, and Brett A. Houk
2012 The Growth and Decline of the Ancient Maya City of La Milpa, Belize: New Data and New Perspectives from the Southern Plazas. *Ancient Mesoamerica* 23(1):143–159.

Zartman, I. William
1995 Introduction: Posing the Problem of State Collapse. In *Collapsed States: The Disintegration and Restoration of Legitimate Authority*, edited by I. William Zartman, pp. 1–14. Lynne Rienner Publishers, Boulder, Colorado.

Zhao, Dingxin
2009 Mandate from Heaven and Performance Legitimation in Historical and Contemporary China. *American Behavioral Scientist* 53:416–433.

Żrałka, Jarosław, and Bernard Hermes
2012 Great Development in Troubled Times: The Terminal Classic at the Maya Site of Nakum, Peten, Guatemala. *Ancient Mesoamerica* 23(1):161–187.

Contributors

Palma J. Buttles is a senior member of the technical staff at the Software Engineering Institute at Carnegie Mellon University and a research fellow of the Center for Archaeological and Tropical Studies at The University of Texas at Austin. She has participated with field projects at Colha, Rio Azul, and Tikal, among other programs.

Arthur A. Demarest holds the Ingram Chair of Anthropology at Vanderbilt University and is director of the Vanderbilt Institute of Mesoamerican Archaeology and Development. He currently divides his efforts between archaeological excavations and exploration in the Maya lowlands and highlands and development programs for indigenous Maya communities.

Héctor Escobedo holds a PhD from Vanderbilt University, has served as minister of culture and sports of Guatemala, and is the coauthor (with Juan Antonio Valdés and Federico Fahsen) of *Ciudades milenarias, reyes, tumbas y palacios: La historia dinástica de Uaxactun*. He has also codirected archaeological projects at Las Pacayas, Arroyo de Piedra, Punta de Chimino, Piedras Negras, and El Perú-Waka' in Guatemala. He has authored or coauthored over sixty articles, chapters, and book reviews.

David Freidel has directed research at Cerro Maya in Belize; Yaxuna in Yucatan, Mexico; and El Peru-Waka' in Guatemala. He has studied Maya divine kingship since 1975, when his project discovered Cache 1 at Cerro Maya, a bundle of Preclassic royal jewels. He is interested in Maya warfare, religion, politics, and economics.

Charles Golden is associate professor of anthropology and Latino American and Latino studies at Brandeis University and has conducted archaeological research in Belize, Honduras, Guatemala, and Mexico. He has worked in the Usumacinta River region since 1977, most recently as codirector of the Sierra del Lacandón

Regional Archaeological Project in Petén and the Proyecto Arqueológico Busilja-Chocolja in Chiapas. His research interests concern the dynamic social and political boundaries between Maya kingdoms and the cultural significance of temporal boundaries, history, and social memory for the ancient Maya. He is coeditor of *Continuities and Changes in Maya Archaeology* (with Greg Borgstede), *Maya Archaeology I* (with Stephen Houston and Joel Skidmore), and *Piedras Negras Archaeology, 1931–1939* (with John Weeks and Jane Hill) and was a 2007–2008 fellow in pre-Columbian studies at Dumbarton Oaks.

Thomas H. Guderjan is associate professor of anthropology and director of the Social Sciences Research Center at the University of Texas at Tyler. He has directed archaeological research in northwestern Belize for more than two decades and has also conducted fieldwork in Peru, Mexico, and the United States. His recent work includes *The Nature of an Ancient Maya City: Resources, Interaction and Power at Blue Creek, Belize*. He is the editor of *Papers on the Archaeology of Blue Creek, Belize* and coeditor (with Jennifer Mathews) of *The Value of Things: Commodities in the Maya Region from Prehistoric to Contemporary*.

C. Colleen Hanratty is a doctoral candidate at Southern Methodist University and the operations manager of the Maya Research Program. She codirects the Blue Creek Archaeological Project and has research interests in Maya ceramics and abandonment processes.

Eleanor Harrison-Buck is associate professor of anthropology at the University of New Hampshire. Her research interests include social identity and power, divine kingship and religious ideology, and technical and stylistic studies of architecture and material culture. She has worked in the Maya area of Belize for over twenty years and directs the Belize River East Archaeology Project. Recent publications include *Power and Identity in Archaeological Theory and Practice: Case Studies from Ancient Mesoamerica* and several recent articles in *American Anthropologist* and the journal *Ethnohistory*.

Brett A. Houk is associate professor of archaeology at Texas Tech University. He holds MA and PhD degrees in anthropology from The University of Texas at Austin and has been teaching at Texas Tech University since 2006. As a student, he worked on archaeological projects in Guatemala and Belize, and he continues to study the ancient Maya in northwestern Belize. He is the author of *Ancient Maya Cities of the Eastern Lowlands* and the director of the Chan Chich Archaeological Project.

Stephen D. Houston serves as Paul Dupee Family Professor of Social Science at Brown University. He is the author of numerous books and articles, including *The*

Life Within: Classic Maya and the Matter of Permanence. Houston, a MacArthur Fellow, also holds the Grand Cross of the Order of the Quetzal, Guatemala's highest decoration.

Gyles Iannone is professor of anthropology at Trent University. He earned degrees at Simon Fraser University (BA), Trent University (MA), and University College London (PhD). His main areas of interest include historical ecology, coupled socio-ecological systems, resilience theory, collapse, and comparative tropical civilizations (especially in Central America and Asia). He conducted archaeological excavations in Belize for twenty-three field seasons (1991–2013) and is currently the director of the Socio-ecological Entanglement in Tropical Societies Project. He is the editor of *The Great Maya Droughts in Cultural Context: Case Studies in Resilience and Vulnerability*.

Takeshi Inomata is professor of anthropology and Agnese Nelms Haury Chair at the University of Arizona. He has been conducting fieldwork at Aguateca and Ceibal, Guatemala, to examine social processes in Maya society. His publications include "Early Ceremonial Constructions at Ceibal" (*Science*), *Life and Politics at the Royal Court of Aguateca*, and *The Classic Maya*.

Melanie Kingsley holds a doctorate in anthropology from Brandeis University. Her research in Guatemala in the Usumacinta River region and at the site of El Zotz has focused on social and economic changes in Postclassic life among the Maya of lowland Guatemala. She currently works and lives in Washington, D.C.

Olivia C. Navarro-Farr is assistant professor of anthropology and archaeology at the College of Wooster. She received her PhD at Southern Methodist University and has directed research at El Perú-Waka's Structure M13-1 since 2003. She recently published a coedited book with Michelle Rich, *Archaeology at El Perú-Waka': Ancient Maya Performances of Ritual, Memory, and Power*. Her current research focuses on social memory and ritual symbolism related to civic-ceremonial architecture at Waka' and across the southern Maya lowlands.

Claudia Quintanilla is a Guatemalan archaeologist and a research specialist in southwestern Petén archaeology, human osteology, and funerary customs at Cancuen. She has a master's degree in management of patrimony and culture with a specialization in museology, which she uses to promote national patrimony to all segments of the public.

Andrew K. Scherer is assistant professor of anthropology at Brown University. He is codirector of the Proyecto Regional Arqueológico Sierra del Lacandón in Petén and the Proyecto Arqueológico Busilja-Chocolja in Chiapas. He is the author of

Mortuary Landscapes of the Classic Maya: Rituals of Body and Soul and coeditor (with John Verano) of *Embattled Bodies, Embattled Places: War in Pre-Columbian Mesoamerica and the Andes.*

Sonja A. Schwake is lecturer in anthropology at Pennsylvania State University–Behrend College. She has conducted research at ancient Maya sites in Belize since 1993 at various sites, including Cahal Pech, Minanha, Pusilha, and Chacben Kax.

José Samuel Suasnavar is vice-director of the Forensic Anthropology Foundation of Guatemala. He has conducted research in Bosnia, Croatia, Kosovo, Democratic Republic of the Congo, Honduras, and Guatemala. He currently develops forensic investigations to clarify the identities of the victims of Guatemala's internal armed conflict.

Christopher Taylor is an anthropologist and an independent scholar who has written extensively on Rwanda. He has studied traditional medicine, sacred kingship, violence, and genocide in that country. He is the author of *Milk, Honey, and Money: Changing Concepts in Rwanda Healing* and *Sacrifice as Terror: The Rwandan Genocide of 1994.*

Fred Valdez Jr. is professor of anthropology at The University of Texas at Austin. He currently directs the Programme for Belize Archaeological Project in northwest Belize. He has done more than thirty years of research in the Maya area.

Index

The letters *f*, *m*, and *t* following page numbers refer to figures, maps, and tables.

Above-floor deposits, 208, 275, 276, 277*f*, 278. *See also* Surface deposits
Abscesses, alveolar, 194
Accession, 126, 279
Accession ceremonies, 87, 162, 276
Achote Black ceramics, 235, 237
Acropoli, 68, 123, 124, 126, 129, 132, 208; Dos Hombres, 15, 204*m*, 208–9, 210–11, 218–19, 222; La Milpa, 214–15, 216*m*; Naranjo, 78; Piedras Negras, 11, 66–69, 115–18, 122, 123–24, 126, 129, 132; Tikal, 75, 76*f*, 271, 278, 279; Yaxuna, 276
Adams, Richard E. W., 189
Adolescent remains, 180, 252–53
Adornment, 179, 181, 221, 255*t*
Adosadas, 246*f*, 251, 267
Africa, kingship in, 28, 29–30, 40–41, 49, 174; Egypt, 26, 28, 29; Ghana, 25, 41; Rwanda, 30, 49; Sudan, 29–30, 41, 49
Agency of stone monuments, 61–63, 87–88
Aggradation, 232, 233
Agricultural ditches, 232–33
Agricultural productivity, declining, 14, 16, 32, 129, 230, 234
Agricultural systems, 227; ditches, 232–33; terraces, 135, 138, 232, 234
Aguateca, 9*m*, 10–11, 67*t*, 92–94*m*, 105–7, 144, 199; social memory, 283; termination deposits, 95–101; termination rituals, 102–5, 177, 276, 278
Aguateca Archaeological Project, 93
Aguateca Restoration Project, 93
Aguila Orange ceramics, 248*t*

*Ahau*s. *See* Kings, Maya
Aimers, James, 225
*Ajaw*s, 44, 168, 169*f*, 272. *See also* Kings, Maya
*Ajk'uhuun*s, 167, 168, 182
Akan (Drunken Death-God), 249
Akropong, kingship in, 41
Akwapim kingship, 25
Alta Verapaz highland trade routes. *See* Verapaz Valley trade route
Altar de Sacrificios, 9*m*, 79*m*, 66, 67*t*, 84, 176, 177, 189, 190, 201
Altar Fine Orange ceramics, 122, 127, 128
Altar Orange ceramics, 248*t*
Altars, 68*t*, 75, 80, 102, 113, 118–19, 120*f*, 168, 169*f*, 182, 259
Altschuler, Milton, 198
Altun Ha, 9*m*, 67*t*, 79*m*, 191*m*
Alveolar abscesses, 194
Amalgams, kings as, 28
Ambergris Caye, 238
Ambrosino, James, 276
Ancestor bundles, 253–54, 263
Ancestor shrines, 139, 140–41, 153–54, 210, 235, 253; Structure 50, 235–37
Ancestor veneration, 145, 217–18, 253
Angkor, kingship in, 25, 28, 30, 36, 37–38, 43, 52
Animal faces, ceramic, 209
Aniruddha, 36–37
Annatto, 184
Annonal Orange Polychrome ceramics, 248*t*
Aquatic themes, 182
"Arab Spring," 201
Archaemenid/Persian Empire, kingship in, 32, 43
Archaeobotanical remains. *See* Floral remains
Armatures, 235

344 · Index

Assassinations, 156–57, 159, 177–83, 186
Assyrian kingship, 28
"Asymmetric reciprocity," 33
Athens, kingship in, 32–33
Atlatl spear tips, 191
Audience chambers, 168, 170f, 178
Audiencias, 168
Aung-Thwin, Michael, 47
Authority, challenges to, 21, 51–53, 154–57, 167–73; royal responses to, 173–75
Autonomy, increases in, 13, 14, 56, 155, 163, 171–72, 185
Axes, 180, 273
Axial stairs, 144, 145
Aztec kingship, 38–39, 40, 43
Aztec new fire ceremonies, 266

Bach'oks, 167
Bagan, kingship in, 47
Bah, 261
Bahlam Tz'am, 264
Bajos and *bajitos*, 227, 233–34, 238, 244m–245m
Balanza Black ceramics, 248t
Bali, kingship in, 30, 39–40
Balkanization, 13, 52, 138, 153, 155, 164–66, 167
Ball court markers, 67t, 137f, 168
Ball courts, 122, 126, 139, 140, 173, 174–175f, 182, 184, 186, 207, 213m, 225, 228
Ballplayers, 168, 169f
Banners, 228
Banner stones, 67t, 69
Bark beaters, 210
Barranca Escondida, 93, 94m, 97, 99t, 100
Barrientos, Tomas, 168
Barrios, 229
Barton Ramie, 199
Basal platforms/courses, 103, 142, 143f
Bayesian probability analyses, 139, 141
Bayonets, 180
Beach, Timothy, 232
Beads, 199, 221, 235, 237, 239, 273
Becan, 9m, 79m, 82, 190, 271
Bedford, Peter, 28
Behavioral residues, 18
Belize. *See* Altun Ha; Blue Creek; Caracol; Chan Chich; Colha; Dos Hombres; Gran Cacao; Lamanai; La Milpa; Minanha; Punta de Cacao; Xunantunich
Belize River, 9m, 79m, 191m, 211

Belize River Valley, 135, 211
Bemba kinghip, 29
Benches, 70, 72, 168, 213–14, 239
Berlin, Heinrich, 274
Bernbeck, Reinhard, 28
Bib heads, royal, 229
Biblical story of Pharaoh's dream, 32
Bichromes, 248t
Bifaces, 208, 209, 213, 237, 238, 252
Bilevel thrones, 144 145
Bird headdresses, 206
Birds of Paradise fields, 232, 240
Bital, 146, 151
Blackman Eddy, 238
Black-on-orange ceramics, 217, 248t
Black stone axes, 273
Black trickle-ware ceramic vessels, 235
Blackware, undesignated waxy, 248t
Blades, obsidian, 69, 151, 210, 213, 235, 237–38, 252
Blanketing of liminal spaces. *See* Doorway depositions
Blau, Peter M., 90
Blocked access, 62, 78, 205; doorways, 12, 15, 16, 150, 151, 182, 210, 218, 234–35; entrances, 13, 75, 159, 181, 209
Blocks, 96, 97
Blood, iconographic/epigraphic, 61, 274
Bloodletting rituals, 35, 63, 88, 106
Blood of Kings (Schele and Miller), 274
Blue Creek, 9m, 67t, 79m, 191m, 207, 225–30, 240–41; Late Classic processes, 230–34; Rosita Group revitalization, 238–40; surface deposits (16, 101, 214, 234–38, 278–79; Special Deposit 1, 206, 215, 217, 218)
Boltco Black-on-orange ceramics, 248t
Bone, incised, 213
Bone and bone fragments: animal, 99, 100, 215, 217; human, 65, 72, 75, 99, 121, 145, 178–83, 186, 196–97, 205, 209, 210–11, 213, 217–19, 251–55
Bone ornaments, 93
Bone pathologies, 179, 194, 254
Book of Chilam Balam of Chumayel, 86
Books of Chilam Balam, 86–87, 133
Bowl lids, 271
Bowls, 213, 219, 235, 237; finger bowls, 144
Brown, Bill, 64, 65
Brumfiel, Elizabeth, 38–39

Budsilha, 127
Burial chambers, 151, 253. *See also* Tombs
Burial of Minanha's royal residential complex, 12–13, 146–52, 153–54, 155
Burial patterns, new, 121
Burials, 213–14; "evil," 65; cremation, 212; primary burials, 62, 140, 151, 196, 210, 253; reentries, 142, 145; secondary burials, 62, 210, 253; shallow burials, 182, 271
Burma/Myanmar, kingship in, 28, 30, 32, 36–37, 41–42, 47, 52, 54–55
Burning, evidence of, 67*t*–68*t*, 95; Aguateca, 93, 95; Altar de Sacrificios, 189; Bital, 146, 190; Chan Chich, 213–14; Colha, 192; Minanha, 142; Piedras Negras, 68; Tonina, 190; Waka', 251, 255*t*
Burning of human bone, 121, 194, 254
Buttles, Palma, 14–15, 187–202, 339
Buyuk Striated ceramics, 217

Cacao, 39, 176, 177, 184, 185
Cache jars, 273
Caches, 72, 118–19, 142, 144, 145, 228, 239, 279, 283; aligned, 140, 157, 210–11; dedicatory, 144, 145, 228, 239
Caciques, highland, 174, 186
"Cadet lineages," 52
Calakmul, 9*m*, 67*t*, 13, 138, 145, 153, 171, 183, 250; hegemony, 160, 162–63, 165*m*, 166
Calculus deposits, 194, 254
Caldero Buff Polychrome ceramics, 248*t*
Cambio Unslipped ceramics, 99*t*
Cambodia, pre-Angkorian kingship in, 54
Cameron Incised ceramics, 248*t*
Campamento Fine Orange ceramics, 173, 184
Cancuen, 9*m*, 13–14, 67*t*, 79*m*, 170*f*, 176; autonomy, 171–72; containment, 173–75; decline of centralization, 160–67; differentiation, 172–73; division of power, 167–71; hegemony, 162, 165*m*, 166; monument defacement, 66, 67*t*, 78, 81; violent termination, 159–60, 177, 178–83, 186, 271, 282
Canine teeth, jaguar or dog, 209, 213, 219
Canoes, 227–28
Capstones, 95
Captives, depictions of, 104
Captive sacrifice, 177
Captors, depictions of, 104, 168

Caracol, 9*m*, 67*t*, 79*m*, 135, 138, 139, 145, 153, 163, 171; shifting affiliations, 141, 146, 151, 155
Caracol shrine, 82
Caribal Red ceramics, 248*t*
Caries, dental, 194, 254
Carmelita Incised ceramics, 248*t*
Case studies, 8–20; Aguateca, 92–107; Blue Creek, 225–41; Cancuen, 159–86; Chan Chich, 207, 211–14, 218, 219, 220*f*, 221, 222; Colha, 187–202; Copan, 73–74; Dos Hombres, 207, 208–11, 218, 219, 220*f*, 221, 222; Dos Pilas, 69; La Milpa, 207, 214–18, 219–220*f*, 221, 222, 278; Minanha, 135–58; Naranjo, 75–78; Palenque, 70–73; Piedras Negras, 108–33; Tikal, 74–75; Waka', 243–69
Categorization of rituals/assemblages, 15–16, 218, 255*t*
Causeways, 93, 94*m*, 97–99*t*, 100, 103, 139, 186, 211, 212*m*
Caves, 160, 135
Cave shrines, 161, 175
Cayo Unslipped ceramics, 235, 237
CCAP excavations, 211–14
Ceibal/Seibal, 79*m*, 84, 106–7, 131, 161*m*, 166, 176, 177, 183, 189
Censors, 98, 100
Central Acropolis Court 5D-2, 75, 76*f*, 278
Centralist, scapegoat king model as, 6, 20
Centralization, challenges to, 160–67, 171, 173
Ceramic animal face, 209
Ceramic appliqués, 235
Ceramic figurines. *See* Figurines
Ceramic frequencies, 84, 99*t*
Ceramic microseriation, 139, 141
Ceramic refits, lack of, 15, 99, 100, 101, 205, 206
Ceramic sequence for Waka', 248*t*
Cerro de las Mesas, 196
Cerros, 9*m*, 191*m*, 238, 274, 275–76, 277*f*, 279
Cervical vertebrae, 194, 253
Ch'ulel, 34–35, 61, 66, 150, 261, 266
Ch'ul/k'ul, glyphic element for, 61, 274
Ch'ul lakamtun, 61
Chablekal Grey ceramics, 248*t*; Fine Grey, 103, 172, 184
Chak, 32
Chak Tok Ich'aak I, 272, 272
Challenges to authority, 21, 51–53, 154–57, 167–73; royal responses to, 173–75
Chan Cahal, 226*m*, 229, 232, 240

Chan Chich, 9*m*, 67*t*, 79*m*, 191*m*, 203, 207, 211, 212*m*; surface deposits, 15, 200, 205, 206–7, 213–14, 218, 219, 220*f*, 221, 222, 278
Chan Chich Archaeological Project. *See* CCAP excavations
Chaquiste Impressed ceramics, 98, 99*t*, 100
Character, patterning in, 19
Charcoal, 144
Check dams, 227, 234
Chert artifacts, 99, 100, 179, 186, 191, 208, 221, 235, 237, 251, 252, 255*t*
Chetumal Bay, 82, 191*m*
Chiapas, 70, 172, 173, 177
Chiapas highlands, 64
Chichén Itzá, 9*m*, 69, 87, 133, 239; Chontal-Itza incursions, 10, 81–85, 87
Chico zapote lintels, 70
Chicxulub Incised ceramics, 248*t*
Chiefs, 24; head chiefs, 86
Child remains, 159, 180, 192–94, 271, 272
China, kingship in, 32–33, 42, 48
Chipped-stone tools, 151, 213, 215, 278
Chola kingship, 26, 28, 34, 42
Cholul Fluted ceramics, 248*t*
Chontal-Itza incursions, 10, 81–85, 87
Chontalpa, 83, 85
Circular structures, 79*m*, 82, 84, 238–239*f*
Cistern deposits, 13, 159, 178*f*–81, 186
Cists, 118, 120*f*
Civic-ceremonial temples. *See* Structure M13-1
Claessen, Henri J. M., 24
Class conflict hypotheses, 199–200, 224
Clay caps, 124
Clayey soils, 227, 233
Clayton, Sarah C., 101, 206
Climate change, role of, 1, 4, 13, 14, 29–30, 45–46, 48–49, 51, 57, 58, 86–87, 110, 131, 140, 153–56, 175–76, 187–88, 198, 224
Cloth, 38, 39; headbands, 87, 271–72; head-resses, 182
Clothing, kingly. *See* Regalia, royal
Clubs, 180
Cobble fill, 208
Cobweb Swamp, 191
Codex Borbonicus, 266
Coe, William R., 279
Co-essences, 63, 65–66, 88

Coffers, stone, 162
Colha, 9*m*, 14–15, 67*t*, 79*m*, 187, 188–89, 190–96, 197–99, 271
"Collapse," definition of, 22, 85
Collapse debris, 14, 96, 213, 217, 219
Collar beads, 273
Column altars, 118–120*f*
Comalcalco, 84
Community continuities, 12, 17, 19, 121–22, 153–54, 243, 268–69
Community-level challenges to authority, 154, 171–72
Conch shells, 162, 176, 179, 271
Conquest warfare, 10, 20, 46, 81
Conservator reconstructions, 68, 115*f*
Consorts, probable, 159, 181, 184
Construction, 138–39; terraces, 234, 237, 250; unfinished construction, 16, 93, 103, 150, 215; upland agricultural systems, 232–34
Construction pens, 146
Construction ramps, 150
Containment strategies, 4, 7, 14, 20, 44–45, 48, 58, 126, 154, 173–74, 176
Continuities, 12, 17, 19, 121–22, 153–54, 243, 268–69
Contour terraces, 234
Contreras Valley, 140
Cooking vessels, 93, 98
Copan, 9*m*, 67*t*, 79*m*, 201, 224, 233, 267; destruction and desecration, 67*t*, 69, 73–74, 88; monument defacement, 62, 66, 67*t*, 79*m*; *wite' naah*, 267
Copan Valley leadership, 167–68
Coral, 229, 237
Cortical erosion, 253, 254
Cosmic energy. *See Ch'ulel*. *See also Tonalli*
Cosmological centrality divine rulers, 18, 281–82
Cotton, 176, 177, 184, 185
Counterweights, 235
Courtyard burials, 12–13, 146–52, 153–54, 155
Courtyard expansion, 138, 208
Covey, R. Alan, 201
Cowgill, George, 83, 85
Cranial shaping, 194, 196, 197
Crania/skulls, 210–11; decapitated, 14, 177, 192*f*–196, 197, 209, 251, 252–55, 263, 271–73; fragments, 179*f*, 209, 251

Cremation, 121
Cribra orbitalia, 194
Cross-cultural comparisons: divine kingship, 24–60, 89, 275; scapegoat king model, 1–21, 24–60, 109–11, 130, 132–35, 157, 186, 240, 261–64, 270, 273
Crown diadems, 272–773
Crowns, 38, 271–73, 280f. See also White headbands
Crypts, 73–74, 144, 145. See also Tombs
Cubeta Incised ceramics, 209
Culbert, T. Patrick, 190, 200
Cultural modifications, 180, 194, 197
Cut blocks, 96, 97
Cut marks, 75, 194, 195f, 253
Cycle 10 iconography, so-called, 82

Dams, 227, 234
Dates of elite abandonment, 67t–68t
Daylight Orange ceramics, 209, 239–40
Deactivation of divine authority, 7, 11, 21, 58–59, 153, 158, 186, 262
Debitage, 213, 235
Decapitated human remains, 14, 177, 180, 192f–196, 197, 252–53, 272–73
Decapitation and flaying events, 14, 66, 187, 191–96
De Casparis, J. G., 29
Decentering of power, 131
Decentralization, 47, 52–53, 160–67, 171, 173
Decommissioning of structures, 12, 95–105, 146–51, 205–7
Dedications, 73, 80, 102, 125, 160, 182, 206, 249, 253, 256, 259
Dedicatory caches, 144, 145, 228, 239
Defaced monuments, 10, 11, 13, 14, 65–66, 67t–68t, 79m, 116, 261
Defensive walls, 93, 170f, 177, 181, 183, 186
Deforestation, 175, 187, 224, 233
Deformations, cranial, 180. See also Cranial shaping
Deification of kings, 28–29
Demarest, Arthur, 13–14, 69, 81, 159–86, 198, 225, 271, 282, 339
Dense deposits, 74, 96–97f, 101, 102, 256. See also Surface deposits
Dental alteration and decoration, 180, 194, 196, 254

Dental pathologies, 192–94, 196, 254
Depopulation, 83, 223–24. See also Populations: declining
Desanctification, symbolic, 11, 12, 13
Desecratory acts, 209, 218; erasure, 150, 151; termination rituals, 17, 255t
Desecratory deposits, 15, 62, 209, 255t. See also Surface deposits
Desecratory termination events, 144–46, 152, 255t
Destruction event #1, 142–46, 152–53
Destruction event #2, 146–152, 153–54
"Destructive event deposits," 209. See also Surface deposits
Dēva suffix, 28
Diadems, 27n–73
Dietary practices. See Food
Differentiation, internal, 172–73
Dirks, Nicholas B., 36, 42, 52
Disarticulated human bones, 14, 75, 196, 255t
Discontinuities, 153
Discourses, 92
Dismemberment, 252–53, 263; monuments, 261
Dismemberment sacrifices, 271
Displacement of souls. See Soul loss
Ditched fields, 226m, 229, 232–33, 240
Divine kingship, cross-cultural comparisons, 25–29
Divine kingship model, utility of, 2, 89–90, 270
Divisible soul ontologies, 64–65. See also Soul loss
Divisions of authority, 167–68, 171, 173–74, 185. See also Joint rulership; Power sharing
Docks, 228
Domestic assemblages, 98
Dominant ideologies: changes in, 106–7; manipulation of, 157; support for, 4–6, 7, 20, 51, 53, 55; resistance to, 56
Doorway depositions, 12, 15, 16, 150, 182, 210, 234–35
Doorways, 18, 87; as liminal thresholds, 88; undermining of, 68–69, 70, 73, 74, 117
Dos Arroyos Orange Polychrome ceramics, 248t
Dos Hombres, 9m, 15, 67t, 79m, 191m, 204m, 207; surface deposits, 203, 205–7, 208–11, 218–19, 220f, 221, 222

Dos Pilas, 9*m*, 67*t*, 79*m*, 80, 83, 161*f*, 172, 177, 181; hegemony, 163, 164*m*, 166; monument defacement, 62, 66, 69, 70, 79*m*; primary capital, 93, 102, 103, 176; termination deposits, 84, 177, 181; under Calakmul hegemony, 162, 250; violent terminations, 178–83
Dos Pilas/Petexbatun hegemony, 163, 164*m*, 166
Double-vaulted architecture, 70, 72
Drained-field farming. *See* ditched fields
Droughts, 13, 14, 131, 155–56, 187–88
Drums, 42, 215
Drunken Death-God (Akan), 249
Dry-stone fill, 146
Duncan, William N., 87
Dunning, Nicholas P., 211
Durbin, Marshall, 274
Durkheimian views of divine kingship, 90
Dyadic gifting, 42
Dynasties, establishment of royal, 122–23, 124, 139

Earflares, 273
Earspools, 124, 221
Eberl, Markus, 171–72, 176
Economic collapse of 2008, 19
Ednza, 9*m*, 171
E-Groups/eastern ancestor shrines, 12, 139–41, 142–54, 157, 210, 235–37; pseudo-E-Groups, 228–29
Egyptian kingship, 26, 28, 29
Ehecatl, 82
El Raudal, 177
El Cayo, 127
Elite artifacts, deposition of, 15, 62. *See also* Chan Chich: surface deposits
Elite goods, 15, 150, 226
Elite identity, ritual termination of, 14
Elites, proliferation of, 167–71, 173
Elite structures, burning of, 142, 189–90, 192, 196, 197, 199
El Perú-Waka'. *See* Waka'
El Porvenir, 122, 127, 128, 129
Elson, Christina M., 201
Emblem glyphs, 80, 96, 167, 274
Emblems, 23, 35, 41, 44
Embodiments, 25, 30, 49, 263
Embodiments of kingdoms, kings as, 1, 11–12, 20, 40–41, 104–5

Embodiments of kings: monuments as, 93, 104–6, 107, 261, 274; royal regalia as, 38–39; symbolic representations as, 89
Enamel hypoplasias, 194, 254
Encanto Striated ceramics, 98, 99*t*, 100
Encapsulations. *See* Courtyard burials
Endemic warfare, 20, 21, 131, 166, 172, 185
Energies. *See Ch'ulel; Tonalli*
Entombment of structures. *See* Burial of Minanha's royal residential complex
Entrances, formal vaulted, 139, 144, 145, 147*f*
Environmental issues, 4, 20, 21, 45–46, 57, 223–24; decline/crises, 4, 11, 20, 48–49, 74, 91, 131–32, 153, 157, 243, 262, 268. *See also* Climate change, role of
Environmental stewards, kings as, 32–33
Epicenters: Aguateca, 11, 93–94*m*; Blue Creek, 16; Cancuen, 13, 159, 173; Dos Pilas, 69; La Milpa, 15; Minanha, 12, 135, 137*f*, 138–40; Piedras Negras, 11, 109, 114*m*, 119*m*
Epic of Gilgamesh, The, 36
Eppich, Keith, 251–52, 254
Erasure, desecration and destruction as, 150, 151
Eroded/undetermined ceramics, 99*t*, 235, 237
Erosion (cortical), 253, 254
Erosion (soil), 96, 230, 232–33
Erosional cuts, 230
Escarpments, 93, 207, 211, 227, 232, 233, 249
Escobedo, Héctor, 80, 108–33, 339
Essentialist, scapegoat king model as, 6
Evans-Pritchard, E. E., 90
"Evil burials," 65
Exclusionary tactics, 16–17, 56, 229, 240–41
Executions, 14, 18, 110, 180, 196. *See also* Violent terminations
Exotic goods, 18, 160, 229; access to, 16, 162, 172, 176–77, 184, 226, 227–28; depositions, 15, 205, 208–9
Extensions of kings. *See* Embodiments of kings
Extrinsic characteristics of kings, 1–2

Facial mutilation, 66, 81. *See also* Defaced monuments
Factionalism, 172–73
FAFG excavations, 179–83
Fagan, Brian, 59
False consciousness, 5

Fash, William L., 266–67
Faunal remains, 15, 144, 205, 206, 209, 213, 219, 220, 237, 238, 278
Feasting ball courts, 174–175f
Feasting remains, 101, 123, 129, 144, 206
Feet, severed, 252–53
Female *ajaws*. *See* Queens, remains of
Female depictions, 258f, 259
Female remains, 13, 159, 180, 181, 192, 271, 272, 280
Fempelle, 48–49
Femurs. *See* Long bones
Fertility, kings' associations with, 2, 3, 17, 26, 27, 29–32, 39, 43, 48, 53–54
Fertility taboos, 31
Fetal remains, 180
Fialko, Vilma, 78, 271–72
Fibulae, 253
Field reconstructions, 68, 115f, 160, 182, 262, 268
Fields, ditched, 226m, 229, 232–33, 240
Fields, Virginia, 26, 272
Figures, illustrative. *See* Illustrations; Maps; Photos; Plan Views
Figurine heads, 209, 220f, 221, 252
Figurines, 123, 210, 211, 213, 215, 220f, 221, 235, 238
Filed teeth, 194, 196, 254
Fill materials, 12, 96, 97, 103, 118, 146, 208, 213
Fill stones, 97
Fine Gray ceramics, 103, 122, 127
Fine-line incisions, 257
Fine Orange ceramics, 15, 113, 122, 127, 128, 173, 184, 213, 215, 217; imitations, 213, 215
Finery, kingly. *See* Regalia, royal
Fine wares, 15, 82, 84, 103, 113, 117, 122, 127, 128, 172–73, 181, 184, 213, 215, 217; imitation, 84, 215
Finger bowls, 144
Fire ceremonies, 266–67
Fire-shattered walls, 192f
Fire shrines (*wite' naah*), 17, 257, 266–67
Firewood bundles, 266
Fish, 39, 129, 182, 197
Fish consumption, 129
Flannery, Kent, 225
Flaying and decapitation events, 14, 66, 187, 191–96

Floral remains, 237, 238, 278
Flor Cream ceramics, 248t
Food: access, 281–82; consumption, 128–29; feasting, 39, 128, 129; production, 32, 197, 198, 202, 234; sacrificial offerings, 34
Food-consumption areas, 99
Food-preparation areas, 99
Food-preparation vessels, 278
Footings, use of buried walls as, 148–49
"Foreign" ceramics, distribution of, 172–73
Forensic Anthropology Foundation of Guatemala. *See* FAFG excavations
Forensic evidence, 178–81, 192–195f, 252–55
Fortes, Meyer, 90
Fortifications, 67t–68t, 69, 171, 172, 176–77; defensive walls, 93, 177, 181, 183, 186
Fragmentary human remains, 252–255, 263, 271–73. *See also* Human skeletal remains
Fragmentation, 13, 52, 160–67
Frazer, James, 1, 31, 48, 90, 106
Freidel, David, 17–18, 26, 75, 162, 259, 262, 270–84, 339
French Revolution, 110
Friezes, 11, 12, 13, 18, 130; Minanha, 144, 145, 148, 149, 150, 151, 157, 261
"Full-service" centers, 138–39
Functionalist explanations, 4, 24, 89
Functionaries as kingly regalia, 20, 39–40, 54
Functionary roles, upstart nobles' assumption of, 13–14, 154, 156

Gann, Thomas, 196
Garber, James F., 206, 275–76, 277f
Garbutt Creek Red ceramics, 235, 237
Garrison, Thomas G., 211
Geertz, Clifford, 39–40, 275
Ghana, kingship in, 25, 41
Gift giving, royal, 33, 34, 41–44, 45, 46, 51–52, 55–56, 128–29, 226
Gilbert, Michelle, 40–41
Gilgamesh, 36
Gill, Richardson B., 187
Glyphic elements, 61, 274
Glyphic texts, 93–94
Glyphs, 10, 68, 72, 82, 87, 209, 266, 268, 274; emblem glyphs, 80, 96, 167, 274
God K, 229
God-kings. *See* Divine kings

Gods and goddesses, 30, 32, 36, 39, 73, 82, 154, 158, 229, 249, 260, 272, 284; depictions of, 27, 73, 82; disgruntled, 45–51; feeding of, 33–35; kings' dressing as/impersonating, 30, 32, 39, 54; references to, 27, 228–29, 249; sacred covenants with, 34–35, 139, 274–75; in scapegoat king models, 3–4, 23, 26–29, 33, 45; symbolism associated with, 272–73; veneration of, 266
Golden, Charles, 11–12, 108–33, 282, 339–40
Golden Bough, The (Frazer), 1
Governance structures as scapegoats, 7, 57–58, 134, 153–54, 156, 157
Grafstein, Robert, 90
Granite, 210, 237
Grave goods, 181–82, 186
Great kings/great kingdoms, 41–44, 135, 141, 145, 146, 153, 155, 157
Greek kingship, 31, 48
Greenstone, 99, 100, 221. *See also* Jade
Grinding stones, 93, 99, 226, 238, 252, 255*t*, 278
Ground stone artifacts, 206, 215, 219
Group J courtyard. *See* Structure 38J
Guatemala. *See* Aguateca; Altar de Sacrificios; Cancuen; Dos Pilas; La Honradez; Naranjo; Piedras Negras; Río Azul; San Bartolo; Seibal/Ceibal; Tikal; Waka'; Xultun; Yaxchilan
Guatemalan highland rituals, 65
Guderjan, Thomas, 16–17, 223–42, 278–79, 340
Guenter, Stanley Paul, 250, 256–57, 264
"Guilt by association," 16, 20, 203
Gypsum, 232, 233
Fine wares, 15, 82, 84, 103, 113, 117, 122, 127, 128, 172–73, 181, 184, 213, 215, 217; imitation, 84, 215

Habermas, Jürgen, 44, 91, 106
Hall, Kenneth, 31
Hamblin, Robert L., 199–200, 224
Hammerstones, 235, 237
Hanratty, Colleen, 16–17, 223–42, 278–79, 340
Hansen, Thomas Blom,, 90
Harrison, Eleanor. *See* Harrison-Buck, Eleanor
Harrison, Peter, 75
Harrison-Buck, Eleanor, 10, 61–88, 213, 148, 200, 205, 213, 214, 218, 238–39, 273–74, 280, 340
Hauberg Stela, 271
Hauser-Schäublin, Brigitta, 30

Haviland, William, 199
Headbands, 87, 271–272, 280*f*
Head chiefs, 86
Headdresses, 39, 96, 182, 206, 209
Head men, 24
Heat exposure, evidence of, 95, 192
Hegemony, challenges to interregional spheres of, 138, 160–67
Heitzman, James, 42
Hematite, 252
"He of the House of Darkness," 44
"He of the Twisted Water," 44
Hershey, 67*t*, 79*m*
Hester, Thomas R., 191
Heusch, Luc de, 28
Hidden transcripts, 91–92
Hieroglyphic texts, 61–62, 63, 80, 209
Hieroglyphs, 10, 68, 72, 82, 87, 209, 266, 268, 274; emblem glyphs, 80
Higham, Charles, 30–31, 43
High *kaloomte'* royal capitals. *See* Cancuen
Highland exchange influences, 160, 162, 173, 184–85
Highland-style feasting ball courts, 174–75*f*
Highland trade route, 131, 160, 161*m*
Hocart, A. M., 90
Hoffman, Michael, 38
Hofling, Charles Andrew, 87
"Holy Lord of Cancuen, Holy Lord of Machaquila." *See* Kan Maax
Holy lords, 182, 186, 281. See also *K'uhul ajaws*
Holy ritual scapegoats, 186
Honduras. *See* Copan
Horus, 26
Houk, Brett A., 1–22, 200, 203–22, 224, 278, 340
House mounds, 230, 231*f*
Houston, Stephen D., 80, 108–33, 230–61, 340–41
Hughes, Donald, 32–33
Human skeletal remains, 15, 65, 67*t*–68*t*, 72, 75, 99, 121, 145, 178–83, 186, 205, 210–11, 213–14, 217–19, 251–55, 271–72; burned, 121; decapitated skulls, 14, 177, 192*f*–196, 197, 252–53, 272–73; disarticulated bone, 14, 75, 196, 255*t*; fragments, 179*f*, 209, 251, 252–55, 263, 271–73
Hun Nal Ye, 162
Hun-Nal-Yeh (One Maize), 32
Huunal jewels, 280
Hypoplasias, dental, 194, 254

Iannone, Gyles, 1–22, 23–60, 89–90, 104, 107, 126, 134–58, 188, 209–10, 270–71, 281, 282, 283, 341
Iberia Orange ceramics, 248*t*
Identity, termination of, 14, 66, 87–88
Ideologies, 4–5; changes in, 106–7; manipulation of, 157; resistance to, 56; support for, 4–6, 7, 20, 51, 53, 55
Illustrations, 77*f*, 101*f*, 169*f*, 175*f*, 178*f*, 193*f*, 195*f*, 220*f*. *See also* Maps; Photos; Plan views
Imaana, 30
Imitation Fine Orange ceramics, 213, 215
Incensarios, 217
Incised bone, 213
Incisors, notching of, 194
Indian kingship. *See* South India, kingship in
Indra, 30, 36
Ineffective governance, scapegoating as response to, 1–21, 24–60, 109–11, 130, 132–35, 157, 186, 240, 261–64, 270, 273
Infant remains, 180, 253
Infierno Black ceramics, 248*t*
Infilling, 12, 13, 18, 50, 78, 109, 146–49, 150–52, 156
Inka kingship, 26, 31–32, 48–49
Inner life force. See *Ch'ulel*
Inomata, Takeshi, 2, 3, 10–11, 89–107, 189–90, 199, 218, 275, 276, 278, 279, 282, 283, 341
Inscribed subroyal titles, increase in, 167
Installation rituals, 19, 20, 25, 44
Instruments, musical, 64; drums, 42; whistles, 209, 211, 213, 220*f*, 235
Intent, patterning in, 18
Interdependence among kingdoms, 15, 198
Interkingdom warfare, 20
Interlocutors, kings as, 281
Intermediaries, kings as, 27, 139
Internal differentiation, 172–73
Internal divisions of power, 167–71, 185
Internal factors leading to collapses, 4, 11–12, 91, 108–9, 167, 187, 190, 198–201
Interpretation, challenges to, 1–3, 17, 19, 63, 75, 108, 111–13, 121, 198–202, 205–7, 210, 221–22, 263, 267
Interregional spheres of hegemony, challenges to, 138, 146, 160–67
Intrasite causeways, 93, 94*m*, 97–99*t*, 100, 103, 139, 186, 211, 212*m*
Intrinsic characteristics of kings, 1–2, 222

Intrusive groups, 80–81: Chontal-Itza Maya, 10, 81–85, 87
Invasion hypotheses, 189; Chontal-Itza incursions reevaluated, 82–85, 87
Isotopic signatures, dietary, 128–29
Itza invaders. *See* Chontal-Itza incursions
Itzamnaaj B'alam III, 80
Itzam-Yeh, 32
Itza nobility as interrogators, 86–87
Ixik uh, 249
Ixtonton, 66, 67*t*, 79*m*

Jade, 124, 131, 162, 172, 174, 175, 176, 177, 184, 225, 251; beads, 199, 239; carved, 181, 271, 272; diadems, 272; fragmented, 252, 255*t*, 275; *huunal* jewels, 280; ornaments, 93, 221, 226
Jadeite, 16, 39, 225
Jaguar or dog teeth, drilled, 209, 213, 219
Jameson, Fredric, 45
Janaab Pakal III, 72
Japan, kingship in, 31
Jars, 93, 98, 99, 235, 237, 273
Java, kingship in, 31, 41, 54
"Jester god," 272
Jewelry, 35, 39, 221
Joint rulership, 145, 146, 151, 152–53. *See also* Divisions of authority; Power sharing
Judges, kings as, 25
Jukun kingship, 29, 49

K'al glyph, 87
Kaloomte's, 160, 166
K'altuun rituals, 87
Kambu, 43
Kaminaljuyu, 9*m*, 177
Kan Maax, 159, 181–82
Kaq ceramic complex, 248*t*
Karstic uplands, 155, 227
K'awiil Chan K'inich (Ruler 4), 69, 102, 126, 163
Khmer kingship, 30, 36, 37–38, 40, 43; Angkorian kingship, 25, 28, 52
K'iche' Maya rituals, 65
K'inich Ahkal Mo' Nahb' III, 70, 71*f*, 72
K'inich appellation, 27
K'inich Bahlam, 257, 283–84
K'inich Bahlam II, 283
K'inich Kan Bahlam III, 72
K'inich K'uk' Bahlam II, 72
K'inich Pakal II, 72

Kidder, A. V., 198
Kilikan Composite ceramics, 248*t*
Kings of kings. See *Kaloomte's*
"Kings of stone," killing of. *See* Defaced monuments
Kings, Maya:
—Aguateca: K'awiil Chan K'inich (Ruler 4), 102; Ruler 3, 102; Tahn Te' K'inich (Ruler 5), 93, 102–5
—Calakmul (Snake Kingdom): Yuknoom Ch'een, 283
—Cancuen: Kan Maax, 159, 181–82, 271; Taj Chan Ahk, 182
—Dos Pilas: K'awiil Chan K'inich (Ruler 4), 69, 163
—Copan: Yax Pasaj, 73–74, 167
—Naranjo: Waxaklajuun Ubaah K'awiil, 75
—Palenque: Janaab Pakal III, 72; K'inich Ahkal Mo' Nahb' III, 70, 71*f*, 72; K'inich Kan Bahlam III, 72; K'inich K'uk' Bahlam II, 72; K'inich Pakal II, 72; Upakal K'inich, 70, 72
—Piedras Negras: Ruler 4, 126; Ruler 7, 68, 80, 109, 112, 113, 115, 125, 126, 129, 130, 132, 153
—Tikal: Chak Tok Ich'aak I, 272, 272; Nuun Ujol Chaak, 282; Siyaj Chan K'awiil, 259; Yik'in Chan K'awiil, 264
—Waka': Bahlam Tz'am, 264; K'inich Bahlam, 257, 283; K'inich Bahlam II, 283; Lady K'ab'el, 258*f*, 259; unknown rulers, 256–60
—Yaxchilan: Itzamnaaj B'alam III, 80
Kingship, cross-cultural perspectives on, 29–44; divine kingship, 25–29; scapegoat kings, 44–53, 1–21, 24–60, 109–11, 130, 132–35, 157, 186, 240, 261–64, 270, 273
Kingsley, Melanie, 108–33, 341
Kín Tan, 16, 226*m*, 229; termination deposits, 234–38
Knives, 235
Korea, kingship in, 31
K'uhul ajaws, 166, 168, 169*f*, 171, 173, 185–86, 281. *See also* Kings
K'uhul Mutal Ajaw, 282
K'ui'k (central precinct), 228, 234
K'ul/ch'ul, glyphic element for, 61, 274

La Corona, 9*m*, 162
"Lady Moon," 249
Laguna del Tigre National Park and Biosphere Reserve, 247

La Joyanca, 127, 128
La Lucha Escarpment, 211
La Lucha uplands, 207
Lamanai, 9*m*, 191*m*, 201, 224–25
La Milpa, 9*m*, 191*m*, 203, 204, 216*m*; surface deposits, 15, 214–18, 219–220*f*, 221, 222, 278
La Milpa Archaeological Project, 214
La Milpa Core Project. *See* LMCP excavations
"Language of Zuyua," 86
La Pasadita, 127
Laporte, Juan Pedro, 271–72
Laythwan maṅgalā, 30
Legitimacy, 24, 90–92, 106, 107, 122, 176, 182
Legitimation crises, 4, 11, 13–14, 20, 23, 44–47, 91, 110–11, 134, 155, 167, 183–86
Legitimation strategies. *See* Containment strategies
Limestone, 95, 135, 146, 155, 227, 232, 233; fire-shattered walls, 192*f*
Limestone, carved, 101*f*; blocks, 96, 192; stelae, 137*f*, 144, 258*f*; tablets, 70, 71*f*
Liminal spaces, 12, 18, 88, 262, 265
Lineages, destruction of, 62–63, 73–74, 88, 145, 240–41
Lineages, multigenerational interactions between, 16, 229–30, 240–41
Lintels, 117, 264; destruction of, 63, 66, 67–68, 70, 72, 74, 78; as "doors' roofs," 87–88
Liquid scrolls, depictions of, 272, 274
Lithic debitage, 213, 235
Little kings/little kingdoms, 41–44, 51–53, 55–56, 171. *See also* Minanha
"Living ancestors," kings as, 26, 260
LMCP excavations, 215–18
Lombriz Orange Polychrome ceramics, 248*t*
Long bones, 210–11, 251, 252, 253
Loofah, 251
Looter's pits, 78
"Lords of the Isles," 31
Lords of the Life Force, 274, 281, 282. See also K'uhul ajaws
"Lords of the Mountain," 31
Low resource areas, expansion into, 230–32
Lucha Incised ceramics, 248*t*
Luzzadder-Beach, Sheryl S., 232

Mabbett, Ian, 29
Machaquila, 161*m*, 168, 177, 183, 184

"Machaquila, Holy Lord of Cancuen, Holy Lord of." *See* Kan Maax
Machetes, 180
Macri, Martha J., 141
Macrobotanical remains. *See* Floral remains
Magical powers of kings, 31
Maize consumption, 128–29
Maize God, 39, 73, 272, 282
Mal entierro rituals, 65
Malevolent rituals, 10, 65
Malay kingship, 31, 54
Mandala, Angkorian, 30–31
Man of Tikal attribution, 282
Manos, 100, 210, 211, 213, 235, 237, 255*t*
Maps, 9*m*, 79*m*, 94*m*, 114*m*, 119*m*, 136*m*, 161*m*, 164*m*–165*m*, 191*m*, 204*m*, 212*m*, 216*m*, 226*m*, 244*m*–245*m*. *See also* Plan views
Marcus, Joyce, 283
Marls, 95, 96, 194, 208, 255*t*, 262, 276
Marriage alliances, 109, 163, 184, 186
Masks, 27, 228
Mason, J. Alden, 111, 130
Massacres. *See* Sacrifice of royal court; Decapitation and flaying events
Mass sacrifices, 159, 178–83, 186
Material correlates, 53–54, 134, 264; kingship, 139–41; scapegoat king model, 3, 7, 10, 59, 132
Material/spatial foci, patterning in, 18
Mathews, Peter, 274
Mat houses, 167
Matillas Fine Orange ceramics, 122, 128
Mat symbols, 271
Maya area, map of, 9*m*
Maya Cosmos (Freidel, Schele, and Parker), 281
Maya kingship. *See* Kings, Maya
McAnany, Patricia, 33, 219, 238
McGuire, Randall, 7, 59
Meat consumption, 128–29
Mesopotamia, 32, 36; kingship in, 28–29
Metatarsals, 252
Metates, 100, 235, 237
Mexicanized Maya invasions/influences, 82–85, 189
Mexico. *See* Becan; Cerro de las Mesas; Chichén Itzá; Palenque; Yaxuna
Microseriation, 139, 141
Middens, 117, 174, 205, 217, 240; "midden-like" deposits, 15–16, 205, 209, 219–20, 278; transposed middens/secondary deposits, 99–101, 114, 206, 217, 276, 278
Middle Pasión exchange route, 166. *See also* Pasión River exchange route
Militarism, symbols of, 171–72
Minanha, 9*m*, 67*t*, 137*f*; caches, 209–10; destruction events (#1, 142–46, 152, 154; #2/ burial of royal residential complex, 12–13, 146–52, 153–54, 155); developmental history, 135–41; social memory, 209–10, 283
Miseria Appliqué ceramics, 248*t*
Mock, Shirley Boteler, 66, 196, 197, 262, 276
Monochrome cream bowls, 237
Monument mutilation. *See* Defaced monuments
Moon goddesses, 249
Morai ceramic complex, 248*t*, 252
Mortuary patterns at M13-1, 252–56
Motagua Valley, monument defacement in, 66, 67*t*, 73–74, 79*m*
Mother of pearl, 181, 182, 237
Mud interments, 13, 159, 181–83
Multigenerational interactions between lineages, 16, 228, 229, 240–41
Muñoz, René, 124
Munson, Jessica L., 141
Murder of institution of kingship, 270
Mutal, 282
Mutal Winik, 282
Myanmar/Burma, kingship in, 28, 30, 32, 36–37, 41–42, 47, 52, 54–55
Mystical constructions of reality, 281

Naba Phase ceramics, 124
Nagual, 65
Nakum, 67*t*, 79*m*, 82, 171
Naranjo, 9*m*, 67*t*, 135, 146, 151; case study, 75–78; monument defacement, 66, 67*t*, 74–75, 77*f*, 78, 79*m*
Narathihapade, 47
Navarro-Farr, Olivia, 17, 205–6, 210, 211, 218, 220–21, 243–69, 275, 276, 278, 283, 341
Neo-Assyrian kingship, 40
Neo-evolutionist, scapegoat king model as, 6
Nephrite, 225
New fire ceremonies, 267
New River lagoon, 224–25
New River, 191*m*
Nohmul, 9*m*, 79*m*, 228, 238

Non-elite contributions to assemblages, 16, 17, 220–21, 265
Nonhuman agency, 61–63, 87–88
Nonlocal "stranger kings," 25, 124, 139, 140–41, 156, 157
Nonreplacement of kings, 20–21, 241
Norman's Temple, 211–13
Normative explanations, 4
Northern ball courts, 174–175f
Northern River Lagoon (NRL), 197, 198
Northwestern Belize case studies. See Chan Chich; Dos Hombres; La Milpa
Notching of incisors, 194
NRL (Northern River Lagoon), 197, 198

Obsidian, 69, 70, 162, 172, 176, 177, 179, 184, 215, 219, 251; Pachuca Green, 84; Zaragoza, 173, 184
Obsidian artifacts: bifaces, 209; blades, 69, 151, 210, 213, 235, 237–38, 252; spear and projectile points, 255t; eccentrics, 118–19, 173, 184; tools, 99, 100, 226
Ocarina fragments, 215
O'Connor, Richard, 40, 42–43, 54
Ollas, 151
Olmec colossal heads, 66
One Maize, 32. See also Maize God
Operation 2012, 196
Orange ground Codex style Palmar ceramics, 248t
Orenstein, Henry, 33
Organic fuels, deposition of, 95
"Original debt," 33–34
Ornaments, 93, 99, 100, 229. See also Adornment
Osteological evidence. See Human skeletal remains
Outset stairs, 144, 145
Overlords/overlordship, 34, 36, 40, 51–53, 55–56, 153, 154, 155, 158. See also Great kings/great kingdoms; Patron-client relationships

Pabellon Modeled-carved ceramics, 82, 84, 248t; Fine Orange, 213, 219
Pachuca Green obsidian, 84
Pacific conch shells, 162, 176, 179, 271
Pagan/Bagan, kingship in, 47
Pagliaro, Jonathan, 62
Paired altars, 68t

Palace gallery J-6 throne room, 67t, 68
Palenque, 9m, 67t, 69, 70–73, 79m, 83, 84, 88, 125, 274; monument defacement, 62, 66, 67t, 69, 70–73, 79m
Pallava kingship, 26
Palmar ceramics, 98, 99t, 209, 248t
Palmar Orange Polychrome ceramics, 209, 248t
Panel 3, 168, 169f
Pantano Impressed ceramics, 98, 99t
Partially reconstructable vessels, 208, 213, 235, 237, 238
Pasión region, decline of, 189
Pasión River, 127, 161m, 162, 177
Pasión River exchange route, 131, 160–165m, 166, 177
Pasión River Valley, 160, 162, 163
Pathologies, 179, 192–94, 196, 254
Patron-client relationships, 41–44, 56, 141, 154, 166, 176, 184
Patron gods, 249
Patterning among case studies, 18–19
PD 2 (Problematic Deposit 2), 204m, 208, 209, 210, 218, 219, 222
Peasant revolts. See Revolts and uprisings
Pedregal Modeled ceramics, 98, 99t, 100
Peregrine, Peter, 44
Perennial springs, 135, 156
Performance platforms, 139, 144, 145, 147f
Perimortem wounds, 179f, 180
Periodontal disease, 194
Perishable construction, 73, 148, 189, 228
Perpetrators, 18, 68, 69, 80, 182; suspects, 177, 183, 210, 250
Persian kingship, 28. See also Archaemenid/Persian Empire, kingship in
Personhood, 62, 261, 263
Peru, kingship in, 26, 31–32, 48–49
Petén, 17, 79m, 135; collapse, 189, 190; decline of, 189, 190; material influences, 160, 162, 172, 184; monument defacement, 66–68t, 74–78, 79m
Petén Gloss ware, 98, 99t
Petexbatun, 171–72, 176–77, 189–90, 224; Dos Pilas hegemony, 163, 164m, 166
Petexbatun/Dos Pilas hegemony, 163, 164m, 166
Petexbatun Regional Archaeological Project, 93
Petty kingdoms. See Little kings/little kingdoms
PfBAP excavations, 214–15
Phalanges, 252

Pharaoh's dream, interpretation of, 32
Photos, 71*f*, 97*f*, 98*f*, 115*f*, 116*f*, 120*f*, 143*f*, 147*f*, 175*f*, 178*f*, 236*f*, 239*f*; human remains, 179*f*, 192*f*, 193*f*, 277*f*, 280*f*; stelae, 149*f*, 257*f*, 258*f*
Picoleros Red-on-orange ceramics, 248*t*
Piedmont and highlands, 14, 162, 163, 172, 174–75, 183, 184–85, 186
Piedras Negras, 9*m*, 11–12, 67*t*, 79*m*, 80, 81, 84, 108–10, 111–22, 125–33, 171, 176, 274, 283; historical context, 122–25; monument defacement, 66–69, 88; social memory, 283
Piehl, Jennifer, 252, 253, 254
Pilgrimages, 85, 162, 217
Pitcher, Brian L., 199–200, 224
Pits. *See* Skull pits; Test Pits
Plank, Shannon, 87
Plan views, 120*f*, 137*f*, 170*f*, 231*f*, 246*f*
Plaster floors, 144, 208, 213
Plates, 209
Platters, 129, 199
Plazas, 16, 37, 207, 208, 228, 249; above-floor deposits in, 276
Plazuelas, 235
Plumbate ceramics, 122, 128
Pochteca, 85
Poite Incised ceramics, 248*t*
Pole-and-thatch structures, 124, 229, 240
Political truncation, 5–6, 134
Polvero Black ceramics, 248*t*
Polychromes, 84, 93, 98, 99*t*, 172, 181, 199, 209, 248*t*, 269
Pomona, 123, 126, 127, 128
Popolna (mat houses), 167
Populations: declining, 85, 109, 121, 128, 130, 172, 177, 187, 199, 230; rising, 14, 16, 49, 83, 84, 138, 140, 153, 154, 155, 176, 198, 199, 230–32
Portrait defacements. *See* Defaced monuments
Ports, 13, 168, 173, 174, 180–81, 183, 186
Post-abandonment behavior, 148, 153–54, 203, 208, 214, 222
Postclassic monument veneration, 217–18
Post-funerary rituals, 121
Power, internal divisions of, 167–71, 185
Powerfacts, 18, 38. *See also* Regalia, royal
Power sharing, 151, 154, 168. *See also* Divisions of authority; Joint rulership
Preah khan, 38
Pregnant woman remains, 159, 180
Presidency, 24; presidents, 157–58

Primary burials, 62, 196, 210, 253
Princesses, 272. *See also* Queens, remains of
Problematic deposits. *See* PD 2. *See also* Surface deposits
Productivity, declining, 14, 16, 230
Programme for Belize Archaeological Project. *See* PfBAP excavations
Projectile point knives, 235
Proskouriakoff, Tatiana, 84, 274
Prosperity, kings as symbols of, 2–3, 23, 27, 29–33, 35–41, 153–55, 188, 242, 243, 266, 281–82
Protracted processes, collapses as, 8, 132, 148, 153–54, 263–64
"Prowess" of kings, 40, 42–43, 53
Proxies, monuments as, 10
Proximate causes, 20
Proyecto Nacional Tikal, 271
Pseudo-E-Groups, 228–29
Public civic-ceremonial shrines. *See* M13-1 fire shrine
Public transcripts, 91–92
Public works as symbols of prosperity and legitimacy, 35–37
Puebla obsidian, 173, 184
Punta de Chimino, 84, 161*m*, 162, 177
Purification rituals, 12, 40–41, 145, 146, 150, 152
"Putun-Itza" hypothesis, 81–82
Pyramid of the Sun, 266
Pyramids and pyramidal structures, 75, 92–93, 95–97*f*, 100–102, 114*m*, 118, 119*m*, 139, 142, 144, 150, 189, 250
Pyrite, 162, 172, 176, 177, 184, 251

Q'an ceramic complex, 248*t*
Q'eq ceramic complex, 248*t*
Queens, remains of, 13, 159, 181, 271, 272
Questionnaires, 10, 86
Questions, volume editors', 7, 8; reflections on, 53–59
Quetzal feathers, 39, 162, 176, 177, 184
Quigley, Declan, 44, 48
Quintanilla, Claudia, 159–86, 341

Raiment, kingly. *See* Regalia, royal
Rain, kings' role in controlling, 3–4, 5, 27, 29–31, 34, 45–46, 48–51, 53
Rainfall, 187, 233, 260; Vaca Plateau, 155, 156; Usumacinta Basin, 131

Rain making glyphs, 274
Ramps and ramplike features, 150
Range structures, 12, 102, 168, 211
Rathje, William L., 185, 282
Rax ceramic complex, 248*t*
Reaggregated and reset monuments, 17, 177, 243, 247, 255*t*, 256–261, 265, 268
Receptacle-bodies, monuments as, 63, 64–65, 88
Reconstructible vessels, 93, 98–99, 101, 213, 255*t*; partially reconstructable vessels, 208, 213, 235, 237, 238
Reconstructions, 68, 115*f*, 160, 182, 262, 268
Rectified isometric plans, 137*f*
Redistribution of prosperity, 23, 33, 41–44
Redistributive mechanisms, 23, 33, 41–44, 128–29
Red-on-orange ceramics, 248*t*
Redware, undesignated waxy, 248*t*
Refits, lack of, 15, 99, 100, 101, 205, 206
Regalia, royal, 35–36, 37–39, 54–55, 159, 271–73; Central Mexican, 125; functionaries as, 20, 39–40, 54
Regicide, cases of, 48–49, 92, 106, 112, 271–73
Rejuvenation attempts, 12, 110, 122, 124–25, 126; scapegoating as, 48
Rempel Group, 226*m*, 240
Reoccupied cities, 196, 201, 225
Resistance, 5–6, 7, 51–52, 55–56, 91, 219, 222
Restricted-orifice jars, 237
Retrospective texts, 133, 283–84
Reused structures, 144, 146–49. *See also* Reaggregated and reset monuments
Reverential acts, 209, 218–19; termination rituals, 17, 152, 156–57, 255*t*
Reverential deposits, 15, 255*t*. *See also* Surface deposits
Revolts and uprisings, 2, 14, 80, 108, 110–11, 198, 201, 224
Revolts, internal, 14, 198–201
Río Azul (river), 191*m*, 207
Río Azul (site), 9*m*, 68*t*, 207
Río Bec region, decline of, 189, 190
Río Bravo, 191*m*, 207, 228, 239
Río Bravo embayment, 207
Río Bravo Escarpment, 207, 232, 233
Río Hondo, 9*m*, 191*m*, 196, 207, 211, 227, 238, 240
Río Usumacinta, 9*m*, 79*m*, 162

Ritual revisitations, 96, 151, 255, 268
Rituals, ideological uses of, 4, 5
Ritual terminations, 12, 17, 159, 178–83, 186; categories of evidence, 255*t*; necessity, 7, 58–59
Ritual water systems, 156, 174, 178. *See also* Water management systems
Rivers: Belize River, 9*m*, 79*m*, 191*m*, 211; New River, 191*m*; Pasión River, 161*m*, 162, 177; Río Azul, 191*m*, 207; Río Bravo, 191*m*, 207, 228, 239; Río Hondo, 9*m*, 191*m*, 196, 207, 211, 227, 238, 240; Río Usumacinta, 9*m*, 79*m*, 114*m*, 119*m*, 162; San Juan River, 247; San Pedro Mártir River, 247
Roller stamps, ceramic, 208–9
Roman Empire, fall of, 32
Romulus Augustulus, 110
Roofs, 87, 88: double-vaulted, 70; perishable, 73, 228; vaulted, 12, 66, 74
Roof supports, deliberate destruction of, 70, 73–74, 78, 150
Rosen, Arlene, 45–46
Rosita Group, 226*m*, 238–40
Round shrines, 79*m*, 82, 84, 238–239*f*
Rovner, Irwin, 190
Royal authority, challenges to, 21, 156–57, 167–71; royal responses to, 173–75
Royal bib heads, 229
"Royal road," 162, 183
Rubble fill, 12, 118, 208, 213
Rulers. *See* Kings, Maya; Kingship, cross-cultural perspectives on
Russian Revolution, 110
Rwanda, kingship in, 30, 49

Sabloff, Jeremy A., 83–84, 189
Sacluc Black-on-orange ceramics, 248*t*
Sacred covenants, 3–4, 34, 35, 139
Sacred kingship, 27–28, 49, 92, 107, 188
Sacrifices, 31, 34–35, 48, 65; auto-sacrifice, 35, 63, 106; captives, 177; elites, 62; kings, 40–41, 45, 48–49, 51, 86, 106. *See also* Assassinations
Sacrificial murder, 271
Sac Witz, 168
Sajals, 81, 167, 168, 171, 182
Sak huunals, 280
Sakka, 30, 36
Salt, 176, 177, 185, 197
San Bartolo, 9*m*, 207, 279
San Blas Red-on-orange ceramics, 248*t*

Sanders, William, 222
San Juan River, 247
San Pedro Mártir River, 247
Santa Amelia, 166
Saq ceramic complex, 248*t*
Satterthwaite, Linton, Jr., 111, 112, 118–21, 130
Saul, Frank, 194, 199
Saul, Julie, 194
Saxche-Palmar ceramics, 98, 99*t*, 248*t*
Sayap Ha, 226*m*, 229
Scapegoat, institution of kingship as, 1–21, 24–60, 109–11, 130, 132–35, 157, 186, 240, 261–64, 270, 273
Scapegoat king model, 1–21, 24–60, 109–11, 130, 132–35, 157, 186, 240, 261–64, 270, 273; applicability, 1–2, 59–60, 133; critiques of explanatory utility, 20
Scarborough, Vernon L., 189, 198
Schaar, John, 90
Scheffer, Marten, 46–47
Schele, Linda, 26, 73, 274, 281
Scherer, Andrew K., 108–33, 127, 341–42
Schortman, Edward, 141, 152
Schwake, Sonja A., 1–22, 134–58, 209–10, 283, 342
"Scorpion kings," 29
Scott, James C., 91
Scrapers, 235
Scribes, depictions of, 229
Scrolls, depictions of, 272, 274
Secondary burials, 62, 210, 253
Secondary deposits. *See* Middens: transposed middens/secondary deposits
Second Pegu/Toungoo dynasty, 52
"Secular" items, 255*t*
Sediment deposition in lowlands, 232–33
Sediments, 146, 210, 233
Segmented shell crowns, 272
Seibal/Ceibal, 79*m*, 84, 106–7, 131, 161*m*, 166, 176, 177, 183, 189
Self, understandings of, 61, 261
Selz Foundation Yaxuna Project, 272
Sepulchers, 271
Service patios, 139, 144, 148, 149
Serving vessels, 98, 99, 144, 174, 235, 237
Sesamoid bones, 252
Severed feet, 252–53
Sexual potency of kings, 92
Shafts, stone-lined, 228

Shallow burials, 182, 271
Shared rule, 151, 154, 168. *See also* Divisions of authority; Joint rulership
Shaw, Justine, 27
Shell and shell fragments, 181, 182, 184, 213, 215, 215, 251, 252; conch, 162, 176, 179, 271; *Spondylus*, 39, 162
Shell disks, 213
Shell ornaments, 93, 99, 100, 229; adornments, 255*t*
Sherds, 62, 99*t*, 101, 127, 135, 183, 206, 209, 213, 215, 217, 234–37, 276–78
Shilluk kingship, 41
Shrines, 73–74, 100, 118, 139, 196, 205, 229, 240; cave shrines, 160, 175; circular, 79*m*, 82, 84, 238–239*f*; E-Groups/eastern ancestor shrines, 12, 102, 139–41, 142–54, 157, 210, 235–37, 253; fire shrines (*wite' naah*), 17, 257, 266–67; mountain shrines, 65; principal public shrines, 243–265, 267–69; pyramidal, 139, 142, 143*f*; stairway shrines, 196, 206; stela shrines, 228
Sierra Red ceramics, 248*t*
Sihyaj K'ahk', 283
Silho Fine Orange plates, 117
Silla kingship, 31
Simonse, Simon, 49
Sinkholes, 135
Site-level differentiation, 172–73
Siva, 26
Siyah K'ahk', 249
Skull cut marks, 194, 195*f*
Skull pits, 14, 177, 192*f*–196, 197–98
Skulls/crania, 210–11; decapitated, 14, 177, 192*f*–196, 197, 209, 251, 252–255, 263, 271–73; fragments, 179*f*, 209, 251
Slate blanks, 237
Slate stelae, 137*f*, 144, 145
Slavery, 83, 85
Snake King, 283
Snake Kingdom. *See* Calakmul
Social change, 4, 91–92, 105, 129
Social contracts, 3, 34–35, 51, 55–56, 57–58
"Social currency," 41
Social memory, 151–52, 209–10, 218, 247, 249, 261, 264–66, 268, 273, 276, 283–84, 340–41; erasure from, 145, 149–50; invocation of, 255–56, 260–61, 266–67
Soil erosion, 96, 230, 232–33

Soils, 95, 96, 155, 227, 230–34
Solidarity, 3–4, 53, 55–56. *See also* Social contracts
Solstice markers, 228
"Soul," concepts of, 61, 63–65; soul force, 263; restoration of, 17, 265
Soul displacement. *See* Soul loss
Soul loss, 10, 62, 64–66, 156
Soul protection, 87
Southeast Asia, kingship in, 26, 43; Bali, 30, 39–40; Burma/Myanmar, 28, 30, 32, 36–37, 41–42, 47, 52, 54–55; Cambodia (54; Angkorian, 25, 28, 52; Khmer, 30, 36, 37–38, 40, 43); Java, 31, 41, 54; among Malay, 31, 54; Thailand, 41, 54–55
South India, kingship in, 26, 28, 34, 36, 41–42, 52
Sowing and the Dawning, The (Mock), 276
Spears, 180, 191
Special Deposit 11, 235–237
Special deposits, 70, 72, 205–6, 218, 235–237. *See also* Surface deposits
Speleothems, 251
Spindle whorls, 221, 235
Spondylus shells, 39, 162
Sponges, 226
Springs, 135, 156, 178
Squared day glyphs, 82
Stairways, 18, 118, 145, 148, 178, 215, 219, 250, 259; axial stairs, 144, 145
Stairways, blocked: burials, 182; deposits, 12, 15, 16, 96–98*f*, 118, 144, 206, 214, 218, 243, 251, 262, 265; infilling, 146, 147*f*, 148
Stairway shrines, 196, 206
Stamps, ceramic, 208–9, 235
"Star wars," 81
State regional authority, challenges to, 171
Status rivalries, 13, 80–82, 167, 176
Stelae, 12, 63, 66, 67*t*–68*t*, 255*t*, 271, 273, 274; Aguateca, 93, 100, 102, 104; Blue Creek, 225, 228; Cancuen, 182; Ceibal, 82; Chan Chich, 207; Copan, 11, 67*t*, 73; Dos Hombres, 207; Ixtonton, 67*t*; La Milpa, 207, 217; Machaquila, 183; Minanha, 12, 13, 137*f*, 139, 144, 149*f*, 150; Naranjo, 67*t*, 75, 77*f*; Palenque, 73–74; Piedras Negras, 116, 274; Tikal, 68*t*, 75, 259, 272; Waka', 243, 246*f*, 247, 249, 251, 252, 256–61, 264, 265, 267, 268, 283; Xultun, 68*t*; Yaxchilan, 68*t*, 80–81, 274

Stemmed blades, 191
Stepputat, Finn, 90
Stewards, kings as, 32–33
Stewardship of kings, 32–33
Stirling, Matthew, 196
Stone-lined shafts, 228
Stone piles, irregular, 97, 98*f*
Stones, exotic, 229
Storage rooms, 94, 95
Storage vessels, 93, 98, 206
"Stranger kings," nonlocal, 25, 124, 139, 140–41, 156, 157
Striated ceramics, 98, 99*t*, 100, 209, 217; unslipped, 235, 237
Structure C-14, 204*m*; surface deposits, 210, 211, 218–19, 220*f*, 221, 222
Structure L8-7, 96–98*f*, 102–3, 104, 105
Structure M13-1, 17, 206, 220–221, 243, 244*m*, 246*f*, 247, 249, 250–51, 283; as fire shrine, 266–67; mortuary patterns, 252–56; scapegoat king model and, 261–64; social memory, 264–66, 283–84; stelae, 243, 246*f*, 247, 249–50, 252, 256–61, 264, 267
Structure O-7, 118–121
Structure 38J, 12, 139, 142, 144*f*, 144–45, 146–49, 150–52
Structure 50, 235–37
Structure 104 deposit, 214–18, 219–220*f*, 221
Stuart, David, 61, 72, 87, 260–61, 274
Stucco fragments, 70, 73, 78, 251, 252, 255*t*
Stucco frieze(s), 130, 144, 145, 148, 149, 150
Stucco replastering, 214
Stucco sculptures, 116, 168, 174, 182, 271; dismantled, 12, 70, 116, 130, 148–50, 151; heads, 116*f*, human figures, 116; masks, 228; upper torsos, 271
Suasnavar, José Samuel, 159–86, 342
Subadult remains, 180, 252–53
Subin Red ceramics, 98, 99*t*, 100
Subroyal elites, rise of, 167–71, 173
Subroyal titles, 167
Subterranean springs
Sudan, kingship in, 29–30, 41, 49
Suhler, Charles K., 75
Sullivan, Lauren A., 217
Summary of volume, 8–22
Sun gods, 26, 27, 228–29, 266
Supernatural forces, kings as link to, 2, 3–4, 26–28, 45, 139, 188

Supreme judges, kings as, 25
Surface deposits, 15–17, 65, 275–76; Aguateca, 95–105; Blue Creek (16, 101, 214, 234–38, 278–79; Special Deposit 1, 206, 215, 217, 218); Chan Chich, 15, 200, 205, 206–7, 213–14, 219, 220*f*, 221, 222, 278; classification, 203, 205–7; Dos Hombres, 208–11, 220*f*, 221, 222; intentionality; La Milpa, 214–18, 220*f*; "near-surface" deposits, 11, 121;Waka', 17, 206, 220–21, 222, 243, 247
Suspects, 177, 183, 210, 250; perpetrators, 18, 68, 69, 80, 182
Swazi kingly regalia, 38
Sweat baths, 117, 122, 126, 283
Sweeping as ritual purification, 144, 145, 146, 150
"Symbolic capital," 41
Symbols, ideological uses of, 4, 5, 24, 35–41, 59, 69, 105–6, 139, 150–51, 200, 228, 247, 272–73

Tabasco, 177, 185; material culture, 172, 173, 184
Tables, 67*t*–68*t*, 99*t*, 248*t*, 255*t*
Tahiti, kingship in, 26, 32
Tahn Te' K'inich (Ruler 5), 93, 102–5
Tainter, Joseph A., 85
Taj Chan Ahk, 182
Tamarindito, 166
Tandem range structures, 148
Targeted portrait mutilation *See* Defaced monuments
Taube, Karl A., 260
Taylor, Christopher, xiii–xv, 29–30, 49, 92, 107, 111, 188, 200, 342
Tecolote, 127
Teeth: jaguar, 213; human, 254. *See also* Dental alteration and decoration; Dental pathologies
Temporal ranges, patterning in, 18
Tenoned stone artifacts, 213, 214, 219
Teotihuacán new fire ceremonies, 266–67
Teotihuacán style influences, 229, 249, 250
Terminal deposits, Maya lowland sites with, 66, 67*t*–68*t*
Termination deposits, 12, 15, 16, 79*m*, 92, 95–105, 181, 200
Termination rituals, 10, 58, 62, 69, 74, 75, 87, 92–93, 95–98, 100–103, 105, 150, 160, 177–79, 182–83, 189–90, 205–6, 209, 262–63, 276–78; categories, 255*t*; as symbolic battles, 105

Terraced fill, 118
Terraces, 32, 148, 149, 150, 155, 227, 231*f*, 232; agricultural, 135, 138, 232, 234; contour, 234
Terrace systems, 37, 135, 138, 140
Tertiary depositions, 254, 265
Test pits, 208
Textiles, 185
Thai kingship, 41, 54–55
Thatch-roofed wooden-pole structures, 124, 229, 240
Thermal alteration of bone, 121
Thompson, J. Eric S., 2, 81–83, 198, 224, 266
Three Rivers adaptive region, 207, 211, 214, 218
Thresholds of interaction, monuments as, 63, 64, 65, 88
Throne 1, 66, 67*t*, 68, 115*f*–116, 132
Throne rooms, 68, 69, 95
Thrones, 11, 18, 63, 69, 70, 72, 95, 130, 167, 170*f*; axially aligned, 144, 145, 147*f*
Tibiae, 253
Tikal, 9*m*, 13, 68*t*, 79*m*, 102, 138, 153, 190, 200, 249–50, 259, 264, 279, 283; hegemony, 160, 162–63, 164*m*, 166; monument defacement, 62, 66, 68*t*, 79*m*; PNT 019, 271–72; terminal deposits, 74–75, 76*f*
Tikal Project, 205
Tikal, decline of, 189, 190
Tinaja ceramics, 99*t*, 235
Tinaja Red ceramics, 98, 99*t*, 237, 248*t*
Tirumalai Cetupati, 42
Ti-sak-hu'ns, 167
Titles, 27, 28, 43, 52, 54, 56; bestowing of, 23, 41–43, 46, 55; proliferation of, 167, 176
Tombs, 140, 142, 228, 229; multiple-entry, 140, 142, 144, 145, 152; royal, 72, 73–74, 121, 122, 126, 228, 271–73, 280
Tonalli, 38–39
Tonalpohualli, 266
Tongan kingship, 26, 31, 43
Tonina, 80, 190
Tools, 219; chert, 99, 100, 191, 221; chipped-stone, 151, 213, 215, 278; obsidian, 99, 100, 226
Torro-Gouged Incised ceramics, 248*t*
Torso depictions, 271
Trade canoes, 227–28
Trade networks, 13, 16, 109, 128, 131, 160–67, 176–78, 183–85, 225, 227–28, 282; shifting, 4, 16, 49–50, 160–67

Trading diasporas, 84–85, 87
Transposed middens. *See* Middens: transposed middens/secondary deposits
Transversal exchange route, 160, 161*m*, 172–73, 177, 184
Trapiche Incised ceramics, 248*t*
Tree roots, 98*f*
Trefoil crowns, 271, 272
Tres Islas, 161*m*, 162, 177
Tres Mujeres bowls, 237
Tres Naciones Fine Gray ceramics, 127, 128
Triadic Acropolis, 78
Trickle-ware ceramic vessel, black, 235
Trigger, Bruce, 37
T600 Maya glyph, 266
Tubular jades, 271
Tumba Black-on-orange ceramics, 217
Turtle carapace, 209
Twisted-cord fire drill, 267
Tzakol influences, 160, 162
Tzotzil Maya, 63, 64

Uaxactun unslipped ceramics, 99*t*
Ucanal, 151
U lob inscriptions, 73
Unburied adult male skeletons, 181, 183, 186
Uncarved stelae, 137*f*, 144
Undermining, 12, 18, 150; doorways/entrances, 68–69, 70, 72–73, 74, 78, 117, 150
Undesignated ceramics, 248*t*
Universal contracts, 34–35. *See also* Social contracts
Unknown god with jaguar ear, 249
Unknown rulers, depictions of, 256–60
Unslipped ceramics, 99*t*, 209, 235, 237
Upakal K'inich, 70, 72
Upland erosion, 230, 232–33
Upper Pasión exchange route, 165*m*, 166. *See also* Pasión River exchange route
Uprisings and revolts, 2, 14, 80, 108, 110–11, 198–201, 224
Urban, Patricia, 141, 152
Uruk, 36
Usajal, 44
Usumacinta-Pasión drainage, monument defacement in, 66–73, 79*m*
Usumacinta River, 9*m*, 79*m*, 114*m*, 119*m*, 162
Utilitarian items, 93, 219, 209, 255*t*, 265, 269
Uxmal, 9*m*, 79*m*, 82

Uxul, 162
U Xulil Beh, 226*m*, 230–32

Vaca Plateau, 12, 135, 136*m*, 138, 155–56
Valdez, Fred, 14–15, 187–202, 342
Vanilla, 184
Vassals/vassal kingdoms, 145, 207, 250, 283
Vaulted architecture: buildings, 74, 78, 80, 103, 139, 148–49; ceilings, 218; formal entrances, 139, 144, 145, 147*f*; roofs (12, 66, 74; double-vaulted, 70); rooms (12, 146, 151, 210, 253; double-vaulted, 72); temples, 103, 104
Vault stones, 78, 103, 213
Veracruz, 177, 185, 196; material culture, 172–73, 184
Verapaz, 163, 174; material culture, 172, 184–85
Verapaz Valley trade route, 160, 162, 163, 166, 172, 175, 177, 184–85
Vertebrae, 180, 194, 253, 271
Violence, 18–19, 267; evidence of, 3, 111–12, 264–65; necessity of, 7, 58–59, 262–63
Violent terminations, 189–90; Cancuen, 178–83, 186; Colha, 187, 192*f*–196, 197–98; Dos Pilas, 177
Visnu, 26
Vogt, Evon Z., 61, 63, 64–65, 88, 274, 281
Volcanic ash–tempered ceramics, 103
Votive offerings, 206, 247, 252, 253, 262–63

Waka' (El Perú-Waka'), 9*m*, 17, 67*t*, 79*m*, 162, 163, 176, 243, 267–69, 272; addressing scapegoat king model, 261–64; *adosadas*, 246*f*, 251, 267; ceramic sequence, 248*t*; deposits, 206, 211, 220–21, 246*f*, 251–52, 276, 278; Structure M13-1 (17, 206, 220–221, 243, 244*m*, 246*f*, 247, 249, 250–51, 283; as fire shrine, 266–67; mortuary patterns, 252–56; political history, 250; social memory, 247, 249, 264–66, 283–84; stelae, 243, 246*f*, 247, 249–50, 252, 256–61, 264, 267)
Waka' ceramic sequence, 248*t*
War captives, depictions of, 104
War crimes, 179
War dance depictions, 73
Warfare, 4, 14, 20, 46, 49, 52, 54, 63, 74, 104, 105, 110, 111–12, 138, 176; changes in practice, 10, 63, 83–85, 87, 224; proxy wars, 168; status rivalries, 13, 80–82, 167, 176
War-related deposits, 276, 277*f*

Warriors, 104, 177, 180, 259; warrior-merchants, 81, 84, 85
Water, 5, 13, 30–31, 32, 33, 135, 155–56, 174, 201; access to, 227; interment in, 179–181
"Water group" prefix, 274
Water lords, depictions of, 14, 168, 169f, 174
Water management systems, 32, 37, 54, 156, 174, 178, 232–34, 239, 140; agricultural ditches, 232–34; ritual water systems, 156, 174, 178
Water tables, rising, 232–33
Wattle-and-daub architecture, 189
Waxaklajuun Ubaah K'awiil, 75
Waxy blackware, undesignated, 248t
Waxy redware, undesignated, 248t
Weberian legitimacy, 90, 91, 92, 106
Webster, David, 222
Western exchange routes, 160–161m, 162, 164m–165m
Whistles, 209, 213, 215, 220f, 235
White, Christine D., 224
"White headbands," 87, 271–272, 280f
White soils, 95
Wilk, Richard, 1
Willey, Gordon, 176
Williams, Raymond, 106
Wind gods, 82
Wing rooms, 139
"Witchcraft," 65
Wite' naah (fire shrines), 17, 257, 266–67
Witz monsters, 257
Wolters, O. W., 40
Woman rulers, 54. See also Queens, remains of
Wright, Lori E., 224

Xkalumkin, 87
Xultun, 66, 68t, 207
Xunantunich, 9m, 68t, 153, 171

Yajaw-k'ahk's, 167
Yajaws, 44, 182
Yalbac Hills, 211
Yashovarman I, 30
Yaxchilan, 9m, 66, 68t, 84, 122, 127, 129, 171, 176, 274; capture of Piedras Negras's ruler, 12, 80–81, 109, 112, 113, 125, 129, 132
Yaxha, 68t
Yaxuna, 68t, 79m, 82, 124, 238, 272–73, 276, 277f, 279–80
Yellow soils, 96
Yik'in Chan K'awiil, 264
Yoffee, Norman, 24, 28, 32
Yucatan, 63, 187–88, 227, 272; ceramic imports, 82, 117, 122, 128; Mexicanized Maya influence, 81–85, 87; Yaxuna research, 276, 277f, 279–80
Yucatecan-style shrines, round, 238–239f. See also Circular structures
Yuknoom Ch'een, 283–84

Zacatel Cream Polychrome ceramics, 248t
Zaragoza obsidian, 173, 184
Zhou Daguan, 37–38, 43
Zinacanteco Maya views: reality, 281; "soul loss," 64–65
Zooarchaeological remains. See Faunal remains
Zuyua, Language of, 86

MAYA STUDIES

Edited by Diane Z. Chase and Arlen F. Chase

The books in this series will focus on both the ancient and the contemporary Maya peoples of Belize, Mexico, Guatemala, Honduras, and El Salvador. The goal of the series is to provide an integrated outlet for scholarly works dealing with Maya archaeology, epigraphy, ethnography, and history. The series will particularly seek cutting-edge theoretical works, methodologically sound site-reports, and tightly organized edited volumes with broad appeal.

Salt: White Gold of the Ancient Maya, by Heather McKillop (2002)
Archaeology and Ethnohistory of Iximché, by C. Roger Nance, Stephen L. Whittington, and Barbara E. Borg (2003)
The Ancient Maya of the Belize Valley: Half a Century of Archaeological Research, edited by James F. Garber (2003; first paperback edition, 2011)
Unconquered Lacandon Maya: Ethnohistory and Archaeology of the Indigenous Culture Change, by Joel W. Palka (2005)
Chocolate in Mesoamerica: A Cultural History of Cacao, edited by Cameron L. McNeil (2006; first paperback printing, 2009)
Maya Christians and Their Churches in Sixteenth-Century Belize, by Elizabeth Graham (2011)
Chan: An Ancient Maya Farming Community, edited by Cynthia Robin (2012; first paperback edition, 2013)
Motul de San José: Politics, History, and Economy in a Maya Polity, edited by Antonia E. Foias and Kitty F. Emery (2012; first paperback edition, 2015)
Ancient Maya Pottery: Classification, Analysis, and Interpretation, edited by James John Aimers (2013; first paperback edition, 2014)
Ancient Maya Political Dynamics, by Antonia E. Foias (2013; first paperback edition, 2014)
Ritual, Violence, and the Fall of the Classic Maya Kings, edited by Gyles Iannone, Brett A. Houk, and Sonja A. Schwake (2016; first paperback edition, 2018)
Perspectives on the Ancient Maya of Chetumal Bay, edited by Debra S. Walker (2016)
Maya E Groups: Calendars, Astronomy, and Urbanism in the Early Lowlands, edited by David A. Freidel, Arlen F. Chase, Anne S. Dowd, and Jerry Murdock (2017)
War Owl Falling: Innovation, Creativity, and Culture Change in Ancient Maya Society, by Markus Eberl (2018)
Pathways to Complexity: A View from the Maya Lowlands, edited by M. Kathryn Brown and George J. Bey III (2017)
Water, Cacao, and the Early Maya of Chocolá, by Jonathan Kaplan and Federico Paredes Umaña (2018)
Maya Salt Works, by Heather McKillop (2019)

www.ingramcontent.com/pod-product-compliance
Lightning Source LLC
Chambersburg PA
CBHW021334230426
43666CB00006B/289